IDEOLOGY
AND
UNDERSTANDING

THE PHENOMENOLOGY OF JUDGMENT AND BELIEF

WESTON ADAM

Ideology and Understanding:
The Phenomenology of Judgment and Belief

Cover painting:
Stan Wiederspan, 080405, 2005. Acrylic on canvas, 45 ¼ x 54 ¼ in. Cedar Rapids Museum of Art, Museum purchase, with gift of the artist, Kathleen and Tom Aller, CRST International and Ann and Henry Royer.
2009.057"

Printed in the United States of America
Paperback ISBN: 978-1-959096-01-6
eBook ISBN: 978-1-959096-02-3

**Canoe Tree
Press**

4697 Main Street
Manchester Center, VT 05255

Canoe Tree Press is a division of DartFrog Books

Спаси и сохрани

Ἰησοῦς Χριστὸς νικᾷ

Quo vadis?

Jumalansynnyttäjä, pelasta meidät

Lord, have mercy

This page intentionally left blank

TABLE OF CONTENTS

SIDE A: IDEOLOGY AND POLITICAL CONTROL

SIDE B: DIALOGUE AND IDENTITY

Acknowledgments

I t's self-evident with any work of this sort the countless debts which its author owes to the intellectual world he draws from. However, often neglected in the West is, for lack of a better term, the living world itself, which is somehow divorced from the intellectual and discarded as if it was of no consequence. A work of this sort however is shaped by a thousand hands – it bears the mark of each who touch it. In fact without the friendship, guidance, instruction, care, time and support that houses, facilitates and engages the kernels, one would be left with rot and disease in the place of a strong and healthy forest. Considering the pen-to-paper origins of this book took place ten years before it was ready for print, the size of the list of people who nourished this forest makes it nearly impossible to speak to in a way that honors their gifts and sacrifices. The list of people who deserve my recognition and gratitude extends beyond what is possible here. Nevertheless, reflecting a challenge as large as that of the text itself, it must still be pursued to the best of my ability: my apologies in advance for its falling short of the honor due to each and all who helped, in ways big and small, this text become what it is today.

First I need to express my heartfelt thanks to my wife, Jessica Hartling for her endless patience, love and support without which the space for this work to grow would have suffocated it; my brother, Bryant Haldeman whose encouragement and loyal reading of many variations of this text helped breathe new life into it; my father, Kurt Haldeman, who took on the role of Devil's advocate to strengthen this work; my mother, Laurie Swanson who provided innumerable opportunities for me to express the ideas of this text in new ways; Dylan (DaddyO) for his sharp mind, friendship and conversation; Beth Haldeman for being the sister I never knew I needed; Logan Simon for the friendship and brotherhood without which I could not stand; Joy Elliott for leading with generosity, support and openness; Ken Hartling Sr. and Pam Hartling for treating me with the grandparently love, care, and conversation that can only come from one's real and true grandparents; Alicia Marshall for her extraordinary kindness and friendship, and for fighting with great might for this text to see the light of day; Dawei Zhang for your endless brotherhood throughout space and time; Mads Hunsaker for being effortlessly more than family: a lifelong blessing; Byrn d. Paul for your kind heart, brilliant mind, and enduring friendship; Wang Dajiang for your brotherhood through a cold and tiring university, for your generosity and your great mind; Jason Hartling for being the patience Uncle that truly everyone needs; Brian White for introducing me to the history of philosophy; Josh Hartling for taking me in as an actual brother, and for your great humor, mind and heart; Ben Davis for challenging me, for your brotherhood, for your heart; Ken Leitza, whose thoughtful conversation and honest sharing in intellectual work shaped many branches of this tree; Miranda Valleroy for your great friendship and camaraderie; Paige Hagemann for your kindness, friendship, and hard work on designing the cover of this book. Paul Higgins for editing this book, for words of wisdom, a keen eye and a kind heart; Ken Hartling Jr. and Jen Ayers for accepting me, for challenging me, for conversations big and small, for your sustained support which leaves one speechless, for your open hearts, for your open ears, for too much to begin listing here; Andrew Huitt, for your ancient brotherhood and endless sense of humor; Dylan Flint, for your art, for your kindness unto others, for your curiousity; Ben Feltes for fighting for what's right, for being the great American man, for your friendship to all, big and small; Jake Marzen for refusing to lose our bond to the sands of time; Michelle Frye for nurturing my curiosities and loves; Neil Goettsch for challenging me, for conversation, for being a truly interesting man; Jack Waugh for his good humor and bright mind; Kailyn Killoran for being an absolute pal; Kaneesha Hughes for her friendship and support; Zoran Knezevic for leading by example; Cara Smith for her honesty and care; Jason Poland for your brotherhood and support, Clint and Susan Ronnenberg for their open hearts and minds; Emily DeBower for her great capacity for care across time and space; Chris Grus for genuinely being one of the most humble, honest and hilarious men I have ever encountered; M. Cassie Goodwin for her friendship and support; Curtis L. Paul for being the father of many young struggling artists; Clarissa Simmons for her camaraderie and longstanding friendship; Andrea Fender for her extraordinary support and kindness which clearly was never due me; Jon Gollnick for his brilliant mind, overflowing generosity, piercing loyalty, and vigorous life; Michael Schultz for his dedication to the craft, and for his kindness to others; Richard Geller for trusting in others, for his kindness, for his humor; Michael McCormick for all things given to me, that I deserved not: faithfulness, hope, knowledge, wisdom, honesty, humility, kindness, love, friendship, patience, humility; Fahaaj MuQeem,Krisztine Bana, Jeremiah Thomas, Jonathan, Cote Keller, Angie Abbott, Steven Black, Michael Gilbride, Matt Hickerson, Austin Bryant and Emily Sauer for your support and trust.

PREFACE

Belief in objective philosophy with an absolute and complete knowledge-based system is alive and well in many of today's leading ideological structures, be they secular or religious. Just as this is the case, so too are relativist ideologies thriving which believe in an absolute lack of universals. In both cases, the fueling desire is one of avoidance of striving. For in objectivist ideologies the task of the individual is mere knowledge of, or scholarly contributions to, the already-existing structures of truth that have been given to us, whereas relativist ideologies clearly, in the face of diverse otherness, avoid grappling with the issue altogether. Neither system allows for individuals to strive to appropriate and translate the truth founded on their relationality such that they may successfully participate in meaningful action. This is all despite the appropriation that these ideologies make of philosophy's champions and their ideas. They fail in a certain fundamental regard to acknowledge the primordial philosophical relation exemplified by Socrates who, as *a midwife of truth*, was one who understood the spectrum of irrationality and rationality within which we all dance.

Despite the aid that discourse offers us in helping to undo deception, there is implicit in the relation a necessity that the individual can strive and access his own rationality in order to contribute to the intersubjective production of understanding. However, due to the nature of ideological interpolation, passivity in all matters has become a position whereby one feels as if one is continually in the process of the greatest striving possible while merely supporting the belief-structures that we have all been in one way or another born into. This is because ideology as a collective structure of knowledge is by definition always-already known to the collective that makes up its actuality. Because of this, and also due to the difficulty of holding a Socratic position, it is remarkably difficult to storm the walls of ideology. It is so difficult in fact, that you will feel as if you already have.

This is, however, only an element of the means by which modern man avoids striving altogether: there is a nearly endless multiplicity of ways in which man is blind unto himself, and capitalizes on said blindness to naturalize both social and personal prejudice. Many who wish to see beyond this struggle claim a type of neutrality as their position, all the while harboring deep animosity toward some particular group. Neutrality is here the bush behind which they are waiting for the right moment to spring from the darkness and press forth their totalizing ideals such that the target of their disdain might be wiped from the earth. Gadamer tells us in his essay "Semantics and Hermeneutics" that

> ideological criticism represents only a particular form of hermeneutical reflection, one that seeks to dispel a certain class of prejudices through critique. Hermeneutical reflection, however, is universal in its possible application. As opposed to the sciences, it must also fight for recognition in those cases where it is a matter, not of the particular problem of uncovering ideology through social criticism, but of self-enlightenment with regard to the methodology of science as such. Any science is based upon the special nature of that which it has made its object through its methods of objectifying. The method of modern science is characterized from the start by a refusal: namely, to exclude all that which actually eludes its own methodology and procedures. Precisely in this way it would prove to itself that is without limits and never wanting for self-justification. Thus it gives the appearance of being total in its knowledge and in this way provides a defense behind which social prejudices and interest lie hidden and thus protected.

One need only think of the role of experts in contemporary society and of the way economics, politics, war, and the implementation of justice are more strongly influenced by the voice of the experts than by the political bodies that represent the will of society.[1]

The individual who seeks emancipation from ideological forms of consciousness must answer to the demand to understand the means by which mediation occurs through language and history *as such*.

As Gadamer himself says, "in every worldview the existence of the world-in-itself is intended. It is the whole to which linguistically schematized experience refers. The multiplicity of these worldviews does not involve any relativization of the 'world.' Rather, the world is not different from the views in which it presents itself."[2] In contrast to what Gadamer's critics would like him to say, he understands the conditions that allow for our very reflection upon our preconceptions of meaning (which are themselves always-already mediated through language) as historically produced. "Tradition is not simply a permanent precondition; rather, we produce it ourselves inasmuch as we understand, participate in the evolution of tradition, and hence further determine it ourselves. The circle of understanding is not a 'methodological' circle, but describes an element of the ontological structure of understanding."[3] In this way, by reflecting upon the nature of our understanding we can recognize that by its very movement, understanding is already itself self-understanding. The participation in understanding must already involve the individual striving to such an extent that it actually brings their Being to bear on their search. And because this process is always open-ended, there is

1 Gadamer, Hans-Georg, and David Linge, "Semantics and Hermeneutics," in Philosophical Hermeneutics (Berkeley: University of California Press, 2008), 93.

2 Gadamer, Hans-Georg, *Truth and Method*, trans. Joel Weinsheimer (London: Continuum, 2011), 444.

3 Ibid., 293-94

never a moment when one can retreat from this search by claiming to have found full and totalizing knowledge (which is in part because of the necessary application of development by the means of interpretation itself). Thus, dialogue must always include a commonality within the heart of the matter that it's aimed at disclosing. Each of the interlocutors must be open to the possibility of the truth of the other regardless of contradiction, for it is from contradiction that the prejudice of the individual may itself be called into question.

Thus, critics such as Jürgen Habermas who try to dismiss Gadamer's complicated philosophy of language and tradition as mute ideology miss the very nature of the items they seek to use for critique. Habermas specifically sought to showcase how Gadamer's understanding of tradition relegates its authority to that of an absolute, and thus its normative structures become impossible to address, and the meaning produced therefrom becomes systematically distorted. Habermas however seems to miss the entire critique of ideal speech free from prejudice and distortion, as well as the reasoned conditionality of acceptance of authority (and tradition) that makes up a major portion of Gadamer's *Truth and Method* (not to mention earlier outline work done in *Philosophical Hermeneutics*). Habermas strangely proceeded to construct an alternative to Gadamer's work by attempting to find the "ideal speech situation" already dismantled by the work it is reacting to, through supplementing hermeneutics with Freudian psychoanalysis. He assumes that Freudian analysis utilizes a fixed theory with a specific methodology which finds each part of analysis related to a predetermined whole. Thus, Habermas risks relegating psychoanalysis to an ideological structure of sorting out prelinguistic and linguistic relations of symbols in a way that seems strangely ignorant of the whole of Lacan's contribution and corrective to the failures of psychoanalysis in his return to Freud.

The type of human striving that the work before you advocates is one which aims to reject overly simplistic and reductive accounts like that of Habermas. It is the very means of avoiding the systematic reproduction of statist dogmatism which is supported through ideological state apparatuses like the scientism of our day. Striving cannot be subsumed to this or other ideologies which extrapolate an objectification of reality and the real-world conditions of its citizens. This is despite the fact that all too often many believe themselves to be engaging in such striving by coming along after the fact and claiming sedimentation as their victory. They champion themselves as having vanquished worldviews taken from their articulation and placed against a system founded on its rejection, thus ignoring the most basic notion of translation dictated by even a semblance of engagement. Thus, the priority of the question in the dialogical relation, which grounds the hermeneutical claim of 'universality' finds that "we can understand precisely *every* ideology as a form of false linguistic consciousness, one that might show itself not only to us as a conscious, manifest, and intelligible meaning but also might be understood in its 'true' meaning."[4]

Habermas-like distinctions between the material conditions of labor and domination, and the linguistic tradition that encapsulates them, are nonsensical. Part of the self-understanding of any given tradition always-already involves the incorporation of those 'extra-linguistic' forces, as in order for them to enter our world at all, they must do so by influencing this self-understanding. Ideology is given meaning *as* ideology through hermeneutic reflection which sees this structure explicitly asserting itself as the answer to whatever question it believes itself to have vanquished.

Thus, the liberation of the question is at the same time the liberation of the interlocutor, crowning him with the status of interpreter once again.

This is what has been at issue throughout the course of the nine years that I have labored over writing this book. With each year, new perspectives and new ways of understanding the problems instigated its coming into being. It is thus a representation of its author's own philosophical upbringing—a beginner's education—a process of moving

---

4 Gadamer, *Philosophical Hermeneutics*, 31.

forward by looking back. The text before you is a working through and working out of the preconditions for the good and the true, as well as their adversaries, at the time of its writing. The work in large part was written as an aid in understanding for its author, and hopes to, through the deployment of dialogical reason, provide a similar aid to its readers. It is through the hard-earned victory of authentic examination that one may discover great self-deception, and thus the single movement of development blooms into a diverse garden, primed for cultivation. Thus, this work acts as an introduction to the art of seeking the good and the true by examining judgment and belief, which are explicated through the problems of ideology, the totalization of knowledge, Otherness as such, mass culture, and the problem of identity and language.

By engaging in this authentic examination, one returns philosophy to its humble position which runs counter to the ideological whore many have made of it. This is because many would like for philosophy to be a means of justification for their particular worldview and set of beliefs, but even popularizers of philosophy explicitly reveal its opposing role; for example, when Rick Roderick tells us that "philosophy . . . does not provide comfort for people who are comfortable, it shouldn't. It doesn't even provide comfort for the afflicted as you may have found out if you are afflicted. It is . . . disconsolate in principle."[5] In what may still be the defining work of philosophy in the centuries since its publication, Hegel's *Phenomenology of Spirit*, we find the life of philosophy giving way to the feeling of being forsaken in the midst of analysis in order that understanding in any real sense make its way forward. It is the achievement of experience which is itself the actualization of true risk.

The life of Spirit is not the life that shrinks from death and keeps itself untouched by devastation, but rather the life that

---

5 Roderick, Rick, "Philosophy and Post-Modern Culture," *Philosophy and Human Values* (1990).

endures it and maintains itself in it. It wins its truth only when, in utter dismemberment, it finds itself. It is this power, not as something positive, which closes its eyes to the negative, as when we say of something that it is nothing or is false, and then, having done with it, turn away and pass on to something else; on the contrary, Spirit is this power only by looking the negative in the face, and tarrying with it. This tarrying with the negative is the magical power that converts it into being.[6]

Thus, in many ways, the years of germination which this work has endured allowed for the ideas held within to be played out against the concrete reality of its author so as to keep them from the folly of the austere theorists who write, in opposition to philosophy, only to sustain beliefs and justify complacency and idleness. In a way, the crystallization of a genre of writing called "philosophy" brings methodology and dogma to bear on the art of analysis claimed as its namesake. In this sense philosophy must die so that Philosophy may be born. This poisonous rebellion against the art of philosophy by the authors of these sorts of works has also spread to other modes of analysis in an attempt to totalize their achievements of understanding into dead knowledge. This corruption of the examined life is unmistakably natural, however, and through efficiently-engineered mass media, which synthetically fulfills the psychic needs of its citizens, this way of life is made ever more challenging to achieve.

This way of Being for man is one that dislodges the very notion of questioning from his concrete existence, thus displacing man from meaning that he can accept as his own. Unfortunately, many believe themselves to be doing this very same analysis when they admit themselves as disciples of the Enlightenment's idealization of reason which denies anything properly Other. Thus, the individual believes

---

6 Hegel, G. W. F., *Phenomenology of Spirit*, trans. J. N. Findlay (Oxford: Clarendon, 1979), 19.

himself to be an heir of total knowledge, which merely adds to its stale treasure all that dare lay before it. The individual who takes the Enlightenment's notions as his own imagines himself to have become a universal individual, the objective measure of all things. One finds then the atomistic relation between universal individuals as one that sees conversational partners diminishing at the express rise of the dual monologue, whereby individuals assume the role of champion in a particular discourse or narrative which they themselves more often than not have simply been *born* into. Thus, the search for the good and the true is displaced by an assertion of ownership and authority of the good and the true.

The dominant activist narrative of our time is to act on behalf of this ownership, forever and always in conflict with one another; all are given an identity and a narrative and set forth to change the world. However, due to the immense range of conditions through which man develops, the structure of critique and explication that lies before the beginner is not the unified theory of virtues and vices sought by those who came earlier. This is because man cannot place examination in a privileged and detached sphere where one vacations before action and belief are committed to: for man is never as Descartes would have liked us to imagine, separable from the constant march of time and demand for attention and action founded therein. The construction of questions and organization of one's beliefs are not something that we work on before entering into the realm of 'serious' philosophy, but are rather something that we are in fact always-already reinterpreting and restructuring. It is by nature of recognizing our thrownness into the world that we might come to an understanding with ourselves, those around us, and those who came before us. In acknowledging the unsuspendable historicity and finitude that condition our positive relation of understanding, we may begin to truly approach man's role in co-constituting meaning. Consequently, the relation of understanding, rather than the methodological knowledge that so many wish to see as its champion, grants us an approach to the

Other that goes beyond abstractions or tautologies (differences which make no difference).

Nearly every aspect of life relies upon some sort of preconditioned justification of belief which, while resembling a reasoned foundation, acts as a sort of cover for the gap that appears by way of the structure of its system. Theoretically the systems of belief through which people align the whole of their Being is meant to be operating passively: the justification for said beliefs is meant to function at every given moment in the background. However, the justification functions *because of* its position as an unexamined background passivity, for in reality it is the very gap which it is meant to cover: it is the very incompleteness that it denies. It is in this regard that this work stands as a translation and development of a beginner's philosophy. It is through authentic examination that its reader may be awakened to mysterious, uncertain, and surprising moments of understanding. In this sense, we must understand that those who authentically seek the true or the good over mere justification are themselves few in number, and as such the task of aligning this way of Being with one's own life will almost assuredly belong to a company of 'radicals.'

Just as this work acted as a beginner's education for its author, thus also does it address the reader. How much more during the course of this book's coming-to-be has the world needed men such as those who undertake the prerogative to usher in fresh speech, of which our tumultuous times are its birth-pangs: and yet did not the call to this examination dwell first among the ancients? Was this not what Plato's Socrates was expressing when he stated that his speech was commanded not only in obedience to the divine, but by nature of it being the 'greatest good'? It is through interpretation and translation then that the truth of this speech is sustained, all the while placing it within the movement of the dialogical relation, which provides the possibility of development? The formation of the right question, which is neither closed nor empty of content, is then the means by which authentic dialogical relations might forge meaning through a shared understanding. This is possible by the relation of maintaining the contingent circumstances of its interlocutors, as well as the structural form of the content as it is in itself. From this there is a subordination of each interlocutor to the subject matter shared by the two, such that the intersubjective relation to the subject matter is the very coming-into-language of the thing itself.

Yet this is a far cry from what the notion of philosophy has come to mean. This is because many would rather measure the strength of their ego in determining who is right and who is wrong, rather than engaging in the real on-the-ground issues that disrupt our everyday lives, the societies we live in, and the types of relations we hold. This mode of egology makes it more and more impossible for conversation to occur that can lead to any positive resolution. This is, in part, due to the insistence of the notion that we are all individual moral agents divorced from an understanding or discussion about a cultural good. Instead, we are all rendered polite yet impotent.

Despite the persistence in significance of a cultural good to each and every one of us, we will forever be driven apart. This is the result of the Enlightenment's idolization of the individual, which makes the empty social and moral life into a virtue: one where an individual can become universal by depriving himself of all positive content. In this way, both the good and the true are tossed aside as well as authentic dialogue, for the individual presumes to have struck gold, concluding that "all evaluative judgments are nothing but expressions of preference, expressions of attitude or feeling, insofar as they are moral or evaluative in character."[7] Thus, the available positions mass-produced for the individuals in any given society are either to have "no necessary social content and no necessary social identity," such that you can "be anything, can assume any role or take any point of view," because this position is "in and for itself nothing."[8]

---

7 MacIntyre, Alasdair, *After Virtue* (Notre Dame, Ind.: University of Notre Dame Press, 1984), 11-12.

8 Ibid., 32

Or, should you opt for having positive content, there is a nearly endless selection of ideologies which come with predetermined content such that you may spend your whole life tirelessly advocating for them. Through ideology you may spend your days obliterating all Otherness, dreaming of a day when your ideals become universalized, and in that state of sublime enjoyment of totality, you may one day find peace. It is easy to imagine that there is a false focus placed on this dichotomy such that truly behind all positions stand masters of one sort or another, who construct for the individual these potential systems of belief or lack thereof, and truly to found victory for oneself. This is the Nietzschean turn whereby all is reduced to a power struggle. This path has found two principal results, the first being that of Foucault who endlessly examines micro-transactions of power in an overall economy too large to exclude anything from its gaze. In endless notation, power here becomes nothing more than the very network of Being whereby resistance and freedom are themselves given through power's conditioning. Thus, this study of power is really part of an attempted scientific mastery via imparting of 'neutral' facts.

The other seeming alternative under this power lens is the elevation of the individual to the arbiter of righteous content, to whom the co-opting of ideology is a tactical role meant to produce the greatest possible chance for the individual to dominate a particular landscape, and amass for himself the greatest possible amount of power. In this respect, they are ideological, but only superficially. It is important to note however that their ideological support need not always be wholly ironic. There is often an attachment of meaning from the notions they claim to champion, and despite the fact that to anyone outside of their ideological system they seem to fly in the face of what they claim as their own, they often still believe themselves to be truly fighting for whatever category is theirs. This is due to the fact that, although power is of course intoxicating enough for man, how much more is it thus when affixed to the self-righteousness granted to those who spread the meaning of their ideology? This is where, in discussing Marx's dictum of religion being the opiate of the people, Žižek reminds us to be careful: "Marx doesn't say opium *for* the people, because this would have meant this primitive idea that there is some evil secret society of priests or whatever which fabricates ideology. No, Marx's basic rule is ideology is not simple external manipulation. You manipulate yourself . . . even cynics secretly believe in some kind of ideology."[9]

Thus, in the writing of a text such as this one, which reflects the path of understanding of these systems and egoisms, there exists the threat of the work becoming a reinforcement of these very things it examines. In this way, the words of the text become trapped like a bug in amber, such that they can be taken to use and abuse as if they belong to an academic or state philosophy. Although it is a New Age notion that the Buddha and the Christ belong together, it is nevertheless worth noting that the two are among the most cited religious teachers of all time, and yet both warned about their teachings being wielded by those who mean harm. It is of course true that man must engage in life regardless—there is no idealized position beyond engagement —and with no guarantee that awakening of any sort for any individual shall occur, or is even possible, there must nevertheless be exertion of the will to find understanding. So is the life of man. For everywhere we look there is an attempt of understanding or else the demand of submission to a totalizing knowledge, one that stretches across every concept that characterizes man from the simplest matters to the most complex and intersecting. It is this dark, slow, and delicate path, fraught with tension from all angles, that this work seeks to tread—searching for a fundamental relationship to understanding such that the individual might begin to navigate the world, himself, and the relation to the Other.

---

9 Žižek, Slavoj, "Disorder Under Heaven," European Graduate School Video
   Lectures, Evening Lecture, June 13, 2019.

This text traces then the logic that has extended from the demand to 'Obey!' all the way to its supplement to 'Enjoy!', refusing all the while to sublimate this beginner's education to the will of the ego, or the command of power, or the cultural structures of belief or desire. This text asks its readers then, as its author did while laboring over its construction, to allow the priority of its questions into their lives, and to examine whether or not they lead toward a path of understanding.

Side A:

Ideology and
Political Control

INTRODUCTION

> *"In the case of all other sciences, arts, skills, and crafts, everyone is convinced that a complex and laborious programme of learning and practice is necessary for competence . . . Let the other sciences try to argue as much as they like without philosophy: without it they can have in them neither life, Spirit, nor truth."*[10]
>
> —*Georg Wilhelm Friedrich Hegel*

I t would appear that since its publication in 1922, and despite its later refutation by its author (as well as the problematic which riddles the text in its totality), the *Tractatus Logico-Philosophicus* has left humanity the purest form of its Humean riddle. If we are to take Wittgenstein seriously in his famous final proclamation therein: "*Wovon man nicht sprechen kann, darüber muss man schweigen*" (Whereof one cannot speak, thereof one must be silent), then we are to remain like its author, without ever being capable of creating any change aside from that which seems empirical and logical, and yet all the while maintaining beliefs about which we cannot speak, nor discuss. This poses a serious threat, for there are very few who possess the razor-sharp perception of Wittgenstein, and as shown by his dismissal of the work, even he was prone to err. As a result we could very well fall into the situation of the hegemonic state pursuing that which expressly benefits our ideological bedfellows while simultaneously convincing those at a lower vantage

---

10 Hegel, *Phenomenology of Spirit*, 41.

point of their scientific aim. As such, it is important to break from the understandably noble declaration of the *Tractatus*.

Instead, though we may be walking into the dark where we are certain to gain footholds on shaky ground, we still might seek to explicate that which already rules our lives quietly. For this invisible grip severely restricts our autonomy, and seeks to rob Plato's famous remark of all its truth:

> If again I say that to talk every day about virtue and the other things about which you hear me talking and examining myself and others is the greatest good to man, and that the unexamined life is not worth living, you will believe me still less.
>
> This is as I say, gentlemen, but it is not easy to convince you. Besides, I am not accustomed to think that I deserve anything bad.[11]

In the final famous words of perhaps the most celebrated thinker of all time we see that his commitment to pursuing wisdom and knowledge was complex. Not only was it the lone favorable alternative to death, but it also came as a result of constant self-scrutiny and mistrust. Thus, the values we hold, the judgments we make, and the intersubjective framework within which we place all our thoughts are not simply something that we upkeep as passively as one maintains comfort by scratching an itch. This passivity, with which one may be engaged, is made worse by often being an *active* passivity, whereby 'investigation' is conducted to supply justification rather than the examination or research by which one seeks to *uncover* what may actually be the case.

Thus, the complicated network which both encourages active passivity and maintains an entangled antagonism which few can traverse,

---

11 Plato, *Plato in Twelve Volumes*, vol. 1, trans. Harold North Fowler (Cambridge, Mass.: Harvard University Press, 1966).

is the Gordian knot which obfuscates our own coding of perception, as well as the application of the values we hold. Unfortunately, there is no immediate resolution, as was the case with Alexander's sword, but instead the labored development of many more tools. So too might these tools take more time in their use, and even become obsolete after serving their purpose, but their development remains necessary, for they are perhaps the sole tools for the task.

Thus, an earnest pursuit of ideology, as that which is unexamined and regulates the individual to the most reductive state possible—the means to pursue that which produces—and thus manipulates the majority of conflicts that arise both today and throughout history. To properly understand the way in which this invisible dimension rules the lives of the vast majority who leave to their past this stage of 'development,' we must make known a psychological function explicated in its basic form by Jean-Paul Sartre, that of the denial of freedom and responsibility.

> There is nothing to prevent consciousness from making a wholly new choice of its way of being. By means of the Ego, consciousness can partially protect itself from this freedom so limitless that it threatens the very bounds of personality. Everything happens as if consciousness constituted the Ego as a false image of itself, as if consciousness were hypnotized by this Ego which it has established and were absorbed in it. Here undeveloped is the origin of bad faith, the possibility which consciousness possesses of wavering back and forth, demanding the privileges of a free consciousness, yet seeking refuge from the responsibilities of freedom by pretending to be concealed and confined in an already established Ego.[12]

12 Sartre, Jean-Paul, "Translator's Introduction," in *Being and Nothingness: An Essay on Phenomenological Ontology* (New York: Philosophical Library, 1956), xii.

This state of being is largely where ideology is maintained with the psychological realm. This undermines man's autonomy over even his own perception of reality. To this extent it seems that man is blinded, for rarely does he cross the boundaries of his own cognition into the relation which finds his emotive state; that is to say that, even if man operates on a level that supersedes the 'purely logical' or otherwise relegates the notion of his *own* autonomy to the realm of the mental, he will rarely reach the depth he places himself within as a fugitive from responsibility. This state allows individuals to function as if they are but a cohabitant in their life, relegating their primary mode of existence to that of an object. This state is a further solidified prereflexive mode of being, from the perspective of the individual wherein thought is so far separated from action that reconciliation is seen as impossible. To break free from this self-imposed determinism, from this radical self-generated state, it very often seems that there must be a brutal confrontation with Otherness. This is because desperation provides the opportunity to choose against one's own fears, such that these fears are subsumed through anxiety into obscurity. This alters the entirety of man's being, and further distances him from his initial experience with freedom by making even his home and body foreign to him. They become uncanny in a sense. This confrontation also denies the experience of man as being-already-in-the-world, reducing his experience to an inauthentic spectacle.

To make sense of this alteration, the Lacanian triad of the Symbolic, Imaginary, and Real orders provide a way to grasp how the world is rendered in some sense 'meaningful' to us. It is from there that we can understand where this disjunction occurs. We look first to the Imaginary Order, which is "the fundamental narcissism by which the human subject creates fantasy images of both himself and his ideal object of desire . . . What must be remembered is that . . . this imaginary realm continues to exert its influence throughout the life of the adult and is not merely

superseded in the child's movement into the symbolic order."[13] This is
the dimension of images, which gives rise to the Ego. Through an individual's identification with the specular image, the Ego is symmetrically
realized against the recognition of the other *as* other such that alienation
co-characterizes the imaginary relation. The imaginary order however
is structured by the symbolic order, which is "the pact which links . .
. subjects together in one action. The human action *par excellence* is
originally founded on the existence of the world of the symbol, namely
on laws and contracts."[14] It is through these first two orders that we
see our psychological model presenting the constitution of man as one
already susceptible to ideology.

This deficiency is not only due to the filtering process established
within our innate psychological system; before we approach language
and establish our linguistic existence with the word 'I,' we are, from the
onset, pursuing that which satisfies our immediate egocentrism. This
egocentrism is what turns man into a combatant when confronted with
Otherness. The reason for this is twofold. First, because of the constitution
of the ego through identification, man imagines himself to have been
whole prior to this alienation upon experiencing the other. In order to
return to this state of unity, we could imagine a means by which we
eliminate this other by placing our life at stake within a struggle to the
death. Secondarily it is through the image of the other's desire whereby
we constitute an ideal object of desire which we can imagine to be the
fulfillment of the other's lack. Thus, we anticipate the knowledge of the
other such that it is from the structure of this 'ideal object of desire'
that we sublimate our encounter with the other into a struggle of desire
for the other's desire. The very process of socialization finds that man is

13 Felluga, Dino, "Terms Used by Psychoanalysis." In *Introductory Guide to Critical
     Theory*. Purdue University, lecture of January 31, 2011.

14 Lacan, Jacques, *Freud's Papers on Technique 1953-1954*, in *The Seminar of Jacques
     Lacan*, Book 1, trans. John Forrester. ed. Jacques-Alain Miller (New York:
     Norton, 1991).

given over to a relation which always-already governs his internal state of Being as performative over and against self-reflexive. In order then to fulfill his desire, man further leans into this self-same performativity, and thus distances himself from the authentic. The cycle of combat begins by turning man toward himself, where in order to achieve that which is separate and distinct from himself (desire), man must alter his own fantasy image.

Yet this fulfillment is aimed at the desire of others, and as such, man finds the impossibility of a reciprocal situation of desire, as it is never the individual who becomes desired, but rather their altered self-presentation: their Ego. This operative of desire not only shows how mankind is innately ready not only to adopt ideology, but to fight for it. This fight is situated within the finite, temporal, and subjective conditions which structure desire. This is how we recognize the demand to act upon natural desire, for it "is the presence of an *absence:* I am thirsty because there is an absence of water in me . . . To desire to drink is to desire something (water) that *is*: hence, it is to act in terms of the present."[15] Yet this is not the desire we have been exploring: this desire is the desire of life itself as mere intuitive biological preservation. Thus, the desire we seek to bring to light is instead "the desire for a *desire* [which] is to act in terms of what does not (yet) exist: that is, in terms of the future. The being that acts thus, therefore, is in a Time in which the Future takes primacy. And inversely, the Future can really take primacy only if, in the real (spatial) World, there is a being capable of acting thus."[16] This being is man who exists always-already in the world, for this future-oriented desire is not a product of conscious reflection, but rather of the social and historical conditions facing him. The 'desire for another desire' here is describing a desire for social or otherwise relational recognition that the individual believes will

---

15 Kojeve, Alexandre, and Raymond Queneau, "In Place of an Introduction," in *Introduction to the Reading of Hegel: Lectures on the Phenomenology of Spirit* (New York: Basic, 1969), 134-35.

16 Ibid.

restore to himself the fullness of Being. This is because the condition of this desire sees the other as unreal, and as an obstacle through which the individual can come to understand himself. This understanding of the self is given as the idea of man as both a subject and an object of knowledge, but not at all in the Cartesian sense wherein self-consciousness is both the starting point of knowledge and the point of delineation of subject and object, for in this case man is both. We understand this concept then in the Heideggerian sense of knowing as a phenomenal character of he who finds himself being-already-alongside-the-world. As a part of this very phenomenal character of knowing, we understand that man self-conceals such that the 'I' loses view of itself as a subject. Thus "the everyday interpretation of the self . . . has a tendency to understand itself in terms of the 'world' with which it is concerned," which means that when man "has itself in view ontically, it *fails to see* itself in relation to the kind of Being of that entity which it is itself. And this holds especially for the basic state of . . . Being-in-the-world."[17]

Man commonly tends to retreat toward the world of things to which he relates, or the 'they' (as in the all-pervasive, but never concrete nor material collective of others against which the individual stands). In determining who is free to orient themselves toward an authentic care of the self, the struggle of this future-oriented desire (which is oriented to another desire, that of recognition) finds the necessity of negation. This negated reality is that of the other to an object, whereupon their interpretation of the self loses the mutual relationality previously established. Instead it maintains a submissive relation toward the *first desirer* or *master* of the 'battle' that took place. We find in the negation of the world that the manifold dimensions of desire are established and differentiated in mankind as both natural and metaphysical. It is in man's status as man that we recognize his unique potential to reach beyond

17 Heidegger, Martin, *Being and Time*, trans. John Macquarrie and Edward Robinson (New York: Harper Collins, 1962), 368.

immediate desire and into a desire which we can label metaphysical in that it is conditioned by a *nonlocal* sphere. This finds its expression in the formation: "Time *is* the History of Man in the World. And indeed, without Man, there would be no Time in the World; Nature that did not shelter Man would be only a real *Space*. To be sure, the animal, too, has desires, and it acts in terms of these desires, by negating the real: it eats and drinks, just like man. But the animal's desires are *natural*; they are directed toward what *is*, and hence they are determined by what is."[18] When speaking then of both natural and metaphysical desire we can say that both are native desires of man because both inhere in his Being as a part of the natural world as well as the symbolic order.

Time, then, as the historical account of man in the world, is fundamental to Being and yet is different from the processes by which its properties may be observed, which both require each other. A helpful parallel is drawn through Heidegger's discussion of the world and the earth in that there is a mutual co-belonging from which its truth may be disclosed. He states that

> world and earth are essentially different from one another and yet are never separated. The world grounds itself on the earth and earth juts through world. Yet the relationship between world and earth does not wither away into the empty unity of opposites unconcerned with one another. The world, in resting upon the earth, strives to surmount it. As self-opening it cannot endure anything closed. The earth, however, as sheltering and concealing, tends always to draw the world into itself and keep it there.[19]

Here we understand the intelligibility of the earth itself as habitually caught within a fundamental dynamic of concealment and unconcealment, from

---

18 Kojeve, "In Place of an Introduction," 138-39.

19 Heidegger, *The Origin of the Work of Art* (Waterloo: University of Waterloo Press, 1977), 174.

which abiding stability in the light of our 'world' signification is merely a dream. In painting this picture of the worlding through which man's actions and meaning itself are understood, we come to see the differentiation of man from nature, for in nature, there are desires and work which are done, but they are in fact cyclical and biological realities alone. They fail to contribute in a way that develops and thus retroactively conditions future interpretation, for such is the temporal-historical Being of man.

It is clear however that the native metaphysical desire of man conditions and is conditioned by a lack in intersubjective relations. Yet because desire is always fueled towards 'something else' (for one cannot desire what one already has), it must habitually defer its object. Thus, this metaphysical desire is itself fundamentally insatiable: dialectically produced as it is through the field of the Other, manifest through the perceived desires of each subject. There is no end to desire *as such*, for it is self-replicating, that is, it is the desire to indefinitely sustain desire. Desire only grows through its consumption, rather than finding satisfaction. Metaphysical desire then is again

a desire that cannot be satisfied. For we speak lightly of desires satisfied, or of sexual needs, or even of moral and religious needs. Love itself is thus taken to be the satisfaction of a sublime hunger. If this language is possible it is because most of our desires and love too are not pure. The desires one can satisfy resemble metaphysical desire only in the deceptions of satisfaction or in the exasperation of non-satisfaction and desire which constitutes voluptuosity itself. The metaphysical desire has another intention; it desires beyond everything that can simply complete it. It is like goodness: the Desire does not fulfill it, but deepens it.[20]

20 Levinas, Emmanuel, *Totality and Infinity: An Essay on Exteriority* (Pittsburgh, Pa.: Duquesne University Press, 1969), 34.

Thus, because desire is constituted from the field of the Other, there is the paradoxical demand that the recognition granted by the Other must stem from a meaningful position of equality as such (for this intuition of equality allows the formation of subjectivity and identification). Yet in this state of desiring from the position of the Other, it is the knowledge of the Other's (supposed) desire which grants whatever series of objects it overdetermines, their surplus desirability. In other words, the lack of being (totally recognized, wholly desired, etc.) is the tension of the multiplicity which makes desire a social product. It is the prohibition of the fulfillment of desire that stimulates its paradoxical replication.

The 'primitive' status of man's self-consciousness is found then to be that which is logically self-defeating. In submission to economic cooperation man's self-consciousness, which determines itself relationally through struggle, finds that the resolution of the desire which grounds his struggle still eludes him, regardless of if he emerges as master or slave. This is because the surplus of response to a demand, that which extends beyond need, is itself the position of desire. It is through discipline, prohibition, and many more discrete relations that man is given over as a subject of desire within the symbolic as well as the imaginary orders. So too, however, it is a necessary reaction against status as barred from the third order, the real, which is "the state of nature from which we have been forever severed by our entrance into language. Only as neo-natal children were we close to this state of nature, a state in which there is nothing but need."[21]

Therefore, in order to determine ourselves in our distinctive separation from the real, the previously established orders give man over to the formation of worlding, and thus production of a sense toward objects, a sense which is entirely human and subjective, and in that very sense confined to human 'creation.' All that exists within the referential totality of each prescriptive 'reality' (or world, or society) necessarily imparts

---

21 Felluga, "Terms Used by Psychoanalysis."

information wholly given by the capacity of man to relate and organize it into a sensible or meaningful idea, concept, or otherwise purposeful object. This is not to say that the information received from man is always necessarily imparted, but rather that the organizational compound from which one can derive the for-the-sake-of-which and the readiness-to-hand of any and all meaningfulness, rationality, sensibleness, or otherwise relational message is somewhere explicated by the existence of the referential totality such that an outsider may be doctored in. Thus, the real remains ever distant, and ever impossible to define or even 'relate' information to or about. It follows that alongside our psychology, our perception too allows for easy submission to ideology. So too does the basic induction of such knowledge prime our understanding as that which structures a foundation for new events and permissive ways of thought.

Having formulated a basic understanding of the conditions through which the natural man is brought into being susceptible to ideology, it is best then to state a working concept of 'ideology,' which is certainly subject to change, but nevertheless forbids us a point of entry. This definition is structured on four separate pillars, which generate the axes from which the rest of its walls and rooms shall then be built and explored. These four pillars are better made explicit by Louis Althusser who orders them (and elaborates on them) as such: "Ideology represents the imaginary relationship of individuals to their real conditions of existence."[22] Instantaneously we see the problematic structure of ideology as that which, instead of attempting reflection of that which is said to be 'real,' choosing the path of representation to dictate structured belief 'about' rather than 'of' that which exists in its real conditions, or even phenomenologically through the ways in which these conditions of existence appear. Ideology then is a fundamental fantasy relation that structures representation, from which discrete narratives are built.

---

22 Althusser, Louis, *Lenin and Philosophy and Other Essays*, trans. Ben Brewster (New York: Monthly Review, 2001), 109.

This is dictated through the language with which we communicate, for it is the fundamental lifeblood that constitutes the social experience of ideology. This is because, as we develop our ability to use language, we find therein "the common domain of the signifieds of connotation is that of ideology which cannot but be single for a given society and history no matter what signifiers of connotation it may use."[23] The use of language then gives rise to a secondary system of connotations, which are attributed blindly to the denotated message that exists as the primary form of communication. It is through this that we find the problematic hidden nature of language, which passively cultivates further distance from authentic communication, and wherein the structures which it erects maintain an appearance of inevitability or an intrinsic character; the admittance of the referential connotation as being 'relative' is hidden by very nature of the referential function to which it attaches itself. This secondary nature, the expressive status of the connotations, is then reflected as being brought on by the one who points it out.

The second pillar through which we come to ideology is by conceding that "ideology has a material existence."[24] This deceptively simple statement seems necessarily wrong, but its truth is found in the explanation that "an ideology always exists in an apparatus, and its practice, or practices."[25] This is to say that we follow the progression from action, to practice, into belief. This is different however from saying that ideology *manifests* itself through the apparatuses, practice, or practices: for this is to say that ideology goes from the metaphysical *into* the physical. To say this is to say that there is but one *true* form, or essential nature which must necessarily find itself in the metaphysical realm. This would mean that in the material world, ideology is always referential towards its metaphysically essential form, and thus *temporally* pointing toward

23 Barthes, Roland, and Stephen Heath, "Rhetoric of the Image," in *Image, Music, Text* (New York: Hill and Wang, 1977).

24 Althusser, *Lenin and Philosophy*, 112.

25 Ibid.

eternity, rather than pointing toward the eternal. This must be wrong, for ideology possesses no history of its own, but instead is eternal in that it is a general omni-historical structure. We find ideology at the end of relationality, and through which belief establishes itself. "Pascal says more or less: 'Kneel down, move your lips in prayer, and you will believe.'"[26] That is not to say that this is the necessary formula through which we might find ourselves ensnared in the fiendish trap of ideology, but simply to make clear the absolute material way through which ideology is 'actualized.' This locates the spectral power of ideology as that of the performative, wherein man finds himself interpolated habitually in relation to institutions or individuals.

The third pillar which we find ourselves confronted with shows that "all ideology hails or interpolates concrete individuals as concrete subjects."[27] This is perhaps the most paradoxical element in understanding ideology. The use of the word "concrete" continues to challenge our perception of ideology as that which is not merely metaphysical, but which also absolutely maintains a material existence; it is also a challenge insofar as the interpolation of individuals is achieved tangibly. The existence of ideology then seems at both times fundamentally obvious, and yet so pervasive that it must always be approximated through inferring the whole of the beast from the observance of its dorsal fin. How is man to speak about that which he is intrinsically encapsulated within, and through which he may never step back and bear witness to the whole of its hideousness? The question itself does not even begin to question one's ability to see accurately or put into words that which is perceived, but simply to be able to look upon. As such, it becomes increasingly clear that a majority of events which transpire among individuals take place under the ever-controlling grip of ideology. This, while maintaining the "practical *denigration* of the ideological character of ideology by

26 Ibid., 114.
27 Ibid., 115

ideology,"[28] this renders as invisible (to the individual) the ideological apparatus through which individuals subscribe.

The third pillar of ideology then effectively denies the first to the ideologue. It maintains its function as invisible, and thus infinitely powerful, until it is made peripherally visible through the limited ability of language. Even through this visibility, instead of being defeated it obfuscates or divorces the visible element in an attempt to relegate all that can be saved back into the 'natural' and 'good' which it was assumed to be prior to the advent of its critique. This is given, as we can come to see through ideology's final pillar, which finds that "individuals are always-already subjects."[29] Thus, perhaps one of the most devastating effects of ideology is made apparent: in conjunction with the development of the 'concrete subject' of ideology, and understanding that man is himself always-already a subject, we find the relationship of man to ideology as defined by symbiosis. This relationship holds the individual's perception of himself and his own self-narrative against the backdrop of ideology, such that it is—to the subject— undifferentiated from Being as such. To restore man to his fullest state of autonomy means literally to deconstruct his own formation as a subject: to approximate the blurred line wherein ideology functions beyond his ascent.

Thus, an openness to change on the most fundamental and *personal* level must be within the realm of possibility for the individual seeking freedom, such that a distance may be founded between the ideological subjectivity man has mistaken for himself, and the true core of his being. The ever-referential deferment to ideology is made ever more evasive through the systematic phenomenon Lacan called the Name-of-the-Father, which in its original French, plays with the near identical articulation of the the-no-of-the-Father. This phenomenon is explicated as "the laws and restrictions that control both your desire and the

---

28 Ibid., 118.
29 Ibid., 119.

rules of communication."[30] It is the system through which a model of identification with the symbolic order is built. It is the means by which signification proceeds, the way in which identity is given to subjects and on which it depends, which grounds the normality from which it proceeds. Thus, self-relation is even indirectly challenged through the language and relationships formed around them. We find that here, even if an individual were open to examining himself in absolute dissection, as well as if by some divine miracle he were to have a trusted external reference point for his own language, his restrictions limit his ability to address his bondage. This is the intimate predicament of the immediacy of ideological interpolation.

---

30 Felluga, "Terms Used by Psychoanalysis."

ABOVE THE BATTLE: INVERTING NAPOLEON

As we have come to understand this formulation of the problem of ideology, the question must turn from the 'what' to the 'how.' If we are to this extent able to communicate about the situation of ideology and our confinement therein, how is one able to benefit from such knowledge, and what steps would be in the right direction of limiting (as much as possible) the restrictions placed upon us by our operation therefrom? The first success would seem to be the existence of a critique in general, for it opens the pathway to reduction by necessity; however, this is not the end goal, for critique itself unfortunately exists within the permitted cycle of the birth and death of all previous lives of ideology. The situation of the critic is then reduced to a member of the class of mere 'intellectuals,' which Kojeve describes as

> a whole category of men who do not actively participate in the historical construction and who are content to live in the constructed edifice and to *talk* about it. These men, who live somehow 'above the battle,' who are content to *talk* about things that they do not create by their *Action,* are Intellectuals who produce intellectuals' *ideologies,* which they take for philosophy (and pass off as such).[31]

---

31 Kojeve, Alexandre, and Raymond Queneau, "Summary of the First Six Chapters of the Phenomenology of Spirit," in *Introduction to the Reading of Hegel,* 33.

Criticism and confrontation are not by themselves enough, for neither allow a point in which one may exit or slow the ride; rather, they merely propel us forward at a faster pace, wherein even less may come of our relationship with ideology as we are no longer even permitted the time to understand the mechanism by which we see the world.

The aim of this text, then, is to succeed by constructing a critique with a built-in ejection system. This text will so successfully object to established ideologies that it will present a thorough explication of not merely hegemonic ideologies, but also 'revolutionary' or 'progressive' ones. This is to be done, of course, without neglecting that which is 'traditional' nor that which maintains a 'conservative' footing. Hence, through the observation of this criticism, we shall find that it eventually achieves its own deconstruction. This will offer one way of transcending critical/textual approaches to ideology, while refraining from calcifying into a dogmatic or ideological methodology. Thus, despite the fact that Napoleon's creation of the citizen has radically transformed the continuation of explicit master/slave relations, we may instead note that the roles carry on, deferred (as action is generally deferred in the post-Napoleonic state) from direct concrete individuals and directly into the symbolic order whereupon we find the positions transmogrified into master and slave ideologies.

Hence the citizen who seeks freedom from rule must in a certain sense begin by seeking freedom from that which is hegemonic. This is because there still exists the battle for recognition, the desire for another's desire, and a failure resulting in subsumption. This transpires at the level of power, but wears the guise of truth. There is certainly some objection to be made that we can achieve a mutually satisfactory result, where those who have been subjects of these shifting mainstream ideologies might find all of our qualms quieted and no longer be divided as a population. However, those who claim that we may find some humane collection of values and structure which is so universal in scope that it obliterates the potential for otherness is pure fantasy. This objection fails to see that as far as social relations go,

> man is not truly *individual*, and that is why he is not fully *satisfied* by his social and political existence. That is also why he actively and freely (i.e., by negation) transforms the given social and political reality, in order to make it such that he can realize his true Individuality in it. And this progressive realization of *Individuality*, by the active and *free* progressive satisfaction of the desire for Recognition, is the "dialectical movement" of *History* which Man himself is.[32]

This passage speaks then to the fundamental means by which man relates his consciousness to the world as the precept from which social or otherwise political reality is navigated and *intentionally* transformed. This is not to suggest that there is a moment where the subsumption of that consciousness is not always-already given over to a collective rationale. This subsumption however strives to negate the individual, rather than negating the social context which birthed him. The resulting loss of the self that was founded by conformity finds the model through which one relates to be inauthentic.

This concern of the individual in light of the conformity to a group structure is mentioned by Heidegger when he states that "*Authentic Being-one's-Self* does not rest upon an exceptional condition of the subject, a condition that has been detached from the 'they'; *it is rather an existentiell modification of the 'they'—of the 'they as an essential existentiale.'*"[33] *Thus,* authentic being-one's-self is an outgrowth of the primordial phenomenon of the they-self. This means that the positive constitution of Dasein relegates both individuality and conformity, authenticity and

---

32 Ibid., 237.

33 Heidegger, *Being and Time*, 168.

inauthenticity to the very ontological structure of man. This is because, insofar as one stands in relation to others, one takes note principally of others as functionaries, who are overwhelmingly interchangeable as regards their social roles. What's worse is that, in this very situation, man understands that his appearance in such a role is broadcast to the very self-same others. This is, as Hegel states, of "twofold significance: first, [because] it has lost itself . . . it finds itself as an *other* being; secondly, in doing so it has superseded the other, for it does not see the other as an essential being, but in the other sees its own self."[34]

Part of what makes ideology so frightening is that it inverts this inherently social and economically defined sense of personhood and maps one's entire meaning and understanding onto it. There is a lack of integration of the specificity of individual experience with what is taught, such that a unique synthesis occurs. Instead, it is within this relationality that one understands that freedom itself is caught essentially within the framework of the authentic. And yet, the recognition from the Other of said freedom necessarily results in the inequality and nonmutual recognition of this very meeting of/against the Other. But it is from this relationality that the paradox the master-slave dialectic begins, for from this point onward the individual "must proceed to supersede the other independent being in order thereby to become certain of *itself* as the essential being . . . in so doing it proceeds to supersede its own self, for this other is itself."[35] Here we encounter the manifold facets involved in the reciprocal inter-discovery of the self and the Other, which have motivated a great deal of both Lacan's and Levinas's work. There is a seeming paradox stemming from this supersession, where an implicit demand is made that the Other negate its own autonomy and independence in order to recognize and thus secure the independence and autonomy of he who is being recognized. Yet, it is from the recognizing

34 Hegel, *Phenomenology of Spirit*, 111.
35 Ibid.

faculties of the other that this independence and autonomy (what we can call certainty) is secured. In Hegel's own words:

> Each is indeed certain of its own self, but not of the other, and therefore its own self-certainty still has no truth. For it would have truth only if its own being-for-self had confronted it as an independent object, or, what is the same thing, if the object had presented itself as this pure self-certainty. But according to the Notion of recognition this is possible only when each is for the other what the other is for it, only when each in its own self through its own action, and again through the action of the other, achieves this pure abstraction of being-for-self.[36]

There are two moments then to take away from this passage, the first of which being the immediacy of the Other as maintaining that which resists the egocentric totality of the self, whereupon the other as Other fails to be pure and simple self-certainty for the individual. Thus, in order that the individual might maintain the pure and simple being of his certainty, a battle must occur to extract by force the absolute recognition from the other. This is played out to an extreme, when we see that

> they must engage in this struggle, for they must raise their certainty of being *for* themselves to truth, both in the case of the other and in their own case. And it is only through staking one's life that freedom is won only thus is it proved that for self-consciousness, its essential being is not [just] being, not the immediate form in which it appears, not its submergence in the expanse of life, but rather that there is nothing present in it which could not be regarded as a vanishing moment,

---

36 Ibid., 113.

that it is only pure being-for-self. The individual who has not risked his life may well be recognized as a *person,* but he has not attained to the truth of this recognition as an independent self-consciousness. Similarly, just as each stakes his own life, so each must seek the other's death, for it values the other no more than itself; its essential being is present to it in the form of an 'other,' it is outside of itself and must rid itself of its self-externality. The other is an *immediate* consciousness entangled in a variety of relationships, and it must regard its otherness as a pure being-for-self or as an absolute negation.[37]

The second moment immediately follows the first in this passage: the core notion that drives human progress forward is this insatiable attempt to weld truth to certainty.

Despite this seemingly eternal struggle, the structure of man's relational totality is still that which is intelligible and significant, providing the opportunity to actively resist the dogmatic structure of contingent conformity; thus the possibility of achieving relative individuality from ideological structures becomes magnified. In Hegel's *Phenomenology* the paradox of the position of servitude is dealt with at length, showcasing that through defeat, the Slave finds his position as slave to be the site containing the very possibility of self-consciousness. Freedom from ideological conformity is here made available in the deep chasm left through the structure of the symbolic order, whereupon the selfsame content of the two is shrouded in a veil. This seems wrong, for how could it be that the possibility of freedom lay at the feet of the slave: is not the slave made into an object and set to servitude as a tool of pleasure and satisfaction of the will of the master? Is not the slave's consciousness degraded and perverted beyond recognition? Hegel states that, as for this self-consciousness, we must

---

37 Ibid., 114.

consider what as such it is in and for itself. To begin with, servitude has the lord for its essential reality; hence the truth for it is the independent consciousness that is for itself. However, servitude is not yet aware that this truth is implicit in it. But it does in fact contain within itself this truth of pure negativity and being-for-self, for it has experienced this its own essential nature. For this consciousness has been fearful, not of this or that particular thing or just at odd moments, but its whole being has been seized with dread; for it has experienced the fear of death, the absolute Lord. In that experience it has been quite un-manned, has trembled in every fibre of its being, and everything solid and stable has been shaken to its foundations. But this pure universal movement, the absolute melting-away of everything stable, is the simple, essential nature of self-consciousness, absolute negativity, pure being-for-self, which consequently is implicit in this consciousness. This moment of pure being-for-self is also explicit for the bondsman, for in the lord it exists for him as his object. Furthermore, his consciousness is not this dissolution of everything stable merely in principle; in his service he actually brings this about. Through his service he rids himself of his attachment to natural existence in every single detail; and gets rid of it by working on it.[38]

It is, for the slave, this self-interest vested in the radical self-identity of the master that allows the slave to become the ideal that is symbolically transposed unto the master. The master thus lacks the determinate productivity, essential transformative nature, and technical skills of the slave, and rather by necessity is bound to consumption, and through this consumption of the object, there is an implicit blinding which causes his identity to further fuse with fantasy as pure enjoyment.

---

38 Ibid., 117.

It would appear that not only is the state of the master that which is necessarily without any further direction up, this state stops itself short upon the desire to be recognized by those who are beneath its reign, and which itself blocks the possibility for the achievement of Being-for-itself. Hence, there must by necessity be within the structure of the master's existence a preoccupation with maintaining a position within the cycle of consumption. This is the means by which revolutionaries and reactionaries misunderstand the reproductive cycle of this level of dialectic, for they find their own definition-of-Being maintained by its contrast with ideologies they claim superiority to. It is from their dependence upon opposing ideologies that they draw their negative definitions, from which they find their own understanding and representation of ideology defined. As abstracted, this concept is as follows:

> If Identity is incarnated in the "A" which is identical to itself (A = A), Negativity is made concrete in and by (or as) the *non* of the "non-A." Taken in itself, this *non* is pure and simple Nothingness: it is something only because of the A which it negates . . . Moreover, as soon as "non-A" exists, the purely negating "non" is just as much an *abstraction* as the purely identical A. What really exists is the unity of the two- that is, the "non-A" as *totality* or entity that is as much one and unique, determined and specific, as the "A" itself = the "non-A" which is a "B." A is preserved in B (= non-A). But the *non* which negates A is equally maintained in it. Therefore A is preserved only in its negation (just as the *non* is maintained only as the non of A).[39]

This showcases the infinite and cyclical regress through which reactionary and revolutionary ideologies are not only defined by that which they

---

39 Kojeve, "Summary of the First Six Chapters," 203-4.

react or revolt against, but are a part of, or in continuation of, that very same ideology, albeit less visibly.

Strange as it is that ideological identity may mirror the dialectical development of the self and/or the concept by positing as a point of contingent historical evil the position of its enemy, and claiming as backwards its identity, this tactic nevertheless fundamentally misses the vital element fueling true development (of the self/concept). Neither the self nor the concept construct their identity around a negated term, but rather the understanding of progress is truth maintaining the history of their constitution as necessary steps that result in the actuality of the form (self/concept). To explicate the event through which the continual relation is established is to reveal the impossibility of ideological sublimation; this is the honest work of negation, which thus draws out the fundamental proposition of the reactionary or revolutionary as nothingness itself embodied.

From this vantage point, we can see that the alternative route through which both moments (the A and non-A) are maintained is equally absurd. For this second path is the necessary confusion of those who believe themselves to operate freely, hyphenated or fragmentary ideologues who makes demands of both camps that are incapable of being reconciled. This is because

> identitarian or minoritarian logic merely proposes a variant on its nominal occlusion by capital. It inveighs against every generic concept of art, putting the concept of culture in its place, conceived as culture of the group, as the subjective or representative glue for the group's existence, a culture that addresses only itself and remains potentially nonuniversalizable. Moreover, it does not hesitate to posit that this culture's constitutive elements are only fully comprehensible on the condition that one belongs to the subset in question. Whence catastrophic pronouncements of the sort: only a homosexual

can "understand" what a homosexual is, only an Arab can understand what an Arab is, and so forth. If, as we believe, only truths (thought) allow man to be distinguished from the human animal that underlies him, it is no exaggeration to say that such minoritarian pronouncements are genuinely *barbaric*. In the case of science, culturalism promotes the technical particularity of subsets to the equivalent of scientific thought, so that antibiotics, Shamanism, the laying on of hands, or emollient herbal teas all become of equal worth. In the case of politics, the consideration of identitarian traits provides the basis for determination, be it the state's or the protestor's, and finally it is a matter of stipulating, through law of brute force, an authoritarian management of these traits (national, religious, sexual, and so on) considered as dominate political operators. Lastly, in the case of love, there will be the complementary demands, either for the genetic right to have such and such a form of specialized sexual behavior recognized as a minoritarian identity; or for the return, pure and simple, to archaic, culturally established conceptions, such as that of strict conjugality, the confinement of women, and so forth. It is perfectly possible to combine the two, as becomes apparent when the homosexual protest concerns the right to be reincluded in the grand traditionalism of marriage and the family, or to take responsibility for the defrocking of a priest with the Pope's blessing.[40]

It is with this hyphenated existence that we see those who find themselves in both camps maintaining a dedication of sorts to two ideological statuses which bring the individual into conflict with himself. Instead of

---

40 Badiou, Alain, "Paul: Our Contemporary," in *Saint Paul: The Foundation of Universalism* (Stanford, Calif.: Stanford University Press, 2003), 12-13.

recognizing the contradiction to be nominal, he instead asserts that the contradiction is in the status of a universal. Instead of deconstructing ideology to present the difficulties in their constitution of its prefabricated identity, there is an ongoing project of specificity on behalf of the subject.

This can be shown to be working within an identitarian commodification of specific identities. As each is deduced from subjective-historical variants to be worn as if to displace the site of particularity within the individual (as is natural), ideology becomes the naturalized guarantee of universality. Thus the 'real nature' of man is seen within the Möbius strip of 'good' and 'bad' without differentiation except in relation to one's identity, which is narrowed further and further with each set of commandments and codas. Instead, unhappy with their place within the universal, there is a need to construct a hyphenated ideology that is more specific toward their conditions of identity, and as such there erupts a tension which the ideological subject cannot tolerate, for his subjectivity still frames the identity as in-relation-to or in-opposition-to, denoting a point of conflicting reference.

> The two components of the articulated whole (abstract homogeneity of capital and identitarian protest) are in a relation of reciprocal maintenance and mirroring. Who will maintain the self-evident superiority of the competent-cultivated-sexually liberated manager? But who will defend the corrupt-religious-polygamist terrorist? Or eulogize the cultural-marginal-homeopathic-media-friendly transsexual? Each figure gains its rotating legitimacy from the other's discredit. Yet at the same time, each draws on the resources of the other, since the transformation of the most typical, most recent communitarian identities into advertising selling points and salable images has for its counterpart the ever more refined competence that the most insular or most violent groups

display when it comes to speculating on the financial markets
or maintaining a large-scale arms commerce.[41]

So it seems that the further we go down the rabbit hole, we find ourselves
still battling for ideological power, only now involving our specific identity as a class from which particular battles are fought, thus only providing
the illusion that our specificity distances us from the dominating totality
that each ideology represents. Hence the shifting of particulars only
solidifies their particularity as relational to their ideological apparatuses.
This brings us back to the idea of the individual as the sole inheritor
of freedom which as a relation provides the opportunity to backpedal
subjectivity's ideological commitments. This is effectively the only means
whereby the actual difference of singularity might come about.

As a result, one acquires an awareness of the compromises of identity
in relation to the demands of ideology. As such we see that the necessary
existence of slave ideology is defined by change, and yet within this change
is the desire to adopt the master's stagnant ideology. This is beyond the
observation that human understanding is constrained to its own desire
to reach beyond itself, for a keen eye sees the identity of one given by
the other, which is to say that within this 'beyond' is but an inversion
of this selfsame desire. It is a desire that finds kinship in the Ouroboros,
the snake that forever feasts upon its own tail. The master ideology
breaking from this form would achieve the impossible: it would need to
achieve independence. To break from its relational identity would mean
to rid itself of the title that its own history gave as its foundation. To
achieve this independence from the position as master would be thrice
the challenge it overcame to inscribe this position as its own within the
symbolic. Doing this would not be to simply announce it, nor is there
even the possibility of a symbolic resignation, but rather to achieve this
position would be to literally force those under its subordination to

41 Ibid., 13.

no longer recognize it as the master, as the hegemonic ideology. In so doing, however, it would be asserting force, which is the most obvious characteristic of the master, so if such a feat were somehow possible, it would have the opposite effect by masking its own presence under the pretense (which all must pretend they go along with) that it is not what it looks like, nor what people say it is, thus strangely granting the ideology far greater power. Therefore, if the impossible was somehow desired, and even more unbelievably achieved, its status as independent would not be legitimate, nor would it be, aside from playacting, recognized.

It would seem to be true that 'freedom' on an individual level would be that which is achievable through means of the position of the slave; however, such an escape is not so easily achieved, for: "before *realizing* Freedom, the Slave imagines a series of ideologies, by which he seeks to justify himself, to justify his slavery, to reconcile the *ideal* of Freedom with the *fact* of Slavery."[42] This is the immediate position noted by Sartre's concept of responsibility and freedom, which the majority of individuals wish to avoid at all cost. It is first through denial that man imagines his freedom actualized, and through this denial he is granted solace through the intellectual justification of Stoic ideology:

> The Slave tries to persuade himself that he is *actually* free simply by *knowing* that he is free: that is, by having the abstract *idea* of Freedom. The *real* conditions of existence would have no importance at all . . . it is sufficient to have the *idea* of freedom, or more precisely, of autonomy, of absolute independence of all *given* conditions of existence.[43]

There is a sleight-of-hand persistent in Stoicism in that there is certainly some degree of psychological freedom offered by the position,

---

42 Kojeve, "Summary of the First Six Chapters," 53.
43 Ibid.

but this psychological operation extends beyond the relief it offers and thus ensnares its followers insofar as it shifts the condition for all freedom from Being to intention alone. The expression of man becomes arbitrary and the dawning of his Stoic perspective represents the completion of his production. He selects intention "as [his] true inner; the intention is supposed to have its more or less *unessential* expression in the deed . . .

[but] the true being of a man is rather his deed; in this the individual is actual."[44] Stoic ideology stops man from action by dictating that the fullness of freedom is achieved merely by its thought. This means to the Stoic that the actual conditions of his existence make no difference: freedom is attained merely by maintaining the open state by which freedom of thought may be exercised. This subjugates man as a *thinker*, and nothing further.

This approach might bring about interpersonal revelation and work well as a therapeutic approach to one's enslavement to a psychological ailment, thus freeing one from psychological bondage with psychological tools. Ultimately, however, maintaining Stoicism as one's own will lead to habitually excusing one's self from the experience and freedom inherent in life. This flips man on his head, for to find himself in this position is to choose for himself absolute stagnation, reducing man to that through which nothing *can* happen, leaving him exactly as he came, save with a psychological coping method to keep him company in his shackles. Should he choose this path his absolute stasis will transform into skeptic-nihilism, fully embracing the resulting solipsism, which negates only himself. Should he progress, however, he will find Stoic ideologies rendered a phase, through which the previously initiated will pass through, having mined the ideology for tools which will aid in the pursuit of freedom, as one recognizes the contradiction present in

---

44 Hegel, Georg Wilhelm Friedrich, *Phenomenology of Spirit*, trans. A. V. Miller (New Delhi: Shri Jainendra, 1998), 193.

the pure Ego of Stoicism [which] though not devoid of content, is inward-turned whatever its content, and has therefore an abstract in-difference to natural being which it leaves to take its own course. The freedom of such Stoicism is not, therefore, a living, contentful freedom, but the mere idea of such freedom, drawn away from life and things into itself. This means that unless content is externally given to this consciousness, it cannot by itself determine the True and the Good. It has no criterion other than the wholly empty, abstract one of the reasonable, a notion as tedious as it is superficially elevated.[45]

Thus, the negation present in Stoic ideology which brought the symbolic realm to a status altogether disregarded rejects all content distinct from its own application, does away with epistemological or ontological grounding, and turns toward pure dumb abjection. Thus, the move to skepticism is one through which absolute certainty of freedom is sought. This freedom is threatened by the 'unreasonable' beliefs that are in some sense necessary for the conduct of ordinary life. The transition from Stoicism to skepticism is from inactive but pure freedom to inactive but pure certainty, neither of which result in freedom or certainty. This is because the predication of purity is intrinsic to the conceptual approaches of either condition.

Thus, because man cannot retreat from Being without resorting to suicide, the life of the skeptic is filled with dissonance, and is "therefore the unconscious, thoughtless rambling which passes back and forth from the one extreme of self-identical self-consciousness to the other extreme of the contingent consciousness that is both bewildered and bewildering."[46] It is from this position where two ends are held apart that

45 Hegel, *Phenomenology of Spirit* (trans. Miller), 523.
46 Ibid., 125.

a solution is sought to join them, and progression from the unbearable friction of skepticism is made. We know this can be done, for

> one can in fact overcome the contradiction of a given existence only by *modifying* the given existence, by transforming it through Action. But in the Slave's case, to transform existence is, again, to fight against the Master. Now, he does not want to do this. He tries, therefore, to justify by a new ideology this contradiction in skeptical existence, which [duplicates,] all things considered, the Stoic—i.e., slavish—contradiction, between the *idea* or the *ideal* of Freedom and the *reality* of Slavery.[47]

It is from this moment that the unhappy consciousness is born, which is the mere container of the disparate halves, and from their perceived dis-unity, the unhappy consciousness conceives of their difference as a fundamental opposition within its Being.

> In this movement . . . consciousness experiences . . . this emergence of individuality in the Unchangable, and of the Unchangeable in individuality. Consciousness becomes aware of individuality in general in the Unchangeable, and at the same time of its *own* individuality in the latter. For the truth of this movement is just the *oneness* of this dual consciousness. This unity, however, in the first instance, becomes for it one in which the *difference* of both is still the dominant feature.[48]

Hence, it is in the observation of both individuality and truth presiding within the unchangeable that the unhappy consciousness "identifies itself with the changeable consciousness, and takes itself to be the unessential

---

47 Kojeve, "Summary of the First Six Chapters," 54-55.
48 Hegel, *Phenomenology of Spirit* (trans. Miller), 127-28.

Being."[49] It is from this faulty perception, this focus away from unity onto difference, that the individual comes to portray in differing models an attempt to reconcile with the unchanging, essential consciousness. The first of these models is that whereby the unhappy consciousness speaks to its opposition with the unchangeable, with the unchangeable itself understood as "an alien Being who passes judgment on the particular individual."[50] It is within this understanding that the unchangeable takes on a position of a mute, cold, and forever-distant icon, a legalistic framework that returns the unhappy consciousness to the beginning of the tension, with no dialectical advance having been won. It is within this mode of opposition that religious institutions support regression.

Here it seems worthwhile to digress so as to offer a lengthy example of the manifestation of this stale moment. Here, we will explore an example from the Christian religion, which may show the death grip it can assume upon the throat of those who find their understanding of the unchangeable in such a light. In Romans 13:1-10, we read:

> Let everyone be subject to the governing authorities, for there is no authority except that which God has established. The authorities that exist have been established by God. Consequently, whoever rebels against the authority is rebelling against what God has instituted, and those who do so will bring judgment on themselves. For rulers hold no terror for those who do right, but for those who do wrong. Do you want to be free from fear of the one in authority? Then do what is right and you will be commended. For the one in authority is God's servant for your good. But if you do wrong, be afraid, for rulers do not bear the sword for no reason. They are God's servants, agents of wrath to bring punishment on

---

49 Ibid., 127
50 Ibid., 128.

the wrongdoer. Therefore, it is necessary to submit to the authorities, not only because of possible punishment but also as a matter of conscience. This is also why you pay taxes, for the authorities are God's servants, who give their full time to governing. Give to everyone what you owe them: If you owe taxes, pay taxes; if revenue, then revenue; if respect, then respect; if honor, then honor. Let no debt remain outstanding, except the continuing debt to love one another, for whoever loves others has fulfilled the law. The commandments, "You shall not commit adultery," "You shall not murder," "You shall not steal," "You shall not covet," and whatever other command there may be, are summed up in this one command: "Love your neighbor as yourself." Love does no harm to a neighbor. Therefore love is the fulfillment of the law.[51]

This passage is often cited in isolation in order to ground Christianity in political quietus or otherwise full-on support for statism, no matter how tyrannical. Comically, when taking Romans 12 into account, the passage is actually meant to temper the politically subversive speech found therein, and as such Romans 13 is rather the antithesis of Jewish Fourth Philosophy. However, part of this subversion persists even into Romans 13 as it recalls Jewish tradition now critically reframing the rule of Caesar as under the authority of, and in responsibility to, God. It is by Christian alignment with a sort of holographic relation to the state and its head that loving one's neighbor as one's self becomes a sort of civil disobedience which refuses the identity of relational antagonism, the likes of which is found in the revolutions that tyrannical states can not only endure (for even should they lose, official tyranny becomes unauthorized tyranny) but depend upon. The cut-and-paste fragmented

51 *The Holy Bible: New International Version* (London: Hodder & Stoughton, 1979).

theology out of which this type of state religion is founded cannot reconcile the critical polemic which makes up the totality of Paul's theology.

Perhaps it is such a grave challenge for our contemporaries to read Paul insofar as their identity often subordinates the radical New Testament vision of Christian life to a political position. However, N. T. Wright clears this up for us when he states that

> the history-of-religions background to Paul's thinking is instructive: Jews holding views broadly analogous to his were quite capable of political activity in the Empire, and of reminding governments of their business. What Paul says is clearly anathema to the totalitarian: the point about totalitarianism is that the ruling power has taken the place of God; that is why it is always *de facto*, and frequently *de jure*, atheist. For Paul, the 'state' is not God. God is God, and the state is thus relativized, as are the powers precisely in Colossians 1:15-20, where they are created and reconciled but not divine.[52]

However, many seek to render institutional the prior statist interpretation which is questioned by few (due to the complex nature of the text), while those who do engage in questioning find themselves at odds with their community. The resulting possibilities then are ostracization or condemnation as a heretic. Such is the devastatingly difficult position of the layman who has little to no knowledge of all the work that goes into the study of the text, i.e., its history and the positioning of authority therefrom. Ultimately, although tradition belongs to the community, and despite its founding revelation which is embodied in the community of the Holy Spirit, it is clear how this radical message of authentic Christian

---

52 Wright, N. T., "The New Testament and the 'State,'" *Theological Studies* (1990); available at theologicalstudies.org.uk/article_state_wright.html.

community can become silently co-opted into a mere spiritual reproduction of hegemony. Thus, the simple shift from recognition of the order of righteousness within the community and the order of political power, to the sanctification of hegemony and its totality, is made almost without notice. The radical command of goodness for a politically disempowered community flowing directly from love is turned into a cover for the spiritual replication of the state. What was a corrective to a community boiling with anti-Roman thought is taken fully to enjoin its higher aims with the gray, stale normativity of state power. Here, spirit truly does become a bone.

Often, however, the demands of such a reading are exposed by a simple explication of its informal commands, thus revealing the *actuality* of a tradition and authentic community separated from the ideology which has previously maintained a monopoly of domination over it. Here, David Chilton offers an astute analysis of the passage in its *actualized* relationship put into direct discussion with the 'ruler' otherwise given the title of "God's minister":

> As God's minister, the ruler has two responsibilities, both of which are mentioned in Romans 13:1. *He must do good.* What is "good"? Is God's minister of justice free to decide that for himself? If so, we cannot condemn anything that rulers have done in the past. Hitler regarded the extermination of Jews as good; Nero thought it was a good idea to tax his citizens in order to fund his private orgies and public slaughters; obviously, we could go on and on. Public health care, minimum wage laws, and state-financed education may all seem "good" to us; but how can we be sure? There is one way: we must go, as Isiah said. "to the law and to the testimony." God's law is "holy, righteous and good" (Romans 7:12; Matthew 23:23). If God's ministers in the state are faithful, they will go to God's Old Testament laws to find out what they should do. Any standard of goodness which is not based on the law of God is not good;

it is mere humanism. A state that departs from God's standard is engaged in a vain and cursed attempt to deify itself. 2. *He must punish evildoers.* What is an "evildoer"? Again we must ask: Is the ruler free to decide the answer for himself? To answer *Yes* is to give a despot a blank check for statist absolutism: he may decide that all babies in Bethlehem are "evildoers," for instance. King Herod was only doing his job, therefore, when he ordered the murder of the infants (Matthew 2:16). Clearly, God has given civil rulers the poster of the sword: obviously they are supposed to execute *somebody.* But whom? If your answer is based on anything but God's law, I repeat: you've just handed the state a blank check—and God's civil minister just might add *you* to his hit list.[53]

Again we find that the prescriptive elements of Romans 13 align with a description of what their current political power looks like. Moreover, the passage asserts the legitimacy of governance with the full weight of Jewish resistances behind it, which are righteously backed by God in the Old Testament. The entire text of Romans is one in which Christian nonconformity and suffering love find the mercy of God overcoming the hostility which was growing toward their community and thus reifying the bonds of said community as a whole. This is all to say that the separation of Christians and the function of a government showcase two separate reactions to evil, one that repays it with good, and one that punishes evil with evil. Thus

> that God orders and uses the powers does not reveal anything
> new about what government should be or how we should

---

53 Chilton, David, "God's Law and the State," in *Productive Christians in an Age of Guilt-manipulators: A Biblical Response to Ronald J. Sider* (Tyler, Tex.: Institute for Christian Economics, 1985), 32-33.

respond to government. A given government is not mandated or saved or made a channel of the will of God; it is simply lined up, used by God in the ordering of the cosmos. It does not mean that what individuals in government do is good human behavior. As we noted, the librarian does not approve of the content of a book he or she shelves; God did not approve morally of the brutality whereby Assyria chastised Israel (Is 10). The immediate concrete meaning of this text for the Christian Jews in Rome, in the face of official anti-Semitism and the rising arbitrariness of the Imperial regime, is to call them away from any notion of revolution or insubordination. The call is to a nonresistant attitude toward a tyrannical government. This is the immediate and concrete meaning of the text . . .[54]

The position herein is a radical one that again gets strangled by the readings given by state religion. For "sometimes doing nothing is the most violent thing to do."[55] This is the space beyond hegemony and its negation which Žižek finds in Melville's Bartleby for

His "I would prefer not to" is to be taken literally: it says "I would prefer not to," *not* "I don't prefer (or care) to"—so we are back at Kant's distinction between negative and infinite judgment. In his refusal of the Master's order, Bartleby does not negate the predicate; rather, he affirms a non-predicate: he does not say that *he doesn't want to do it*; he says that *he prefers (wants) not to do it*. This is how we pass from the politics of "resistance" or "protestation," which parasitizes upon what it negates, to a politics which opens up a new space outside the hegemonic

54 John Howard Yoder, "Let Every Soul Be Subject," in *The Politics of Jesus: Vicit Agnus Noster* (Grand Rapids, Mich.: Eerdmans, 2008), 202–3.

55 Žižek, Slavoj, "Epilogue," in *Violence: Six Sideways Reflections* (New York: Picador, 2008), 217.

position *and* its negation. We can imagine the varieties of such a gesture in today's public space: not only the obvious "There are great chances of a new career here! Join us!"—"I would prefer not to"; but also "Discover the depths of your true self, find inner peace!"—"I would prefer not to"; or "Are you aware how our environment is endangered? Do something for ecology!"—"I would prefer not to"; or "What about all the racial and sexual injustices that we witness all around us? Isn't it time to do more?"—"I would prefer not to." This is the gesture of subtraction at its purest, the reduction of all qualitative differences to a purely formal minimal difference.[56]

In the tension between subordination and moral judgment, the position of Bartleby becomes a clear alternative to a state religion which seeks to define any arbitrary activity as 'sin.' Thus, if we are to understand Romans, and more largely the Bible and Christian tradition as a whole, in this way the *justice* of God seems to falter, and its defining feature becomes one of arbitrariness. This arbitrary nature is the *essential* character by which the unchangeable in this regressive form of dialectic, by its very own mute and distant nature, may be interchanged with any other arbiter, and thus only the *form* remains, where the epistemological condition authorizing this form is bottomless. This anachronistic repositing of authentic Christian belief places the Bible and the whole of Christian tradition into contradiction with its own statist support. Thus, the hyphenated nature of the individual's ideological position reveals the rendering of Christianity into a state ideology (e.g., American-Christian, or even more specified, African-American-Christian). This modifier is often used to harness a more primal identification, forever displacing responsibility into the realm of the unchangeable.

---

56 Žižek, Slavoj, "The Obscene Knot of Ideology, and How to Untie It," in *The Parallax View* (Cambridge, Mass.: MIT Press, 2009), 381–82.

This returns us from the digression, for it becomes obvious that the solution found here, to the question of dialectic in relation to the unchanging, is unsatisfactory. This implicit hope in ideology will prove futile, for it is necessarily dishonest in its approach to the divine, which places man in such a manipulable position. This is the life-hating asceticism which rejects all before it in order to ground man's worries about freedom in the eternal and unchangeable. It is through whatever conceptual manifestation the unchangeable takes that man will have found a much more complicated state of affairs, which he still comes to believe as truth (precisely as he did in his previous Stoic dabbling), but now he no longer roots his *ideal* of freedom in his mind, but in something external. With no progress to show for his laborious struggle against unifying his self-certainty and the truth, man merely shifts the narrative of his ideological slavishness. He is now not only in the position of total submission, for his biological survival is not all that is at stake anymore, but so too are his certainty, individuality, and relation to truth eternally subject to the identity of the unchangeable. This is not to say they are aligned, for man's identity is not found within the unchangeable, but rather is subject to absolute stasis in relation to it. Man then denies himself and the world, holding his slavish decimation as his pure and only value. As such, inaction is now that which is sustainable, for there are psychological justifications as to his newly dawned transcendental reality, through which he has found himself free, and equal to all that live, including those who maintain hegemony. This is the condition of the unhappy consciousness *par excellence.* Even if the unhappy consciousness seeks to understand individuality as belonging to the unchangeable *as such,* the unchangeable assumes the status as one standing over and against the unhappy consciousness as individuality incarnate, rather than mere alien Being (universality).

The reason that this alone fails to resolve the previous impasse (as far as this reflection is ours and ours alone) is that the unchangeable consciousness also retains in its very form the basic character of divided-ness and being-for-self in contrast to the individual consciousness. Consequently, for the latter, the fact that the Unchangeable receives the form of individuality is only a contingent happening; just as it also merely finds itself opposed to it, so that the relation seems to result from its own nature. That, finally, it does find itself in the Unchangeable, appears to it to be brought about partly, no doubt, by itself, or to take place because it is itself an individual; but this unity, both as regards its origin and the fact that it is, appears partly due to the Unchangeable; and the antithesis persists within this unity itself. In fact, through the Unchangeable assuming a definite form, the moment of the beyond not only persists, but really is more firmly established; for if the beyond seems to have been brought closer to the individual consciousness through the form of an actuality that is individual, it henceforth on the other hand confronts him as an opaque sensuous unit with all the obstinacy of what is actual. The hope of becoming one with it must remain a hope, i.e. without fulfillment and present fruition, for between the hope and its fulfillment there stands precisely the absolute contingency or inflexible indifference which lies in the very assumption of definite form, which was the ground of hope. By the nature of this immediately present unit, through the actual existence in which it has clothed itself, it necessarily follows that in the world of time it has vanished, and that in space it had a remote existence and remains utterly remote.[57]

Through this second attempt at reconciliation, we find that the modality of legalism, which in the first stage sought to bring about spiritual support

---

57 Hegel, *Phenomenology of Spirit* (trans. Miller), 129.

for a statist agenda, here too may be utilized. This is because the appearance of reconciliation is how the unhappy consciousness resumes a slave mentality, seeking only to serve the unchangeable itself, whether this is king, emperor, or pope, rather than race, gender, a state, the church, etc. The unhappy consciousness here cannot be satisfied, for it has no way to internalize the mediation which was found previously in the external and which made the individual's existence object-like. As he learns in continuing to pursue reconciliation, his desired objective is beyond both the previously conceived alien Being as well as incarnate Being alone. The dialectic is pressed forward from this desire for reconciliation by calling the unhappy consciousness to, through the dawn of reason, "find its own self as this particular individual or the unchangeable."[58] However, this calling is itself far beyond this dialectical moment, and as such, the individual finds himself considering turning away from religion altogether.

At this point of rejecting religious ideology, man has the potential to actively take part in the reduction of ideology's grip upon his life. However, the majority of those who begin this journey do not have so explicit a goal in mind, even should they tell themselves that they are aiming at something like maximal freedom. This is because freedom unto itself, while a pleasant ideal, is a mere abstraction which can manifest absolutely nothing without interacting with, and being conditioned by, the world before it. Thus, this pursuit of freedom dashes to and fro, blindly attributing that which restricts or debilitates to whatever institution, community, or group surrounds it. Often the rebellion against ideology is merely a brief excursion that one embarks upon such that they might feel free in relation to the tradition that bore them. Often the truth of such rebellion is merely another name for the arrogance of youth. In taking this turn away from religious ideology, the individual seems destined to again unite with a parasitic ideology, which is perhaps more difficult to escape than those previously mentioned.

---

58 Ibid.

In ideological atheism, belief is constructed upon the idea of there being no God, rather than the lack of a belief in God. This is also the case with scientism or other such forms of positivism, where negative belief within a dualistic system is constructed purely in contrast to religious ideology. This then forms a structure through which all other information must pass, wherein man will find himself lacking the freedom he assumed as his due after having escaped what he previously understood as the limits of ideology. This is because he mistakenly believed that the content structured the system, without understanding the largely irrelevant role that content plays in an ideological system. It is thus important to carefully differentiate the abstracted non-belief of atheism, which as a blanket term encapsulates all lack of belief in a deity, and ideological atheism. Ideological atheism is positively contrasted with religion, rather than a lack which would be filled by theism. Its implementation is a structured set of beliefs that are intrinsically ideological. The individual who has fallen prey to this secondary ideology finds himself in a position where said ideology has made itself all the more invisible, retreating further into the darkness, away from the light which shone previously upon its limbs. This retreat is just as much the pursuit of a stronghold for ideology, in that the further it ventures from its basic functions the more power its ironic self-disavowal gains. This particular ideology has found itself so adapted to previous attempts at its exposure that it has now hidden itself as a primarily abstracted term, through which its induction point is now much harder to dialectically discern. This is not only because it has an immediate refutation of those who wish to speak to its ideological function—the semantic (not merely syntactic) bait-and-switch—but also due to the fact that through its perceived variety it slips away, as if it were merely another background operation of particular Being.

However, we can perceive its sedimentation in just as many fundamentalist sects as its religious counterpart. Perhaps the clearest example is that of the New Atheists, who are primarily a reactionary phenomenon, one that responds to religion with the same venomous ire with which religious fundamentalists respond to atheism. What one finds in the writings of anti-theist ideologues . . . is the same sense of utter certainty, the same claim to a monopoly on truth, the same close-mindedness that views one's own position as unequivocally good and one's opponent's views as not just wrong but irrational and even stupid, the same intolerance for alternative explanations, the same rabid adherents . . . and, most shockingly, the same proselytizing fervor that one sees in any fundamentalist community.[59]

It should be quite clear then that we speak not of a simple aspect of disbelief which many maintain as merely another aspect of their lives, but of the ideological evolution of such an idea. One can trace the development of these ideological structures, but the common man finds himself at odds, habitually evaluating with limited access towards the information present as to this monopolization of truth. The hand of the common man is forced then to accept, swap, or generate subsequent hyphenated ideologies. This further limits man's relation to the truth, and instead busies him in a continual battle with surface information, wherein he cannot even adopt an honest answer toward the problems that he supposes he has.

However, there is perhaps an easier way to follow this 'becoming' of ideas as that which 'evolve,' by utilizing the notion of memes. Richard Dawkins defines this concept in his *The Selfish Gene* (1976) as being

conceived of [as] an entity (specifically, a "unit of cultural transmission"), similar in action to a gene, that both replicated

---

59 Aslan, Reza, "Why Richard Dawkins, Sam Harris and the 'New Atheists' Aren't Really Atheists," *Alternet* (November 21, 2014).

itself and evolved. It might be considered the cultural equivalent
of a gene, residing in the 'mind' and replicating itself through
interpersonal communication, evolving in the process. We
might consider a meme as an 'idea' that 'catches on' (is
imitated) like a 'contagious thought,' with memes functioning
as its smallest units. Combinations of memes might form the
basis of a religion, a philosophy, or any of society's numerous
'isms' in the form of 'meme bundles' or 'complexes'[60]

It seems then with this new perspective in mind that our search for
understanding and pursuit of ideology springs up again as that which one
possesses in terms of limits and controls, as opposed to that which we can
fully eliminate or grasp absolutely. This relegates the notion of atheism as
an ideological apparatus immediately to the status which other ideologies
have had to work to achieve: the notion of symbiosis with a subject, where
the desire of the ideology takes control and replaces the desire of the
individual to the point where it becomes unknowable to the individual.
The desire of the individual (which is no longer his in its origins, nor in
its goals) has become the unknowable phantasmatic relation of the self to
the self. Thus, in this way the presence of the ego implies that "in as much
as he is committed to a play of symbols, to a symbolic world, that man is
a decentred subject."[61] This relation of the self to the self, the *presentation*
of the transparency of consciousness to itself, is the very plane whereby
ideology expresses itself as the subject's most intimate being.

This is also one way of specifying the meaning of Lacan's
assertion of the subject's constitutive 'decentrement': its point

---

60 Grimes, Robert G., "GENERAL SEMANTICS AND MEMETICS: A Tentative
   Relationship?," *ETC: A Review of General Semantics* 55, no. 1 (1998): 30-31.

61 Lacan, Jacques, "A Materialist Definition of the Phenomenon of Consciousness,"
   in *The Ego in Freud's Theory and in the Technique of Psychoanalysis: 1954-1955*,
   trans. Jacques-Alain Miller (New York: Norton, 1991), 47.

is not that my subjective experience is regulated by objective unconscious mechanisms that are 'decentered' with regard to my self-experience and, as such, beyond my control (a point asserted by every materialist); but, rather, something much more unsettling —I am deprived of even my most intimate 'subjective' experience, the way things 'really seem to me', that of the fundamental fantasy which constitutes and guarantees the core of my being, since I can never consciously experience and assume it.[62]

Immediately there is an attempt at justification in lieu of such a radical claim, when we are confronted with "the bizarre category of the objectively subjective—the way things actually, objectively seem to you even if they don't seem to seem that way to you!"[63] This is because the ontological paradox implied by the categorical defiance of ideology is a serious blow to the arrogant beliefs that man has about himself as the measure of all things. Contained within the very fundamental ideological relation is the scandal of "the notion of *fantasy* [which] lies in the fact that it subverts the standard opposition of 'subjective' and 'objective': of course fantasy is by definition not 'objective' (in the naive sense of 'existing independently of the subject's perceptions'); however, it is not 'subjective' either (in the sense of being reducible to the subject's consciously experienced intuitions)."[64] It is through self-narrative that ideology is naturalized, and thus its reification is founded in the relation of the self to itself through the replacement of the desire of the individual with the desire of ideology.

We may begin to see the collective means of this desire manifest within the relation to the other, through which the individual communes

62 Žižek, Slavoj, "Of Stones, Lizards and Men," in *The Fragile Absolute, Or, Why Is the Christian Legacy Worth Fighting For?* (London: Verso, 2000), 76-77.

63 Dennett, D. C., "Multiple Drafts Versus the Cartesian Theater," in *Consciousness Explained* (Boston: Little, Brown, 1991), 132.

64 Žižek, "Of Stones, Lizards and Men," 76.

with himself via his relation to the other. It is not through the strategies of thought reform, coercive persuasion, or other forms of proselytization which the most powerful ideologies find success, but rather in the totalizing reflection throughout the complexities of the social condition of man where the only intelligible notion of ideology is found. This is because self-deception is founded on the very relation of the desire of ideology. which is sustained by mutual conviction. This is why we find that

> deceiving others is often an important method for deceiving oneself. Someone who fears that X is true, but wants to believe it is false, may strive to convince others that X is false and, if they do accept that belief, the person can more easily dismiss his or her fears and believe that X is indeed false. Haight distinguished this from hypocrisy or lying in that the person is sincerely trying to believe what he or she seeks to convince others.[65]

As Pascal remarked, the more you want to believe, the more you shall—and what compacts the belief is man's desire for recognition, which is itself fused within the biological survival instinct, thus rendering ideology a biological necessity. Within the very basic functions of man seeking meaning and truth in direct relation to himself, even if he knows himself as constructed to function in a way shaped by ideology, that ideology is already mediating said search. The ensnaring trap of ideology only seems to become deeper and more controlling the more a person makes any movement toward or away from it.

Ideology solidifies its hold at a basic level, for in pursuing a critique of ideology one must recognize that convinced ideologies will always attempt to claim as their own, or else reduce the individual to the opposing ideological camp. The function of ideological fantasy necessitates an

---

65 Sedikides, Constantine, and Marilynn B. Brewer, "The Primacy of the Interpersonal Self," in *Individual Self, Relational Self, Collective Self* (Philadelphia: Psychology, 2001), 79.

immediate investment in the othering of everyone who exists outside the structure, thus reducing the infinite multiplicity of human life to a mere dichotomy. It forces those who imagine peace to be a possibility within such a system to make a decision regarding the newly perceived threatened status of such solace: is this 'other' within my camp, or do they subscribe to an 'enemy' ideology? After which it becomes a question of conversion: if they are not in the same camp, it no longer becomes important to listen to their ideas, but merely their words, to try to find an issue where they might be open to conversion. This allows for the ideologues to have the tool of rejecting all that the other might believe or share on behalf of their status outside of the ideologue's camp. Due to the other's disconnection from what the ideologue views as being the fundamental link to Truth (despite the fact that every so often the two might arrive at a similar conclusion), it is not a real conclusion with otherness formed on the grounds of that-which-is-not Truth.

This effect can be seen in Wittgenstein's discussion of the noncontradicting nature of a believer and a nonbeliever:

> If you ask me whether or not I believe in a Judgment Day, in the sense in which religious people have belief in it, I wouldn't say: "No. I don't believe there will be such a thing." It would seem to me utterly crazy to say this. And then I give an explanation: "I don't believe in . . .," but then the religious person never believes what I describe. I can't say. I can't contradict that person. In one sense, I understand all he says—the English words "God," "separate," etc. I understand. I could say: "I don't believe in this" and this would be true, meaning I haven't got these thoughts or anything that hangs together with them. But not that I could contradict the thing. You might say: "Well, if you can't contradict him, that means you don't understand him. If you did understand him, then you might." That again is Greek to me. My normal technique

of language leaves me. I don't know whether to say they understand one another or not.[66]

Now, a theological formation of belief is not qualitatively reducible to that of an ideological belief, and it is important to note that Wittgenstein is, in this passage, concerned with theological belief. This is so because, as both Hegel's *Phenomenology of Spirit* as well as Wittgenstein's *Lecture on Ethics* both show, theological belief (as I am calling it here) does not pretend that its method is that of the Enlightenment, and as such it seeks not to deploy reason in the same way, nor to stake out empirical claims.

However, ideology often seeks to self-authenticate by appealing to the most naturalized method possible, so as to maximize its spread. This passage from Wittgenstein showcases the difference between ideological beliefs and a belief divorced from the totalizing system of ideology. It is important to hold these distinctions in mind as we note, from an ideological perspective, that the deployment of reason here is subservient to a belief which itself acts as its guiding concept. Conceptually, the significant and fundamental difference is found to be not merely linguistic but somehow ontologically constitutive. This difference is so ingrained within the epistemic network of ideological belief that it is very difficult for the two to separate themselves from what they perceive to be the nature of their conversation—the ideas, traditions, and language within which they attempt to meet. As such, it seems to be a real challenge to those who exist within ideology to perceive their interlocutor's relation to truth, which to the nondogmatic interlocutor is free to be plucked wherever it should blossom. To the dogmatic ideologue, this state is but the performance of a rival ideology. Thus, despite the occasion of an appearance of identical conclusions, albeit one from an opposing source, there is total rejection from the

---

66 Wittgenstein, Ludwig, and Cyril Barrett, *Lectures & Conversations on Aesthetics, Psychology, and Religious Belief* (Berkeley: University of California Press, 1966), 55.

ideologue, for he imagines that although the answer remains the same, there must be some metaphysical specter who haunts the conclusion of the other. Thus, rhetorical syntax becomes the signifying aspect of ideology. This aspect of ideological thought functions at a psychological level, restricting the individual from pursuing understanding, and instead leaving him with self-referential knowledge. One can find this notion pointing the finger back to a metaphysical gap constituted by the conceptual structure of belief for the ideologue which retains for itself the hard kernel of minimal difference. It is through the referential totality that the ideologue finds himself within that the denotations of everyday experience are always deferred back toward the hidden drive of ideology. Thus is the ideological consumption of man.

It seems that in the face of this notion of difference, which is within itself no difference, one who seeks freedom from ideology (inasmuch as this is possible) must recognize that contradiction does not mean the same thing to him that it does to the ideologue. Paradox is not necessarily something to be overcome, as much as it is something which unfolds his knowledge as always-already incomplete. The ideologue however has a sworn commitment to what he has come to believe are fundamental axioms of the absolute system under which all truth fits perfectly, and from which no conclusions can contradict each other. In this absolute system, then, all ideas must fall under a black-or-white classification, even if occasionally such reasoning becomes obscure to the public. Ideology maintains its power in the lineage it claims as its own, and as such there is always an assertion of reasoning to supplement its obscurity.

It is through the retroactively implemented linking of its authority with historical figures or events that ideology legitimizes and obscures its genesis. Its power is naturalized through establishing a historical lineage and ideological intersectionality, such as claiming, for example, the Christian mystic Meister Eckhart as a feminist.[67] This example showcases

---

67 Eckhart, Meister, *Meditations with Meister Eckhart*, trans. Matthew Fox (Santa Fe, N.M.: Bear, 1983).

clearly the ways through which power is sought by those who make such claims, for not only is it anachronistic in that the establishment of feminist ideology can be found squarely within the twentieth century, but also as it seeks to hide the ideological structure of feminism while granting to it the monopolization of the treatment of women as human beings, and the 'history' therein where it is purported to be a modern 'realization.' This is the perverted formation of morality found in naming and ownership, which Nietzsche posits as "the lordly right of giving names [which] extends so far that one should allow oneself to conceive the origin of language itself as an expression of power on the part of the rules: they say 'this *is* this and this,' they seal every thing and event with a sound and, as it were, take possession of it."[68] The significant accusation often missed in this sentiment is that every event is regarded as a possession, from which we find the hegemonic paradigm of asserting domination over the past (directly in terms of that which is *no longer the present*).

This power over language and naming (an assertion of ownership of the symbolic order) is that which manipulates and dictates the desires of the individual, and which flies in the face of any understanding of Dasein as the bearer or enactor of time. It is this very control over language that seeks to censor or police it such that it may be molded to naturalize their ideological stance. When an ideology is considered even indirectly through its influence during the course of our daily social interaction, it is phenomenologically revealed to be a performance of hollow moralizing and self-declared virtue. Through its abstract relationship to the individual, information is manipulated by the process of naming through which not only is his expression contorted, but so too are his innermost desires. This illustrates how ideology treats those who do not subscribe to its lineage of thought as infantile: they need to be told not only how to think, but how to feel; an experience need

---

68 Nietzsche, Friedrich Wilhelm, *On the Genealogy of Morals / Ecce Homo*, trans. Walter Kaufmann and R. J. Hollingdale (New York: Vintage, 1989), 26.

not change, but it is instead framed and moralized, and if that is not enough, a new idea is created to hold it.

Strict control must then be in place to purify and sanction such a lineage. This express control of the symbolic order through which ideology dominates the individual who submits to it can be shown working in and through examples that are typically seen as diametrically opposed ideological systems. We can see that they have both set about maintaining an all-consuming framework of reference through which the world is categorized and judged in relation to its absolute system. The first of these two is that of neo-conservative Christianity, of which it is important to note that the specificity here is not to say that there are many approaches to Christianity which escape ideology. Certainly many thinkers have put forth such ideas, trying to reclaim the title, but inadvertently assume it for simply another ideology, one which comes through the necessity of taking with seriousness a canonizing process. However, upon examining the qualifying descriptor, one finds an explicit function of ideology in general to be working from two opposing sides. Through the specificity of each in their opposition we may begin to see the general role that ideology takes in regulating the individual on behalf of whatever virtue it claims. As anachronistic as a modern political qualifier of a religious community might have once seemed, it is now commonly presumed as *de facto* religious functioning. These qualifiers can in fact supersede biblical evidence to the contrary, as the ideological claim is that which foregrounds the textual. The qualifiers limit and sanction language which sinks well past consciousness into that which is immediate and reactionary. This sanction on language seeks to draw the Christian away from the secular, not merely in an anointed epistemological condition toward such a series of topics, themes, images, and the like, but so too to keep the ideologue pure and chaste by not entertaining such things. Hence, to employ the language or subject matter would disrupt the collaborative effort to maintain and promote a prosperous, healthy, and wide-reaching life of the absolute system of ideology. The purity of ideology is pursued just as other conquerors hope to maintain the purity of their empire through expulsion of access points from which the individual can 'see the empire from above.'

The opposing example would be the liberal humanists of the Western English-speaking world who report that, in the same fashion as Christians, evil lurks about in language outside of the policed safe-zones of their liberal authorities. To touch it with one's lips, mind, or pen without immediate repentance is to give way to the foundation, and consequently, the safety of the absolute system. To entertain otherness as is to taint the essence of a person, such that its evil state will take hold. This policing is done through a humanitarian rather than a spiritual assertion of righteousness, but retaining the same state of ethical superiority. This state maintains an avoidance of certain topics and ideas which will best cleanse the world of sexism, racism, and other such "isms" that denote hateful and ignorant traits under this ideology. Since in both cases the arguments for such policing vary in appeal it is a given that one's disposition grants a degree of play in how far subsumed they will be by the ideological system. Though the strategy may remain the same, it will begin to exert its power the more an individual believes in the moralizing polemic which the ideology seeks to naturalize within the notion. The individual freely severing other relations is a characteristic relation to dogmatic belief; the semblance of autonomy granted to him is subverted for the sake of ideological purity.

This is the means by which the unconscious is subverted to a state controlled by means of ideological representation, which utilizes its primacy of the symbolic order such that the fantasies which sustain the life of the individual are effectively dictated by ideology. As is being hinted at here, the degree to which ideology fills out man's epistemological framework is so far-reaching, that so too are the most simple of good deeds perverted by ideology. So inborn are the tenets of every action to the absolute system that even doing a good deed for another is turned into that of charity in service to this selfsame system in any of its capacities. This ranges from the distribution of knowledge to the act of helping another, subtly altering and consuming even the arts, industry, and welfare. Due then to charity's discrete ontological difference and moral veil, the individual comes to imagine that it is an action taken on the behalf of oneself, and as such a true expression of their heart. It is through one's position within whatever given ideology that the relation of self to other becomes parasitical, and produces the poverty of the other by way of his ideological lack. It is through the moral self-superiority of an ideological system that the anxiety of its apologetics is installed within the individual. In this way charity becomes the pure feeling and need for ideological replication of the individual. Charity is then a staged event, through which ideological performativity establishes its drive within eternal reference toward the self. It is a deployment of the structure through which the individual's relation to his self is concealed ideologically by reference to the totality of its beliefs, which install the signification of its 'truth' as representative of the real. An event through which one may understand and offer comfort or solace to another is rendered a conversional process, through which the ideologue attempts to subsume the other, and render a solution to his own moralizing process. Thus, there is no ideological opportunity for doing good.

As has been alluded to: ideology of any nature establishes the transactional relation of the ideologue to those outside of it. There is a giver and receiver, as well as the matter-at-hand, the character of which is radically hindered through the transaction. The very structure of ideology insists that an action through which one man helps another must be translated into a universal standard through which all subsumed by ideology can participate in. The moral maxims of ideology contrast the ethical in that they no longer consider ethical action at all, for ideological morality is merely a totalizing epistemology in that it is premeditated: it is mediated by the ideology. The ethical then is rendered incomprehensible to ideology, for ethics denies totalizing systematization. Ideology insists that without adherence to it one lacks the very possibility of a relation to the good and the true. It states that we are lacking the ability to interpret that which is in and around us, and that in submitting to it, even if we fumble and fail again, it matters not, for we finally have the system through which we can purge ourselves of meaninglessness and absorb the knowledge for what it really is, which is coincidentally defined as meaningful by fitting within the confines of the structure. In addition to truth, the acceptable framework for interpretation and the limitations of its products are founded by the ideological structure such that traversing them grants excommunication. Should this come to pass however, the individual will become sterilized from their own life and work and *reconciled* as a pillar of support for that which suffocated them.

Ideology grasps onto the ideas of many great men, but supplements the wisdom with a second helping of knowledge: completely disregarding the challenges presented in the original thoughts, in place of easy-to-digest aphorisms or general and confusingly basic axioms such as the interpretation of the commandment "thou shalt not take the Lord's name in vain" to mean "thou shalt not utter the word 'God' outside of an ideologically sanctified context." Such is the nature of ideology, to adopt ideas with little to no regard as to their implications, even should their most basic assertions be antithetical to the very foundations of ideology. Ideology is then the separate worship of knowledge in that it creates a false duality whereby truth as a formal structure exists apart from man and thus it is by way of ideological submission that he can confer meaning upon each act, symbol, and relation. This usefulness provided by ideology further creates tension between man and its caused truth such that it gains a weight with which it has become an *object*. Paradoxically freedom from ideology is not the final goal for one who wishes freedom from it, but rather to attain the position of a new beginning, a state of openness achieved in tandem with a fundamental rupture in the ideological chain of signifiers. This exposes the brutal nature of ideology as that which adopts external phenomena, internal supposition, and ideas and while ripping from them vital elements of their own nature so that they should fit within its confines. This not only supposes a lot about the natures of truth, phenomena, and experience, but generates strange reflections of them through misinterpretation of their deliberate inversion. There can however still be information gained from those who despite recognizing the entanglement they've found themselves caught within, still submit to radicalization. To those who exist outside of such a system, the ideas which form the real kernel of ideology can be known more fully. This is because such ideas are far from a righteous interpretation of their original framework. (The Buddha was not a Buddhist, Marx was not a Marxist, nor Hegel a Hegelian, etc.)

A new idea is born, but it remains important to note that its radicalization is not a representative outgrowth of prior ideology, its followers, or the ideas which are claimed as foundational. The heroism garnered from newly established canonization is a very real threat to ideology, and what is often not seen is how ideology creates division through the establishment of a paradigm. That is, no matter what ideology garners hegemony, it will disrupt society by providing a supplemental yet artificial antagonism. This antagonism is artificial not in that it is external to immediate Being, but rather because it is an antagonism by virtue of its assertion of splitting society into those who agree and those who disagree. This is expressed even with notions as basic and seemingly universal as Christ's "do unto others as you would have them do upon you" as well as Kant's "act only according to that maxim whereby you can, at the same time, will that it should become a universal law," for there are disagreements with even these.

There is a sense then that Freud and Lacan are to be read with the same hermeneutic humbleness with which one approaches the Bible. To read psychoanalysis or theology through any presumed 'natural' lens of another (i.e., scientific positivism) is necessarily to miss the crucial benefit of enacting the labor: it gives to the reader an affirmation of this belief in the lens, which is necessarily abject and isolated from the text as its only reified 'benefit.' What, then, is the purpose in the veneration of such a distant, abstract, and meaningless tool save renewing the content by which its cyclical, 'external' justification is silently made? By naturalizing this tool, one assumes its predicate, which justifies its conclusion. Ideological lenses then are not the modes of critique they claim to be, for a mode of critique surveys the strengths and shortcomings under fire against its own totality, and against that of the 'objective facts.' 'Critique' with a lens then merely supplies naturalized supplemental conclusions about the world which justify the supposition of the predicate. So then, the 'benefit' of using such a lens is to habitually assert a model which finds its ideology undergirding the world wherein its meaning becomes the only thing that exists. This singular grip of a lens is not equivalent then to those who adopt and shift through lenses in order to open up further the possibility of relational meaning so as to give them the largest possible relation to that of the true. The two functions are entirely different.

The lenses of ideology may exist separate from the mainframe of ideology itself, and persist as localized phenomena much as we see ideology placed upon self-narrative in a historical ideological apparatus. This can be seen functioning in the ideologies of Romanticism which separate men from one another, as a result not only solidifying but also falsely supporting the ideology from which this self-narrative is itself rendered. Romanticism functions as a means of mediating relations through literal objectification and instrumentalizing of other human beings, not necessarily benefitting from their relation as Being itself. Rather there is an egoist mediation, that is essentially the function of performative ideology, which after turning upon itself turns to others as relational *to himself.* This symbolically positions the individual as God in representation to what his ideology defines as truth but also in relation to the Other, as adopted within this egoist fantasy, whose agency has been destroyed through the filter. This is not to say that the ideologue sublimates the world in terms of a power-relation toward himself, for to do such a thing would be to recognize himself in terms of pure individuality and freedom, which is not something accessible to the ideologue. This is because the power, freedom, and individuality that the ideologue possesses are granted to him explicitly on behalf of his ideology. For even if he ends up at this positive outcome, whereupon 'objectively' one might be able to look upon himself and his state and suggest that he has indeed achieved that which is outside of himself, he may never reap the legitimate benefit for *his individuality*. Because this achievement is always gained in terms of its synthesis with its ideology, it is signified through the conversion process, wherein the converter solidifies his position only through further establishing the regime of ideology he converts on the behalf of.

This bypass gives the ideologue the feeling of power, sublimated by means of an ordered establishment such that one may partake in power while being displaced from the crushing weight of having to explore all for themselves. This alignment with power however ontologically displaces the individual from the concrete existing set of relations that make up their communities outside of this ideology. So the alignment with power necessarily delineates them from the genuine struggles with antagonism that constitute their concrete community, for this ideological relation is the conviction of freedom-by-chains. It maintains the illusion of freedom without the dizzying openness expressed via the very nature of its concept. The ideological fleeing from freedom goes even further than that of Sartre's bad faith, for it avoids the re-instating of newer answers that maintain the very existence of the problem itself. Those who follow suit with 'political correctness' for example, "far from being a disguised expression of the extreme Left, the pc attitude is the main ideological protective shield of the bourgeois liberalism against a genuine leftist alternative."[69] Thus, the ways through which ideology sustains itself, and uses others as a shield for criticism are meant to sustain the fantasy which structures our desire, such that it remains identical to itself. The felicitous social analysis of ideology is the very thing which upholds the very object of that same critique.

---

69 Žižek, Slavoj, "Enjoy Your Nation as Yourself," in *Tarrying with the Negative: Kant, Hegel, and the Critique of Ideology* (Durham, N.C.: Duke University Press, 1993), 214

This fantasy too finds itself expressed through the trinitarian nature by which nationalism, ethnicity, and culture interplay. Nationalism, that is, the ideological representation one has of the grouping of their 'people,' romanticizes the positive elements of that grouping, in clear opposition to the rest of humanity. This differs certainly from an ethnicity which sustains the true biological multiplicity of man. There is a difference too between a cultural heritage and an ethnic heritage: a cultural heritage is specific to a creature's Being and time, and maintains no relationality in terms of other cultures but maintains instead the differences, thus having no concrete relationality to the 'universal' which a nation-state claims for itself, while in ethnic representation the 'biological' is given credence somehow through the linking of man to a biological 'law' which governs all. A cultural heritage is not prideful, but instead maintains an acceptance of man's sensible collectivization and organization whose context values him specifically. Nationalism, and consequently ethnicity, seem instead to value individuals based upon their utility, for these ideologies hold themselves up in opposition to other nation-states and in contrast to other ethnicities. Man maintains only a warlike 'duty' to place himself in alignment with the 'effort.' This is how racism and nationalism function in terms of relationality towards otherwise ambiguous (or undifferentiated outside of pure biological iconography) characteristics by immediately assigning a moral function to them, and as a result reducing man to a statistical existence.

Queries based on one's biological or otherwise transcultural nature is insulting only to one's ideological relation; that is, a 'moral' judgment is based on a distinction that is then given the modification of relationality. The problem here exists within the positing of one *in relation* to another, for this mediates an internal projection or directionality, and as such maintains a subjectivity that forces a moralizing experience upon the subjects of the relation. Instead, distinctiveness is an externally verifiable mode of one's existence, which cannot offend one's ideological relationship due to the fact that it maintains no separate information metaphysically clinging to the facts *as they present themselves*: there is no interpretation of this distinctiveness save *misinterpretation* which exists as the mode of using interpretation to draw facts into a system of knowledge. The man who feels deeply for and is moved by nationhood or ethnicity falsely replaces the self (the subjective) with the nation or ethnicity (the universal) which can never become subjectivized, and as such it is always a perversion or miscalculation of the potency of one's singularity, and as such condemns him to the position of a necessarily false God. This ideology is formalized through ideological and repressive ideological state apparatuses. The first of these, the ideological state apparatus (ISA),

> is a system of defined institutions, organizations, and the corresponding practices. Realized in the institutions, organizations, and practices of this system is all or part (generally speaking, a typical combination of certain elements) of the state ideology. The ideology realized in an ISA ensures its systemic unity on the basis of an 'anchoring' in material functions specific to each ISA; these functions are not reducible to that ideology, but serve it as a 'support.'[70]

We can understand institutions such as schools, political structures, religions, news organizations, and publishers as the means by which we are given a fitted spot in the larger umbrella of culture; and it is often through these that broader relational ridicule is founded. It is through these apparatuses that one may only occasionally sense the hidden constituents of ideological goals which are fitted behind the self-professed liberating qualities of the ideology that are presented as inconspicuous. Ideological state apparatuses are fitted to the social setting of man, who finds himself always-already predisposed to ideology, and as such they take the form of every possible solace that man may find from it.

---

70 Althusser, Louis, "The States," in *On the Reproduction of Capitalism: Ideology and Ideological State Apparatuses* (London: Verso, 2014), 77.

PERSISTENCE, PERFORMATIVITY, AND AUTONOMY

Reactionary ideological 'revolutions' rise up only to press into the hegemonic field what initially stood in 'resistance,' simultaneously betraying those who stood in honest pursuit of freedom initially, and creating a *new* reactionary movement from those freshly 'disenfranchised' by this set of normalized behavior and thought. As collectives smash against each other in the recurring waves to create a totalizing system of pure sameness, those who lay no stake in the outcome find themselves at odds with the combative social positions around them. Here, then, it is important to draw a distinction between the autonomy found in the liberation of the self in awareness of ideology, and the promise of autonomy that is said to lie in the *fulfillment* of ideology. This second type of autonomy is presented in stark dichotomous opposition to what it narrativized as historical in the present hegemonic ideology.

For example, see the characterization of gender as radically performative in the position of Judith Butler. As a feminist, Butler seeks to explain how we as individuals have been 'gendered' through a "grid of cultural intelligibility" which exists as a matrix: a binary found only in the actualizing of heteronormativity which must only exist as a congealment of historical anticipation, repetition, and ritualization of norms. This states that gender, while not necessarily *fully* chosen in any sense, is instead a product achieved through "violence imposed by restrictive bodily norms" which give way to categories of identity, thus generating further bodily norms which we are hoped to, at some point, somehow transcend.[71] What we are then presented with is a reaction that narrativizes gender in relation to the hegemonic paradigm in the historical field of feminism. As is the case with most ideologies whose rise to power threatens hegemony, its power comes from a theory which frames said paradigm as a source of abuse or violence which it contrasts with itself as a false dilemma. We are here careful to note that what is left is not simply a criticism, or even the underlining of the present narrative as such, but rather a direct battle for power, for the sake of power. This ideology is that whereby all information, including sensory or empirical information, is directly filtered through the theoretical framework of the narrative project of feminism, which stands in an attempt to make history in its own image. This stands as a refuge for those already seemingly marginalized and acts as a categorical critique, seeking to find justification for what it purports to believe as an institutional form of violence and oppression. This adds credence to its own rise as a reactionary movement opposed to hegemonic ideology and thus weaponizes the feelings of the marginalized for its own gain.

Here, just as in any form of ideology, there is a demonizing of the other through a secular formalized worldview that groups individuals into those who possess historically inherited troubles which are functionally similar to the Christian doctrine of original or ancestral sin. This moralizing which takes place is not only a stepping stone upon which, at the expense of others, an ideology establishes its legitimacy, but also establishes (based on the sphere of influence and its strength of a memetic reproduction) the narrative foundation of its emotional attachment. Not only does this affect those who have bought into the plight of morality, but as it garners more weight within ideological state apparatuses, so too do we find that morality transitions into legality. Once institutionalized, we find that anxiety has been instilled within

---

71 Butler, Judith, *Gender Trouble: Feminism and the Subversion of Identity* (New York: Routledge, 1990).

the very core of the individual regardless of his status or relation to the now-hegemonic ideology. This also codifies ideological history, which not only demonizes the now-faltering post-hegemonic ideology, but also establishes a universal appeal to its own belief structure, which generates a framework for 'hereditary sin' of which, as Kierkegaard proposed, is inferred from its presupposition: anxiety.[72] The demonization of the previous hegemonic ideology is done tenderly as it claims it was really just a shell to be shed, of which the reactionary is the true inheritor of the movement of the 'right side of history.' It establishes the ranges of acceptable behavior and is quick to make judgment claims regarding other cultures and ways of life. It also flattens the ideas it seeks to negate through moralization and quickly creates its own discourse wherein the previously held ideology is put on trial. With none to defend the true origin of the now-demonized ideas, they become mythologized and anyone found in agreement with or sympathetic toward those ideas find themselves branded a savage under the new ideological rule. Like most informational processes found in Western-analytic traditions, alignment of people into 'groups' is as highly reductive and flattening as moralizing. This seems to be the cost of producing ideological discourse. Even when arguing against the reductive categorization of a group, often one will notice the very same ideology presenting a counterclaim utilizing the same techniques, augmented with justification as to why it is acceptable to the technique that the 'revolutionaries' abhor. These justifications often boil down to either a negative quid pro quo, a retaliation backed by power, or the presentation of a new definition which seeks to rewrite the past in its own image.

Another way that this insincerity is discernible is through the partnership of diametrically opposed ideological movements. Perhaps the easiest example of this to see is the continued support found among

---

72 Kierkegaard, Søren, *The Concept of Anxiety: A Simple Psychologically Orienting Deliberation on the Dogmatic Issue of Hereditary Sin*, trans. Reidar Thomte and Albert Anderson (Princeton, N.J.: Princeton University Press, 1980).

third-wave feminists and Islamists (this is narrower than the category of Muslims, and denotes the colonial or socially politicized form of Islam). They both have an outlook on society that finds themselves 'displaced' therein, even if the displacement belongs not to them but their parents, or their grandparents, or their great-grandparents, and so on. Though their justification for demonization of the hegemonic paradigm is starkly dichotomous, these outlooks group together so as to create the highest potential for power. They may function cross-dialogically so that they may overlook the particulars of misogyny or Islamophobia for a common ground in an anti-Western ideology (in terms of its ideologically narrativized 'historical' sense). While the two find themselves in a bid for power, here too they are capable of presenting themselves as truly humanitarian efforts and thus seek to free the other from their collective enemy. The two partner so long as they both consider the other to have the same relationship of power within the hegemonic field, for anything else would present the other as a threat and as a result, bring to the forefront their differences rather than what unites them. This of course would be a problem for the ideologue, seeing as tolerance fits with the goal of power and domination only as an ideological category.

It is to this end that a variety of techniques are employed, which are similar to those employed during the course of any non-sanctioned forms of warfare. These techniques are often forms of seduction wherein subjects are interpolated in a state of compliance rather than through force, thus producing much more devout subjects, for they believe themselves to be freely choosing their beliefs and desires with full access to the truth. These tactics are effective because they can be ejected by their employers once discovered, like most other means of subversion, despite their contribution to the cause itself. The flip-side of the employment of these tactics is found in a large-scale approach to ideology wherein there is a continued effort to return or renew the ideology, often as a means of reformation. This approach seeks to find a pure or otherwise original mode of said ideology in spite of a branched or denominational approach to its informational center. This might not seem to be a problem in terms of the evolutionary lineage of an idea or culture, but in terms of the legitimate discussion or criticism thereof, the problem is immense. This is because of the opportunity for displacing responsibility that this grants an ideology when presented to an outsider, which makes the discourse surrounding and emanating from it, malleable for it. It is through the multiplicity of power relations maintained by an ideology that credence is given to it. For example, an appeal to definition wherein a genuine understanding of an ideology's *telos* is masked with a soft and otherwise agreeable abbreviation of its initial memetic appeal (i.e., equal treatment of people groups and feminism, or loving kindness towards others and Christianity). With this tactic, criticism is avoided by means of assigning the criticism to extremities 'barely' fitting within the ideological spectrum and advising their critics to check sources whose definition they've supplied. This approach is backed by those ingrained from the start of their lives as subjects who assume their identity through nothing other than their having been birthed into it, and as such assign their own moral standing or personalized ontology to the ideology, and pledge their support from within. Even should they share little in common with the ideology born unto them, they still find themselves with selective vision assigning their commendable properties with that of their ideology, which is one of the proudest achievements of any successful ideology.

Another way that ideology spreads its deceptive wings across the plane of the uninitiated is by claiming that the definitional ideas are exclusive to its approach. For example, if one were to state that they agree people should be treated equally under the law in terms of their sex, regardless of whether one agrees with any other tenet (or the framework under which the host of theories and narrativization occurs) of the ideology, feminists would be quick to speak up and claim that said egalitarian is indeed a feminist. This is because their claim is that the belief that both sexes should be treated with equality and opportunity is exclusively a feminist belief structure, and that despite the words of the individual themselves, they belong to the ideology: it *claims* them as subjects. Beyond the threshold of a given ideology however, once named as in its house, courtship truly begins. For example, once named as a subject of feminism, many feminists would claim that feminism requires an observation of women as an oppressed class, and that to retract from the ideology and claim yourself a supporter of equality and equal opportunity is to deny the support to specific instances of oppression in favor of abstract platitudes. The moral imperative of the renaming accepted by the individual presses forth, immediately sliding him deeper within said ideology.

However, within the ideological frameworks that view the power and oppression used against classes, such as in the example of feminism just used, intersectionality states that not only are there multiple oppressing forces operating from within power-relations towards those marginalized, but that it shifts throughout space and time such that there are higher burdened categories of individuals who suffer from accumulated oppression from a variety of ideological fields. Not only does this immediately point to the dark underbelly which propagates abuse protected by the exclusive association with oppressed groups (which struggle within a loosely held hierarchical system resulting supposedly in the class of most oppressed), but also it points to the question of a theoretical approach to oppression which states that only those who hold privilege and power might enact or engage in an oppressive action, attitude, lifestyle, discourse, etc., against another. This is because there is often an ideological definitional distinction drawn which supposes the category of focus (racism, sexism, etc.) to be a matter retained by ideological sanction, such that morality remains a tool in the hands of the ideologue. This belief system is a complicated defense strategy on behalf of an ideology, for not only does it garner strength in terms of those who share a commitment against the hegemonic ideology, as well as gaining a rich discursive element therein, but it also has the memetic weight of shame of a fallen ideology (we find here again a moralizing that foists 'sin' upon another). This strategy need not apply exclusively to those with 'hard' disagreements, but also to those who deny the 'right to power' that an ideology seeks to claim for itself.

This is in opposition to what in actuality appears as the phenomeno-logical existence of such oppressive operations as highlighted by David Pilgrim (in terms of the conception of racism in opposition to those who use its existence as an ideological tool) when he states:

> The quirky part of this story is that there were two groups of people, both desperately poor and treated as outcasts, who used their hatred of the Other as bonding mechanisms. I want it said loudly and clearly that we can define racism in many ways, but it is, in my opinion, intellectually disingenuous to define it in a way that trivializes the role that racial hatred plays. Certainly, not all racism is hate-driven, but to ignore the connection between racial hate and racism is to reduce the concept of racism to a useless theoretical abstraction. Definitions of racism have clearly become battlegrounds. I have attended academic conferences where it was professionally chic to accept definitions of racism that only focused on white privilege or dominant group privilege. In chats with scholars, many of them white, I heard a disdain for social scientific, especially psychological, definitions that characterize racism as an attitude. For those who share this disdain, racism could only be viewed as an organized system of group privilege, and since blacks collectively lacked that privilege, they could not be racists. This tautological reasoning remains problematic for me.[73]

---

73 Pilgrim, David, "Question of the Month," Jim Crow Museum (March 2009).

It appears then that no matter the necessary quantifiers used to find this line of thought not only acceptable but correct, in any approach thereby constituted one must continue the flattening process found in this employment of morals. It must then continue the promotion of a theoretical approach to oppression which is reducible to a logical formula coincidentally identical to the historically oppressive nature of the ideology it claims to be in opposition to.

We see here the full reduction of an individual's autonomy from personal choice of association with an ideology into their loss of freedom of psychological responses (the instilling of sin and the memetic production of guilt and anxiety), all the way to their appointed savagery and flattened social self should they be in oppositional relation to the ideology. This is because ideology seeks to dictate the symbolic and imaginary realms through which all things, including the innermost feelings and desires of the individual, are filtered. If this line of thought is followed, we find the ability to positively appraise the actions of any given individual only so long as they find themselves in the parameters given by the ideology. Once one looks outside the moralizing sphere, at the logical formula devoid of any of the ideological terminology or aestheticization, one finds that the rules that an ideology establishes are often in conflict with themselves.

For example, in terms of race relations, as far as one looks to categorize others that the ideology seeks to 'free,' the lines are blurred on behalf of the ideology: gender and sex are broken down and legitimized on behalf of the 'oppressed' class, and demonized in terms of these narrativized as an 'oppressive' class masked by hegemony. This is, for example, why men are allowed to follow feminist ideological approaches to sex and gender so long as they break from the paradigmatic masculine representation previously given (i.e., homosexuals, transgenders, all the way to artists and other 'appropriately feminized' men). Yet when one looks at the moralizing process, one finds the theoretical framework for such theories as 'the patriarchy' to center around sex and gender as necessarily concrete apparatuses from which the two must be reconciled by attributing the 'false' assertion of concrete reality to the previously held hegemonic ideology. However, in so doing, the 'reactionary' ideology continues to play by the same rules, and as such continues to support that which it demonizes in the prior field.

This leads to Hegel's *Aufhebung*, which can be seen as an absorption of the 'reactionary' ideology into what was maintained as hegemonic, and hence the continuation of and contribution

to the ideology they are 'fighting against.' We find this particular mode of *Aufhebung* as a 'negation of the negation' wherein affirmation is the resulting conclusion:

> Method is the consciousness of the form of the inner self–movement of the content of logic . . . Besides, the *immanent coming-to-be* of the distinctions and the *necessity* of their connection with each other must present themselves in the exposition of the subject matter itself for it falls within the spontaneous progressive determination of the Notion . . . It is in this dialectic as it is here understood, that is, in the grasping of opposites in their unity or of the positive in the negative, that speculative thought consists.[74]

This view can also be seen in the historic lineage through which the works of the Stoics and Epicureans are procured by Sextus in terms of a literal continuation of a previously found dialectic. Neither perspective of said dialectic produces anything, however, save that of the phenomena divorced from the noumena and presented to us as pure dialectic. This in turn drives home the point that truth, right action, loving kindness,

---

74 "Introduction" in G. W. F. Hegel, *The Science of Logic*, trans. George Di Giovanni (Cambridge: Cambridge University Press, 2015), §64-§69.

etc., are not the end-goals of a particular ideology; rather, ideology seeks after power and privilege alone.

Another problem that presents itself is the nature of debate which stands around the idea of the ideologue *as such*: as shown through a denominational approach to ideology, it becomes difficult to discern whether or not one falls into any specific ideology by means of an ideology's own masking effect. However, this too is pressed further into obscurity by means of the argument of degree or consistency, wherein there is either a grade to which one falls into an ideology, producing a form of ideology-lite, or popular manifestation of said ideology. The other option tightens the question to a stark black and white dichotomy of being either a good (and as such 'genuine') ideologue, or a bad (and as such 'false') ideologue. The point in contention is not whether or not either is the correct approach, but merely that both present another way through which ideology slips away from criticism or any other such critical eye turned towards it. This is perhaps most commonly seen in the previously mentioned ambiguous formal defense from criticism, and beautification process for recruiting: i.e., "they're not a *real* Christian" or "the only required approach to being a Republican is wanting financial responsibility." Here there is only a continued lack of responsibility for the groups themselves, for they rarely police themselves, due to the fact that the core group benefits from 'radicals,' as seen above. This is also seen in the continued employment of techniques which, when labeling the group, broaden the definition to such an extremity that all fit the criteria listed, and therefore the grouping loses all possible substance save that of which garners and subjugates individuals, and generates more power for said ideology.

If one seeks an authentic definition of any particular ideology, often there is a hybridization of approach, which seeks to understand the necessity of flexibility within an ideological structure, and yet finds the stark contrast ever-present in definitional accounts. With the presence of the definitional contrast, there looms the blurred threat which continues to limit the autonomy of those interpolated by expecting them to perform their ideology either in line with the dominant narrative or to risk starting their own denomination. This is not to say that ideologues who fit within the nature of the revolutionized form of this ideology can be discerned from the general form of said ideology, but merely that there is that which is held to be true within the eyes of the public (not necessarily readily available, but within the collected knowledge of the mainstream) in contrast with what the group is seen to be as filtered through that of the hegemonic ideology of the time. The other problem with the persistence of an ideology is that there will often be a radical transformation that takes place, turning the category against itself almost in terms of direct opposition, somehow maintaining a vague 'existential essence.' A formal break can only be noticed retroactively, from which the two are categorically juxtaposed. Like all great power struggles, it functions through progressive flux, wherein it is always gathered after its dispersal. In this way, we find ideological approaches to succession of hegemonic rule to be the hidden rule of a group, where even political or familial rule act under this influence. The question then arises: to what extent are the spheres of influence and evolution of ideological progress influenced by private interests?

The conditions of ideology rest on the compulsory belief of the symbolic order as a necessary replacement of the real, that conceptual language replaces the reality described. It assumes a metaphysical plane, confusing the map for the territory, and assuming reality as evoked or accurately prescribed by language. This shows why ideology is so pervasive: its immediate relation to man is a power game which establishes the rules itself and ever in deference to itself, so that to deny the substantiative qualities is to present a counter-intuitive approach to life. Any idea which does not stem from ideology or as an argumentative reaction to ideology can only initially be viewed as pointless abstractions. It is in ideology's assertion of itself as the totality of real relations that we find the complete disregard for (or reduction of) language to

simplified or abstracted categorical mediators of our relation to reality. This shapes our ability to create meaning that is manifest only in terms of its dialectic: this then posits Being as free to be repurposed, and the entirety of Being's nature as explicitly contingent upon these moralized metaphysical planes of ideology. The feedback loop created between the functionality of ideological state apparatuses and ideological private interests, wherein media and intellectual support domineer the space around these theories, also consumes the reactions against it and splays it between the two, displaying singularity as multiplicity of difference, again confining Being to a theoretical plane. Because of this the specific performativity of the individual who, through the subconscious inflection of guilt and the dutiful moralizing of his actions, ultimately reflects the nature of the ideology that stands around him.

Through understanding the nature of conformism contrasted with that of conformity, we see that man finds the constructed nature of his surroundings such that his participation therein is necessary in order to find himself in a communal sense, no matter his relation to ideology. Here too one sees that he senses through his conscience a need to participate in an individuating formality such that he achieves success, popularity, love, or anything else he desires by means of his communal life. His individuation is galvanized and isolated in terms of its limits, thus allowing a site wherefrom we see the walls of ideology in their strictest sense in terms of communal relationality and reactions therein. This is not to say, however, that there is no way to approach language or other abstracted mediators in a way that makes navigation and intelligibility therein possible, nor that the impression on the singular from that symbolic order cannot be more accurate or freeing respectively. Rather, the difference between reading the map and mistaking it for the territory is similar in respect to the difference between conformity and conformism.

In utilizing either approach, one maintains passivity and a seriousness absurdly attributed therein which allows for a monopoly of one's autonomy by means of a false association of individual dependency maintained through one's adoption of moralization and communal manipulation. These approaches forge such strong bonds that men structure their lives and livelihood around them. In this way we see again the situation of reaching a correct conclusion by way of desecrating the notion of truth itself into information transferrable by its supporting ideological teleology. Despite the appearance of an acceptance of truth, the ideological culture which surrounds the nature of the notion by means of dogmatizing it within the canon of ideological thought, such that it prescribes a moral value to the conditions of acceptance. This is perhaps the strongest mode whereby ideology attempts to establish its substantiated qualities as reality itself, wherein all relations direct the individual back unto itself; the ideology assumes for itself exclusivity of the ideas or objects in question, whereupon they are moralized and prescribed a 'definitive' relation to Being. We again trace this approach to information as a commodity or as power-relation (as historical ascription) formulated exclusively under the societal or relational form of language. This notion of language as bearer of a positive epistemology is guarded and awarded by means of willful submission to ideology. This is another path through which the dimensionality of Being is controlled, and by which power is located as the central access through which man relates to ideology, and through which Being's relations are controlled by ideological state apparatuses. It is by way of ideology's habitual appeal to the freedom and truth that Being gains from its relation to ideology, that they are both stripped from it. Here truth is sacrificed on the altar of its certainty.

REFUTATION OF ALL
JUDGMENT

A
s one continues to note the form and function of ideology, one must at some point confront the necessary condition of presupposed narrative buy-ins of ideology in general. For those who disregard such narratives in pursuit of a life as free from ideology as possible, the question raised in opposition toward dogma is this: how does one conduct a relationship with what exists while aiming at a lack of holding to one's beliefs in a moralizing or dogmatic way? To maintain that there is a prescriptive way through which one can look to an authoritative value of such a way of life seems an impossibility. This seeming impossibility springs from our discussion on reactionary ideologies, as well as the conditions of our psychology seemingly habituating dogma from any truth we may find. The way by means of which ideology is minimized, however, can be aided, not guided, by means of the employment of tools with which one notes both the function of ideology as well as determinate Being's susceptibility to it. This can be done through the acknowledgment (not acceptance nor admittance of any character outside of their functionality as tools) of a negative (or negating) epistemology: the function of self-canceling refutation that is found in the work of Sextus Empiricus, as well as in some propositions of the work of D. T. Suzuki and the Buddha, or even directly self-defeating quips, the likes of which Marcel Duchamp employed.

As we have also found, the ideologue and his other can arrive at the same conclusion due to the mediation of language and its relation to reality. But he who seeks escape by means of climbing the discardable ladder holds neither judgment in terms of a dogmatic belief towards language or reality, nor a moral prescription from its ideological relation. It is the modality of one who looks to escape from ideology which utilizes refutation to demount one's 'beliefs.' It seems like freedom from ideology is thus a paradoxical task resulting in self-alienation. Through closely examining the means by which the task is sought, we find that the refutation of oneself is revealed not in actuality against oneself, but rather toward the societal ideological constructs surrounding oneself, which is how ideology installs itself so as to make itself seem impossible to escape from or deny as reality. This is where the sense of confusion comes in, for one realizes that one's own beliefs are in a sense installed, and not necessarily within some relation to or contrast with other beliefs, for there may be none. The question of purpose underlies the instability of continued acceptance of these beliefs, for without the possibility of an individual taking a stand for themselves in terms of (or through) social roles or performativity, he rather finds these beliefs as the product of an *other's* stance on themselves, and thus the recognition of the instillation of beliefs cannot help but create unrest within the individual who was set forth upon this path. For even though they might wind up at the same set of ideas (which look very much like the previously held beliefs), freedom for and knowledge of the individual can never be attained without this selfsame stance being taken *for* one's self. However, the adaptive capacity of ideology finds that to those who recognize themselves in this predicament, ideological state apparatuses can cater their tactics. Ideology has the potential to lose power by means of this sort of negating epistemology, and as such it adapts mere representation to quiet the worry of the individual without worry of having actual change effected.

It is this adaptive nature, which clings so tight to its chest that ideology goes unnoticed, that is propagated with such desperate necessity. Not only does reactionary ideology slip into that which it protests, but so too is the worry of turning a flight from ideology into an ideology, an anti-ideology ideology, attributing the sought-after freedom to a dogmatic approach to one's life solidified through belief. This is not to say that he who flees does not have the potential to maintain a persistent view of a series of ideas, but his views are never given the 'weight' of a belief, nor its sedimentation; that is, he never confuses the view of a linguistic ontology of an argument as a presentation of reality. He understands the real as unavoidably excessive, slipping from the story we agree or disagree on, or which we symbolically represent it as. If the prescription of narrative is maintained as such, there is no worry in adjusting, nor in disregarding it if a seemingly more reasonable, clear, or 'precise' story should make itself visible.

However, the individual is concretely interpolated such that the constitution and desire of the individual are themselves adjusted against the moving adaptive function of morality, which serves the private interest of those whose power relation is thereby maintained. However, here "rather than thinking of the social struggle in terms of 'justice' one has to emphasize justice in terms of social struggle." In terms of ideological morality, it engages in the struggle for power not "because it considers such a war to be just," but rather because "it wants to take power." It becomes evident that "one makes war to win, not because it is just."[75] For in ideological struggle all such justification is instrumental for or against the achievement of the position of power for one's self. Morality is the ideological ascription of what *ought* to seek after in one's own life, dictating even romantic and sexual desire, as well as the individual's own livelihood and self-preservation. This is often how we find that revolutionary ideology as a consumed faction of the hegemonic is revealed to man. For example, many of the demands of the supposed far left of American politics settle for demands of representation as a detached fantasy image of oneself within the narrative frame of reference *from* the hegemonic

---

75 Chomsky, Noam, and Michel Foucault, *The Chomsky-Foucault Debate: On Human Nature* (New York: New Press, 2006).

narrative. Just as ideological identity is compounded through the media of the hegemonic, so too is difference illustrated.

This difference takes the ideological Other and castigates the totality of a people through a singular (and thus necessarily fictional) representation. This function also satisfies those with mild resentment towards the hegemonic by representing them through a figure occupying space in its spectacle. It is in this form of representation as satiation of an alienated consciousness which functions as "a means by which workers obtain a redress of grievances . . . rather than an instrument for its transformation."[76] This is the process of false legitimization through which immediate participation within the spectacle of ideology consumes the desire and action of those who would otherwise transform the *society itself.* That is, there is a subsumption of the revolutionary or reactionary ideology under the hegemony of spectacle in terms of their literal reappropriation as new avenues of ideological power. This is again shown to us by the growing weight of the imagery and rhetoric of the hegemonic such that man's very relationality is transmogrified and the individual becomes further subjugated. It is through these means that "the social and family life of the community are weakened, new branches of production are brought into being to fill the resulting gap and new services and commodities provide substitutes for human relations in the form of market relationships, social and family life are further weakened."[77] Through this sleight-of-hand, the reactionary/revolutionary ideologue gains the role of an apologist by having taken the mediating token of the hegemonic ideology, and in terms of their own relationality, speaking to the progress of the hegemonic ideology as being in line with their own project.

This is often the most direct presentation of inter-ideological power-relations, where ideological content is not changed, or even discussed,

---

76 Aronowitz, Stanley, *False Promises: The Shaping of American Working Class Consciousness* (New York: McGraw-Hill, 1973), 51.

77 Braverman, Harry, *Labor and Monopoly Capital* (New York: Monthly Review Press, 1974), 277.

but instead simply presented as a direct change in visual identity. This essentially falls to a relative, moralized aesthetic, from which ethical queries are made by way of form, rather than function or content, due to a belief of signifiers in place of what constitutes a 'legitimate' ideologically transcendent experience. That is, somehow through a shift in formal iconographic features, the displayed effect seems to the ideologue to be one of power which relates (fundamentally and unconsciously) the undeniable and innate truth of the revolutionary or reactionary ideology being represented. However, in actuality, the display is, rather than relating some truth or affirming some positive character, instead merely the accepted method through which the claims of the alienated against either camp of ideology are silenced. This is Homeric mastery at its finest, rhetorical and aesthetic packaging to self-endorse one's predisposition to enjoy or celebrate by way of an ideological devotion. In this way, there is a cyclical conformation of ideology, whose instillation within the symbolic order is elevated to mythological status and presumed as self-evident, thus evoking the idea that truth, or at least relative morality, are 'eternal' elements exclusive to one's own ideology. It is here where they may present the ideals of their ideology in postmodern succession, denying these 'external' elements to their rhetorical stratagems, and immediately continuing to enact the labor demanded by the absolute system.

The subjugation of the ideologue also presents itself by means of a conceptual or linguistic domination in sets of ideas eternally retreating back into said ideology. This not only limits the quality or quantity of individual expressions or reactions, but also their perspectives on and care for each other. This type of ideological slipperiness sets apart categorical resignations for ideologically identified groups and attempts to concretize such groupings under an acceptable substructure, defining them as merely a representation of the ideologue in various images and rhetorical presentations, as if such a thing were a virtue in and of itself. We also find that through this categorization individuals are stripped of the very individuation which is their taking-a-stand-on-their-Being. Ideology removes from man that which makes him distinct from other living organisms. This is because the necessity of directly interpolating the individual as subject requires the identification of the self with a ready-made categorization or subcategorization dictated by the ideology. This interpolation is in part done through the presentation of options deviating from the ideologically acceptable as incompatible with the present power paradigm, and from which the inferred deduction is a prescription of categorical oughts. These dictates are the adaptive means by which a group of would-be subjects are delineated and categorized in a way that distinctly targets them so as to best interpolate them through systemized historiographical representation. This is systematically distorted communication wherein not only the categorical impositions and dogmatic reliance are placed on the false prescriptive nature of their dialectic, but also are placed against the theoretical and phantasmatic framework under which all linguistic or semantic presentations of opinions are given value, and from which the moralizing process flows. Here again we note the disregard for entire worlds by means of their moral or mere intellectual reconstitution.

Being is compressed into ready-made identities which stand as an authentic representation of the most intimate 'version' of the self. The freedom so passionately sought after by the individual then is presupposed by their beliefs, limiting their search to mere reconnaissance for their ideology's colonial expanse. The ideologue, having superseded the social agreement of language, asserts their own rhetorical approach, which is backed by the power given to it by the ideology wherefrom the rich universe of worlds necessarily devolves into mere subscription to localized semantics. The ideological grouping of people allows for its content to be so loosely defined, yet with categorical boundaries so oppositionally rigid in their definition that the attempt to force engagement with it brings out the contextual agreement of presuppositions of said identity, resulting in the mere presentation of ideological chains of signification. Through the employment of these self-referential categories, an ideology seeks to establish historiographical referents which narrativize its generative qualities through a sociopolitical ontology. Ideological identity reflects the structure's lack in terms of the very 'truth-factors' with which it concerns itself. The eternality of an ideology is founded throughout a network of narratives whose truth-functions are preserved only by their nature as self-referential, and by which ideologues have present in their ideas a presumption of ignorance within reasoning itself.

It is through this expert knowledge that men constantly build their network of knowledge, which is in essence mere narrativization, which by its nature habituates man to the realm of faith while maintaining knowledge without understanding. It seems, by this very nature of narrative self-support, and through its prior hypocritical assault upon opposing ideologies, that we find the moral commands of oughts and ought-nots to be unaware of their ironic element. This ironic element is due to their internal logic which is valued at a higher level than all else. And yet the very same irony is more likely to play into the hands of the ruling powers than to discomfort them, as Slavoj Žižek observes: "in contemporary societies, democratic or totalitarian, . . .cynical distance, laughter, irony, are, so to speak, part of the game. The ruling ideology is not meant to be taken seriously or literally."[78] It is as though the ruling ideology has already accommodated the fact that we will be skeptical of it, and reorganized its discourses accordingly. Even when it comes to the belief in the principles of an ideology itself, adaptation is already able to invent its representation in order that power be maintained. This is again to show that the demand of representation is itself already a sign of submission, one which stems from the overall moralizing procedures of the ideology. This moralizing process of othering and flattening fails to "manifest exteriority and the other as the other; it destroys the identity

---

78 Žižek, Slavoj, *The Sublime Object of Ideology* (London: Verso, 1989), 28.

of the same."[79] The moralizing process of ideology is antithetical to an authentic ethical relation, and instead

> individuals are reduced to ring bearers of forces that command them unbeknown to themselves. The meaning of individuals (invisible outside of this totality) is derived from the totality. The unicity of each present is incessantly sacrificed to a future appealed to bring forth its objective meaning. For the ultimate meaning alone counts; the last act alone changes beings into themselves. They are what they will appear to be in the already plastic forms of the epic.[80]

Just as before we find desire projected upon *no-thing*, which promises so great a historical or otherwise spiritual reward that those who see this meaning are willing to grant fuller submission to their commanding ideology.

It is from this devotion that we find the very reason these instilled ideas truly become that of warfare: life or death unto the ideologue. One identifies the success of an ideology that they have been interpolated into for various reasons as their own, and strictly alter their Being, values, and relations in a strategy to yield the greatest potential for success in their life as a tool, seeking to propel their ideology into the realm of the hegemonic, hoping to thereby preserve themselves eternally. This is made all the more compelling to the ideologue due to the level where the particular ideology installs itself: that of the unconscious. It seems to many who find themselves interpolated that the event of interpolation sneaks in through the ways of individual choices, which in many instances pretend to be divorced from the overarching ideological warfare, and instead take on the self-affirming migration

---

79 Levinas, "Preface," in *Totality and Infinity*, 21.
80 Ibid., 22.

trail from which the individual travels from their initial ontological consideration. To the ideologue, it seems as though the fight for the successful recognition of their particular ideology is fundamentally no different than that of their own survival. This is the totalizing character or the moralizing process of ideology, which adorns war itself with the mask of true moral content.

A TEMPORARY STAY

Perhaps one of the most important keys to understanding ideology and its critique is through one of the many modes of self-identification. This particular mode is that whereby the self is contrasted with the 'I.' This contrast is brought to consciousness by means of the primordial relationship of man in the world. This brings understanding of the very possibility of identification as drawn by staying here, a place where one differentiates oneself from that which offers or resists possession. Yet, through the relationality of the self to the other, there is a potential for affect and/or change, whereby through this relational effect one finds within themselves the appearance of a seeming alterity. This unity of both unity and difference is constituted by the transcendental character of Being. The notion is described by Hegel in a way where form nearly mirrors content: "I distinguish myself from myself; and therein I am immediately aware that this factor distinguished from me is not distinguished. I, the selfsame being, thrust myself away from myself; but this which is distinguished, which is set up as unlike me, is immediately on its being distinguished no distinction from me."[81] This very play that one finds within oneself allows for the maintaining of differentiation of thought: in this way we find that those who recognize this double thought, this turning of the self, are granted a way to distance the personalization that ideology finds itself habituated within. What transpires then is the distinguishing from hard-fast, clung-to 'belief' which manifests itself as a personalization of ideology and concludes exterior to the self, and that of soft 'belief' wherein ideas follow from that of a formulated thought to

---

81 Hegel, G. W. F., *The Phenomenology of Mind,* trans. J. B. Bailleie, 2nd ed. (New York: Humanities Press, 1964), 211.

generalized abstraction. This soft 'belief' mediates emotional response and generalized notions of value while formally lacking belief in the epistemic sense; thus this modality of 'belief' is a formulation of thoughts which relate to the garnering of intelligibility from their cultural matrix.

What this means is that, through this separation, one rewrites one's own history as a narrative through which is generated an epistemology only understood by way of reference to the totality of narrativization habitually used as a supplement for Being. The problem with this narrativization is that it never generates ontically what exists for a being in-and-of itself, but rather generates the ontology of an identity or identities, through which we find the individual's understanding of himself as intrinsic to that which they differentiate, and in this understanding there is no difference any longer separating the individual from that which they have constructed. Another way to understand this is in contrast to the theological idea of there 'being something in a name' and against which we understand this discussion as centered through

> the effort to secure its identity and establish its presence, [through which] the self discovers its unavoidable difference and irrepressible absence . . . The search for self-presence in self-consciousness leads to the discovery of the absence of the self. Once again self-affirmation and self-negation prove to be indivisibly bound. Apparent 'selving' is actual 'unselving.' The journey to selfhood turns out to be a dangerous voyage— nothing is shattered and opened.' The shattering of the subject is registered by the trace.[82]

In the continued narrativizing of one's life, one finds oneself constructing that which is made concrete only through difference, and it is by

---

82 Taylor, Mark C., "Disappearance of the Self," in *Erring: A Postmodern A/theology* (Chicago: University of Chicago Press, 1984), 50-51.

difference through which it establishes itself within the narrative, and through this narrative, the individual ceases to *exist*. This is made clearer through the explication of the idea of the trace which Derrida tells us is

> the opening of the first exteriority in general, the enigmatic relationship of the living to its other and of an inside to an outside: spacing. The outside, 'spatial' and 'objective' exteriority which we believe we know as the most familiar thing in the world, as familiarity itself, would not appear without the grammē, without difference as temporalization, without the nonpresence of the other inscribed within the meaning of the present, without the relation to death as the concrete structure of the living present . . . The presence-absence of the trace . . .[83]

Hence, this 'shattering of the subject' is itself Being registered with this other *in itself,* inscribed in its *name* wherein we find clarity as to this self-differentiation. Hence, to those unable to navigate the complexities of this self-differentiation, ideology may seem forever inescapable. This self-differentiation is a necessary development of those who wish to escape the grip of ideology, for despite the contained nature of the 'I' within the self, without this process there is no divorcing the coded software which has been impressed onto the hardware of Being (as we have seen: the two were adapted to be *as such*).

This coding is guessed at by Richard Dawkins when he states that life itself as a structure subsists "by the differential survival of replicating entities."[84] This idea is reconsidered near the end of his book wherein he asks the question hiding in the shadows: outside of the genetic replicat-

---

83 Derrida, Jacques, "Linguistics and Grammatology," in *Of Grammatology* (Baltimore: Johns Hopkins University Press, 1976), 42-43.

84 Dawkins, Richard, *The Selfish Gene* (Oxford: Oxford University Press, 1989), 192.

ing entities which the rest of the book focuses on, there is a set of other replicators outside of genetics, which are perhaps never addressed as such. This notion locates the primordial function of imitation which Susan Blackmore explicates by pointing out that "all the words in your vocabulary, the stories you know, the skills and habits you have picked up from others and the games you like to play. It includes the songs you sing and the rules you obey . . . each of these memes has evolved in its own unique way with its own history, but each of them is using your behavior to get itself copied."[85] This means to say that aspects of culture are seeking to replicate themselves by means of coding themselves into relationality in such a way that promotes their continued well-being, in much the same way that genes seek to propagate themselves. It is through memeplexes (groups of memes, often found together in the same individual) that memes join together in a fashion that benefits their reproduction and their reproduction alone, much as feminist ideology supports the ideology of the Islamists such that each gains potency, despite their conceptual opposition to each other.

This set of structures helps to keep ideology from imploding under the weight of diverse vehicles, and maintains a frame of legitimacy for their individual parts. This is because memeplexes are metaphysically in-affectual and thus apathetic, which, because they can maintain negative, positive, or neutral value in the individual, must have some form of structure apart from the content of the individual or the values of the ideology. This is not to suggest that memeplexes or their ideological superstructures have providence or an abstract plan, for they possess no sentience separate from man, but rather variation, acquisition, and selection offer significant avenues through which their replicatory process plays itself out. In this way, we may begin to understand how ideologies establish themselves as progressive without any real progression made. In some sense, then, autonomy, as being free to take a side

---

85 Blackmore, Susan J., "Strange Creatures," in *The Meme Machine* (Oxford: Oxford University Press, 1999), 7.

in this ideological war, itself becomes something constructed as a mere means by which memes replicate themselves. In this way, too, yet another angle is revealed through which reactionary or revolutionary ideologies parasitize power, which in a way is merely a continuation of the hegemonic. Through a type of memetic survival, this battle of ideas that is held in one's own mind, wherein the individual can recognize opposing ideals within himself, is mere dictation from these cultural replicators such that the next generation may carry on as many copies of that meme as possible. To use perhaps a kitsch example, Daniel Dennett looks at parasitic memes from an evolutionary biological perspective when he asks one to

> think about symbionts again. Parasites are (by definition) those symbionts that are deleterious to the fitness of the host. Consider the most obvious meme example: the meme for celibacy (and chastity, I might add, to close a notorious loophole). This meme complex inhabits the brains of many a priest and nun. From the point of view of evolutionary biology, this complex is deleterious to fitness by definition: anything that virtually guarantees that the host's germ line is a cul-de-sac, with no further issue, lowers fitness. "But so what?" a priest might retort. "*I* don't want to have progeny!" Exactly. But, you might say, his body still does. He has distanced himself somewhat from his own body, in which the machinery designed by Mother Nature keeps right on running, sometimes giving him problems of self-control. How did this self or ego with the divergent goal get constituted? . . . whenever and however it happened, it has been incorporated by the priest—at least for the time being—into his identity.[86]

---

86 Ibid., 365.

This notion of identification when meditated upon however reveals itself to be "ambiguous between incorporation and endorsement."[87] The question of the relation between identity and the self is complicated, as we recognize the self as being neither the "cognitive relations directed towards the past or by actions [as they are] fulfilled in the present . . . [but] instead, the self is integrated in a network of practical and productive relationships projected toward the future . . . [as well as] the peculiar irreducibility of the first-person givenness manifested in the phenomenon of the call of conscience."[88]

To understand the entirety of identity as the particular aspect of mind caught in mimetic relations, to be consumed to a point of no return, eternally shifting from one ideological superstructure to another, seems too simple an understanding. It seems more likely that individuals, while engaging in this ideological warfare, possess by way of the same faculty which led to their interpolation, the potentiality to wake up to their seduction, and indeed resist. It would seem that there is a more challenging structure of manipulation beyond the funhouse imaginings of revolutionaries who position themselves within a gnostic universe against the wicked logic of a monolithic leader. Instead it would seem there is a manipulator of he who is manipulating: the process which his power generates is not his satisfaction, but rather the development of the ideological forces themselves: "the manipulator himself is always-already manipulated."[89]

Hegel's *The Philosophy of History* poses the concept of the 'cunning of reason,' where we can begin to see the complexities through which

---

87 Berofsky, Bernard, "Values and the Self," in *Liberation from Self: A Theory of Personal Autonomy* (Cambridge: Cambridge University Press, 1995), 99.

88 Escudero, Jesús Adrián, "Heidegger on Selfhood," *American International Journal of Contemporary Research* 4, no. 2 (February 2014): 7-8.

89 Žizek, Slavoj, "I or He or It (the Thing) Which Thinks," in *Tarrying with the Negative: Kant, Hegel, and the Critique of Ideology* (Durham, N.C.: Duke University Press, 1993), 33.

this notion highlights a fundamental aspect characterizing ideological superstructures:

> It is not the general idea that is implicated in opposition and combat and that is exposed to danger. It remains in the background, untouched and uninjured. This may be called the *cunning of reason*—that it sets the passions to work for itself, while that which develops is existence through such impulsion pays the penalty, and suffers loss . . . the particular is for the most part of too trifling value as compared with the general: individuals are sacrificed and abandoned. The Idea pays the penalty of determinate existence and corruptibility, not from itself, but from the passions of individuals.[90]

By "the moving force of the productive Idea" man might stand beyond or outside of the cultural division of ideology. This is of importance in part due to the possibility of conflict between the selfish replication of one's genes and of memes.

The glaring suggestion here is that memetics unfolded in parallel to genetic structures through the most fundamental of replication processes: sexual selection. That is to say that (without even commenting here on the role in which ideological stressors affect sexual selection) those who best imitated the culturally significant memes of their era would have a more diverse lot of sexually available individuals from whom to select. The memetic drive would become amplified, through the combined reinforcement the chemical element of sexual reproduction provides in tandem with the habituation of memetic information. Erotic and otherwise sexual content becomes the protein through which a memeplex is strengthened. It is understood then how sexual liberation and political control are often intertwined in the way that feminists have claimed

---

90 Hegel, *The Philosophy of History* (New York: Dover, 1956), 33.

famously that the "personal is political."[91] These expressions of one's 'personal desires' are often seen by those within the group promoting such expression as the revolutionary action which will finally install their freedom within the mainstream, and support the people whom the group considers to be oppressed by giving them unlimited access to this desire.

This, however, is a false assumption which misunderstands the aspects of ideological struggle that they claim informs their movement, for when installed within the mainstream, the group that seeks to offer freedom ultimately discovers themselves offering this freedom only for those who find themselves always-already in the group itself. When installed in the arena of power which their striving runs up against, instead of offering freedom for all (their original stated goal) they offer a mere intellectual reaffirmation to what they have already believed to be true, and as such they create and insulate messages they themselves wish to be true. This creation of insulated messages finds its audience within itself, and thus its consumers are made up from its own body such that they believe that refinement of thought is reducible to its inevitable reaffirmation. Tolerance becomes an ideological category wherein, as Žižek puts it,

> the liberal idea of a "free choice" thus always gets caught in a deadlock. If the subject wants it, he or she can opt for the parochial tradition into which they were born, but they have first to be presented with alternatives and then make a free choice among them. Amish adolescents, on the other hand, are formally given a free choice, but the conditions they find themselves in while they are making the choice make the

91 Carol, Hanisch, "The Personal Is Political: The Original Feminist Theory Paper at the Author's Web Site," *Carol Hanisch of the Women's Liberation Movement*, December 20, 2016.

choice unfree. In order for them to have a genuine free choice, they would have to be properly informed on all the options and educated in them. But the only way to do this would be to extract them from their embeddedness in the Amish community and Americanise them.[92]

Žižek here seems to be facetiously suggesting that 'Amercanising' is more than a modification which would leave intact all unfreedom found in embeddedness. Beyond that, his use of the terms "properly informed" and "educated" recall the ironic underbelly found therein through the presenting of information on oppositional perspectives, for those in power seek to represent the opposing ideas by way of their preconceived notion of them.

    This representation is one of information about the ideology currently in power instead of anything about any other group. This effect seems to be fully visible when we observe the groups that sprang forth from the sexual revolution of the 1960s, who altered the way media and culture broadly discuss and consume sex and sexualization. This form of sexual representation ultimately speaks of its own virtue, citing freedom alone, while simultaneously using its representation as a moralized condemnation against the free choices of sexuality that do not constantly allow individuals to always be sexually open.[93] Both freedom and sexuality are embedded as ideological categories, where differing worlds can be seen as only modifiers to the given ontology. This is because, as we have seen before, media as a cultural representation is a literal staging of fantasy by way of a projection of commanding desires. Žižek tells us

    What the fantasy stages is not a scene in which our desire is fulfilled, fully satisfied, but on the contrary, a scene that

---

92 Žižek, Slavoj, "Tolerance as an Ideological Category," in *Violence: Six Sideways Reflections*, 145.

93 Brown, Jane D., "Mass Media Influences on Sexuality," *The Journal of Sex Research* 39, no. 1 (2002): 42–45.

realizes, stages the desire as such . . . desire is not something given in advance, but something that has to be constructed — and it is precisely the role of fantasy to give the coordinates of the subject's desire, to specify its object, to locate the position the subject assumes in it. It is only through fantasy that the subject is constituted as desiring: through fantasy we learn how to desire.[94]

This is the element of desire which popular media necessarily habituates: not the fulfillment or satisfaction of desire, but instead its reproduction *ad infinitum*. Through popular culture and media this desire is understood as a retroactive desire which is generated as a mediator between the self and an object/other by means of the fetishistic provocation of one's own gaze.

It is then by keeping distance from realizing the objects in one's own life that the desire itself is sustained: desire is a positive constitution of a lack. This desire is that phantasmagorical element which makes ideology so potent, for within its background operation is the escapist impulse needed for the individual to keep from saying the truth about his own desire. Installed within the emotional content of the individual in relation to the ideological narrative they call their own is the character of avoidance of reality. This is because desire is fueled by its own impossibility. It is by way of misrecognition of the fullness of the object and the separation of man from what truly matters to him that the fantasy of ideology is sustained. For man "to remain in this state, they must block outside stimuli . . . and what is it that they are doing? They are visualizing, analyzing, experiencing a fantasy not their own but which . . . they believe in some provisional way to be true—true enough to draw conclusions, form moral opinions, and even shape their own lives to fit."[95] This very analysis and

---

94 Žižek, Slavoj, "From Reality to a Real," in *Looking Awry: An Introduction to Jacques Lacan through Popular Culture* (Cambridge, Mass.: MIT Press, 1991), 6.

95 Davis, Lennard J., "Resisting the Novel," in *Resisting Novels: Ideology and Fiction* (New York: Methuen, 1987), 2.

inner experience are traced alongside the formation of the very first form of mass-produced media: the novel. It seems as though the novel (and analogously, the film and other meta-narrative media) stands as perhaps the least questioned and most influential (albeit invisible) form of ideological and dogmatic persuasion. This seems in part due to the way in which it subsumes the individuals who consume novels, whom we can seek to understand through the ways in which the individual's ideological defenses are constructed psychologically. This is because it is through these means that viability is maintained and illusory resolutions to social, political, or individual tensions founded. We understand these defenses as operating as an innate characteristic of the novel itself: this integrated quality continues to provide a deepened instillation of the subject through the ideological process. These processes are first understood by way of the very necessary conditions for reading a novel: that of isolation.

> In order to read, we have to ascribe a certain validity to what we read. If we were truly skeptical, we would be saying, along with our Puritan forbears, "This is false, this is a lie," and we would ultimately be unable to read a novel. To be able to read, then, we must cut off, as it were, or isolate certain features of our ideational life and separate them from the demands of reality.[96]

The form and function of the novel introverts consciousness, and orients the individual towards that of the fictional, which is itself "alienated from lived experience, their subject matter is heavily oriented towards the ideological, and their function is to help humans adapt to the fragmentation and isolation of the modern world."[97]

In this way, not only does the novel parallel the function of ideological narratives, but so too does it mirror desire, for isolation is sustained by

---

96 Ibid., 20.
97 Ibid., 12.

way of distancing ourselves from *reality*. Isolation lends itself to function alongside projection, which is another innate defense mechanism of the novel. This is the action by which people "attribute to others wishes and impulses of their own which are unacceptable to them and which they unconsciously try to get rid of."[98] In this way it is also revealed that the individual is consumed by desires which he allows himself to feel on behalf of those who he disavows as fictional. Therefore, since the individual has a psychological barrier between themselves and the emotions that they would otherwise not allow themselves to feel, they blur the distinction between what is fiction and what is real, and in some way enjoy the emotions which they themselves attribute to others. As such they can convince themselves *emotively* that they are testing reality in a safe space, while never stopping to realize the contradictions that their systematization of emotive projection is riddled with. We can understand if the mechanism is nurtured into adult life, and therein used with great frequency such that "the user's perception of external reality will be seriously distorted, or to put it in other words, his ego's capacity for reality testing will be considerably impaired."[99] As fiction is celebrated for having often been cited as encouraging the capacity for sympathies, it seems as though the way it inversely impacts the individual's rendering of reality has been greatly neglected.

The last of the major defense mechanisms intrinsic to the reading of novels is identification. Identification is perhaps more invisible than the others in that it seems straightforward but requires a great deal of work pre-engaging with the text itself. This is because identification operates on the basis of

> the very act of believing that there is space and claiming it
> is at root [the] ideological . . . dimension of formal elements

---

98 Brenner, Charles, *An Elementary Textbook of Psychoanalysis* (New York: International Universities, 1973), 102.

99 Ibid., 101.

. . . [by which we assume] novels can and should be filled with 'living human beings.' The feeling we have that living, changing people are what novelists create is a mass cultural assumption—not a universal given—and requires a major perceptual and defensive change of the kind that the novel as a discourse encourages and requires.[100]

This assumption is how we go about understanding that the characters, and as a whole the signs and symbols, are arranged throughout the novel such that those who read and are instructed by way of its very form and function defensively identify with the totality of experience. This is all done by way of understanding that "the simplification of personality required to produce a character in a novel is itself once again an ideological statement about the role of the individual in relation to society."[101] And this statement is one which rarely goes recognized, for as has been seen, the defense mechanisms involved with the reading of a novel make it so that the consumption of the novel itself renders this very statement invisible to the reader, instead formalizing its *moral* subsumption so that the individual who reads the novel fails to recognize the statement as one of a subjective author functioning through their own artifice to create a 'truth' which holds only to their own 'universe,' and alternatively interprets this experience as an objective signifier. Identification as a defensive mechanism intrinsic to the novel is substantiated by way of beauty, passivity, and invitation, which all serve to inform the reader ideologically. Now, when identification is taken into consideration regarding fictitious media, we understand that those who engage with the work formally already possess the preceding desire of identification. That is, before a reader picks up a novel, he *desires* to identify with a character who he can put himself in the place of.

---

100 Davis, "Resisting the Novel," 103.
101 Ibid., 102.

One sets out in a novel to identify with a character—even before meeting that character or any character, novelistic characters exist because they are designed to entice us to identify with them. Readers do identify with characters as diverse as Jude Fawley, Tom Jones, Verloc, or Maggie Verver. In novel reading, the desire to identify precedes the particularity of the characters. In other words, it is not a question of liking a character, or finding reminders of our own early relationships in that character, but simply the fact that the form of the novel itself evokes identification. While Freudian identification is largely dependent on the particular personality of the object with whom we will identify, novelistic identification is indiscriminate and promiscuous, if you will, since all objects, all protagonists, have been or will be objects of desire.[102]

This is not to say that we cannot like the presentation or find reminders of ourselves in the portrayals of characters we read in novels, but rather based on the format and necessary conditions of the novel, and preceding the novel (that is, intrinsic to the action of *reading a novel*), that these factors are largely irrelevant to the identification process of reading. The fact that we are *invited* to identify is that process by which these emotive associations occur, but whether they may or may not occur has no relation to the prior invitation aside from their concluding possibility therein.

This invitation is what is necessary to place ourselves in relation to the protagonist (or in other works, the author), wherein a collective wish-fulfilling fantasy proceeds such that the reader might find psychological 'escape' from their own reality. Part of what entices people to read novels is a beauty which encourages this desire (which is performed) to grow, much as those who seek a particular product are enticed further by

102 Ibid., 126-27.

advertisers who utilize a physically attractive model to subtly convince the onlooker to purchase their product over others. We may understand then the motivation behind using beauty as an ideological tool of the novelist

> since the physical beauty of most protagonists is not accidental but taken as a functioning requirement of the classic novel . . . In effect, it is not so much that we identify with a character, but that we desire that character in some nonspecific . . . way. In this sense, part of novel reading is the process of falling in love with characters or making friends with signs. This desire for novelistic characters provides a way in which the defensive nature of ideological constructs can be understood. The novel as an ideological form requires attraction as much as pornography requires attraction to succeed. By the connection through identification, ideologies can ebb and flow through a populace.[103]

This means that there is no neutrality when it comes to beauty or ugliness in novels or other novelistic forms, but instead these symbolic elements take their power, in part, through the totality of meaning systematized through the ideological considerations of the novelist himself, and not simply as an accidental relation.

Novels then maintain a strict parallel with pornography, for we understand that for the novel to succeed you need not find anything about the characters, signs or symbols to be anything save sufficiently attractive. So long as it draws you in, and since a prerequisite of novel reading is this desire to be drawn in, the process is streamlined and naturalized, hence seductive yet invisible, and thus, like pornography, novel reading is necessarily narcissistic. This narcissism is the drive that encourages ownership by way of Marx's commodity-fetishism, whereby

---

103 Ibid., 127.

the products of the human brain appear as autonomous figures endowed with a life of their own, which enter into relations both with each other and with the human race. So it is in the world of commodities with the products of men's hands. I call this the fetishism which attaches itself to the products of labour as soon as they are produced as commodities, and is therefore inseparable from the production of commodities.[104]

This is to say that the subjective elements of a novel and the psychological intimacy they provide are merely commodities packaged as discrete experiences that reorganize individual thought processes as a narrativization by which those who read understand themselves. This form of fetishization is that whereby man's very Being is itself made a commodity to be capitalized on, and exported in a consumable manner, whereby all relations become potential transactions of one sort or another. This form of isolation works in tandem with the further desire, and at some level, *need*, for the reader to lose themselves in the novel, for this escapism is also driven by the foundation of the way in which their individuality has been defined. This is understood not only through this psychological commodification, but in every way through which the novel works, for we understand that

the novel works not only by transforming space into controlled property but by turning personality into controlled character. In effect, personality is rendered a form of property quite literally if you consider the author's ownership of his or her creation through copyright laws—and a commodity in the sense that readers buy novels in some sense to have access to

104 Marx, Karl, "The Commodity," in *Capital: A Critique of Political Economy*, trans. Ben Fowkes, vol. 1 (New York: Vintage, 1976), 165.

these controlled personalities. By placing so much emphasis on
the process of desire, and the feeling that this activity of novel
reading is so dependent on Eros to solve personal problems and
reshape character, the novel in effect becomes a social form that
changes the complexity of personality into a rather simplified
commodity of desire. Like a desirable commodity that seems
to offer the promise of an improved life, or like an objectified
fashion model who beckons the user of the targeted product
into the frame of an advertisement, character holds out the
possibility of personal fulfillment in a world.[105]

This makes obvious the cycle in which these commodities are used for
the narcissistic ends of the user, further installing the individual's need
for escape, as the desires/needs are not fulfilled and/or issues persist,
where the individual finds himself that much more easily subsumed.
This cycle prolongs itself, for while they are inside of the fantasy their
original situation is exacerbated by persisting and yet remaining stagnant,
and as such might even grow and/or become more obscured by way of
taking the fictitious solutions at face value and attempting to resolve
their dissonance by way of symbols and icons. This is because

in effect, reading novels is a solitary activity in which readers
define themselves by what they are not, put themselves into
locations they have never been, and celebrate values that often
they would never endorse. The activity is also the ultimate
in reification. Rather than actually seeing and perceiving the
sensual reality of human life, a patent simulacrum of a human
being made up purely of linguistic symbols with certain rules
of recurrence is presented as if it were human. And what is
more to the point, it is conceived as an object of desire. We

---

105 Davis, "Resisting the Novel," 128.

seek to locate ourselves in the character and to merge with the character. We read to make friends with signs.[106]

This is ultimately a way in which ideological conversion may occur, for it is in this way that we see the individual abandon his present 'reality' and place on hold their convictions such that they assume the nature of the simulacrum to be that of reality, and take the company of symbols to be their own, transforming their reality to match that of the fictitious. For some, the reading of any text is considered beneficial due to the ability for change to occur in the reader in part due to the intellectual priority given to the written word, regardless of its qualitative effect. This is also due to the fact that an individual's propensity for testing reality has been disabled and as such they cease qualitatively testing the content of the novel as it relates to the beauty with which the text has been endowed. This beauty is not only convincing, as in an advertised image of the escapist desire to embody the life of the work of fiction, but also as an embodiment of morality itself. In this way, the ideological transference of a novel is, on the immediate surface, threefold in its fortification. Without ever having peered into the psychological strongholds making an individual, without diving into issues one may be facing that could further open oneself up, it is easy to see that the fortification of the subsuming ideological qualities with which the novel convinces the consumer is brilliantly structured, and in and of itself a study of memetic replication nearly unparalleled historically. Authors in many instances create characters whom they find to be beautiful, and those who read find their desire instigated by identification with these characters, as if this quality is given to them by reading fiction embodying that quality.

We would do well to take note here that man is not free from these traps should he turn his eyes from the written word and instead live a life of solitude, finding no psychological projection by way of the fictitious.

---

106 Ibid., 135-36.

This is because even in the words of the nonfiction author, history and truth have been touched by the blade of meaning. Historians too form signification from the static register of material history, and as such plot structure "has its implication for the cognitive operations by which the historian seeks to 'explain' what was 'really happening' during the process of which it provides an image of its true form."[107] We understand that the narrative relation people share with the events of their time make this sort of narrative ontology invisible and isolating in that, upon inspecting the narratives of the past to be so dissimilar to those in contemporary practice, a metanarrative is constructed as to how they had achieved their initial beliefs. Narratives have the ability to transform history by way of revelation, which ultimately fails to understand itself as such, for

> the paradox is that while novels participate in a revisionistic view of history in which the past can be changed, that view must be mutated through the ideological or defensive modality. Massive social change is, after all, a disturbing idea to middle-class sensibilities, even if that same class had to get its own power through some such upheaval . . . So, what plot does is refocus these cultural concepts through the lens of the novel into less threatening visions of personal and familial reform. That personalization of reformation is the accepted mode through which novels can bring change to life.[108]

It is then through the ideological notion that the personal is political that we can see how personal desire can be an overriding function of the ideological struggle on behalf of the individual. For it can thus become a shared desire through the public dream of fiction, and the individual who consumes it consumes this desire as their own.

---

107 White, Hayden, "Introduction," in *Metahistory: The Historical Imagination in Nineteenth-Century Europe* (Baltimore: Johns Hopkins University Press, 1975), 11.
108 Davis, "Resisting the Novel," 218-19.

This is a way in which ideological explanations and explications of private life are given a rich narrative justification, and is also a way in which metaphysical alterations are made to people's private desires and convictions. Due to the ways in which individuals engage with narratives (especially if such engagement is mere escapism), these private desires and convictions are given a passion and strength unrivaled in even the most radical of paradigm shifts. This is due to not only all the defense mechanisms which insulate the individual, but also the intimate nature and invisibility of the ideological guide, wherein despite the very fact that the reader is exterior to every aspect of the text they feel as though they themselves have generated all of the change that they claim as their own. This is the endpoint of the fiction, perhaps the greatest landmark of any ideological subsumption.

> Therefore, since readers are not involved at all in the process of story-telling—the way a collective audience would be if only on the level of body language and reaction . . . In other words, precisely to the degree that the novel is reified and alienated from life, it has to create the further illusion, along with its use of the technique of realism, that the reader is actually part of the making or unmaking of the plot.[109]

This process is far from simple however, for it is with the subjective character of, and differential narrative interpretations for, words in the written text that there is left enough room for what amounts to very real denominational struggles in relation to fictions themselves. Despite the dominance of hegemonic memetic transference, it is still important to note that

> replicability, then, is not the same as replication; replicability is different from and logically prior to its empirical instantiations in the form of actual replications, actual duplications. If

---

109 Ibid., 212.

replication can be either exact or inexact and still be replication, then that is because there is something more fundamental than replication, something that facilitates the transfer not primarily of the (exact) copy but of this copy's copyability, something that thereby is always able in principle to interfere with the transfer of the (exact) copy.[110]

This is also made obvious in the fact that individuals are complex and intricate organisms, with the greatest of possibilities to be pushed and pulled in innumerable directions, and with an unlimited range of choices that could alter any aspect of their life, ideological or not.

110 Kimball, A. Samuel, "Replicability versus Replication: A Derridean View of Mutability," in *The Infanticidal Logic of Evolution and Culture* (Newark: University of Delaware Press, 2007), 83.

A New Development?

I n contemporary culture, the fading of the novel, instead of granting
an alternative to the demand to enjoy, merely gave way to ideology's
evolutionary development of one of the chief ways in which many
live and verify their lives against an external source. This is done through
media in its comforting whisper, which has found its way into our hearts
as a much more subtle moralizer of the people, and in this way remaining
much more invisible both to those interpolated, and those exterior to this
subsumption. In this way, many of the debates over morality, political
theory, and conduct of the layman are mediated through the figures we
see presented through media. In fact, as one study notes:

> Fact-related information contained in fictional narratives
> may induce substantial changes in readers' real-world beliefs.
> Current models of persuasion through fiction assume that these
> effects occur because readers are psychologically transported
> into the fictional world of the narrative. Contrary to general
> dual-process models of persuasion, models of persuasion
> through fiction also imply that persuasive effects of fictional
> narratives are persistent and even increase over time (absolute
> sleeper effect).[111]

It seems that man has sought wrongly the target of Marx's famous
proclamation of 'the opium of the masses' in the past, believing that

---

111 Appel, Markus, and Tobias Richter, "Persuasive Effects of Fictional Narratives
Increase Over Time," *Media Psychology* 10, no. 1 (2007): 113-34.

they have conquered the problem of which it spoke. However, since we have seen the process of ideological interpolation, we note the charge as speaking simultaneously to characteristics everyone sees working on a day-to-day basis.

By looking at the statement without a Marxist (opposed to Marx's) presupposition we begin to see the ways in which it lives on as a critique of the society man still constructs and lives in. We can accurately pinpoint then the enduring effects which his critique still carries in our society of ideology, keeping this grand perspective in mind as over and against its substantiation. Marx states that within religion

> the foundation of irreligious criticism is: *Man makes religion*, religion does not make man. Religion is, indeed, the self-consciousness and self-esteem of man who has either not yet won through to himself, or has already lost himself again. But *man* is no abstract being squatting outside the world. Man is *the world of man* —state, society. This state and this society produce religion, which is an *inverted consciousness of the world*, because they are an *inverted world*. Religion is the general theory of this world, its encyclopaedic compendium, its logic in popular form, its spiritual *point d'honneur*, its enthusiasm, its moral sanction, its solemn complement, and its universal basis of consolation and justification. It is the *fantastic realization* of the human essence since the *human essence* has not acquired any true reality. The struggle against religion is, therefore, indirectly the struggle *against that world* whose spiritual *aroma* is religion. *Religious* suffering is, at one and the same time, the *expression* of real suffering and a *protest* against real suffering. Religion is the sigh of the oppressed creature, the heart of a heartless world, and the soul of soulless conditions. It is the *opium* of the people. The abolition of religion as the *illusory* happiness of the people is the demand for their *real*

happiness. To call on them to give up their illusions about their condition is to call on them to *give up a condition that requires illusions*. The criticism of religion is, therefore, *in embryo, the criticism of that vale of tears* of which religion is the *halo*. Criticism has plucked the imaginary flowers on the chain not in order that man shall continue to bear that chain without fantasy or consolation, but so that he shall throw off the chain and pluck the living flower. The criticism of religion disillusions man, so that he will think, act, and fashion his reality like a man who has discarded his illusions and regained his senses, so that he will move around himself as his own true Sun. Religion is only the illusory Sun which revolves around man as long as he does not revolve around himself.[112]

Religion then as an instantiated moment of ideology itself possesses a double function as its outlet to and dwelling through which the hidden moment of desire and identification is maintained. The lives of 'average citizens' are kept unexamined and automatic and without maintaining more than a production's required amount of autonomy. This allows those who generate the structure of any particular instance of these innumerable outlets to maintain a monopoly on power and influence. One of the most fundamental ways this is done is in the portrayals and unilateral moral prescription of the past.

We can see this easily in the way that the media co-opts previously established genres or conventional items in storytelling such that the entire weight of the production adds to this necessary understanding of the media relating information about characters. This relationality, under which there is necessitated no factual or immediate understanding of the way things are *in actuality*, finds historical sympathy for its

---

112 Marx, Karl, *Introduction to A Contribution to the Critique of Hegel's Philosophy of Right*, in *Collected Works*, vol. 3 (New York: Oxford University Press, 1976).

consumer's plight. This is made all the more successful through cross-platform mass media presentations such as that of *Game of Thrones*, which enable consumers to 'become a part of the experience' no matter what their preferred mode of media consumption. The producers of *Game of Thrones* are all too aware of this relational tactic, however, and so, while guiding the viewer from the entry point of comparative neoliberal values, they downplay the power structure that gave way for the moralizing process used therein. It downplays this structure by way of pointing back to those rigid power roles in the series through which their habituation would have been historically achieved, and thus things are no longer simply named by those in power, but created and forced to exhibit themselves a certain way. Through this process, *Game of Thrones* downplays the fundamental relationship of scarcity and choice, benefiting from the moralizing process which it condemns in characters like Joffrey Baratheon, Roose and Ramsay Bolton, Tywin and Cersei Lannister, Walder Frey, and the like, while glorifying characters who have found themselves the victims of the times they live in: disempowered and against which a system has seemingly been set up. Hence there remains that modality of pure ideology through which we find the impossibility of the situation existing solely so that the fiction is intended to historically reify said ideological belief system. This is done to such a degree that the fictional world which the audience member is transported to is ripe for subtly shifting their real-world beliefs.

An example through which this real-world effect can be seen is in the drastic shift in the relationality between genders found in the phenomena of "infidelity overload" wherein the plotlines of the majority of narratives that pass through the screens in our homes in any given week present extramarital sex more often than not.[113] Through the disavowal seen previously in relation to the novel, it is perhaps because

---

113 Drexler, Peggy, "The New Face of Infidelity," *The Wall Street Journal* (October 19, 2012).

viewers understand these characters and their situations to be the work of creative fiction that they find themselves nevertheless brought into a belief structure wherein cheating is an inevitability, and from which they understand their situation within the world to be one wherein cheating is not only permissible, or sexual promiscuity merely a fact of life, but are also promoted *as such*. It is through a bombardment of the passions which one finds ideological structures influencing the hegemonic totality which subsumes all individuals who live within its supra-cultural reach, and against which obvious reactionary ideologies flow. This is the reversal of the Oedipal paternal authority figure, for we are now no longer commanded to conform to society and participate within its structures of meaning, but instead led by the obscene primal figure who commands us to enjoy. We are no longer forbidden to indulge in perverse or excessive pleasure, but commanded to do so.

This bombardment maintains a restriction from critical examination or understanding of these passions, and instead it is through manipulation of these passions that the justification of belief is ever-returning toward an ideological backdrop. This can be seen in the reversal of concern, through which we find our culture's understanding of romantic relationality. It was once seen through the lens of the hegemonic structure of the past that sexual relations were the end-all-be-all in the setting of a serious romantic partner, and that this was what was to be guarded semantically. However this emphasis seems to have shifted with hegemonic sexuality dictated as merely another product whose free exchange is justified by a stronger feeling of freedom, and labeled as such with the term liberation. In its stead, the previously enjoined notion of commitment which sexual consummation symbolized is now transformed into a free-floating signifier which seeks a restrictive force wherein individuals may find their relationality tested against representatives of their community. Culturally many find the counter-point of sex to be commitment of an emotional or spiritual order, wherein the individual might themselves invert the commandment, and instead sacrifice their *freedom to enjoy*.

However, since technological normalization occupies the developed nations where this shift has occurred, and despite being given access to a near-unlimited scope of information, individuals still buy in to what is readily presented and habituated such that even a majority of 'alternative' understandings 'against' said hegemonic structure are built *into* it, as an anticipatory setting. In many cases those who think they are understanding different 'alternative' ways of human life are merely buying into a facet of the preexisting structure that maintains its legacy and historicity while hiding its all-encompassing grasp of the individual. What's more is that this structure co-developed alongside the dramatic drop in the average age of the onset of puberty and the radical prolonging of marriage and reproduction such that a significant gap ripe for biopsychosocial exploitation can occur.

Media, in its use as an ideological tool, is Guy Debord's "spectacle" wherein one finds Marx's critique of the modern era failing to grasp the scope of its offerings of alienation and the diffusion of social organization; for we find that the critique has shifted from recognizing the transformation of 'being' to 'having' to what it has become in later modernity, shifting even further from 'having' to 'appearing,' wherein we discover that

> the spectacle consists in the reunification of separate aspects at the level of the *image*. Everything life lacks is to be found within the spectacle, conceived of as an ensemble of independent representations . . . for the spectacle monopolizes all communication to its own advantage and makes it one way only. The spectacle speaks, 'social atoms' listen. And the message is One: an incessant justification of the existing society, which is to say the spectacle itself, or the mode of production that has given rise to it. For this purpose the spectacle has no need of sophisticated arguments; all it needs is to be the only voice . . . its first prerequisite, therefore, and at the same time

its chief product, is the passivity of a contemplative attitude. Only an individual "isolated" amidst the "atomized masses" could feel any need for the spectacle, and consequently the spectacle must bend every effort to reinforce the individual's isolation.[114]

The spectacle is the form of ideological subversion of the novel made global. It follows along the interconnected revolution of technology such that, despite individual access to the tools which make up the image, there remains a barring of the diverse set of responses to the epoch it inaugurates, for participation therein continues to aid in the transformation from life to representation.

The monopoly is maintained in terms of its relation to the 'social atoms' of those who have been separated and alienated, only to be reassembled 'socially' by the common stream through which detached images converge. This is, then, only to reiterate the accommodating nature of ideological power whereby the totalizing effect of the spectacle is the very means whereby Otherness is represented, that is, destroyed. To understand the spectacle as mere propaganda then is to misunderstand

the entirety of social activity that is appropriated by the spectacle for its own ends. From city planning to political parties of every tendency, from art to science, from everyday life to human passions and desires, everywhere we find reality replaced by images. In the process, images end up by becoming real, and reality ends up transformed into images.[115]

Man is essentially transformed in his understanding of himself relating to others and to the world expressly through direct image-based ideo-

114 Jappe, Anselm, "The Concept of the Spectacle," in *Guy Debord* (Berkeley: University of California Press, 1999), 7.

115 Ibid., 7.

logical interpolation. As previously understood, when those who exist outside the direct regard of the hegemonic ideology beg for a way in, or in what is ultimately the same thing, beg to be understood in terms of that ideology's recognition as a subject rather than an object, we find 'admission' therein to give way to a flattening and totalizing representation. Yet this can only be achieved by the sacrifice of identity upon the altar of ideology, for where art still offers engagement in dialogical reason, whereby the individual is called to engage, the spectacle instead is independent from this relation, and stands in ideological domination over man. Thus

> the problem lies not, however, in the 'image' or 'representation' as such, as so many twentieth-century philosophies argue, but rather in the society that needs such images. It is true that the spectacle makes particular use of sight . . . but the problem resides in the *independence* achieved by representations that, having escaped from the control of human beings, proceed to address them in a monologue that eliminates all possible dialogue from human life. Such representations, though born of social practice, behave as independent beings.[116]

That is to say that these images dominate and subsume man, and he finds himself sympathizing more easily with concepts that go directly against his survival and/or happiness, seeing as there is again a fundamental misrecognition of these images as reality. This misrecognition leads man to attribute the real-life worries he has with the images themselves, and since he has been socialized into the realm of images, these representations are of the most significant order. This is not only significant for the ideological institution of the spectacle, which supplies it with more power and understanding as to the attainment of the passivity of social

116 Ibid., 8.

atoms or the buy-in of entire ideological groups that have yet to serve the rule of the hegemonic, but also for the individual, for now having understood image and spectacle as reality incarnate, we begin to see how desire and fantasy have been adopted as the most intimate form of control. To repeat, "the mechanical reproduction of representations of the human body both abstracts from the sensuous nature of human experience and provides a breeding ground for sadistic desires and fantasies. The alienating effect of modern forms of communication both produces pathological side effects and acts as a means of domination."[117] The ideological constructs through which the individual is intimately recast in the image of ideology have found on a global level the most effective and efficient achievements in the spectacle. The false community of the image has become for man the event-site of his actualization, which in reality is mere servitude. The command over one's own destiny has become the demand for the proper staging of fantasy within the spectacle of hegemony. The good, the just, and the true are, in this logic, modes of consumption whereby representational demands are demands of those within the pure and total grip of Stockholm syndrome.

This logic continues to unfold when we understand that these representations have their own form and autonomy which exist in some sort of collective individuated abstraction. Thus "in a society where individuals encounter one another solely through exchange, the transformation of the products of human labor and of the relations that preside over it into something apparently 'natural' further implies that the whole of social life seems to be independent of human volition and that it manifests itself as a seemingly autonomous and 'given' entity that is subject to no rules but its own."[118] It is from man's relation to this seemingly naturalized, autonomous, and semi-divine entity that individuals believe not only

---

117 Stevenson, Nick, "Marshall McLuhan and the Cultural Medium," in
     Understanding Media Cultures: Social Theory and Mass Communication, 2nd ed.
     (London: Sage, 2006), 122.

118 Jappe, *Guy Debord*, 16.

that the fulfillment of their desires and fantasies are to be found, but that truth will be spoken into their lives which can be verified against an external source. They believe truth and certainty to be finally found. It is within this spectacle that they understand themselves finding a way into the objective sphere of reality wherein they are not only verified but given an image that allows them to feel as though they have escaped alienation. This belief grants that those who feel underrepresented might somehow earnestly discuss and present themselves by submitting to the power of the spectacle such that those who are not at present accepting of them will thereby understand and surrender power to these individuals by way of their phantasmatic presence in the spectacle.

This showcases that "the spectacle is not a collection of images; rather, it is a social relationship between people that is mediated by images."[119] Ideology through the spectacle maintains a material form, through which it "'attends to' the whole man and appears to lavish on him, in the spheres of consumption and free time, all the attention that in reality is refused him both in the sphere of work and everywhere else . . . even dissatisfaction and rebellion are liable to become cogs in the machinery of the spectacle."[120] There is a direct functionality of the role of the spectacle such that what takes place on abstract ideological grounds is given concrete materialization through the spectacle itself. 'Dissatisfaction and rebellion' are directly of the order of reactionary ideologies which engage in the power struggle founded by the very essential formation of ideological structures of any sort and thus are presupposed necessarily within the hegemonic. This is not even to begin to understand that the *act* of consuming in the society of the spectacle is that which "confirms individuals in passive, isolated, privatized roles,"[121]

119 Debord, Guy, *The Society of the Spectacle,* trans. Donald Nicholson-Smith (New York: Zone Books, 1995), 12.

120 Ibid., 25.

121 Eagleton, Terry, "Ideological Strategies," in *Ideology: An Introduction* (London: Verso, 1991), 35.

hence reducing community proper to more specified niche cliques of consumers, who find the whole of their Being reified against similarly desiring consumers. The function of the spectacle as an ideological apparatus is to produce social control, where dominance and habitual self-replication are naturalized on behalf of the hegemonic ideology, which habitually produces more power to justify itself, and at the same time using consumption to create patterns of dissatisfaction and rebellion such that its control may be expanded to grasp the demographics who might stir in their seats.

A key stratagem, then, of ideological enterprise is that of historical control, which through the functionality of the spectacle becomes that much easier to grasp. This is an obvious extension of the Marxist critique of labor, wherein there is a temporal surplus value that is extracted for the masters of these societies to possess a private ownership of history. From this it is clear that those who labor under such a regime find their "time-as-commodity" expropriated by the hegemonic to produce a new diverse set of products that allow them their seats in power.[122] With this process's finding maximal exploitation in the spectacle, this control over time is expanded to the periphery of reason's gaze, for

> the spectacle must deny history, because history proves that laws are nothing, whereas process and struggle are all. The spectacle is the reign of an eternal present that claims to be history's last word. Under Stalinism, it took the form of a systematic manipulation and rewriting of the past. In countries where the diffuse spectacular system holds sway, by contrast, the mechanism is subtler. To begin with, it eliminates all opportunities for people to share experiences or projects without intermediaries or to recognize themselves in their own actions and in the effects of those actions. The complete

---

122 Jappe, *Guy Debord*, 34.

disappearance of historical intelligence creates socially atomized individuals with no choice but to contemplate the seemingly unalterable progression of blind forces. All those faculties that might allow such individuals to perceive the contrast between the falsification wrought by the spectacle and earlier forms are likewise eradicated.[123]

Under the reign and warfare of ideology in the society of the spectacle, very often access to historical truths is suppressed not by a direct severance to it through book burnings, bans, and other material events, but rather through ideological buy-ins which falsely relate destiny and truth to the ideological and away from historical accuracy. Information is obscured and becomes an echo of the subjective worldview, where the information supplied by any ideological camp is presumed to be true without question, for should they be confronted with opposing information, it is denied as the ideological conjecture which it itself maintains.

Secondarily, information is habituated through an obsessive retreat from reality into the escapism provided by series-programs. After the individual has found himself relating to the characters and their situations, the empathy and relationality that the real-life user experiences toward the fictional environment in which he is participating is augmented such that the environment shared with other real humans becomes mediated by the fantastic. A displacement occurs wherein the hopes, desires, ambitions, and loves which carry them through real-life conflicts are transposed onto the fictional world, which carries such a sense of care to the individual that their world may be consumed by it. This may occur to such a degree that their buy-in to an ideological system is informed not only through the extensive grounding of ideals in the program's ontological and epistemic source of comfort, but this cycle is habituated in its apparent variety, which finds its source

---

123 Ibid., 34-35.

identically through those who exist in power. This presents modes of ideological consumption which map onto capitalist structures of profit to continually structure a cycle of repetition through which consumers demand the ideological perspective that sinks them further into the characters, and which allows them to feel more in terms of empathetic and relational content. This is further problematized through the shift in intimacy wherein interpersonal relationships become dictated in large part by an ideological buy-in. These buy-ins are performed by those who, having become fully subsumed by that which they consume, allow this to dictate part of their personal identity and play a large part in their own narrativization. Through this particular aspect of an ideological buy-in, individuals place their relationality *behind* the ideological buy-in, that is, if those who engage with them should resist any element of the totality of ideological content placed first and foremost upon the heart of the individual, they will be cast out and judged by the network of ideologues which relationally reinforces this ideological position. This is the means by which the restrictions that individuals place upon themselves tighten even further. As such, their foundational understanding of their position in relation to their subscribed ideology is strengthened. This understanding of the way individuals posit their relationality might too be understood by way of justification of aspects pertaining to their individuation within the ideological framework that might have once been more concerning to the individual.

REPRESENTATION AND REPRODUCTION

As we have seen, and despite the claims of a majority of those who belong to minoritarian ideologies, representation via hegemonic-sanctified media works is simply another masking technique of the hegemonic ideology in order to operate on behalf of those represented. It could not be further from the truth that securing solid representations is amongst the most significant steps in the dialectic toward autonomy and selfhood of those identifying with said minoritarian ideologies. This is due to the fact that the (mis)recognition of fantasy objects (qua cultural figures) as (re)presentations of the self, or more specifically, the ego, are merely an extension of the mirror stage which we understand as a continuation of the rehabituating chronology of overlapping images which the individual carries with them throughout their entire life. The mass-produced images are as unreal as the ideal unity the child sees in the mirror, produced by the framing by which they are seen, and are just as impossible in their demand of desire. The demand of the hegemonic ideological state apparatuses to 'properly' create and display these images are, in effect, "man ident[ifying] himself with the specular image in order to make up for his original helplessness."[124] This "*organic insufficiency . . . is supplemented by an ideal imaginary unity*"[125] through which ideology extends its reach into man's identification and imposes a superficial solution to the fundamental sorrow of his alienation. This

---

124 Lacan, Jacques, *Ecrits: A Selection* (New York: W. W. Norton, 1977), 4.

125 Chiesa, Lorenzo, "The Subject of the Imaginary (Other)," in *Subjectivity and Otherness* (Cambridge, Mass.: MIT Press, 2007), 18.

is done in exchange for the individual's submission to hegemonic rule by way of this double recognition, which reinforces itself as master over man's own self-consciousness. We find that it is "forever impossible for the subject to achieve the perfect self-identity of the external alienated image with which he identifies."[126] The individual who seeks identity through this mode of representation bypasses their own self-narrative by way of reducing their identity to information no longer contingent upon actual existence, recalling the insulation of the Stoic when confronted with the conditions of his being. This ideological operation is about control, in this instance used as a tool of silencing. Psychologically speaking, the act of feigned understanding and listening on the behalf of hegemony (which the minoritarian group understands not so much as an ideological grouping themselves, but as 'the mainstream,' that is, 'the rest of the world') is such that it allows for full control of the group who grants them their image while also maintaining control of the stage of dialectic by means of the minoritarian group's appeal to power. This buy-in is the discrete contract whereby hegemony continues to ignore diversity of thought and ideas (even within the ideological community) for the sake of directing virtue and morality by projecting role-models that individuals should strive to achieve, encapsulated in the mantra 'if you can see it you can be it.'

When subsumed by the hegemonic, the minoritarian ideology has its tools of warfare co-opted to make it easier to sway others via social and psychological influence. Aside from being an obvious example of Nietzschean power exertion by way of naming and categorizing (a tool of those in power that Foucault himself recognized as "the dividing practices," wherein the individual is objectified through the process of dividing himself internally or externally from others[127]) it is also the way in which the ego internalizes this self-narrativization of the idealized fantasy images it receives from the hegemonic. In terms of consumption

---

126 Ibid.

127 Foucault, Michel, "The Subject and Power," in *Art after Modernism: Rethinking Representation* (New York: New Museum of Contemporary Art, 1984), 417.

and reproduction via media, we can understand that the state of ideology in our current society, having been adopted directly into our 'day-to-day reality,' is not the end of ideology as some had previously supposed it would be. Rather, with the advance of technology we have found the possibility to make society *more* ideological. The prevailing technological rationality which guides the culture industry finds "the material process of production . . . finally unveil[ing] itself as that which it always was . . . [i.e.,] ideology."[128] This is to state that the genesis and distribution of mass-produced culture by exclusive institutions (such as in America as of the year 2000, where over 90 percent of media was owned by just six companies[129]) is consumed largely by those who, after having years and years of differentiation put to rest as a result of subsumption by ideological warfare, have become homogenized, and are all the result of a monopoly held by the nation-state that "integrates its consumers from above."[130]

In feigning demand to participate in economic and social repro-duction, hegemony affords a group partial command thereof, which is announced with eagerness as 'good business' by cultural icons from its institutions. In this approach, the moral becomes opened up as potential within the iconographic status of items. This is strange in that the content possesses a dual meaning: on the one hand, it is filled out with the content demanded by the individual, which mirrors his superficial appearance so as to create the potentiality of mirror-stage identification, such that the appearance becomes the means by which a product's purchase is encouraged. However, in connection with the item's purchase is a discrete shift in narrative power, whereby the acknowledgment of the relation of identity and consumption leads to the synergistic co-option of one's

128 Adorno, Theodor W., *Prisms* (London: N. Spearman, 1967), 100.

129 Wright, Erik Olin, and Joel Rogers, "Corporate Control of the Media," in
    American Society: How It Really Works (New York: W. W. Norton, 2011), 3.

130 Adorno, Theodor W., and J. Bernstein, "Culture Industry Reconsidered,"
    in *The Culture Industry: Selected Essays on Mass Culture* (London: Routledge, 2001), 98.

self-narrative. Instead of branded worlds being simply the relegation of a corporation to a ready-made identity, those who invest their self-narratives with this consumptive relation to representation find their identity relegated to the authority of the state hegemonic media. This is the means by which ideology turns the ego of the individual into a brand. No matter how you divide your ego and its relations, the state media is ready and willing to adopt (rather than adapt).

Further, the cultural elites who benefit from the production of hegemony work to reframe this identity buy-out as a moral issue. In this way man is kept in line by the identities through which he can be marketed to. The ever-specific formation of new identities is not the rebellion against late modernity's status quo, but a looping acceleration thereof. This is important due to the fact that

> the productive apparatus and the goods and services which it produces 'sell' or impose the social system as a whole. The means of mass transportation and communication, the commodities of lodging, food and clothing, the irresistible output of the entertainment and information industry carry with them prescribed attitudes and habits, certain intellectual and emotional reactions which bind the consumers more or less pleasantly to the producers and, through the latter, to the whole. The products indoctrinate and manipulate; they promote a false consciousness which is immune against its falsehood . . . Thus emerges a pattern of *one-dimensional thought and behavior* in which ideas, aspirations, and objectives . . . are redefined by the rationality of the given system and of its quantitative extension.[131]

---

131 Marcuse, Herbert, "The New Forms of Control," in *One-Dimensional Man: Studies in the Ideology of Advanced Industrial Society* (Boston: Beacon, 1964), 11-12.

A surrendering of a minoritarian ideology to hegemony presents an opportunity then to rectify demands with its obvious paradoxical conclusion: either there is a continued state of constant reinterpretation of their identity by those who are not included within it (i.e., people who do not self-narrate in a similar fashion) or the issue is resolved by way of mass exposure. This either elevates the information to the realm of the public or sells previously-minoritarian ideologies, which would result in the 'turning' of more and more individuals to the viewpoint of those who were demanding in the first place, hence homogenizing and saturating the market and creating more products which reflect their demanded existence.

This is why, where Samuel Huntington claims that "the fundamental source of conflict in this new world will not be primarily ideological or primarily economic" and that "the great divisions among humankind and the dominating source of conflict will be cultural,"[132] he seems to make the mistake of thinking that a hard line exists between ideology and the culture from which individuals originate. Many who argue from this perspective suggest that intolerance comes from a cultural realm, where particulars face the paradoxical threat of the individual, who somehow iconographically embodies the universal. With culture being a constraint that is socially transmitted through discrete influences, culture becomes often a direct extension of ideology, elements of which contrast with each other and form social factions, much as ideology does.

However, this idea of 'accurate representation' is ultimately a hopeful rebellion against the Lacanian notion that "Desire is the desire of the *other*."[133] The ego of those who gaze with desire toward the *iconic*, whose

---

132 Huntington, Samuel P., "The Clash of Civilizations?," in *The Clash of Civilizations and the Remaking of World Order* (New York: Simon & Schuster, 1996), 22.

133 Lacan, Jacques, "Of the Subject Who Is Supposed to Know," ed. Jacques-Alain Miller, trans. Alan Sheridan, in *Seminar XI: The Four Fundamental Concepts of Psycho-Analysis* (New York: W. W. Norton, 1981), 235.

status has been dictated to them, have found the other desirable only insofar as they have recognized the desirability of the position they occupy: and as such, the 'rightful' place of the individual's ego has been fundamentally displaced. However, through self-narrativization many have considered the possibility that to eliminate the imaginary icon that stands in the way of achieving and fulfilling their own autonomous desire is to represent themselves through those imaginary icons in what is deemed to be an accurate enough narrative presentation. They suppose that "I do not want to destroy the other because he *has* the object of my desire; on the contrary, I want to destroy him because he is the object of my primordial desire: the other *qua* specular image literally stands in my place, there where I desire to be a unity, and supersede alienation."[134] However, the information is adapted incorrectly, such that the individual believes somehow through a representation of their choosing, i.e., one that aligns with their self-narrative, the specular image will find its resolution, and that this will somehow lead to the individual's desire achieving autonomy and fulfillment. This seems to be simply drawing the imaginary ideal unity closer to the individual, and as ideology does on a grander scale, blurring the distinction between the two.

Nevertheless, from this movement the individual is much less likely to find a way out of that which he initially understood as alienating. It is as though just as soon as the individual discovers the source of his discomfort he is told, via the exact medium which alienated him to begin with, that the issue lies in wait through a resolution via the same specular image, and as such they are redirected back inward. Despite the fact that "no object that causes primordial desire can be refound . . . the object is hallucinated on the basis of a primary anguishing reality; the loss of traits that amalgamate them into a Thing of *jouissance*."[135]

134 Chiesa, Lorenzo, "The Subject of the Imaginary (Other)," in *Subjectivity and Otherness* (Cambridge, Mass.: MIT Press, 2007), 25.

135 Ragland-Sullivan, Ellie, "The a as Signifier of the Void," in *Jacques Lacan and the Logic of Structure: Topology and Language in Psychoanalysis* (London:

The cycle completes itself, again with the promise of unfulfillable pleasure by way of neurotic illusion masking the paradox of the entire problem: "having recognized the other as other, I do not desire to *be* the other—with whom I identify—but I desire what the other desires, or, I contradictorily desire to be exactly like the other *without* wanting to be (the) other."[136] Part of the issue with this element of representation is that it demands, at some level, that the individual's own narrative-identity is the implicit notion of self that is grasped by this representation. While one might come close enough in presenting what a majority of people within a group might claim is at least historically their ideological image/ heritage, the distinction between the presentation of the individual *as such* and the individual as an ideological representation becomes difficult to distinguish thanks to the depth and breadth in which ideology installs itself in the individual.

Žižek points out a level of difficulty in distinguishing the two by stating that "innermost beliefs are all 'out there,' embodied in the practices which reach up to the immediate materiality of my body."[137] This further exemplifies the blurred extension of culture and ideology, whereby we understand that the systematization of ideas and ideals physically manifest themselves through nearly any means possible. It is through the complex demands and needs of the alienated man whereby ideology and culture meet to sublimate desire into their own productive forces. In a single movement the coding *by which* we desire, and *ought* to desire, is refracted throughout the cosmos of the social and the epistemological. Social reinforcement of this moralized desire is then founded within the level of self-policing, wherein loneliness and alienation are alleviated on the behalf of the individual investing in the *moral* or otherwise *ideological*

Routledge, 2015), 84.

136 Chiesa, Lorenzo, "The Subject of the Imaginary (Other)," in *Subjectivity and Otherness* (Cambridge, Mass.: MIT Press, 2007), 25.

137 Žizek, "Tolerance as an Ideological Category," 166.

elements advertised through their embodiment in the representations of the community's practices. Hence, desire becomes not only that which is subsumed and installed in the community of ideologues, but it also becomes a tool by which those outside the ideological circle become initiated.

In this way, for ideological power to function, the subject is taught to desire through abstract representation. Yet this learning is set at the competency of the subject therein; the truth of the desire is kept from articulation such that the endless suspension of its fulfillment will support the economic and cultural dimensions by which ideology can thrive. This is the means by which hegemony as sold to the individual becomes personalized. Not only because the individual feels as though they are the master of their destiny, freely participating in individualist materialism, but also in the exploitation of dopamine, which results in its higher forms as an anticipation of pleasure rather than its direct attainment. Joyful memories then become memories of consumption, which when related to the media of mass culture this exploitation becomes all the more personal and as such pleasurable in relating them to a representation which grants them fuller self-access. This demand is one whereby the subject announces: "I myself am included into the picture constituted by me."[138] Yet, once more, this identity is a means of relating towards one's commodified ego as it mediates the products and mode of Being that is advertised to him, so as to continually reproduce the power that grants the conditions of possibility for the sale of such identities.

---

138 Žizek, *The Parallax View*, 17.

THE QUESTION OF EXPERTISE

If the understanding of a non-ideological stance is to be one that maintains a delineation toward epistemic information, then it seems as though there must be some degree of a commitment to attacking expertise on all fronts, yet benefiting from the "skills" procured therein. Such is the paradoxical position that ideology has left mankind in. It is beneficial to take an extended look toward the past, as historical reactions toward the dogmatism that ideology has inspired find skepticism of one sort or another at their heart. In Hegel's lectures on the history of philosophy, he highlights at the end of the first period of Greek philosophy the air being choked by "a dogmatism that divides into two philosophies, Stoicism and Epicureanism, and the third philosophy, in which they both participate but which is nonetheless their 'other,' or contrary, Skepticism."[139] However, in so noting that for contemporary thought, as was the case for Hegel, skepticism is the modality of dialectic and thus contrary to the popular image of the skeptic as a pure nihilist, the position he occupies is cognitively productive. This means that the criterion which falls apart does not leave the dialectician in a starting position all over again, for the sublation of the notion contains within it the shortcomings of that which it sublated. This is "the seriousness, the suffering, the patience, and the labour of the negative."[140] The production of the negative is not ontologically barren. This must be kept in mind when looking towards the Pyrrhonian skeptics in their attempt to achieve the robust equanimity of *ataraxia*.

---

139 Hegel, "Dogmatic and Skeptical Philosophy," in *Lectures on the History of Philosophy 1825-26*, trans. Robert F. Brown (Oxford: Clarendon Press, 2006), 263.

140 Hegel, *Phenomenology of Spirit* (trans. Findlay), 10.

Central to this question is how the notion of a belief can be navigated without breaking the law of noncontradiction, as well as how expertise and its products may be divorced. For Sextus Empiricus, perhaps the most well-known Pyrrhonian, there seems to be a level of erudition admitted within his own texts. In fact, the first handful of paragraphs in *Against the Professors* find Sextus taking pride in his sectarians for just that: "the School of Pyrrho . . . [was] not moved either by the view that these subjects are of no help to gaining wisdom (for that is a 'dogmatic' assertion) or by any lack of culture attaching to themselves; for in addition to their culture and their superiority to all other philosophers in breadth of experience they are also indifferent to the opinion of the multitude."[141] It seems as though the extent to which one can be 'learned' by way of Sextus's account is related to amassing a varied and rich amount of experience. Yet they claim that this approach gives them this 'learning' without them gaining wisdom, or generating an epistemological claim. That is to say that if there is a degree to which this Pyrrhonian stance might maintain a degree of expertise, it is one that exists *without knowledge.*

The expertise of the Pyrrhonian must be such that it cannot exist by way of the transference of true beliefs from one who is learned to one who is not; rather, it is understood as that which is learned on the basis of a technical form, like those who learn one artform or another. This is due to the fact that one cannot verify the nontechnical truth-factors by which the epistemic structure of beliefs claim to be supported. This impasse results in the Pyrrhonian suspending judgment on the issue. However, due to the technical quality which informs the expertise of certain artforms, they may be understood as in line with a distinction Sextus drew between beliefs. This distinction sought to speak to beliefs which merely separate that which is beneficial from that which is harmful

---

141 Sextus Empiricus, *Against the Professors*, trans. Robert Gregg Bury (Cambridge, Mass.: Harvard University Press, 1961), 1:5

within the nominal everyday life that the Pyrrhonian is said to lead. Sextus explicates this by stating

> that the standard of Skeptical persuasion is what is apparent, implicitly meaning by this the appearances; for they depend on passive and unwilled feelings and are not objects of investigation. (Hence no-one, presumably, will raise a controversy over whether an existing thing appears this way or that; rather, they investigate whether it is such as it appears.) Thus, attending to what is apparent, we live in accordance with everyday observations, without holding opinions—for we are not able to be utterly inactive. These everyday observations seem to be fourfold, and to consist in guidance by nature, necessitation by feelings, handing down of laws and customs, and teachings of kinds of expertise. By nature's guidance we are naturally capable of perceiving and thinking. By the necessitation of feelings, hunger conducts us to food and thirst to drink. By the handing down of customs and laws, we accept from an everyday point of view, that piety is good and impiety bad. By teachings of kinds of expertise we are not inactive to those which we accept.[142]

This leads us to see that it is by way of appearances and passive, unwilled feelings that there is an understanding of that which is worthwhile and advantageous to our everyday experience of the world. These understandings would not be truth statements that are made, nor opinions held on the matter of that which is produced by way of technical expertise, but rather observations that refer exclusively to the appearance through which the objects establish themselves. It seems as though the fourfold observations

---

142 Sextus Empiricus, *Outlines of Scepticism*, trans. Julia Annas and Jonathan Barnes (Cambridge: Cambridge University Press, 1994), 1:22-24.

allow a great deal of room for qualitative judgments such that the percep-tion and thought immediately available might provide comfort in place of distress. For example, one might set apart a pair of shoes that allow a person to walk across rough terrain with comfort, rather than shoes that have the bottoms falling out, which would provide perhaps nothing but discomfort to the individual on his journey. It is care with regard to efficacy which is sought, for effect maintains no relation to the true, but merely to man's perception in dealing with the world. Judgments that affect his perception need not violate the Pyrrhonian's ability to refrain from holding opinions.

As such there cannot be found a conclusion as to the standards assessing everyday life, for there is no assessment in the ascension to appearances. This is by way of objects appearing to affect end goals in a desired way, much as the consumption of food produced the desired effect of satisfying hunger, about which there is also no qualitative assessment. This seems to be in line with the teleology of Pyrrhonian life, which aims at the tranquility achieved by the suspension of beliefs (*kata doxan*) and moderate affection (*metriopatheia*) placed upon the matters bestowed upon us by of passive and unwilled feelings such as the matter of the comforting shoes for the journey.[143] This makes way for the "breadth of experience" with which the Pyrrhonian assumes a 'superior' position to that of the other philosophers. In Pyrrhonian life, one may "attend to what is apparent" and "live in accordance with everyday observation" to a greater degree than those who spend their time dwelling upon qualitative assessments in a vain attempt to understand truth. Since the Pyrrhonian merely suspends judgment on these matters, it seems as though the amount of time he spends living his 'ordinary life' almost immediately affords such 'breadth' of experience. The individual is capable of reporting that which appears to them at the very moment without adopting the position of assessment,[144] in such a way that their

143 Ibid., 1:25-29.
144 Ibid., 1:4.

relation to appearances can be passed on as technical observation as if from one watching a master at work. In this way the 'student' can understand that the suspension of judgment does afford the Pyrrhonian the time required to observe that which is apparent.

When we understand the extent of the consensus that occurs during the production of certain products via artforms or technical expertise, we may understand the beneficial aspects of those products as evident. For example, navigability makes international mercantilism achievable,[145] astronomy makes us able to predict poor weather,[146] as well as Sextus's own medical expertise, which makes the sick well again.[147] This shows that the benefits of technical expertise of the artforms in question in no way maintain any relationship to a truth-value, but instead function via "the guidance of nature and necessitation by feeling."[148] Their beneficial contributions are not under dispute, and are understood to be evidently helpful insofar as there is an undisputed utility (by way of the artform). This moderate affection (*metriopatheia*) placed upon these objects indicates that the consensus itself seems apparent. However, more often than not, artforms fall outside of the apparent utility of the technical arts which produce items immediately recognizable as beneficial in our ordinary lives.

For example, we see the Pythagorean mathematicians suggest that all of life's fundamental building blocks come from the mathematics they prescribe.[149] In opposition, however, Sextus is able to find major discord as to the immediate utility and beneficial aspects of this practice. Obviously that is not to say that the Pyrrhonians either affirm or deny such things as Pythagorean mathematics, but simply present a counterpoint

---

145 Sextus Empiricus, *Against the Professors*, 1:51.
146 Ibid., 5:20.
147 Ibid., 2:49.
148 Sextus Empiricus, *Outlines of Scepticism*, 2:63.
149 Sextus Empiricus, *Against the Professors*, 4:39.

against the dogmatic theories that are put forth by the Pythagoreans. Here we find a crossroad, for it seems from this point of view that the Pyrrhonians themselves maintain some kind of appreciation for an expertise of living, through which the breadth of experience is garnered; however, simultaneously maintaining doubt about any kind of expertise that lies outside of that which is immediately recognizable as beneficial. This is not as prickly as it may seem however, as Sextus attacks the Stoics for this very notion:

> There also could not be a craft of living. For if there is such a craft, then it is a craft of contemplating things good and bad and indifferent; and since these are non-existent, the craft of living is non-existent. Moreover, since the dogmatists do not all agree in locating the craft of living in one thing, but some hypothesize one craft, some another, they stand accused of disagreeing, and are held to account by the argument from disagreement . . . But even if, for the sake of hypothesis, they were to say that the craft of living is one craft, for example, the notorious craft of 'prudence,' which is fantasized about by the Stoics, and seems more impressive than the rest, still no less absurd consequences follow. For since prudence is a virtue, and only the wise man has virtue, the Stoics, not being wise men, will not possess the craft of living.[150]

It is important to note here that there are no negative epistemological claims made here by Sextus, but merely a counterpoint to that which has been asserted by the Stoics. This attack seems to be in line with the over-arching teleology of the path which Sextus himself walked,[151] wherein he undertook the life of philosophy in order to find truth, but in fact found

---

150 Sextus Empiricus, *Outlines of Scepticism*, 3:239-40.
151 Ibid., 3:280-81.

equipollent arguments and disputes as to that which is true, thus resulting in the suspension of judgment.[152] The Stoic means by which expertise is understood with regards to living is just as confused on the approach to living and the language that it uses as is any other nontechnical artform.

It may seem that to the Pyrrhonians, all subject matter with which expertise concerns itself is without merit. However, as Sextus approaches the artform of grammar, he greets his audience with a surprise, and one which seems to suggest that these other nontechnical artforms might still be practiced to some worthwhile degree. He maintains that, so long as the practitioner himself refrains from appealing to dogmatic beliefs or belief-structures, there may be a way of practicing with no beliefs about the objects or rule-systems of said artform.[153] This could be done via recollective rather than indicative signs.[154] This suggestion is manifest through Sextus's approach to grammar:

> Since grammar is twofold, one form professing to teach the elements and their combinations and generally, being a certain skill of writing and reading, the other being a more profound ability than this, not based in bare knowledge of letters, but also in the examination of their discovery and nature, and, in addition, the parts of speech which are organized from them, and anything else if it is perceived to have the same form, it is our intention now, not to speak against the former— for it is harmoniously agreed to be useful by everyone, among whom one must even include Epicurus, even though he seems to hate the professors of the disciplines. In the treatise *On Gifts and Gratitude*, he tried sufficiently to teach that it is necessary for wise people to learn their letters. Even we ourselves, in another

---

152 Sextus Empiricus, *Against the Professors*, 1:6.

153 Ibid., 8:156-58.

154 Sextus Empiricus, *Outlines of Scepticism*, 2:102.

THE QUESTION OF EXPERTISE

way, should say that, not only the wise, but all people should learn their letters. For, clearly, the end [*telos*] of every form of expertise is useful in life. Some forms of expertise aim at the avoidance of things that are troublesome, and others at the discovery of beneficial things. And, medicine is of the first type, since it is a skill for healing and relieving patients of pain. Navigation is of the second type, for all people are especially in need of goods [*chreias*] from other nations. Therefore, since grammatistic through its understanding of letters heals a most lazy passion—forgetfulness—and conjoins with a most necessary actuality —memory—everything is based on it more or less, and it is not possible to teach others any necessary thing without it, nor will it be possible to learn from someone else anything profitable. So grammatistic, in this sense, is one of the most useful forms of expertise.[155]

Grammar is here that which is seemingly essential to life itself, and its beneficial aspects appeal to all, not only the wise. Sextus does not find disdain toward the professors, which it seems Epicurus did, but instead confirms that instruction and reception are necessary skills for Pyrrhonians to operate in and navigate the world surrounding them; it is fundamental even in establishing memory.

Since grammatistics are the foundation of all that is, and the means by which all expertise is established, they comprise the most significant order that one may become familiarized with. Grammar is not exclusively celebrated as "one of the most useful forms of expertise" due to its immediate use for navigability, but also as that which gives way to avoidance of those things which are meddlesome or irritating, which is also listed as a goal of the Pyrrhonian approach to life.[156] Not only

---

155 Sextus Empiricus, *Against the Professors*, 1:49-52.
156 Sextus Empiricus, *Outlines of Scepticism*, 1:25.

does language provide navigability and the opportunity to learn, but it also allows for the possibility of the avoidance of that which is bad. The study of grammar provides technical and navigation skills allowing for interaction and thought, as well as the groundwork for living the average everyday life that the Pyrrhonian wishes to pursue. Sextus does not, however, state that grammatistic pursuit is a stepping stone to wisdom (as in Epicurus), but rather that it is a necessary supplier of all possibility, including, but not limited to, Sextus's own Pyrrhonian pursuit and his own medical practice. He also further defends this area of expertise by suggesting that to attack it as such would be to contradict one's self the moment the argument was formulated, for how else could the argument be framed except by way of grammatistic pursuit?[157] The study of grammar needs no appeal to theoretical foundations then, and is simply the foundation of possibility as such. As said before, this would be recollective rather than indicative, functioning by way of the senses and other technical tools.[158] One finds here that expertise is taught by way of imitation such that one does not maintain an epistemic approach to that which one is "learning" but rather that one maintains a "disposition" which is aimed at that into which they are inducted.[159]

Hence it is not the knowledge that one retains in order to maintain one's status as an expert, but rather their acts, which are observable. In this manner, one may note two actions taking place side-by-side and observe that one seems to be the action of an expert by way of its expediency and effectiveness. This too is how the expert's acts are brought about, for it is this phenomenological perception that allows him to mediate the experience more effectively, but not, as stated before, by some appeal to epistemology.[160] The Pyrrhonian understanding as such is merely the

---

157 Sextus Empiricus, *Against the Professors*, 1:53.

158 Sextus Empiricus, *Outlines of Scepticism*, 2:14-15.

159 Sextus Empiricus, *Against the Professors*, 1:188.

160 Sextus Empiricus, *Outlines of Scepticism*, 1:236.

suspension of judgment, and the immediacy of action mediated by that which is phenomenologically present.

However, we find limitations to any such study for Sextus. For example, the study of grammar finds that Sextus suggests that reading and writing are the stopping points of grammatical literacy such that once attained we need not go any further.[161] This is because it maintains a contribution to the Pyrrhonian goal of *ataraxia* and provides the technical tools needed to mediate the experience of life without ever having to delve into metaphysical speculation or abstract theoretical epistemologies. The Pyrrhonian need not explain what precisely the mediation and technical prowess are that grammar offers or is aimed at, but merely that these operate on such a necessary functional level, like that of eating, that one need not pursue it either dogmatically or epistemologically. It appears as though there are two modes of expertise: that which is fundamentally dogmatic, and as such has no appeal to the Pyrrhonian, and that which procures a skill or a "disposition" which lends itself to phenomenological mediation. This disposition then would maintain a degree to which it is beneficial (whose application does not lend itself to judgment, and as such refrains from becoming dogmatic).[162] It is important to note here that Sextus himself may still attack the grammaticians by way of their epistemic beliefs about their art, for in so doing they have deceived themselves by way of an ever-deeper buy-in of their own constructed understanding of grammar.[163]

We are here led to believe that the Pyrrhonian areas of expertise, so long as they maintain no epistemological structure, aim at that which is beneficial rather than that which is true. Hence, the Pyrrhonian approach may produce a disposition which is understood as a way to mediate the applicative phenomena to which it is aimed, and as such maintain no ultimate end goal, but rather a positive approach to the suspension of

---

161 Sextus Empiricus, *Against the Professors*, 1:53-54.

162 Ibid., 1:5.

163 Ibid., 1:41-56.

judgment. We understand the expertise which is acknowledged by the Pyrrhonian to be that which offers a navigation and an avoidance of the adverse, while giving accessibility to that which the individual seeks out.

It seems then that the beliefs which a skeptic maintains are those through which one navigates the world, and not those with which one knows something about it. These beliefs are actualized through the non-epistemic sense of belief, wherein one might operate in a way with objects, language, or others to make navigation possible, while maintaining no truth-values beyond that of a relational tool. They may function much like one uses a word from hearing it used in other conversations; one might have no knowledge as to what the word directly means, nor of its origin, nor of its connotations, nor anything about the word save that it functions at an operational level to move from point A to point B. It is here then that we find Sextus's argument for a radical degree to which the skeptic maintains beliefs which possess no theoretical or scientific value, nor conformity with logic. He asserts that this is even the case when forced into a situation wherein there seems to be no alternative. He brings up the idea of a skeptic charged by a tyrant to commit unspeakable deeds or face execution. He maintains this assertion even in the most extreme of cases such as this, for he states that a skeptic will not at any point maintain a belief which carries epistemic or theoretical weight. Instead, the Pyrrhonist will merely find solace from choice by simply going along with the beliefs taught to him by his parents, or other child-rearing figures, which fall squarely under the umbrella of chance. Though there is discrimination regarding what choice is made, there is no belief as to the suffering that awaits physically on one end, and perhaps mentally on the other. In its stead, however, there is merely a retreat to conditioning of thought. It is also important to note that in Sextus's account of the skeptic's custom, it does not dictate the skeptic's struggle to determine what he *ought* to do; instead there is immediacy in choice. This holds that there is no necessity of theoretical or logical belief to which the skeptic must subscribe, and instead there is an immediacy of action and navigation through which the skeptic finds himself managing the world around him.

Many here will miss a major element of this approach as they ignore the case of the devil's advocate, wherein one can operate within a field of information without holding to it or maintaining some truth-value in the information being sifted through. That is, a skeptic might maintain some criterion of truth without holding to it. This mistakes a suspension of judgment with an inability or complete refusal to judge. This is not a metaphysically abstract point: a great majority of people deal with the world by this negative relationship with the activities they are engaged in on a daily basis. It seems then that one type of belief, that which the dogmatists hold, is a belief with a positive epistemological value, which makes claims and takes a position on matters beyond 'ordinary' beliefs. The other belief surrounding Sextus is this secondary relationship through which we find the individual able to possess a way of using the experience around him despite not being wed to any of the information that he uses. It is in this way that he can maintain 'beliefs' about brushing his teeth and the prosperity therein without having to accept or 'believe' in the information to which he assents in order to navigate the world.

The word 'belief' is contested here, wherein a vast amount of meaning or value is seen to be held. If this point is ceded, it can only be done so by acknowledging that, if this 'belief' is to count on any definition, it must be one that strips the definition of relating knowledge down to the one who holds it. It seems that a much better way of going about this is through the humble word 'faith' which, despite its many con-notations, would accurately describe the use of information within the world without necessarily having a direct attachment to an epistemology of any kind. This can be seen in the way that a layman has faith that gravity will produce the same results on him when he acts in a way toward it, yet needs no positive epistemological understanding of it. This sort of faith is inherently a philosophical one, however, for it is the result of a philosophical struggle, rather than a biological disposition.

Sextus seems to suggest that we are to arrive at this banausic life in a completely circuitous way. This is achieved through first engaging in the laborious struggle of attempting to live a life that will answer some of the questions which plague man. Only after this can he find himself developing an extremely specialized method through which he will eventually lead this banausic life. It is still somehow these impressions of information or teachings through which the skeptics life is molded, and while he may lead a banausic life, he remains uncommitted to anything, and thus maintains no 'beliefs.' While engaging in philosophical debate, Sextus and the Pyrrhonian skeptics like him may indeed live a life of the layman and philosopher while not once maintaining a 'belief' outside of this secondary form. In this way, and without intending to, perhaps the skeptic journey speaks to us about the relationship of faith, belief, and the dialogue with others that seems to bring them about. In this way we may come to an understanding about appropriate belief which aligns the earnest quest for knowledge found in Socrates and Aristotle with the recognition and rejection of the unthinking nature of the ideologue. The deep agreement found here will be further explicated later on through Plato and Aristotle's approach to philosophy as elucidated by Hans-Georg Gadamer. For now it is enough to take notice of the tension at the heart of foundations of belief, and its formal manifestation in our day-to-day activity by which the negative work of dialectic negates its own negation, and thus sublates its substantial categories into the life of dialogical relationality.

LANGUAGE AND THE EXISTENCE OF OBJECTS

In 1981, the French philosopher Jean Baudrillard published a treatise on signs, symbols, and reality: *Simulacra and Simulation*. In this work, he speaks of the disorder of postmodernity, wherein the signs and symbols constructing the shared reality of a given society precede and eventually do away with the original objects and people which they seek to represent. This form of society causes the distinction that previously divided reality and its signifiers to vanish, and heightens the absurdity of the individual's relation to his concrete reality, his own works, and even the self, to the point where there is little hope for meaning in any shape or form. Baudrillard instructs us that, following the work of Jorge Luis Borges, this given society uses its signs and symbols in such a way that the 'maps' replace the very reality they sought to help us navigate. In this 'reality,' labor is reoriented toward establishing and securing a place within the representation itself, and as people devote themselves to this representation, reality itself is displaced one step further. This state is one from which language is often confused for reality; we presume that we understand the world as existing in relation to these signifiers, but it seems that there exists an equipollent argument that these concepts, their form and structure, do not exist in actuality. That goes to say that language is structurally significant primarily as a tool of communication and navigation. This, the question of macroscopic nihilism, is structured around the nature of a negative or negating epistemology. This argument does not suggest that those who claim the existence of objects, such as that of a statue "[have] hallucinated, been the victim of a prank, or mistaken something for a statue that, upon further inspection he would agree was not really a statue at all."[164] This suggestion would be reserved for those who make extravagantly hysterical claims such that they have been confused or otherwise convinced of an appearance that metaphysically deviates from our everyday experience. Instead the claim for macrophysical nihilism suggests that indeed, "one's 'seemingly seeing a statue' is caused—in a non-hallucinatory, non-prankish way—by things *arranged statuewise.*"[165] Such matter exists on some unperceivable level, and structures itself into an exceedingly panoptic 'complex object' where the unperceivable matter occupies space-time but the occupation and arrangement of it in actuality does not constitute the *existence* of the 'object' itself. This position leaves intact navigability and usage while remaining skeptical about the positive epistemology or dogmatic structure of 'belief systems' involved therein, so as to leave untouched the openness of man's ability to know and his relationship in the world, as well as the potential for meaning produced therein. Much in the same way that the paradigm of quantum physics has shaped man's understanding of the world without changing his day-to-day navigability, so too do we find that in the macrophysical nihilistic view, "for practical purposes, the bulk of everyday uses of 'statue'—as well as, for example, '*Michelangelo's David*' and '*The Statue of Liberty*'—can remain unchanged, even if the claims such uses express are false because eliminativism is true."[166]

There are many cases through which this theory is understood to be working in daily activity and in relation to objects; the understanding of the way language socializes man to make the world navigable is easier to grasp and as such it retroactively explicates the theory on a much more fundamental level. For example, those who wish to deny macrophysical

---

164 Merricks, Trenton, "Explaining Eliminativism," in *Objects and Persons* (Oxford: Clarendon, 2001), 2.

165 Ibid.

166 Ibid., 7.

nihilism, upon speaking of water in a swimming pool, must within their language contain the belief "in a kind of entity called 'a mass'—[such that to] say that 'the water in the swimming pool' refers to a big material object."[167] This example makes it clear that when we refer to the water in the pool, we are referring to the conceptual totality through which no 'object' is *actualized* and instead is merely an easy way with which we refer to a collected group of nonvisible *things*. This is a conceptual necessity, for through their interaction the relational whole performs a phenomenological experience that can be repeated enough times to warrant terminology which identifies a group of related experiences (that is related through linguistic explanations which maintain peak navigability).

Another concerning item which casts considerable doubt against those who maintain the objectivist notion of conceptual objects is that of perfumery. This is especially problematic when considering batches, bottling errors, as well as clones of original scents. In this case, what constitutes the object itself? If one appeals to a formula through which a noted amount of combined smells constitutes the aroma of a perfume, and from which we consider the perfume to be actualized, what then are we to do if the aroma is found naturally, or if a competing company reproduces this same aroma with differing levels of constituent parts? What then are we to do if the original producer of this aroma reformulates his original work and presents it again under the same name? Or if a batch is changed from its initial production to its very last? Are we then to consider perfumery a collection of objects, wherein each bottle represents its own individual object? But how then are we to come to terms with the impossibility of differentiation between the smells themselves? Or with the smell itself aged as in a vintage as opposed to a new bottle? Certainly with the conditions of each location where an individual bottle is stored there are variations in light, temperature, pressure, and the like. All of this can no doubt be accounted for by modifying terms indefinitely, but

---

167 Merricks, *Objects and Persons* (Oxford: Clarendon, 2001), 2.

the identity is retained by conceptual relationality. This is not to affirm or deny a metaphysical claim about the really existing structure of the items retained by any particular conceptual totality, but rather that the nature of perceptual belief in either use of the term always-already includes the application of concepts. Naturalizing concepts thus grants counterintuitive thoughts and an overcomplication of our relationality in general.

That is to say, even should one hold greater metaphysical beliefs about reality, should one reify one's beliefs by drawing them within discourse, we find the conceptual tools remaining, and simply modified *ad infinitum*, not for the sake of clarity (for this only occurs upon breakdown of communication,) but as if somehow achieving something within language that is *more real* than the 'merely' conceptual. The idealist and realist perspectives that dominate perception both absolutize a reduction of reality to the material or the rational at the expense of the other. Hence despite the truth which may arise from their particular horizon, they cut the legs out from under them and forget their origin. The exclusivity with which each perspective chastises the other is reflected in the limit of the content with which their own particular view is restricted. Both do away with the truth of ambiguity in order to satisfy their need for certainty, yet in the end they achieve only a partial helping of either. Through notions like Merleau-Ponty's "incarnate consciousness" we can begin to see the ways in which the fundamental ambiguity of lived experience spills out past and beyond the closed conceptual systems that affirm themselves as the totality of the true. Incarnate consciousness is the ambiguous position that, throughout its development in *Phenomenology of Perception*, appears at one moment to be purely material and at the next subjective and idealist. The reason for this is to reveal to the reader the fundamental contradictions which either position must confront due to their reduction of the complexity and depth of human being.

However, at the same time, this is not to suggest that there is such a thing as a pure relation to objective truth, such that one may achieve the fullness of truth beyond the possibility of perspective as such, for the condition of the appearance of truth is this very perspective. It is via the condition of being open that human reality is able to go outside and beyond itself: it is the condition of openness to experience as such, to perception, which mediates the freedom and determinism absolutized by one or the other notion of man's freedom that dominated the topic. Again, openness to lived experience reveals the situatedness of transcendence within human reality as such, and thus it is 'both-and' more than the reduced totalizations founded by the hegemony of dichotomies proposed by society's experts. Once more this is because the notion of a theory already goes beyond the realm of philosophical pursuit, and thus totalizes that which it speaks of. The openness with which the true is pursued is that which prioritizes the question in a way which truly respects otherness by privileging the dialogical relation as that which reveals the excess which the method or theory has cast into oblivion. The openness with which one respects this otherness is one which can hold it within its gaze without at the same time totalizing it within the confines of yet another theoretical prison. In this way, it is the living relation by which we can bypass the footholds which such ideological repositioning of realist or idealist methods would affix as the totality from which truth and certainty find their union. The openness and privileging of the question fundamentally transform the perspectives we take with us in everyday experience.

The case of perfumery brings to light the issue of how we think about average everyday objects, which is often one of convenience rather than the impossibility of a formal and accurate portrayal of totalizing facts given within reality itself. This is what Lacan's notion of the real helps to showcase, for the real is the ever-existing excess bifurcated to unutterable obscurity by the closed totality of the concept in use. Despite the ease with which we use language to talk about objects, it seems irrational to claim that this is the way in which we understand language and its relationship to reality (as a direct representation thereof), for the mere multiplicity of systems seem to confirm this. Far beyond any example that could be given is the state of each and every man as restricted to experiencing the outside world from within himself as a subjective individual. In this sense we are relying exclusively on the language with which we communicate about things to *experience* understanding at all. Any further questioning in terms of the legitimacy of objects seems to make language fall apart into an extraneous list of definitions and the like. If this were the case, we would have a habitual need to explain the lack of consistency between the definition of an object and what we consider as objects by way of their founding ontology, which essentially relocates macrophysical nihilism in a great deal many more words. If the relationship of language and reality were in fact constitutive of a one-to-one ratio, knowledge would be little more than the understanding of language itself, and the whole of human history, a joke.

Yet as Merleau-Ponty tells us, "at the elementary level of sensibility, we catch sight of a collaboration among partial stimuli and between the sensorial system and the motor system that, through a variable physiological constellation, keeps the sensation constant, and thus rules out any definition of the nervous process as the simple transmission of a given message."[168] It is this very complicated process which is mistaken for a simple impression that directly relates true information to the sensor, and thus this confusion embeds itself into our language. By so doing, it breaks down the misunderstanding into discrete affirmations wherein our language cements perceptions as such, and from which complex arguments are built in such a way that to even understand the initial misnomer is a radical move. Yet Merleau-Ponty describes language's continued support of communication due to the fact that

> knowledge appears as a system of substitutions in which
> one impression announces others without ever providing

---

168 Merleau-Ponty, Maurice, *Phenomenology of Perception* (New York: Routledge, 2014), 9.

a justification, in which words evoke an expectation of sensations . . . The signification of the perceived is nothing but a constellation of images that begin to reappear . . . The most simple images or sensations are ultimately all there is to be understood through words; concepts are but a complicated manner of designating them, and like images and sensations, they are themselves inexpressible impressions.[169]

All this is to say that "the supposed evidence of sensing is not grounded upon the testimony of consciousness, but rather upon the unquestioned belief in the world,"[170] thus committing the psychological fallacy of "the experience error" which is to "build perception out of the perceived. And since the perceived is obviously only accessible through perception, in the end we understand neither."[171]

Ideology, then, like this mode of experience error, maintains a fundamental prejudice from which it exerts the complete and unambiguous determination of the things of the world toward consciousness, and yet confuses its theoretical data-points with these things, thus forcing the notion of determination onto the theory of the ideology itself. However, these things of the world are in fact not objects of perception, but rather are idealized, nearly Neoplatonic objects of ideas. This transformation of perception then is that through which "a reversal has taken place: the concept, itself founded on the precept, becomes the model and measure of the precept . . . The authentic experience of perception has been obscured, and perceptual reality has been displaced by an idea of reality."[172] From this it is easy to see the lack hidden by the nature of

---

169 Ibid., 16.

170 Ibid., 5.

171 Ibid.

172 Dillon, M. C., *Merleau-Ponty's Ontology* (Evanston, Ill.: Northwestern University Press, 1988), 62.

ideology as well as man's desire for the understanding and simplicity of relationality. In order that man can stray from this domination of totalizing knowledge it is clear that sensing must be returned to its place as the "living communication with the world that makes it present to us as the familiar place of our life. The perceived object and the perceiving subject owe their thickness to sensing. It is the intentional fabric that the work of knowledge will seek to decompose."[173]

Initial openness and active engagement are positioned against the dead totality of knowledge. Rather than a dichotomous set of concrete principles, these are modes of being which show extremes in relation to the productive co-creative understanding produced by the relation of sensing. The body in connection with the world (which is "in the world just as the heart is in the organism"[174]) achieves this understanding through question and answer whereby

> a sensible that is about to be sensed poses to my body a sort of confused problem.
>
> I must find the attitude that *will* provide it with the means to become determinate . . . I must find the response to a poorly formed question. And yet, I only do this in response to its solicitation. My attitude is never sufficient to make me truly see blue or truly touch a hard surface. The sensible gives back to me what I had lent to it, but I received it from the sensible in the first place. Myself as the one contemplating the blue of the sky is not an acosmic subject *standing before* it, I do not possess it in thought, I do not lay out in front of it an idea of blue that would give me its secret. Rather, I abandon myself to it, I plunge into this mystery and it 'thinks itself in me.'[175]

173 Merleau-Ponty, *Phenomenology of Perception*, 53.
174 Ibid., 209
175 Ibid., 222.

It is thus that senses find unification in that the body is itself co-natural (to use Merleau-Ponty's word) with the world; it is an active inherence therein which finds the correlative position that relates the truth of the matter through a process analogical to the way that understanding is produced intersubjectively. Through the position of always-already being alongside the world, our communication reveals the need with which we remain "open to phenomena that transcend me and that, nevertheless, only exist to the extent that I take them up and live them."[176] In other words, this understanding exists only as it stands between idealism and realism, for "idealism, by making the exterior immanent in me, and realism, by subjecting me to a causal action, both falsify the relations of motivation that exist between the exterior and the interior and render this relation incomprehensible."[177] The relationality infused with openness and active participation reveals the art of Being which itself is the actualization of truth as such.

---

176 Ibid., 381.
177 Ibid.

JUDGMENT OF JUDGMENT?

At the very heart of criticism of ideology is the problematic of the biased nature of the critic, as well as mankind's penchant for pattern seeking and confirmation bias which work in tandem to suggest that ideology is something that may be bad on a generalized front, but somehow worse when it has active replicating power. Unfortunately for those who cut down 'enemy' ideologies, this strategy serves only to make more space for other ideologies to flourish; even further and worse still is that they miss the fundamental memetic quality which ideology uses to its advantage, instead falsely attributing this quality to specific ideologies, and using it to justify where they stand in relation to those who maintain hegemony. As Daniel Dennett states, "the first rule of memes, as it is for genes, is that replication is not necessarily for the good of anything; replicators flourish that are good at . . . replicating! . . . the important point is that there is no *necessary* connection between a meme's replicative power, its 'fitness' from *its* point of view, and its contribution to our fitness (by whatever standard we judge that)."[178] This is to say that there is no internal logic hardwired into ideologies, save that of the logic of replication. Following this logic, however, will never arrive at the 'source' of the ideology but rather into a den of mirrors, for "a single occurrence of the sign is not possible. In consequence, there can never have been a pure 'first' appearance of the sign: any sign must appear from out of a repeatability that in some sense precedes any actual repetition, indeed that precedes the sign's very first appearance."[179]

---

178 Dennett, *Consciousness Explained*, 203.
179 Kimball, *The Infanticidal Logic*, 84.

Derrida relays in *Speech and Phenomena* that "a sign which would take place but 'once' would not be a sign; a purely idiomatic sign would not be a sign . . . it can function as a sign, and in general as language, only if a formal identity enables it to be issued again and to be recognized."[180] Memes, whose formal elements mirror those found in genes, function "independent of what the sign designates, of what it is intended to mean or is believed to refer to."[181] A sign, a meme, or an ideology need nothing to "determine its repeatability" and is thus "always able in principle to be separated from the sender's intention and therefore . . . always able in principle to lose their original meaning in the course of their sending."[182] This does not necessarily denote that mankind is merely the puppet through which memetic replication performs its own private show, but rather it should indicate the narrative lineage through which individuals habitually shape, divide, or denominalize ideological information. It also makes the relations of form and content explicit whereby the recognizable iterability of the form itself establishes the virtual relation to both its originary intention and the multiplicity of oppositional intentions. This subsumption of the relation under ideological rule gives birth to a concept whose referent is retroactively motivated by its opposition. It is the horizon of ideological meaning whereby multiple layers of reference are 'decoded' within the relation of the individual to whatever particular ideological discourse.

Worries concerning ideological criticism that excuses ideologies not currently in power, or disregards qualities as a whole based on their associative relationship, or disregards ideological critiques based on the critic's (or the critic's critic) past alignment, still showcase the possibility of ideological criticism (or worse, anti-ideological memeplexes) turning inversely toward the structure of an ideology all their own. For here power

---

180 Derrida, Jacques, *Speech and Phenomena: And Other Essays on Husserl's Theory of Signs* (Evanston, Ill.: Northwestern University Press, 1973), 50.

181 Kimball, *The Infanticidal Logic*, 84.

182 Ibid.

may also co-opt criticism as a deplatforming tool and in the popular eye reduce words and ideas to signifiers with nothing signified (or too many things signified unjustly as to reduce the seriousness with which the word is understood to be used). This may be an approach of turning the idea into an ideological structure by blowing out the terminology and associations toward unjustified targets or uses such that the idea is disregarded in favor of being non-ideological despite the associations and non-necessary attachments of the idea. This is not to suggest that there is an obligation, morally or otherwise, to equally share the stage with others based solely off their very existence, but merely a way through which 'anti-ideological' or 'non-ideological' goals can turn ideological by way of otherwise distancing from the subsuming popular qualities of ideologies. It seems as though in this way, as with reactionary ideologies, the difference that those who believe in 'non-ideologies' or 'anti-ideologies' through criticism can find themselves unknowingly drawn into ideological superstructures by way of ideology posing as 'philosophical investigation.' This is to say that the way in which reactionary ideologies seek to undermine the hegemonic (but ultimately find themselves giving way to similar and less readily criticism-worthy ideologies, hence ensnaring them rather than 'freeing' them) allows for a modality which separates the meaning attached by its sender to logical or 'necessary' relations between ideas themselves. It is from this modality that there is a disregard based off the individual's criticism of ideology, which is, in itself, ideological and unwittingly goes the same way as the reactionary. This is part of what Žizek means when he says that "what really matters is not the asserted content as such but the way this content is related to the subjective position implied by its own process of enunciation."[183] This is not even taking into account the fact that information not related to ideological structures undergoes the possibility of the loss of relation when transmitted, and may immediately be interpolated and installed ideologically, or at least used, mirrored, and accredited by ideologies writ large.

---

183 Žizek, Slavoj, *Mapping Ideology* (London: Verso, 2012), 5.

This ideological confusion, the turn through which those who oppose an ideological stance altogether fall into a more discretely packaged ideology, is brought about by way of the social pressures and linguistic bait-and-switches that those who grapple with ideological formations must traverse, which ideologies themselves are nestled against. This is because of the way in which the 'textual' or symbolic presence of the ideology fails to account for its own 'frame' which functions ultimately as a mode of 'the framed' itself made invisible.

> Žizek makes this clear when he says that ideology is a systematically distorted communication: a text in which, under the influence of unavowed social interests (of domination, etc.), a gap separates its 'official', public meaning from its actual intention—that is to say, in which we are dealing with an unreflected tension between the explicit enunciated content of the text and its pragmatic presuppositions.[184]

This means that prejudice, not necessarily in some nefarious sense, permeates all relationality, such that there is no neutral access point which grants delineation between reality and its appearance. This is the trap by which those who seek to deny ideology fall into, for they claim this impossible access point as their own, and thus embark upon their own ideological evangelism. The position which imagines itself to have found the point of access to the good and the true, who asserts that only others have been tricked into ideology, is the position situated within the chief moment of pure ideology.

In this way we find that

> one cannot draw a clear line of separation between descriptive and argumentative levels of language: there is no neutral

---

184 Ibid., 7.

descriptive content; every description (designation) is already a moment of some argumentative scheme; descriptive predicates themselves are ultimately reified-naturalized argumentative gestures.

This argumentative thrust relies on topoi, on the 'commonplaces' that operate only as naturalized, only in so far as we apply them in an automatic, 'unconscious' way —a successful argumentation presupposes the invisibility of the mechanisms that regulate its efficiency.[185]

To the anti- or non-ideological individual then, there is not only formulation in opposition to specific tenets of ideologies, but an entire ideology of opposition, therein creating a mirror-opposite ideology whose generative quality is that of blind negation: but, as we have seen, language is preceded in its own actualization by way of practices, rituals, and institutions. We understand this by means of one of the most readily available and popularly (mis)understood examples of religion, wherein first we see the ideologically negating route in atheism, which, as an anti-ideology ideology, often refuses to investigate spiritual matters altogether after having encountered ideology which claims a monopoly on spiritual matters. Secondarily, as alluded to, we understand "religious belief . . . not merely or even primarily [as] an inner conviction, but the Church as an institution and its rituals (prayer, baptism, confirmation, confession . . .) which, far from being a mere secondary externalization of the inner belief, stand for the very mechanisms that generate it."[186] This is not to say that the matters which are framed (spiritual matters) are 'appropriated' *necessarily* by the frame popularly seen, as much as that which is framed rather than the frame itself (religion) maintains 'discursive hegemony,' and the frame itself acts not as a supplementary

---

185 Ibid., 7-8.
186 Ibid., 8.

meaning, but rather "retroactively (re)defin[ining] the very nature of 'literal' identity."[187] The fantasy and the ideology that gives expression to it are but aspects of the same movement: the fantasy is both the origin and the supplement by which power is given to its ideology. This means that when we are calling this ideological frame into question we

> delineate . . . an intricate reflective mechanism of retroactive, 'autopoetic' foundation that far exceeds the reductionist assertion of the dependence of inner belief on external behaviour. That is to say, the implicit logic of [Althusser's (following Pascal's)] argument is: kneel down and you shall believe that you knelt down because of your belief—that is, your following the ritual is an expression/effect of your inner belief; in short, the 'external' ritual performatively generates its own ideological foundation.[188]

As far as the alternatives to this type of ideological subsumption are concerned, one of primary interest is that of the approach of Michel Foucault, whose theories of power attempt to bypass ideology and maintain distance in his approach to power. For Foucault this power is "inscribed directly into the body," and its material manifestation circumvents the 'domination' and 'exploitation' except at the levels *in view* at his social theory's structure. However in "abandoning the problematic of Ideology," Foucault sets the stage for a new explication of said ontology of power, which he never attempts. Instead, Foucault's career becomes the tireless repetition of

> how power constitutes itself 'from below', how it does not emanate from some unique summit: this very semblance

---

187 Ibid.
188 Ibid.

of a Summit (the Monarch or some other embodiment of Sovereignty) emerges as the secondary effect of the plurality of micro-practices, of the complex network of their interrelations. However, when he is compelled to display the concrete mechanism of this emergence, Foucault resorts to the extremely suspect rhetoric of complexity, evoking the intricate network of lateral links, left and right, up and down . . . a clear case of patching up, since one can never arrive at Power this way—the abyss that separates microprocedures from the spectre of Power remains unbridgeable. Althusser's advantage over Foucault seems evident: Althusser proceeds in exactly the opposite direction—from the very outset, he conceives these micro-procedures as parts of the ISA; that is to say, as mechanisms which, in order to be operative, to 'seize' the individual, always-already presuppose the massive presence of the state, the transferential relationship of the individual towards state power, or—in Althusser's terms—towards the ideological big Other in whom the interpolation originates.[189]

This type of disregard for the power relation which maintains interpolation leads to an eternal game of catch-up wherein one can only address the instances of 'microprocedures' as sterile, and ignore the regulation externally manifest in the big Other. This radically underestimates the repressive apparatuses which both the state and the law use to exercise explicit violence. This move seeks to suggest that ideology has becomes so pervasive that it is the horizon of all of man's possibilities, and that ideology is itself the soft exterior often directly bypassed so as to reproduce material and economic conditions.

This 'escape from ideology' then follows the same pattern of disregard as those who believe in the capability of themselves wholeheartedly

---

189 Ibid., 9

bypassing ideology altogether. However, once again we see that this act is the purest act of ideology, for to

> denounce as ideological the very attempt to draw a clear line of demarcation between ideology and actual reality, this inevitably seems to impose the conclusion that the only non-ideological position is to renounce the very notion of extra-ideological reality and accept that all we are dealing with are symbolic fictions, the plurality of discursive universes, never 'reality'—such a quick, slick 'postmodern' solution, however, is ideology par excellence. It all hinges on our persisting in this impossible position: although no clear line of demarcation separates ideology from reality, although ideology is already at work in everything we experience as 'reality', we must none the less maintain the tension that keeps the critique of ideology alive. Perhaps, following Kant, we could designate this impasse the 'antinomy of critic-ideological reason': ideology is not all; it is possible to assume a place that enables us to maintain a distance from it, but this place from which one can denounce ideology must remain empty, it cannot be occupied by any positively determined reality—the moment we yield to this temptation, we are back in ideology.[190]

If we are to follow Žižek's argument, the non-ideological position is not a position at all, but rather a non-position from the void. If one chooses 'a philosophy,' it is the one through which reactionary and otherwise 'non-ideological' ideologies establish themselves as differentiated or delineated from ideologies contrasting their *truthful* position. This seems to be the matter of any ideology wholly distinct from others, as opposed to denominational 'reformation,' the differences found in either location

---

190 Ibid., 11.

are not too far separate, for in some way they are using the ideology as a referent from which they establish *their* 'reality' against. The primary difference is the view through which the individual substantiates between the original ideology and its relationship to reality, for he who delineates himself views the past ideology as exactly that: ideology, and that through their step 'outside and beyond' they have somehow stepped into reality itself, no longer in the throes of ideology.

The 'reformer' thinks himself to be within the truth itself as well, and that the unreformed others are the ones corrupted by ideology, which he and other reformers kept their group belief safe from. As such, often those critical of ideology find themselves in a social-symbolic or otherwise rhetorical distancing game wherein they are defined by and ever in argument with ideologies, and as such fail to encounter the 'reality' of their situation wherein they are an ideologically defined warrior specifically entranced by the stratagems of those ideologies they most frequently oppose. This is yet another way in which truth itself, as an important factor in subsuming individuals, seems to reveal information which is framed. This is the effect of an unfolding of the facts 'speaking for themselves.' This then, is what informs the network of related information and the frame which seems to 'reveal truth,' and which convinces others it is indeed the objective itself and the self-grounding floor from which the entire structure of reality unfolds. The 'true' nature of reality is that which is easily accessible to the ideologue, and what's more startling, is that it is mere appearance as such which is the genesis of its own 'virtual appearance' standing over and against itself—it is that which is disclosed that in actuality is represented, rather than that which represents giving a surplus over and against its representations within the individual ideologue.

THE QUESTION OF SOCIAL ANTAGONISM

Escapism, like a private deification of one's side in a deadlocked social antagonism, represents an inability to rectify an ideological perspective with the nontotalizable reality of class struggle as a phenomenon. "The real achievement of hegemony is crystallized in the concept of social antagonism: far from reducing all reality to a kind of language-game, the socio-symbolic field is conceived as structured around a certain traumatic impossibility."[191] This is obviously due to the 'subject-position' being filled out with the illusion of achieving the full self-identity that one believes to be blocked by the ideological bogeyman that their particular ideology specifies, it always locates this bogeyman as the oppressive force maintaining the impossibility of contradicting overlap between two structures of social reality. The illusion here is "that after the eventual annihilation of the antagonistic enemy, I will finally abolish the antagonism and arrive at an identity with myself."[192] This is because we notice that the identity of an observer with a membership to a group is always-already marked by its own impossibility, and as such marked with limits denoting its end and its beginning. This is what Mouffe and Laclau mean when they use the word 'society' in stating this very idea about identity and ideology (or social grouping): "society never manages fully to be society, because everything in it is penetrated by its limits,

---

191 Žižek, Slavoj, Rex Butler, and Scott Stephens, "Beyond Discourse Analysis," in *Interrogating the Real* (London: Bloomsbury Academic, 2013), 249.
192 Ibid., 251.

which prevent it from constituting itself as an objective reality."[193] This specifies the conditions of social relations that generate "mutually exclusive endeavors to cope with this traumatic antagonism, to heal its wound via the imposition of a balanced symbolic structure."[194] That is to say that there is no neutral point in which this division can be described, for it is the obstacle itself wherein reality is falsified into a symbolic system.

It then becomes clear what Žizek means when he points out, reading Lacan, that "distortion and/or dissimulation is in itself revealing," wherein the real can be discerned as a value differentiated from "objective reality" in the sense that the real is the symbolically untranslatable, and its production highlights the differences and masks the sameness of those classes caught in conflict and around which social reality is constructed. This is also because, regardless of material dispersion, man as historical Being (as one in a state of becoming) maintains a unified perception: one which denies the prismatic refraction into the now. This does not deny the relational aspect shared by many things that he investigates, but merely asserts that understanding as such is ever pervaded in one way or another by the real of Lacanian psychoanalysis:

> This Real, however, is not the inaccessible Thing, but the gap which prevents our access to it, the "rock" of the antagonism which distorts our view of the perceived object through a partial perspective. And, again, the "truth" is not the "real" state of things, that is, the "direct" view of the object without perspectival distortion, but the very Real of the antagonism which causes perspectival distortion. The site of truth is not the way "things really are in themselves," beyond their perspectival distortions, but the very gap, passage, which

---

193 Laclau, Ernesto, and Chantal Mouffe, "Antagonism and Objectivity," in *Hegemony and Socialist Strategy: Towards a Radical Democratic Politics* (London: Verso, 2014), 102.

194 Žizek, *Mapping Ideology*, 16.

separates one perspective from another, the gap (in this case: social antagonism) which makes the two perspectives radically incommensurable. The "Real as impossible" is the cause of the impossibility of ever attaining the "neutral" non-perspectival view of the object.[195]

There is no 'ultimate' ideology which achieves a permanent state of hegemony and ultimately succeeds in creating the 'best possible world for all,' which should be protected as the ultimate achievement of human life. Instead, there is always-already a differentiated value that ensures the 'continuation' of social antagonism as a characteristic of any number of groups of people. Social antagonism is a corroborator with desire in its Lacanian state, described earlier as that which replicates itself and seeks not its satisfaction but its *reproduction*. In speaking of an end goal, Žizek states that

one should thus abandon . . . the opposition between the 'normal' run of things and the 'state of exception' characterized by fidelity to an Event which disrupts the 'normal' run of things. In the 'normal' run of things, life just goes on following its inertia; we are immersed in our daily cares and rituals, and then something happens: an eventual Awakening, a secular version of a miracle (social emancipatory explosion, traumatic love encounter). If we opt for fidelity to this event, our entire life changes, we are engaged in the 'work of love' and endeavor to inscribe the Event into our reality. At some point, then, the eventual sequence is exhausted and we return to the 'normal' flow of things.[196]

195 Žizek, *The Parallax View*, 281.
196 Žizek, Slavoj, "Addressing the Impossible," *RETHINKING REVOLUTION: Socialist Register 2017* (Halifax: Fernwood, 2016), 343.

It is with the 'normal' flow of things, this situation wherein there is no neutral point to stand upon, that we understand the shift from one discourse to another as merely a variance by which the social antagonism continues; this is true of course even when a newly balanced imposition is erected, for it is erected as a co-opted subset of the hegemonic super-structure. As social antagonism permeates the relationships that occupy any groupings of people (for the notion of a people, no matter what axis they are founded upon, maintains the radical multiplicities which fosters said antagonism), we should understand that the event which the non-hegemonic ideology seeks to bring forth is one that ultimately fails to bring about the full identity of those involved in achieving its success. Their wrath will become redirected at some other target that they can blame for this blockage of their success.

And yet these limits of society are felt not from a singular reflection, but at every turn as an ideology seeks to achieve hegemony and repro-duce power in its own terms. This is because there is a failure to see the impossibility it seeks to actualize, as it installs its own variances on the symbolic order believing that this somehow covers the gap of the real which will be realized once hegemony is achieved. Yet as this transition is finalized, social antagonism is felt at its most raw, for through its now highest expression of power it must give expression to the mounting pressure of its claims which now realize that "every identity is already in itself blocked, marked by an impossibility, and the external enemy is simply the small piece, the rest of reality upon which we 'project' or 'externalize' this intrinsic, immanent impossibility."[197] We can see this play out in the way that identities are always-already embedded in the relationships subjects have with each other, wherein they constitute each other as a differentiated substance which, when enacted authentically, finds the other as open to the infinite. Instead this relation which ideology

197 Žižek, Slavoj, *Interrogating the Real* (London: Bloomsbury Academic, 2013), 252.

often parasitizes is one that imagines the other to, by mere nature of their being other, undermine the essential characteristics of the individual's self-represented identity. Hence, as we see these identities politicized and make their demands known, it allows for that ideology which they claim to be in opposition to the possibility to appropriate and recommodify these very elements of their now-politicized identities. These identities were originally bought into, in large part, for their subversive or critical perspectives on power, which are now effectively redistributed back under the province of hegemony, only with their politics modified ever so slightly. Thus

> the groups installing the hegemonic group do not share the same relationship to that group: each group has its own point of identification with the hegemonic group, because each experiences social antagonism in a specific way, and so every group has a unique fantasy about the way the hegemonic group can remedy its particular lack (not the lack in the social field per se) or is stealing its *jouissance*. If the specificity of these transferential relations is not taken into account, we have no way to analyze the historical forms that the attribution of the loss of *objet a* takes. It is not, as Laclau would have it, that a specific group loses its particularity in its rejection or elevation of the hegemonic group. Rather, it relates transferentially to the hegemonic group in its own way. The fact that a group takes another group as its transferential object makes it possible to analyze the specificity of that group's fantasies about what is missing in the social field from the point of view of that group. The group's specificity, rather than its equivalence, is the key to this historical dimension, but not in the same way that multiculturalist historicism imagines. We need not attribute any positive properties to these groups, no essential identities,

and no perduring qualities. The "groupness" of the group is a function of its retroversive relations to the other groups and its relationship to its own split. More importantly, we do not take the group "at its word": we accord no special knowledge of itself to the group, nor do we accept that group's analysis of the reasons for its dissatisfaction. The unconscious (Real) register is our concern. The historicist dimension enters into the analysis when retroversion and fantasmatic identifications take center stage.[198]

As political relations, there are two ways in which these identities favor ideological foundations. Laclau defines these forms as hand-in-hand with certain particularities, that of the 'positive' and 'negative.' The 'negative' form of identity politics is that which seeks to establish itself via the subordination of others, yet maintains universalist language and engages in universalist politics, thus maintaining a contradiction by way of relating this set of universals to its own particular self-realization. 'Positive' identity politics are those which collaborate, joining their demands in a "chain of equivalence" which expresses and identifies with the struggle across the aisle, as we saw with feminists and Islam earlier under global left/liberal political schemas.[199]

It remains difficult to see how either option does more than merely help to enable the ideology in control, and, furthermore, to help mask and hide it from criticism. This masking seems to be part of the naturalization process which the hegemonic undergoes when co-opting the narratives of those who place demands on it, and thus the consciousness of the other's particularity is lost amidst a sea of 'solidarity' giving way to the

---

198 Rothenberg, Molly Anne, "Laclau's Radical Democracy," in *The Excessive Subject: A New Theory of Social Change* (London: Polity, 2013), 151–52.

199 Laclau, Ernesto, and Chantal Mouffe, "Preface to the Second Edition," in *Hegemony and Socialist Strategy: Towards a Radical Democratic Politics* (London: Verso, 2014), 9-10.

autonomy being traded for acquiescence which ultimately goes about reinforcing the dominant ideological force as eternal. This is not to say however, as many do, that this relegates us to identifying the ideologies which remain out of power as those who are oppressed or victimized and thus deserve a chance at power, for as we have seen this results in the habituation of power reactualizing itself as a universal. Thus,

> as long as we are fixated—as happens in multiculturalism and identity politics— on the symbolic identifiers of our personal identities, we obscure the link between the subject and the drive as the true engine of the subject's existence. For when we focus on the symbolic dimension of identity, we are conceiving of the subject as a subject of desire, perpetually seeking to overcome its lack by finding its object of desire. Any political action founded on this premise dooms the actors to a futile search for a utopia which, of necessity, must always be deferred.[200]

---

200 Rothenberg, *The Excessive Subject*, 176.

SEX AND THE
REPRODUCTION OF VALUES

In regard to the weakening of defenses on an individual level, wherein ideological replication may be most wholly imparted, there is but one approach which might lay bare not only emotional but also psychological footholds that are otherwise well guarded: sex. The relationship of sex to power is something that many theories have been constructed around, and yet there is often very little produced outside of dogmatic and unreflective assertions already expounded through ideology. This, it seems, is due not only to the mysterious and primordial nature of sex, but also in part due to its symbiotic relation to ideological development, where a unified understanding is one in which sex may act as a powerful drug and thus may find itself inadvertently used as a tool of reward in romantic love's already compromising situation. This compromising situation is the bedrock of romantic relationships growing and persisting throughout time, whereupon an individual's sense of self begins to shift in multiple directions, which begin to encompass the 'other' as a consideration upon one's own self.[201] The inclusion of new (or the expansion of existing) traits as positive, as well as the avoidance or loss of other traits, may begin to occur alongside positive affirmation. This need not mean that this affirmation comes from the significant other involved, but perhaps from the social experiences that are surrounding the two as they grow. It seems obvious, then, that there may be a positive or negative association with growth or loss depending on a variety of complications, such as the ideological biases already present

---

201 Agnew et al., "Cognitive Interdependence."

when entering into the relationship, if the expansion or loss was organic, etc. Both the self-concept and ideological positioning of the individuals involved in the romantic relationship always-already affect the relationship as well as the self-concept of the other.

When religious figures attempt to insulate their young from engaging in relationships with those who exist outside of their community, it is due in part to the implication of their children in a situation harboring a potential ideological or value-specific conversion, or at a minimum a shifting of one's faculties toward a more susceptible position. Even if the specifics are not understood *as such*, generally there is an awareness of this tendency for romance and sex to *persuade* ideological convictions and transform the values they hold therein. Furthermore, as a reproduction of appreciation and affection, sex in the pursuit of pleasure deepens the bond between the two, and in turn furthers persuasion by way of habituation in this state. This is the reason why both pornography and the sexualized figures in the media are to be understood with a great deal of skepticism. It is also the obvious reason why the seemingly contradictory values of feminist heroines portrayed in films are constantly given an ideological space of justification such that they may still be sexualized in great detail, for it is not with *the act* of sexualizing women on screen that the feminist ideological criticism would have us believe it has a problem, but rather that this devastating and subtle tool is being used by an opposing ideological system which does not directly benefit them. This is because there is an understanding of sex as amongst the most immediate approaches to deep psychological attachment; it also coincides with the physiological through hormones and other natural, chemical, and even neurological events taking place in the prefrontal cortex which help to establish interaction therein as a positive and self-habituating reward. It is also at the heart of social attitudes about the self and one's own conceptual self-understanding, for esteem and connection may also be greatly impacted by one's relationship to sexual preferences, arousal, and the act itself.

It seems easy to spot the ways in which not only preferences but also thoughts and desires might be manipulated such that the reproduction of power and hegemony in a particular society might be secured. The identity of those who participate in said culture is constituted by the very fundamental act from which life both begins and is maintained. Sexual socialization occurs, in part, by way of recurrent rewards being received in a direct psychological manner, or by perceiving trends in rewards across social peers, media, and reinforced ideological signifiers. It seems worthwhile to repeat that not only do the physiological conditions of estrogen, dopamine, oxytocin, serotonin, testosterone, and prostaglandin coincide with a predisposition whereupon sex may be used as the illusory fulfillment of its related condition of desiring, but so too does one's self-esteem, social status, identification within media representations and so on become reinforced as a primary way through which individuals might fortify said illusory pursuit. This is not to say, however, that *all* sexual contact is an illusory resolve originating in a condition of real suffering as such, but rather to speak on the ways through which the ideological hegemony of the twenty-first century might indeed provoke and install approaches to sexuality that persist primarily as illusions, the pursuit of which results in the reproduction of hegemony. An instance whereby one may be called to give up the condition that requires these illusions can be found at the pen of Immanuel Kant.

Kant was a moral philosopher of the most rigorous sort, and in thus estimating the bounds of morality which man should find to be his compass throughout life, so too it becomes apparent that at some point, sex and its use must have been addressed (as has been a central theme in the historical approach of those who posit moral philosophy or ideology). Kant was among the first to formalize a theory preconceptualizing sexual objectification, which details a modality of perception, thought, and desire ultimately aimed at utilizing the body of another for one's own gratification, all the while disregarding their humanity as actual. He formulates the conditions upon which man encounters himself as such by stating that man has an impulse directed to others, not so that he may enjoy their works and circumstances, but immediately to others as objects of his enjoyment. He has, indeed, no inclination to enjoy the flesh of another, and where that occurs, it is more a matter of warlike vengeance than an inclination; but there remains in him an inclination that may be called appetite, and is directed to enjoyment of the other. This is the sexual impulse. Man can certainly enjoy the other as an instrument for his service; he can utilize the others' hands or feet to serve him, though by the latter's free choice. But we never find that a human being can be the object of another's enjoyment, save through the sexual impulse.[202]

Immediately what we find in this opening passage is the differentiation of the sexual impulse from the other relations that man has by the term 'appetite': Kant here by this differentiation sets out to show that this appetite is one which necessarily extends from objectification, and which disregards in some way the free choice of the other. At the heart of this appetite is the inversion of man's relationality such that he misunderstands the nature by which he shares this relation with an other.

When an appetite shifts its focus from the considerate-less consumption of a thing to an other we understand that a fundamental displacement has occurred. Not only does man conceptually remove from the other that which truly allows him his place as the other, but he who possesses this appetite also by virtue of its deployment denies himself this autonomy. This already speaks to Marx's account of alienation, which he would come to articulate many years later, but from which we might begin to see the ways in which the notion of objectification may bloom from this secondary theory. This is because Marx draws the conception from speaking of production and labor, when he states that to produce as humans we find

---

202 Kant, *Lectures on Ethics*, 155-56.

each of us would have, in two ways, affirmed himself, and the other person. (i) In my production I would have objectified my individuality, its specific character, and, therefore, enjoyed not only an individual manifestation of my life during the activity, but also, when looking at the object, I would have the individual pleasure of knowing my personality to be objective, visible to the senses, and, hence, a power beyond all doubt. (ii) In your enjoyment, or use, of my product I would have the direct enjoyment both of being conscious of having satisfied a human need by my work, that is, of having objectified man's essential nature, and of having thus created an object corresponding to the need of another man's essential nature . . . Our products would be so many mirrors in which we saw reflected our essential nature.[203]

Marx furthered this theory in his later work, the *Economic and Philosophic Manuscripts of 1844*, whereby he lays out two key elements of alienation of the laborer from his labor which we may find helpful to observe in relation to our study. The first point is that the infrastructure of the product and its production itself is determined neither by those who labor or those who benefit from the objects and works of said laborer, but rather those who maintain hegemonic dominance in a society. This is because, in addition to structuring the labor and the individual, they structure the taste of those consuming the product *as such* by means of a monopoly on institutions and the social capital therein. This all maximizes the amount of exploitable labor on an intimate level.

Sexually, this plays out in much the same way, wherein individual sexual situatedness is exploited not just as a way through which products

203 Marx, Karl, and Friedrich Engels, "Comments on James Mill., Élémens D'économie Politique," in *The Collected Works of Karl Marx and Frederick Engels: Early Works 1835-1844, vol. 3* (Charlottesville, Va.: InteLex Corporation, 2001), 227-28.

may be sold and capital maintained, but also a way through which sex itself is situated qua institutes and representation, so that the very *act itself* is but a way through which individuals may be stimulated as social agents. Sex becomes subtracted from itself and given as a commodity unto itself which, rather than allowing those who participate *in it* to use its reflection as a mirror, is instead a way by which those who manage its replication and representation are able to profit. In this sense, there is a cynical distance maintained already by those who consume such products; it is already understood by its subjects that 'sex sells.' This 'sale' is founded by a new mode of commodity which masks the inherent antagonism present in its surface appearance. That is to say that this mode of commodification perfectly capitalizes and exploits the 'need' of the drive to infinitely suspend its articulated pathology, thus creating an image which denies itself to be read as such. This maps onto the 'direct' form of manipulative production. This is because labor is an endless cycle, which maintains itself via 'unmediated' relations between labor and compensation that naturalize themselves in the contingent necessity of labor as survival within the late modernist society.[204] So too does this blind approach to sexuality conduct itself via a naturalized necessity which maps itself by its demand that mirrors biological drives in maintaining a similar withholding of psychological reprieve. Kant's reading of it understands the great extent to which sexuality may sit as the most intimate relation between individuals, as well as with one toward and for oneself, and thus might at its very core be a way through which the rest of societal relations, hegemony, and one's own relation to ideology might be persuaded. He continues this exploration by stating that

> there is a sort of sense underlying this . . . whereby one human being is pleasing to the appetite of another . . . Love, as human affection, is the love that wishes well, is amicably disposed,

---

204 Ibid., 237-38.

promotes the happiness of others and rejoices in it. But now it is plain that those who merely have sexual inclination love the person from none of the foregoing motives of true human affection, are quite unconcerned for their happiness, and will even plunge them into the greatest unhappiness, simply to satisfy their own inclination and appetite . . . The sexual impulse can admittedly be combined with human affection, and then it also carries with it the aims of the latter, but if it is taken in and by itself, it is nothing more than appetite. But, so considered, there lies in this inclination a degradation of man; for as soon as anyone becomes an object of another's appetite, all motives of moral relationship fall away; as object of the other's appetite, that person is in fact a thing, whereby the other's appetite is sated, and can be misused as such a thing by anybody.[205]

The justification whereby sexual objectification is rendered reasonable in modernity and beyond is the mere atomistic category of consent which, despite leaving the formulation of the relation untouched, suggests that the individual by nature of his agreement to the free subjugation or sale of his body sidesteps the plunge into the great unhappiness. However, the issue at stake in the question of this freedom of consent is to what degree voluntary slavery is possible. This question does not take into account the morality of such a choice, but rather its possibility as such. This is significant not only for matters of prostitution or pornography wherein the use of one's body as an object for sale is a pure and singular choice for the individual (not to mention either's fundamental relation to sex trafficking) but so too does it direct its gaze toward the use of one's sex in Hollywood or other similar industry's 'casting couches' and beyond into casual sex which persists outside of a 'committed' relationship. This is because

---

205 Kant, *Lectures on Ethics*, 156.

the sexual impulse is not an inclination that one human has
for another, qua human, but an inclination for their sex, it
is therefore a principium of the debasement of humanity,
a source for the preference of one sex over the other, and
the dishonouring of that sex by satisfying the inclination.
The desire of a man for a woman is not directed to her as a
human being; on the contrary, the woman's humanity is of
no concern to him, and the only object of his desire is her
sex. So humanity here is set aside. The consequence is, that
any man or woman will endeavour to lend attraction, not to
their humanity, but to their sex, and to direct all actions and
desires entirely towards it. If this is the case, humanity will be
sacrificed to sex. So if a man wishes to satisfy his inclination,
and a woman hers, they each attract the other's inclination to
themselves, and both urges impinge on one another, and are
directed, not to humanity at all, but to sex, and each partner
dishonours the humanity of the other. Thus humanity becomes
an instrument for satisfying desires and inclinations; but by
this it is dishonoured and put on a par with animal nature.[206]

Here, it seems as though Kant speaks in anticipation of man's penchant
for turning himself, his desires, his thoughts, and characteristics into
commodities that are to be exchanged in return for other goods and
services, as in later Marxist thought.[207] This foresight itself preceded
the notion of love as an ideological category developed in later modern
thought, which society at large came to understand as driving factors of
relationships: that of true love, marriage for true love, and the under-

206 Ibid., 155-56.
207 Lukács, György, "Reification and the Consciousness of the Proletariat," in
    History and Class Consciousness Studies in Marxist Dialectics (London: Merlin,
    1971), 100.

standing of true love as that which conquers all[208] as well as, perhaps more directly confounding, the eroticism or sexualization of that love.

Perhaps following on the heels of Kant's influential position was the notion that reciprocal sexual satisfaction was a primary function of marriage, and as such it was believed that matrimonial intimacy would grow as a result, while the previous notions of "duty, moral character, personal sacrifice, and spiritual union were fast losing their appeal as the defining characteristics of . . . the conjugal relationship."[209] Kant's understanding of sexual intercourse speaks to the ways in which social sexualization would become a normative presumption of one's identity in late capitalism. When Kant mentions giving oneself to another sexually without giving over all of one's self *in its totality*, this is the complete state of objectifying oneself with no resolve, for this is forsaking oneself to another's usage, and indeed becomes exclusively an exchange of sexual attributes. For it is an impossibility to "acquire a member of a human being," as that "is at the same time acquiring the whole person, since a person is an absolute unity."[210] By this, he states, only one individual may be traded for another *in their entirety*, and for the entirety of another, which, in Kantian terms, has no dissolution save that of death. This all hinges upon Kant's notion of surrender (or submission) in which sexuality finds itself as an incarnated action. For in Kant's mind, there is either submission/surrender, or there is not: there isn't a middle ground whereupon one may partially submit/surrender, or submit/surrender for

---

208 Lantz, Herman R., et al., "The American Family in the Preindustrial Period: From Base Lines in History to Change," *American Sociological Review* 40, no. 1 (1975): 21–36.

209 D'Emilio, John, and Estelle B. Freedman, "The Rise and Fall of Sexual Liberalism, 1920 to the Present," in *Intimate Matters: A History of Sexuality in America* (Chicago: University of Chicago Press, 2012), 265.

210 Kant, Immanuel, "On the Right of Domestic Society Title I: Marriage Right," in *The Metaphysics of Morals*, trans. Mary Gregor (Cambridge: Cambridge University Press, 1991), 97.

a set period of time that allows for a reversal at a specified point. This brings resolution to the nature of the 'giving over of oneself' involved within sexual intercourse by actually marrying the two in the sense of combining two to one, for as one exchanges, they receive their 'humanity,' and in that sense "one person is acquired by the other as if it were a thing, the one who is acquired acquires the other in turn; for in this way each reclaims itself and restores its personality."[211]

It seems then that our 'humanity,' freedom from restriction by another's choice and the 'giving' of 'bodies' into the possession of others, are all wrapped up in the ways through which sexual contact exists and as such is incompatible with another's external independence, whereupon the only result is the habituation of one's own objectification for the use of pleasure. This is further confounded by the ways in which gender within sexual relations is exaggerated as an exploitable element to be capitalized on, furthering objectification and dissociation of the intimate within sexual intercourse and thus furthering the alienation of individuals as subjects of ideological rule. This market value speaks of the ways in which male and female sexuality seem diametrically opposed and are detrimental to the formation of relational approaches more likely to promote prosperity of the individual when not governed by those who wish to reproduce hegemony. Sex becomes neither confirmation nor expression of the real lives of those engaging in it, nor does it grant the action or its place within one's self-narrative within the world that *they themselves understand*, but instead it persists as that which is alien, external to those who engage in said action, reproducing the normalization of cultural and social affairs that are ever present in the messages installed in nearly every aspect of the images and symbols which occupy the external world we inhabit. These are not only linguistic messages (which break apart the textual information into connoted and denoted messages) or iconic non-coded messages (literal or denoted image-messages), but also

---

211 Ibid.

coded iconic messages (symbolic or connoted image-messages) of which Roland Barthes speaks.[212]

These exploitable biological drives and niche pleasure-centers are taken hold of and utilized, perhaps not consciously, but to an end that does indeed contribute to alienation as Marx articulated it. This is because man's sexuality has been interconnected with his status as a socioeconomic entity, whereby direction of one's goals and activities as they exist in themselves are dictated by instruments promoting, defining, and vying for sexual capital within various ideological institutions. Henceforth man understands himself as autonomous and self-realized, yet at the same time makes sexual choices which invariably speak to his loss of determination and orientation as regards his most intimate and fundamental self-relations. This affect is directed toward one of hegemony's key productions, those positive assertions of social relations, ideas, and ideologies which help to constitute norms that are generated by these social relations in order to stimulate social or material agents. Here too, as is one of the principal aims of ideology, it is itself made invisible by procuring itself upon the back of ideologically founded 'freedoms,' and as such we are no less Puritan in believing that these cultural constraints constitute our true freedom in any legitimate way. This is also done in part by an appeal to 'natural' drives and desires through an unrestrained and 'pure' approach to sexuality, which are not 'left alone to persist as they would in nature,' but instead promoted as the most desirable approach to sexuality as is possible: for here, too, it is said that 'freedom' is constituted more perfectly. Despite the system of socialization, assent to its values and the resort to justifying ideological 'revolutions' that constitute the hidden nature of the *movement* of hegemony within naturalized fields and theories, this interplay between men and women constitutes a reinscription of the hegemonic in a way more challenging to see, and all in the name of freedom.

---

212 Barthes, Roland, "The Rhetoric of the Image," in *Image-Music-Text*, trans. S. Heath (London: Wm. Collins Sons and Co., 1964), 32-51.

Historical Clues; or,
What Happens Now?

Hegel, in the preface to *The Phenomenology of Spirit*, speaks to the fact that we should not disregard entire philosophical systems: the diversity found therein should not be approached by means of wholesale negation, but instead should be celebrated as the progressive unfolding of truth. As such there is a process of refinement that takes place whereupon systems of thought take the aspects of a previous philosophy that were working, and instead of disregarding the totality of the system itself, they restructure and advance those ideas. This is, in part, a reason for giving the most robust readings of philosophies rather than disregarding them in haste so as to bolster our own name upon the mantle of history. Here is then a way in which philosophy may be approached without losing elements of possibility, and which reproduces a true Hegelian synthesis wherein the expectation is to give way to the progressive arising of the truth.

Hegel uses the metaphor of the flower, where the bud gives way to the flower, and the flower to the fruit, where each is unique in their individuality, and stand as their own observable substances *as such*, but each are necessarily connected and contrived *by* that which came before them.[213] It is important to consider when thinking of language, symbols, storytelling, and more broadly ideology, is that the ways in which meaning appears on the face of language or symbol-systems may cease to exist from one moment to another. Indeed ideology, as a symbol in itself, has undergone a considerable transformation from its conception

---

213 Hegel, *Phenomenology of Spirit* (trans. Findlay), 2.

to what it has referred to throughout the entirety of this text. We can see this in action when we look historically to the inventor of the term 'ideology,' Antoine Louise Destutt de Tracy. In Cristea Ioana's study on the term, she notes that

> [t]he word appears for the first time in his study titled "Memoires sur la faculté de penser", published in *Memoires de l'Institut National des Sciences et des Arts pour l'An IV de la République* [in 1803.] The author's goal was to overturn the old classifications in order to introduce a new "science of ideas." The purpose of this new science was to replace the old type of "metaphysical" knowledge with a new kind of knowledge, namely, "scientific" knowledge. Destutt's thoughts were influenced by Claude Adrien Helvetius' materialism. In Helvetius' view, ideas are essentially the result of the influences that the society in which we live has on the individual. People's representations derive from the sensations that the surrounding objects produce on their senses. Thus, ideology must conduct an objective study of ideas and their origins.[214]

This is obviously contradictory to nearly every sentiment in this text, however there is a historical reconciliation within the fact that when mankind involves itself in 'objective studies,' this is often an overstep into the presumption of objectivity, which might prove useful initially, but reveals with exposure to history how great its overstep was. As Terry Eagleton states, ideology is a symbol following the fate of a great deal many '-ology's whereby "a curious process of inversion 'ology' words often end up meaning the phenomenon studied rather than the sys-

---

214 Ioana, Cristea, "Antonio Gramsci's Concept of Ideology," *South-East European Journal of Political Science* 1, no. 3 (2013).

tematic knowledge of it."[215] We see then that from the outset, ideology sought to remove doubts or inconsistencies as to the 'exact' study of human thought and the ideas that it generates, which Dustett thought to be capable of delineating from the effects of degeneration brought about by their attachment alongside the human body and mind. He presumes that, as a continuation of zoology in some respect, ideology would be capable of "defining the sources of human knowledge, its limitations, and the degree of its certainty."[216]

Ideology then was originally the attempt at systematizing the material grounds from which ideas and human thought were revealed to reason itself. Yet from the very outset ideology as a scientific practice and its adherents, 'ideologists,' were accused of the exact opposite goal by Destutt's major political rival at the time, Napoleon Bonaparte. Bonaparte saw Destutt's philosophy as hand-in-hand with his political and economic beliefs, which favored the form of American Republicanism that was just then coming to full term. Bonaparte used the terms in a derogatory way to point out the theoretical implications of his opponents' epistemological and ontological foundations which he claimed were invalid "with reference to practice."[217] We then understand that by labeling those who opposed his imperial vision with their critical thought reflected back at them, Napoleon sought to undermine the pure contemplation that, by contrast, he claims as his direct political and personal experience with reality. Bonaparte's critique revealed what we have seen many times throughout this text, that Destutt's aim, which is itself parallel to the Enlightenment's attempt to free reason

215 Eagleton, Terry, "From the Enlightenment to the Second International," in *Ideology: An Introduction* (New York: Verso, 2007), 63.

216 Barth, Hans, "The Ideology of Destutt De Tracy and Its Conflict with Napoleon Bonaparte," in *Truth and Ideology* (Berkeley: University of California Press, 1977), 2.

217 Mannheim, Karl, *Ideology and Utopia* (London: Routledge & Kegan Paul, 1966), 64.

from unwarranted prejudice, instead found that he merely cast off the burden of guilt while maintaining prejudice. This is because he still held onto Locke's idea of individuals as "passive and discrete" as well as "the appeal to a disinterested nature, science and reason, as opposed to religion, tradition and political authority, [which] simply masked the power interests which these noble notions secretly served."[218] Yet, despite ideological critique's initial servicing of those already in power (as in Napoleon's case,) further in its historical development it would take another sharp turn and become the tool of the Marxist proletariat whose use of ideological analysis sought to expose the hidden agendas of their particular adversaries. This reveals that, in a society where ideological capital is maintained by mass consumption, one of the ways in which subsumption occurs is by constantly consuming subversion *as such* and reaffirming hegemony without regard for content.

It is at the pens of Marx and Engels that ideology's conceptual development finds its most well-known contribution. This movement of the theory's historical unfolding has its roots in their theories of alien-ation, inversion, and production, which begin to step into pre-memetic thoughts that speak on "human powers, products and processes [which] escape from the control of human subjects and come to assume an apparently autonomous existence."[219] It is from this stage that Marx and Engels elaborate on what, in their view of ideology, constitutes its most precious and powerful secret, which is its masking ability to naturalize and dehistoricize ideas and their systems whereupon consciousness itself becomes separate and inverted from the social realm where its ties were formed, and becomes fetishized as a thing-unto-itself which generates and constitutes historical life. They consider consciousness to be socially determined, and thus ideas are a historical product to be examined as such. They state that

---

218 Eagleton, *Ideology*, 64.
219 Ibid., 70.

men are the producers of their conceptions, ideas, etc.—real, active men, as they are conditioned by the definite development of their productive forces and of the intercourse corresponding to these, up to its furthest forms. Consciousness can never be anything else than conscious existence, and the existence of men in their actual life-process. If in all ideology men and their circumstances appear upside down as in a camera obscura, this phenomenon arises just as much from their historical life-process as the inversion of objects on the retina does from their physical life-process. In direct contrast to German philosophy which descends from heaven to earth, here we ascend from earth to heaven. This is to say, we do not set out from what men say, imagine, conceive, no from men as narrated, thought of, imagined, conceived, in order to arrive at men in the flesh. We set out from real, active men, and on the basis of their real life-process we demonstrate the development of the ideological reflexes and echos of this life-process . . . Life is not determined by consciousness, but consciousness by life.[220]

Here we see something familiar through the camera obscura metaphor which returns us to a critical eye aimed at the epistemological foundations of ideology. Resting in the center of this sharp turn by Marx is his conception of consciousness as, in its relation to the world, that which produces the theoretical realm of ideas (as well as that of ideology itself). Consciousness itself, when relating to the social 'reality' produced by human material praxis (which showcases the intentional nature of man's existence, as well as intertwining the nature of action and meaning) and its relations, constitutes the genesis of ideas *from* material practice. This is eventually reconciled with his concept of the efficacy of thought *upon*

220 Marx, Karl, and Friedrich Engels, *The German Ideology* (Moscow: Progress, 1976), 47.

material practice itself, in a sort of agreement between primacy and necessity. This is illustrated in his *Selected Writings* when Marx states that "the mode of production, the relations in which productive forces are developed, are anything but eternal laws, but that they correspond to a definite development of men and of their productive forces, and that a change in men's productive forces necessarily brings about a change in their relations of production."[221]

This formally demonstrates how social relations of production and productive forces work hand in hand to produce consciousness, which, in turn, continues to affect social relations of production and thus ideas. Ideology becomes false consciousness generated by these social relations in order to stimulate social or material agents. Here then we see Marx's critique of ideology culminating in that which intends to delineate false from true consciousness by transmogrifying the practical activity in which the *real contradictions* subsist, in order to abolish these social phantasies. This false consciousness is the way in which consciousness can invisibly privilege the interests of a particular grouping of people over all others in the same historical moment. That is, these interests are naturalized and universalized, wherein those who do not benefit from the hegemonic ideology are led to believe that their domination and lack of beneficial social positioning is merely the effect of the 'real world' they exist in, and that these conditions are in fact universal. When we say that Marx and Engels have established themselves as possessing "a materialist theory of ideology," we understand this as being "inseparable from a revolutionary politics."[222]

These revolutionary politics regard true change as that which results from economic class struggle, yet whose material history has ultimately resulted in socialist and communist political states, where the validity of and their relationship toward 'authentic' or otherwise 'pure' Marxist

---

221 Marx, Karl, "The Materialist Conception of History 1844–1847," in *Selected Writings* (New York: Oxford University Press, 2000), 227.

222 Eagleton, *Ideology*, 72.

politics has been theoretically debated at such great length that one would be forgiven for imagining it to be a purely theoretical activity. Regardless, the other contribution from this conception of Marx's materialistic theory of ideology is that of consciousness in ideology, both in its initial understanding to those who see the word as a sort of private mental life-process, but also persisting through a secondary meaning which speaks of "historically specific forms of consciousness [that] become separated out from productive activity, and can best be explained in terms of their functional role in sustaining it."[223] Epistemologically speaking, it seems as though there would have to be two modes of ideological critique for a society which divides labor into mental and physical, and one that does not. However, this schism is resolved when looked at more closely, for it is "a dislocation internal to social reality itself, in specific historical conditions. It may be an illusion to believe that ideas are the essence of social life; but it is not an illusion to believe that they are relatively autonomous of it, since this is itself a material fact with particular social determinations."[224]

This viewpoint allows self-knowledge to be a referential mirror, as it were, contained within the totality of the system which is itself not entirely secondary, thus refraining from a delegation to a database against which conception sits internal to the action which we perform. Therefore, the 'imagery' of the "language of 'reflexes,' 'echoes' and 'sublimates'"[225] generates a space for false consciousness and self-deception. This leads to the camera obscura metaphor, which speaks of 'truth' as an experiential force in the world, which, when given to one with 'true consciousness,' is purely related to them without mediation.[226] Marx's formulation of the problem and critique of ideology makes it clear why his name was left as the primary symbol of the historical development of the concept.

---

223 Ibid., 74.
224 Ibid., 75.
225 Ibid.
226 Ibid., 77.

However, we must also make clear his integration of political critique, which shows the material side of ideology, as well as an active edge that encourages action as the primary mode of critical movement against that which dominates us. Although his name is the most synonymous with ideological critique still to this day, much thought encapsulated under the title of 'Marxism' ultimately generates and is governed by its own larger sense of ideological thought, more often than not resulting in its own grandiose metaphysical system. However, for a great deal of those engaged with or having seriously thought through ideological or political criticism, Marx's thought is that which forms, either in parallel with or in opposition to, the formation of many of its most vital elements. As such, Marx and his tradition of criticism stands in history as a great example of ideology and its strange relationship to truth. It speaks in-and-of-itself to the ways in which narratives and systematic self-groupings may well maintain true elements that help to infuse them into the groundwork of their ideological superstructure.

Marx's critique of ideology as separate and distinct from 'Marxism' progressed parallel to the global trend of modern capitalism, most notably through György Lukács, Antonio Gramsci, the Frankfurt School, Louis Althusser, and Slavoj Žižek chronologically. We can see this progression starting from war and revolution which laid fertile groundwork in many countries for Communist and Marxist thought to grow from their roots. Because of the movement of history, it became a most opportune time to take hold of the original commentary of Marx himself and elaborate further upon what political theorists saw on the horizon for the world. This was an opportunity not forsaken by one of the most notable Stalinist-era intellectuals, György Lukács. Lukács progressed in his Leninist philosophy, pursuing Marx's analysis wholeheartedly, while abandoning the modernist and anti-positivist positions he otherwise previously maintained. During his Leninist era of authorship, he produced his magnum opus, *History and Class Consciousness,* which not only laid a substantial philosophic groundwork for Lenin's particular brand of Communism, but which also housed Lukács's two major contributions to ideological criticism: *reification* and *class consciousness*. The first term, reification, came about via a close reading of Marx's discussion of commodity fetishism, which is the transformation of relationships between individuals from *social* to *economic*.

The philosophical underpinnings of this perception continue to follow the material vision of ideological critique by outlining the ways in which the social organization of labor is structured as well as showcasing a primary way in which individuals who live under capitalist rule find themselves socially alienated. This perception inhabits a larger phenomenon that encapsulates commodity fetishism as a specific form of reification which is in line with an orthodox reading of Marx. Since Lukács's form of analysis highlights the Hegelian elements persisting beyond his forced headstand, it draws said theory further into the actual work of Hegel. This can be seen through the notion of commodity fetishism, and as a larger whole, Marx's work on reification, which works as a dialectical relationship between social consciousness and social reality whereby perception and the objective conditions of social relationships are dominated by commodities and their production. Lukács understood Marx's approach to reification as lacking, however, for it restricted consciousness dominated by fetishism as only related to commodities, whereas Lukács saw reification as a fundamental aspect of all of man's social relations under capitalism. Under Lukács we see that reification recognizes the phenomenon of appearance as regards to holdings, relations, and acts of man as coming from the commodities themselves (which also appear to not have their origin in man either), and as such they govern every aspect of man's life and indeed transform him into a thing-unto-itself which dwells among the commodities as if it were one of them.

The specific set of social relations generated by this phenomenon are deemed natural and intrinsic to the life of man, and as such ensures the reproduction of the conditions whereupon its genesis is founded, dominating near every area of life:

Even when commodities have this impact on the internal structure of a society, this does not suffice to make them constitutive of that society. To achieve that it would be necessary . . . for the commodity structure to penetrate society in all its aspects and to remould it in its own image. It is not enough merely to establish an external link within dependent processes concerned with the production of exchange values. The qualitative difference between the commodity as one for among many regulating the metabolism of human society and the commodity as the universal structuring principle has effects over and above the fact that the commodity relation as an isolated phenomenon exerts a negative influence at best on the structure and organization of society.[227]

Lukács believed that this kind of social and cognitive organization is essentially ingrained in the consciousness of man from the nineteenth century onward, and as such, fields like law, science, and even philosophy begin to mirror the fetishistic tendencies that Marx outlined in his treatise on commodity fetishism. He explains the far-reaching grip of ideology by stating that

[i]t stamps its imprint upon the whole consciousness of man; his qualities and abilities are no longer an organic part of his personality, they are things which he can 'own' or 'dispose of' like the various objects of the external world. And there is no natural form in which human relations can be cast, no way in which man can bring his physical and psychic 'qualities' into play without their being subjected increasingly to this reifying process.[228]

227 Lukács, György, "Reification and the Consciousness of the Proletariat", in *History and Class Consciousness Studies in Marxist Dialectics* (London: Merlin, 1971), 85.

228 Ibid., 100.

Where Marx imposed limits, and spoke of the concrete relations of production and its goods as well as the transformation of human relationships, Lukács chose to speak more broadly, and primarily through analogy of the "diffusion" of reification from commodity fetishism to a universal trait. He spoke of its "rationality" as a modified Aristotelian essence that permeates the form of man who lives with this "universal structuring principle" ingrained upon its every moment. The appearance of this pathology in any society dominated by this form of reification leads to the disappearance of formal reasoning and logic and instead bisects and categorizes man into a fundamental dichotomy of consciousness: that of the proletariat and the bourgeois.

Lukács argues that the fundamental antagonism which structures modern capitalist societies is that of the proletariat fighting to achieve its particular class consciousness (that of the revolutionary) in opposition to ideology, which is a projection of bourgeois class consciousness. The understanding of the proletariat as the revolutionary class from which reification may be overcome takes its foundation from dialectical materialism, which speaks of an understanding of the concrete and material totality of the historical process. This understanding illuminates the proletariat as the producer of this totality, and thereby is in the unique position which poses the possibility of transforming society, thus maintaining the possibility of revolution, which for Lukács remained forever the notion of a communist revolution. However, perhaps the most overlooked element of these concepts that Lukács elaborated is that the struggle for class consciousness against reification is never-ending, and thus when he speaks of "the act of consciousness overthrow[ing] the objective form of its object"[229] it is surely constant realization, rather than *the* final action itself.

Lukács's thought projects far into the future, whereby it directly lays the groundwork for Adorno and his contribution to the philosophical history of ideology. However, due to the rhizomatic nature of its develop-

---

229 Ibid., 178.

ment we must stop first at the steps of the Italian philosopher Antonio Gramsci if we are to remain chronological. Gramsci broke from orthodox Marxism by attempting to utilize Marxist thought while subtracting the deterministic economic elements, and as such became a key thinker in what is known as neo-Marxism, which still maintains such a large scope that it is largely un-unified, save for potentially the influences or reformations of Marxist theory by other intellectual traditions. Gramsci was a celebrated figure amongst the revolutionary and radical left in Italy during the rise of fascism under Mussolini, known early on for his socialist periodical *L'Ordine Nuovo: Rassegna Settimanale di Cultura Socialista* and position as general secretary in the Italian Socialist Party, which, by way of culminating a strong opposition to Mussolini and his politics, resulted in Gramsci's eventual imprisonment, where a majority of his serious philosophical writing was done.

From his journals we notice that he makes a move similar to that of Lukács in that he again pushes the scope of his critique even wider, and thus generates a theory that is of a broader category of ideology, and so speaks to the relations of ideology. We are presented then with the theory of hegemony, which he uses to mean

> the ways in which a governing power wins consent to its rule from those it subjugates . . . hegemony [is associated] with the arena of 'civil society,' by which he means the whole range of institutions intermediate between state and economy . . . To win hegemony, in Gramsci's view, is to establish moral, political and intellectual leadership in social life by diffusing one's own 'world view' throughout the fabric of society as a whole, thus equating one's own interests with the interests of society at large.[230]

---

230 Eagleton, *Ideology*, 112-16.

In instituting the thought of a *cultural* hegemony, Gramsci saw that the best way of creating a resistance that utilizes value systems opposite that of the hegemonic (bourgeois) was by instructing others through the particulars of revolutionary historical analysis as well as proletariat theories of emancipation, so as to encourage intellectuals to grow from the movement, and thus allowing for the material growth of the social classes against the hegemonic. This growth results from constant observation and pointing out the constructed nature of the social institutions and beliefs held by those in the hegemonic class as well as theorizing as to the real reason behind these constructs as those which continue to affirm the domination of all outside the hegemonic. For Gramsci

> a dominant ideology reflects not just the world view of the rules, but the relations between governing and dominated classes in society *as a whole*. Its task is to recreate, at an 'imaginary' level, the unity of the entire social formation, not just to lend coherence to the consciousness of its rulers. The relation between a hegemonic class and a dominant ideology is thus indirect: it passes . . . through the mediation of the total social structure. Such an ideology cannot be deciphered from the consciousness of the governing bloc taken in isolation, but must be grasped from the standpoint of the whole field of class struggle.[231]

Gramsci operated with the idea that the enemy of his enemy was his friend, and constructed a theory that, through a unified will of (even seemingly disparate) ideological bedfellows, true revolution may come to actualize itself, and liberate those living under domination. In this way, Gramsci runs parallel to the Marxist tradition of the indistinguishable nature of theory and radical politics, for ideology then is not necessarily

---

231 Ibid., 122.

the focus of frustration within a society, but more a tool through which power is manipulated to keep culture in reproduction.

Thus far we have seen how the history of the notion of ideology mirrors the struggle of an ideology itself. We have seen philosophers adopt positions of reformation and revolution, utilize power and accusations, and fail to account for biases and blind spots wherefrom we might see the external workings of these internal theories manifest brilliantly before us; and so too does this parallel expression continue as Marxists established an institute devoted to social research in 1923 which came to be known as the "Frankfurt School." This grouping became the first major group of Marxists divorced from the working class, as well as from communist parties of any variety. Here Marxism came to infuse itself with the bourgeois ideologies which had established themselves in academia, and thus, as a new wave of Marxist thought developed, it situated itself internally alongside those ideologies which governed and helped to reproduce cultural hegemony. Here, Marxism sought to continue the tradition (in whatever form that may be) by working from within the ISA of the university, armed with the end goal of developing cross-disciplinary research from a wide range of differing Marxist perspectives.

Two of the most influential figures in this school were the German philosophers Theodor Adorno and Max Horkheimer, who worked together to address pop culture as the primary mode through which cultural goods are produced *en masse*. They saw pop culture as a principal form through which the masses may be deceived and co-opted into an ideological framework, as outlined in their opus, *Dialectic of Enlightenment*. In one of the essays contained therein, "The Culture Industry," the two speak on how conformity is encouraged through reproductive cycles using the same schema which allows for easy digestion by those who are consuming the product such that active engagement with the work may be wholly disregarded. They approach the culture industry as one which is driven by money and power via the logic of late capitalist rationality (unlike that of art, which maintains some semblance of autonomy according to the authors), such that "amusement has become an extension of labor under late capitalism."[232] This extension finds culture commodified, and by extension, human consciousness.

And yet, perhaps the most novel contribution found here is the utilization of the cross-disciplinary approach procured by the Frankfurt school where, at the crux of the chapter, the two speak of desire as the principal drive exploited for capital to continue in its growth and towards the reproduction (and hiding) of ideological principles driving cultural hegemony:

> The culture industry perpetually cheats its consumers of what it perpetually promises. The promissory note which, with its plots and staging, it draws on pleasure is endlessly prolonged; the promise, which is actually all the spectacle consists of, is illusory: all it actually confirms is that the real point will never be reached, that the diner must be satisfied with the menu . . . The secret of aesthetic sublimation is its representation of fulfillment as a broken promise. The culture industry does not sublimate; it represses. By repeatedly exposing the objects of desire, breasts in a clinging sweater or the naked torso of the athletic hero, it only stimulates the unsublimated forepleasure which habitual deprivation has long since reduced to a masochistic semblance . . . The mechanical reproduction of beauty, which reactionary cultural fanaticism wholeheartedly serves in its methodical idolization of individuality, leaves no room for that unconscious idolatry which was once essential to beauty.[233]

---

232 Adorno, Theodor W., and Max Horkheimer, "Culture Industry: Enlightenment as Mass Deception," in *Dialectic of Enlightenment* (Frankfurt am Main: Fischer Verlag, 2006), 145.

233 Ibid.

Not only do we see the criticism of the superstructure of cultural repro-duction neatly represented from the Marxist tradition, so too this shows the psychological implications of how capital is built into the psyches of those who consume its productions. The language of masochism, desire, and sublimation gives credence to the theories generated by entangling them with other schools of thought. This radical combination of cultural commentary, philosophical argumentation, psychological diagnoses, and literary analysis generate a twofold image of the historical foundation of modernity. It is through this double image that the potentiality of fundamental change is found, such that the resistance thereby outlined to this recognition of potency is cast both toward the past with myths of fate and toward the present with an idolization of *the facts*.

This recognition of that which is differentiated theoretically is pre-cisely what Adorno addresses as the primary fear of ideological hegemony in his text *Negative Dialectics*, where he states that "reconciliation would release the non-identical, would rid it of coercion, including spiritualized coercion; it would open the road to the multiplicity of different things and strip dialectics of its power over them."[234] The identity-centric fascist ideology that the majority of those leading the Frankfurt School saw in Nazi Germany became projected onto all ideological subsumptions, which sought to suppress all contradictions and social antagonisms by dissolving them in the hegemonic identity that it carried along. This polemic of identity as an oppositional differentiation is one of the key elements generating critical theory as a practice, and as such establishing itself in opposition to traditional theory using this very controversy, where traditional theory is charged with this same regulatory system, which hides and dissolves difference in lieu of simply furthering late capitalist reproduction. This repositioning of the problem of ideol-ogy, as Terry Eagleton points out, "is what the system would *like* to

---

234 Adorno, Theodor W., *Negative Dialectics* (London: Routledge & Kegan Paul, 1973), 6.

be told,"[235] rendering the problems presented by those early to work within the Frankfurt School as, more often than not, misidentifying the ideological conditions associated with the reproduction of Western late capitalism at large.

While the Frankfurt School might have produced totalizing theories which neglect the complexity and active nature of modernity, the concepts which they provided served as tools that fostered a continuation of theoretical approaches to the problem of the established Western ideologies. When Jürgen Habermas arrived on the scene, he

> follow[ed] Adorno in dismissing the concept of a Marxist science, and in refusing to assign any particular privilege to the consciousness of the revolutionary proletariat. But whereas Adorno is then left with little to pit against the system but art and negative dialectics, Habermas turns instead to the resources of communicative language.[236]

This shift was made at the express interest of resolving the impossibility of critique which the first generation of the Frankfurt School had founded by granting that reason is, in itself, totalitarian. Habermas developed a theory wherein the discursive system at hand is always-already in service of normalizing the hegemonic ideology keeping intact the radical nature of hegemony while reopening the possibility of autonomy. This fight against what Habermas constantly refers to as systematically distorted communication is an approach that has inspired waves of philosophy after it by approaching the problem as a communicative rationality, and moving the frame of the issue back yet another step. For Habermas, ideological critique necessarily became a critique of the conditions of communication. This approach is

---

235 Eagleton, *Ideology*, 128.
236 Ibid.

another way of securing an internal bond between present and future, and so, like Marxism itself, is a form of 'immanent' critique . . . it installs itself *within* the present in order to decipher those fault lines where the ruling social logic presses up against its own structural limits, and so could potentially surpass itself. There is a clear parallel between such immanent critique and what is nowadays known as deconstruction, which seeks similarly to occupy a system from the inside in order to expose those points of impasse or indeterminacy where its governing conventions begin to unravel.[237]

Habermas's studies were such that they broadcast Marxist thought and stratagems across disciplines, for just as he and those associated with the Frankfurt school sought to gain influence, so too did this influence blur the lines traditionally isolating Marxist theory. From this critique, a commentary on the superstructure involved in the reproduction of language *as such* developed, for it appears as though, through an emancipatory form of Freudian analysis (continuing to muddle the distinctions previously kept in place), we discover that

> pathological behavior, in which our words belie our actions, is thus roughly equivalent to ideology's 'performative contradictions.' Just as the neurotic may vehemently deny a wish which nevertheless manifests itself in symbolic form on the body, so a ruling class may proclaim its belief in liberty while obstructing it in practice.[238]

Just as in psychoanalysis, an understanding of the symptom itself is important, but so too is the origin of such a symptom, so as to be

---

237 Ibid., 131.
238 Ibid., 133.

capable of treatment. This approach is one that attempts to cause a hiccup whereupon the 'manifest content' of the language itself becomes disjointed from that which it naturalizes, and brings the contradicting or otherwise complacent force into view as the hiccup itself. Habermas would spend a great deal of time and later work grappling with issues of ethics which he saw as unifying his theory of communicative rationality, and thus honing his arguments as far as they could go.

The interest in the use of psychoanalysis in approaching ideological critiques did not however die with Habermas, for so too did Freud (and Lacan) influence one of the final giants who made his mark upon the historical development of the critique of ideology: the Algerian-born philosopher Louis Althusser. Althusser's theoretical approach to such a critique took a further step back in rejecting a great deal many presumptions which, at this point in Marxist history, naturalized themselves within the context of Marxist thought. The presumption of humanism was most difficult for Althusser to agree with, as he believed this to be a rigidly ideological notion that unjustly elevated human status, infused with Aristotelian essentialism. However, despite their similarities, the spheres of influence between Habermas and Althusser could not be more disparate, for where Habermas described deconstruction as one of the primary tools of 'uncovering' ideological governance, Althusser took the complete opposite direction as the primary architect of structural Marxism, a train of Marxist thought that utilized the tools of structuralism, which can be described as

> fundamentally a way of thinking about the world which is predominantly concerned with the perception and description of structures . . . As a developing concern of modern thinkers . . . it is the result of a momentous historic shift in the nature of perception . . . particularly in the field of the physical sciences . . . The 'new' perception involved the realization that despite appearances to the contrary the world does not consist of

independently existing objects, whose concrete features can be perceived clearly and individually, and whose nature can be classified accordingly. In fact, every perceiver's method of perceiving can be shown to contain an inherent bias which affects what is perceived to a significant degree. A wholly objective perception of individual entities is therefore not possible: any structuralism and semiotics observer is bound to create something of what he observes. Accordingly, the relationship between observer and observed achieves a kind of primacy. It becomes the only thing that can be observed. It becomes the stuff of reality itself. Moreover the principle involved must invest the whole of reality. In consequence, the true nature of things may be said to lie not in things themselves, but in the relationships which we construct, and then perceive, between them . . . It follows that the ultimate quarry of structuralist thinking will be the permanent structures into which individual human acts, perceptions, stances fit, and from which they derive their final nature. This will finally involve what Fredric Jameson has described as 'an explicit search for the permanent structures of the mind itself, the organizational categories and forms through which the mind is able to experience the world, or to organize a meaning in what is essentially in itself meaningless.'[239]

Social structures and the relations which produce them become the focus of study, rather than the subjective and individualistic approach which Marxists had largely been taking until the advent of Althusser's work. One of his primary goals was to create an objective science of history, defending Marx's thesis that class struggle is the motor of history as a

---

239 Hawkes, Terence, "Introduction," in *Structuralism and Semiotics* (London: Routledge, 2005), 6-7.

fundamental building block thereof. This is possible due to Althusser's rigid belief that science is differentiated from ideology as some type of 'pure' labor which somehow exists outside of the conditions of history and is free from subjection to human ideological imposition. In this science of history, man is constituted as a subject by ideological social relations which impose this subject-form so as to allow ideology's persistence through history itself, and thus is the principal aim of criticism (especially turned toward the increasingly humanistic approaches which historical Marxism had adopted).

All of this led Althusser to approach the formation of a concept of *interpellation*, which describes how formalized institutions and restrictions in a society give way to the condition of individuals as subjects unto themselves whose very identities are constituted through the social interactions that are always-already predisposing individuals to their classification as an ideological subject. He argued that ideology has a material existence which manifests itself through actions, and that this notion of interpolation transpires through a material chain of relations rather than something that happens to an individual in their pure state of being upon encountering an ideological grip around its throat. He thus seeks to elaborate the notion of the material existence of ideology as the process through which a society establishes its subjects by way of ISAs and Repressive State Apparatuses (RSAs). These infrastructural systems are maintained by the ruling class so as to dominate the working class by force; e.g., the RSA which functions by way of political, legislative, or armed repression of politics and organizing strategies. Those who threaten to upend the social order which maintains the class distinctions favoring those already in power are also targeted through social ridicule and self-repression by the expression and imposition of the ideological order of hegemony. This is primarily done through ISAs, which function by definition in a more diverse and wide-ranging mode of operation. These are prototypically schools, media outlets, churches, clubs, and all the way down to the family, and are thus divided from the formal measure of the state as in the RSAs. ISAs function at more of a psychological level, and have a self-distancing feature whereby they naturalize and narrativize the formal oppressive nature of the state as found in the RSAs.

All of this he posits at the same time that he elaborates the backdrop of Marx's conception of historical materialism stating that "history is a process without a Subject or a Goal where the given circumstances in which 'men' act as subjects under the determination of social *relations* are the product of class struggles. History therefore does not have a Subject, in the philosophical sense of the term, but a *motor*: that very class struggle."[240] This reproach of the Hegelian Absolute's effect upon earlier Marxists, as well as the Western brand of Marxism which now flourished amongst his peers, was a way through which Althusser's constant dismissal of humanitarian excess carried his thought and differentiated it from the influx of popular Marxist thinkers at the time. It also marked a shift from his early works, which tried to reconcile Marxism and Christianity as well as maintaining a somewhat positive outlook on Hegel, which he would later denounce even in its slightest appearance in Marx's early work (down to Althusser's later admission that Marx never truly escaped Hegel's dialectic). It also, however, left his theories with a constant set of tensions, which allowed for Marxists on either side as well as intellectuals outside the tradition to approach his work with heavy criticism. They argued that Althusser's work maintained an ideological character all of its own (such as when he theorizes the eternal qualities of ideology as well as its persistence in communist communities[241]) and that he conflated and was ambiguous regarding already-vague Marxist terms.[242]

As this history enters the twenty-first century, the theory of ideology will receive mainstream popular attention. This is granted by a major facelift to its otherwise formal intellectual approach, having previously arrived there by divorcing itself from being at the forefront of the working

---

240 Althusser, Louis, *Essays in Self-Criticism* (London: New Left, 1976), 99.

241 Eagleton, *Ideology*, 149.

242 Kolakowski, Leszek, "Althusser's Marx," *Socialist Register* (1971), 111–28.

man's mind, as it had taken itself to be with Marx and those immediately following. This popularizing is due to the work of the Slovenian philosopher, Slavoj Žizek, who infused the lineage of Marxist theory with film criticism and cultural theory, as well as being involved in the creation of films which themselves serve as introductions to his work. His approach to a criticism of ideology is necessarily concerned first with Lacan and Hegel, although more often than not his approach is quite unorthodox, bringing many philosophers to suggest that Žizek is not in fact writing about Hegel at all. Yet at the same time, those devout psychoanalytic thinkers who approach his text suggest the very same for Lacan, that Žizek is using Lacanian psychoanalysis as a mouthpiece for his very own Hegelian philosophy. While Žizek has agreed that he maintains a very unorthodox Hegelian approach to philosophy, it is clear that through reading his work, the questions of the value of an 'authentic' reading of Hegel, as well as the authority behind such an articulation become reversals of the investigation into his work, which in and of itself is a microcosmic example of the philosophic games that he so often plays with his audience, navigating his own complex relationships with the material he speaks from.

Nevertheless, this approach has become one of the most influential and wide-spreading conceptions of ideology, one that in many ways echoes Althusser, stating that ideology is an unconscious endeavor that is justified through symbolic rituals and apparatuses, which in turn generate the social conditions necessary for the reproduction of the authorities already in power. This unconscious endeavor maintains the hegemonic representation and reproduction of subjects by a dominating and self-organizing power. In this way Žizek's approach to the concept itself is strictly Marxist. He says

> [f]or me, ideology is defined only by how the coordinates
> of your meaningful experience of the world, and your place
> within society, relate to the basic tensions and antagonisms

of social orders. Which is why for me no attitude is *a priori* ideological. You can be an extreme materialist, thinking that economic development ultimately determines everything; then you are truly ideological. You can be a fanatical millennialist religious mystic, and you are, in a certain way, not outside of ideology. Your position can be that of perfectly describing the data and nonetheless your point is ideological. For example, I would like to use the wonderful model of Lacan. Let's say that you are married and you are pathologically jealous, thinking that your wife is sleeping around with other men. And let's say that you are totally right, she is cheating. Lacan says that your jealousy is still pathological. Even if everything is true it is pathological, because what makes it pathological is not the fact that is it true or not true, but why you invest so much in it—what needs does it fulfill? It's the same with the Jews and the Nazis. It is not a question that they attributed false properties to the Jews; the point is why did the Nazis need the figure of the Jew as part of their ideological project? It is clear why: their project was to have capitalism without individualism, without tensions, capitalism which would magically maintain what they thought previous eras shared, a sense of organic community and so on, so in order to have this, you must locate the source of evil not in capitalism as such, but in some foreign intruder, that through its profiteering just introduces imbalance and disturbs the natural cooperation between productive capital and labor.[243]

This explication of ideology is not only one that notes our necessary participation in ideology as always-already acting subjects with a given idealized persona, but also that we maintain some cynical distance

---

243 Dilworth, Dianna, "Interview with Slavoj Žižek," *The Believer* (July 2004).

wherein a correction is given to the well-known Marxist formula, "they don't know it, but they are doing it," but rather that "they know that, in their activity, they are following an illusion, but still, they are doing it."[244] This is a formulation of ideology in a postmodern society, wherein Marxist thought is regularly taught in high schools, and more cerebrally in universities and colleges, and yet ideology persists regardless, and perhaps as even more illusory.

This kind of self-awareness that ideologies tend to participate in merely acts as a register against which those who act in the name of ideology might seek to disregard or discredit criticism more readily, while actively propagating ideological end goals. This becomes the fetish-object of ideology, the "ideological disidentification"[245] whereupon the subject recognizes the authorities' power as derived from a symbol alone, and yet the subject nevertheless deems it fundamental to his own life and as such continues participating in ideology with his cynical distance intact. This all works together in a way that situates the subject as one who both recognizes those in authoritative positions as operating from a purely symbolic standpoint but also understands himself as restricted from this access by way of a deeper truth, which is disclosed by way of the master's signifiers. For Žižek these signifiers become the sublime objects which move the people to action, and consume their lives to such an extent that they might lay down their lives at an opportunity to serve this big Other.

This position may appear too reactionary or 'false' due to his dissent from new Left politics which claim Marxism as its own. Many from his 'own side' speak out against his strongly controversial and nontraditional approaches to politics which fly in the face of what they consider to be a continuation of the 'real' revolution advanced by Marxist thought, which is supposedly incompatible with psychoanalysis of any sort

---

244 Žižek, *The Sublime Object of Ideology*, 33.
245 Žižek, Slavoj, *Welcome to the Desert of the Real* (London: Verso, 2013), 218.

whatsoever. So too it appears that Žižek may be considered to be missing the pathological character of a traditional Marxist, and indeed due to this lack, it appears that he too might be yet another example of an ideological break in the utilization of a theory. This has caused many to consider Žižek's approach as something of a post-Marxist critique, which states that ideology cannot be directly confronted at the current stage it occupies due to the interminable deferral of power and its restructuring in alterior loci which resituate "the dynamics of ideology [which] reveal that power is not so much everywhere, but fundamentally elsewhere."[246] Power in this light becomes simply a secondary characteristic of "the intersubjective relation between king and subjects."[247]

One of the key focal points of this repositing of the condition of hegemony is that maintaining reluctance toward power regardless of where it is located provides an opportunity for a break to occur in the concealed cycle of reproduction. Žižek's heroic figure of Bartleby presents his argument as a

> kind of absolute impassivity against the Symbolic links the revolutionary potential of the political Act to the inertness of the acephalous subject through the gesture of self-aestheticization. By deliberately identifying with the extimate cause, the subject changes its relationship to its own drive determinants *athwart* any Symbolic constraints. This neosubject does not seek to act *on* the social field but rather to reveal its true relation *to* the social field—the relation of nonrelation—by explicitly appearing as the excessive dimension in itself and making visible what cannot be accommodated within the encyclopedia of the situation. In Badiou's terms, we might say that the

---

246 Poulard, Étienne, "Shakespeare's Politics of Invisibility: Power and Ideology in The Tempest," *International Journal of Žižek Studies* 4, no. 1 (2010).

247 Ibid.

subject makes of itself the *Event* of the revelation of the hidden dimension of the situation and, at the same time, transforms itself into the subject of the process of fidelity by sticking to its self-aestheticization.[248]

This seems to be what one can hope for in a 'post-ideological' era, wherein ideology is ever-present and always retreating from the finger pointing it out; where ideology is not expected to be wholly discarded, but maintained in such a way that its effects are minimized.

248 Rothenberg, *The Excessive Subject*, 186.

SIDE B:

DIALOGUE AND IDENTITY

INTRODUCTION

....

"This Logos holds always but humans always prove unable to understand it, both before hearing it and when they have first heard it. For though all things come to be in accordance with this logos, humans are like the inexperienced when they experience such words and deeds as I set out, distinguishing each in accordance with its nature and saying how it is. But other people fail to notice what they do when awake, just as they forget what they do while asleep."

—Heraclitus[249]

....

Upon recognizing the basic movement of ideology, one seeks to transition from unconscious devotion for an unrelated and detached universal to the development of authenticity and potential for phenomenological freedom in constituting their associations, relations, and perspectives. However, there exists a longing not yet realized, for in these developments' realization there comes nothing of a truly concrete character, and as such the individual in question seeks to form this substance (as it can only be found) extending outside themselves and into the community they find themselves always-already existing within. The individual sought to differentiate himself by resistance to absolute Otherness, which he understood as functioning through ideology as the rearticulation of each element of the individual. This is done while aiming at a totalizing habituation of function such that the only authentic element

---

249 Diels-Kranz 22B1.

the individual might find as it is in-and-for-itself is the very form through which this function is articulated. In some cases, as we have seen, this very form itself is called into question as a thing unto itself, as a part of the world which was oriented toward the negating capacities of the individual himself. Nevertheless the individual finds that he is not an island, and cannot diffuse this substantiation of unity that had come with his understanding of individuality or identity: for, upon seeking to actualize his understanding as an absolutely particular individual, he is confronted with a fundamental contradiction of his being, for his immediate approach in forming this substance is subject to cause the very identity to fall into the ideologies that they are attempting to flee. This is because this substantiation of identity is that which speaks to the experiences of a group within a given society as the bedrock which supports the pebble. This group as an identity is stumbled upon by way of an initial alienation and reflection back onto the self, occurring as the result of the specific contradictions of the individual in relation to the universal represented in any given society as conceptually present in either notion. As the individual turns toward politics and social structure to find through work a resolution to this internal antagonism, he will find that rather than what we find in the historic past, where such a group would seek to structure their politics around explicit manifestos guiding through principles of thought, those who engage in the politics controlled by identity aim at utilizing this identity as the foundation from which politics should be corrected. Indeed these sympathies seek to 'make the political, personal' as the feminist slogan preaches, thus inverting the universal/individual toward that which obliterates the particular at the cost of this individual identity.

The individual, in seeking a community through which his individuality might find expression in the form of a substance, offers up this very in-itself identity to a group, which promises a syllogistic fulfillment for the identity to achieve its for-itself. This results necessarily in the subsumption of the individual himself, because the for-itself cannot be purchased, as if through a transactional service it could find its fulfillment through the mere identification with one end of a syllogism. For the in-itself to achieve its content as well as its self-certainty by the achievement of the for-itself radically misunderstands both, which are won by the hard labor of Geist, and as such this guarantee sold to the individual is but an a-theistic indulgence. This is, in part, because both receive their actualization through the working out of the drive of understanding, and as such arrive conceptually or notionally whole through the process of the dialogical relation. This results from the deep immersion of one's self in the work at hand in fleshing out the antagonism present in the conditional relation. For instead of the work being done on the behalf of the individual, those who structure the group utilize an understanding of identity that flows from the purchase and homogenization of those within the group itself as a mere political tool to undermine and replace characterizations from hegemonic iconography: reflecting and representing their position as one which is controlled and policed by *the group itself.* This political tool thus remains the corpse of a system, speaking only with the surface tongue of the Old Law. Those involved with this type of political organization believe its actualization to be the primary way in which autonomy is restored to those disenfranchised and mislabeled by a society, and by way of such a group the individual is convinced that this is perhaps the only way in which self-determination may be granted. What this type of political motivation seeks to accomplish then is to generate a recognition via differentiation as a mirrored image of the struggle with ideology and the individual's own self-unity—and yet, by the very process through which the action of recognition is posited (explicitly qua differentiation *as such*) we come to understand that these politics seek not to find identity within the universal concept, but rather to be universally individual.

One of the reasons for this is that a central governing principle within identity politics proper is the belief in a Marxist false consciousness given to each member within a 'group identity' by the hegemonic, which distorts the ways in which groups understand their identity to be not only constructed, but led astray so as to habitually reproduce a situation of power whereupon those who benefit from the current paradigm will always continue to do so. The universally individual operates such that experience is the bedrock of their political organization, and as such a group might maintain virtue so long as there is a community which experiences the world and their professed identity's struggles as they do. This belief is one which fractures identity into politically volatile tools to be divorced from every related phenomenon until it is abstracted to a notion barely recognizable without utilizing the hegemonic narrative that said group believes bars them from achieving identity proper. This viewpoint finds identity capable of being universally constructed by a group in-itself, and through which an individual's totalized identity is constituted. This is asserted while maintaining that each particular unit of identity might be subtracted from the whole of one's being and utilized as a mask which the individual wears to represent the abstracted universal of the group as their own individual totality; or, as is the case with intersectional group thought, they might solder units from two or more identities together to represent a newer universal individual identity.

These formal and external compositions of identity are used without regard, but are given to the individual as if in fact authentically representing them, beyond even the individuals' capabilities, in the hands of the 'community' at large. Thus the radical idealism informing said group disregards the other's particularity and presumes that since identity is the wellspring from which their politics stem, they cannot, without possessing false consciousness, consist of particularity but rather mere individuality. It neglects to ask whether the individual can in fact deploy practical or moral reasoning, and in its stead presumes this as an eminent feature of all those who participate in their community *as such* by nature of their identity as it stands in-itself. As feminist philosopher Sonia Kruks puts it:

What makes identity politics a significant departure from earlier, pre-identarian forms of the politics of recognition is its demand for recognition on the basis of the very grounds on which recognition has previously been denied: it is *qua* women, *qua* blacks, *qua* lesbians that groups demand recognition. This demand is made irrespective of whether identities are viewed in essentialist terms, as inerasable natural traits, or whether they are viewed as socially, culturally, or discursively constructed.[250]

This is how we understand the notion put forward by many feminists who declare in varied terms that whatever your 'brand' of feminism is, it is justified by the very nature of its name, as long as the name and identity of the individual find some form of syllogistic relationality. Thus, there is a radical contingency that informs the feminist who fills out his or her content through whatever means *feels* representative to the individual himself. Kruks continues by stating that

the demand is not for inclusion within the fold of "universal humankind" on the basis of shared, human attributes; nor is it for respect "in spite of" one's differences. Rather, what is demanded is respect for oneself *as* different . . . identity politics tends toward what I call an epistemology of provenance. By this, I mean it tends toward an epistemological and ethical relativism . . . this tendency is grounded in claims about the group specificity of experiences and the exclusive capacity of particular identity groups to evaluate those experiences. Although important in enabling previously marginalized and silenced groups to speak, an epistemology of provenance can also be problematic. For it threatens to undercut notions of shared (or even communicable) experience to such an extent

---

250 Kruks, Sonia, "The Politics of Recognition," in *Retrieving Experience: Subjectivity and Recognition in Feminist Politics* (Ithaca, N.Y.: Cornell University Press, 2001), 85.

that possibilities for a broadly based emancipatory politics are de facto subverted. This often occurs even as calls for solidarity and coalition across differences are being made.[251]

Identity becomes merely a form, a signification of what the individuals themselves sought to manifest substantially, and as such the demand is not one for recognition but one of power (or one of tolerance on the road to power). This is so because recognition would be in relation to the individual hidden beneath the signification, for the obligations under this 'identity' no longer imply treating the particularity of the individual themselves through the mediation of their syllogistic status, but rather that of their signification itself (which is distant and detached from the particular by means of a feigned psychological dependency on the feedback cycle from hegemony to the projected signifier therein).

'Their place' in society denies the specific normativity which they find those outside of identity politics utilizing, for it is the presence of this lack that gives way to the process through which the individual's relationship toward himself is inversely invested into that of their in-group identity in total. Yet, as the group grows, there will be an increase in members who find themselves no longer represented under the primary title, or as the identity itself is fractured by the incredible number of particularities seeking their own image where now only one stands (as universal). The position of dictatorial power over their own representation is, however, prone and ready to collapse, for utilizing ethical and epistemological relativism, there is no bedrock upon which this 'substance' actualized by and in a community can be sustained, for if there exists an exclusive capacity of individual identity groups to evaluate those experiences, then the unifying claims as to the epistemological content of politics which reach out to a group of people diverse by definition must necessarily diverge from the particular elements of those who possess such a

---

251 Ibid.

capacity, and what's worse, the ethical charges which they carry against those they claim did them a disservice maintain relativity, and as such cannot be in any sense truly unifying.

This systematic distortion nevertheless must call to a reality in which things *really are in-and-for-themselves,* which ultimately grounds itself in an epistemological and ethical order which must be universalized in some capacity, such that recognizing it would be a possibility and acting upon it would be a necessity, both of which require interpretation through a particular series of concepts which necessarily are derived from those already articulating them as for-other. As a series of views through which concepts crystallize as universal individuals, there rises a natural defense of the group against critique and debate through a conglomerate of voices articulating the same individuality, which, in the views of those articulating, seems the hidden reality of the hegemony prior, which disgusted them to the point of their own genesis. Part of the 'armor' of the group's identity comes from the ways in which the category of identity is utilized in identity-based politics, where there is a propensity to flatten out identities wherein singular discrete parts of an individual's total identity are utilized as if divorced from the rest of the person. It makes up the target 'whole' of the 'universalized particular' which it says it represents, from each and every one of the individuals who make up said group, and mobilizes this iconography such that those who fit within the 'universal' of the form, but not the 'particular' of the group, suddenly are enemies of the 'universal' itself.

Within the group there are those who become aware of this fact and seek to reduce the flattening effect on identity caused by mobilizing a 'universal' or essentialist identity for political or social gains. They seek to do so by reorganizing the way the group represents itself and its members such that its initial homogenous character, around which the collective rally, becomes destabilized for the goal or aim of preserving uniquely heterogeneous sub-identities or intersectional identities such that they might exist in authentic relation to their identity without being consumed alive by the total identity materialized in name alone. However, despite the potential for this awareness, it is a double-edged sword by way of the fact that its understanding brings with it a knowledge that necessarily cuts at the foundations which the group itself established, and as such its adoption would require a major reworking of the total group formation as it stood in-and-for-itself. At the expense of the certainty with which the group understood itself and identified (around the individual), adopting this strategy pursues instead the truth of the particularity of all identity found within itself. Even should this revelation occur to those seeking to mobilize identity politics, the notion itself is something that can only be taken on by those who exist already under the umbrella of the initial concept, and what's worse for those who benefit from the operation of the group as it was established, such a reworking means losing out on all of the power which they had garnered for themselves, thus starting from close to ground zero.

With its internal prospects in mind, the group instead might seek to ground its sense of identity in that which was presented within the hegemonic understanding of identity, but here they find that an infinite regress awaits them. This is the case because this possibility of an identity directly for-themselves as such is barred by the consequential negating critique that caused a reflection into their own group identity. For example, the notion of biological determinism as largely responsible for the identity of a particularized group is asserted to be, by identitarian groups, either a pseudoscientific construct of the hegemonic in order to keep those of a separatist identity in line, or as that which cherry picks information aligning those who deviate with negative features so as to create a false consciousness relating in-and-for those within said group. More often than not there is an abstraction which takes place in the symbolic icon of the group, which is hollowed out of actuality and replaced with an unending potentiality relating toward positive features, and a disregard of potentiality for negative features. As such, more often than not, there is a universalizing of a particular understanding of said icon as it stands in-and-for those within said group, yet without particu-larizing the universality such that it might become concrete and capable of maintaining the quintessential quality of its function. What does this ultimately look like? Since there is an impossibility in the relation toward the concrete of the icon itself, and yet simultaneously a necessity involved in the utilizing of said icon in order to mobilize those underneath its shadow, there is a sense in which those under the icon are kept at a distance from the object, maintaining that it is simply a social icon ascribed to them involuntarily, which despite maintaining no element of Truth itself is necessarily taken up by them in relation to everything within society as it stands. The experience of the icon itself to those that it is ascribed to reverses the predicates of the social and biological such that it becomes the experience of a *necessary* social relation rather than of a *contingent* biological condition; iniquity is derived from a function of society which utilizes icons in order to subordinate individuals and their universal conditions under the domination of a series of icons that dictate a society at large. This is not to say that the necessity with which social relations are imbued is granted as truth, but rather, since in the eyes of the group as it stands, truth has been relegated to the sphere of relativity itself, it is merely a rule of engagement as such—one which does not reach back to any transcendent truth but rather a contingency in-and-of-itself, with the condition of being interlocked into a social relation, which itself stands as simply 'what is' until a revolutionary relation itself is formulated and implemented as its replacement.

As such, these icons in the field of universality which the individuals under them relate to (while maintaining the distance with which those who persist in their social usage feel) allow for an attempt at subverting the specific original notion within the universal such that the icon might become that which, while still constructed to serve a function within a giving society, now relays power into the hands of those who have reconstructed them as such. Rather than espousing virtue or articulat-ing a universal manifesto, attention is instead drawn toward the radical contingency of universal identity or social concepts, such that power itself might be reorganized and hegemony subverted directly. All actuality is reduced to mere potentiality; potentiality which is rendered by this transformation not just impotent, but sterile. However, since the signifiers which they seek to liberate through subversion of (or revolution against) permeate the totality of potential relations within a society as it exists, those within a revolutionary group seek to find themselves in opposition to the dominant narrative while using that which came to them *a priori* installed in society, language, history, iconography, etc. Their revolt is essentially always-already within the realm of the dominant narrative as such. Rather than being an empty signifier for each individual to fill with their own particularized actuality, they become notions related directly to those who stand in a position of power to dictate their content: that is, either they maintain and subvert the universal they thought they were fighting against within the public sphere, or they create a new notion which has the same limits but becomes redirected to that which they sought to actualize within their own life.

It seems if the path traversed is one whereupon the original signifier's continued use is sought, there must be a habituation of its usage as universalized and which must constantly be filled with content through those in power such that those who seek solace under its name might still find it in some sense fitting despite how society, iconography, and the like might evolve. If this path is denied, then the group must, it seems, habituate themselves as revolutionary against any cause as it may stand. Through this second path there is a constant need to denaturalize and obliterate the positive content within any epistemology that establishes notions of identity or of essentialist persistence of any form. This path then ostensibly hopes to keep the notion of a representation into or through hegemony from ever becoming actualized: yet this habitual revolutionary is kept from fully adopting a view this radical, for there remains a necessity involved in the utilization of these discrete notions. This is because, despite their claims that the use of these notions exists only by way of communicating through hegemony from which oppression and inequality result, there is nevertheless the whole of their self-consciousness which persists beyond them as an ineffable quality threatening to obliterate all they hold dear. Identitarian groups first find themselves in a situation whereupon their identity might be called upon in order to create a group in the first place, and second, habituate the relational limit of access by responding thereto. As such the nature of such a group structures its identity "in part by *ressentiment* resubjugating itself through its investment in its own pain, through its refusal to make itself in the present, memory is the house of this activity and this refusal."[252] Identitarian groups which are formed around this notion have within their very *being* an insistence upon the habituation of "entrenching, restating, dramatizing, and inscribing its pain in politics; it can hold out no future—for itself or others—that triumphs over this pain."[253]

The notion of such politics comes full circle as that which is again grounded in identity of a *universal individuality,* and is by way of this very grounding, one which misunderstands the relationality from said identity as that which one holds *toward* all that is Other, understanding this Other as he who restricts freedom and imposes limitations. This identity is one that believes it passively maintains a lived experience as the individual identity that the group speaks on the behalf of, and yet at the same time is able to step back out, over and against this particular identity itself in order to gain or achieve a holistic picture of the total presentation of the identity as it stands in its universality. The identity-based consciousness understands this totality as that through which the individual absolutely related to the identity at hand would become supremely free, autonomous, and yet simultaneously equal to all of those who maintain their own separate identities through their own group

---

252 Brown, Wendy, "Wounded Attachments," in *States of Injury: Power and Freedom in Late Modernity* (Princeton, N.J.: Princeton University Press, 1995), 74.

253 Ibid.

politics. They consider this identity somehow fundamentally parallel to their own cause, and as such the individual and the universal may both find actualization through each other without any core conflict. At the same time the explicit claim is that all that stands in their way is this Otherness itself: that is, the identity which is utilized within the praxis of identitarian thought in the first place seeks to "establish its identity by simple opposition *to the other* . . . it would already be a part of a totality encompassing the same and the other." In other words, "every representation is essentially interpretable as a transcendental constitution."[254] This transcendental constitution refers to the cognitive activities through which the object of consciousness's study is determined as that which the particular consciousness addresses it as. The conditions of knowledge are such that the immediacy of constitutional action does not itself fall within the constituted object of knowledge *for consciousness,* but is rather the groundwork from whence the two sprang.

Yet despite this, as Levinas writes,

> The collectivity in which I say 'you' or 'we' is not a plural of the 'I.' I, you—these are not individuals of a common concept— neither possession nor the unity of number nor the unity of concepts link me to the Stranger, the Stranger who disturbs the being at home with oneself. But Stranger also means the free one. Over him I have no *power.* He escapes my grasp by an essential dimension even if I have him at my disposal. He is not wholly in my site. But I, who have no concept in common with the Stranger, am, like him, without genus. We are the same and the other. The conjunction *and* here designates neither addition nor power of one term over the other. We shall try to show that the *relation* between the same and the other—upon which we seem to impose such extraordinary conditions—is language.

---

254 Levinas, *Totality and Infinity,* 38.

For language accomplishes a relation such that the terms are not limitrophe within this relation, such that the other, despite the relationship with the same, remains transcendent to the same. The relation between the same and the other, metaphysics, is primordially enacted as conversation where the same, gathered up in its ipseity as an 'I,' as a particular existent unique and autochthonous, leaves itself.[255]

It is understood that the relation between the same and the other need not form a totality *as such*, but rather can persist in the possibility of infinity. It is the call of an earnest engagement to transcend the rudimentary egoism involved in the most abstract and basic modes of being, which operate from that "famous naivete of its thought, which thinks 'straight on' as one 'follows one's nose.'"[256] This naivete is that which misunderstands its genesis, which sprang from pleasure *itself*, and what's more while living out and actualizing this particular totality, the individual who seeks to engage the world 'directly' thus continues misunderstanding the genesis of all that surrounds it. Despite this, the individual attempts to traverse all that resists his totalizing gaze while operating from a rigid sentimentality, and neglecting discipline. He neglects the conditioned nature by which his own existence operates, due to its formation within the force and understanding that transpire as a result of the Other's action and expression, thus causing affect, rather than mere effect. The desire to draw all within our own will is this desire for control and mastery as a totality derived from egoism.

It is thus *ipso facto* a reduction of human existence, and one which accounts for nothing beyond the scope of one's solipsistic sensual desires (try as many might to intellectualize them through largely unsuccessful and incoherent ontologies or doctrines of metaphysical groundwork).

255 Ibid., 39.
256 Ibid., 36.

This totality which gives meaning to identitarian politics denies the constitution of Being through an always-already situated state relating to the Other, and neglects the possibilities of intersubjective fraternity while maintaining emphasis on an ever-shifting individualization. It may be said that such identitarian politics deny responsibility outside of a solipsistic representation of mere totalizing identity. This is, in part, what Hegel refers to when he speaks of "the realization of the immediate *undisciplined* nature [which] passes for a display of its excellence and as productive of the welfare of humanity."[257] This of course operates directly in opposition to the 'alien necessity' which orders the structure of the real world as such and against _____ which is thrown the negative content that this realization seeks to undermine by relegating it into the alien necessity's essence. It presumes, in its naivete, that the humanity that suffers and cannot help itself against the hand of this alien necessity (which to those under the identitarian political banner is the embodiment of irrationality itself) must be helped by way of reorganizing the real world, such that it reflects the sentimentality felt within their very hearts.

It is obvious to anyone who has understood the preceding analysis that this modicum of relationality maintains a dissonance within the individual, such that, to use Hegel's terms, the law of the heart from which they operate is at odds with the "alien necessity" of the law structuring the real world as such. Those under the law of the heart find that their

> humanity which is bound by this law does not live in the blessed unity of the law with the heart; but either lives in their cruel separation and in suffering, or at least dispenses with the enjoyment *of itself* obeying the law, and lacks the consciousness of its own excellence in *transgressing* it. Because that authoritative divine and human ordinance is separated

257 Hegel, *Phenomenology of Spirit* (trans. Findlay), 222.

from the heart, it is for the latter a mere show which ought to lose what is still associated with it, viz. the power of authority and reality. In its *content* it may well by chance agree with the law of the heart, and then the latter can submit to it; but for the heart, what is essential is not the bare conformity to law as such, but that in the law it has the consciousness of *itself*, that therein it has satisfied *itself*. Where, however, the content of universal necessity does not agree with the heart then necessity, even as regards its content, is in itself nothing and must give way before the law of the heart.[258]

It would be hard to find many who would be pleased to involve themselves knowingly with bare conformity for its own sake, but it is nevertheless upon utilizing this sentimentality that those involved think that its utilization will arrive at something greater than itself. This is what is promised to those persuaded into this sentimentality through empathy. This something greater is of course principle or virtue as such, no longer merely guided by sentimentality: the necessity involved in the law they oppose counter-posed to their sentimentality acting *as if* it were in fact principle or virtue in-and-for-itself. What's more, in order to install the law of the heart into the ethical community surrounding them (this same alien necessity) we find that what divines the law of the heart as such is its relation to direct subjective sentimentality, which, of course, when installed in a community as law, finds itself transposed in such a way that the relation dictating its existence in the first place has all but vanished.

The individual must face the alterity found in relation to this 'unity of the law' which they themselves have established, while understanding that their previous attempts to resolve the tension of harboring such sentimentality within their being have all but failed, and as such there is

---

258 Ibid., 222.

always the demand that they make for themselves which plunges them head first into their own projects attempting to fulfill this demand. At this point they have convinced themselves entirely that they are to renounce their individual happiness and seek to transform the world such that it conforms to the image found within the demands of the law of the heart. They seek to establish the expression of the law of the heart within the law of the world itself, and as such to revolutionize the established institutions and traditions such that they refract the well-being of humanity as they see it (pre-conceptually). As such, they become the individual who "speaks of the universal order as a perversion of the law of the heart and of its happiness, a perversion invented by fanatical priests, gluttonous despots and their minions, who compensate themselves for their own degradation by degrading and oppressing others, a perversion which has led to the nameless misery of deluded humanity."[259] Yet this sentimentality is one which always-already sets the individual against himself in its development. They desire to liberate the oppressed humanity, and yet at the same time recognize the sentimentality which constructed the law of the heart as what is and will be valid for all, yet from this we find that "what the individual brings into being through the realization of his law, is not his law."[260] This realization of the law of the heart which the individual believes that he alone has found is deceptive on both fronts, for not only is his transposition of individual law to universal law immediately contradicting universal law *as such*, but it also contradicts the individuality that it itself was founded by, for "others do not find in this content the fulfillment of the law of their hearts."[261]

This law, brought from the individual law of the heart and transposed into that of the universal, is the institutionalization of that state of the

---

259 Ibid., 226.
260 Ibid., 223.
261 Ibid., 224.

ethical substance whereby any and all who possess a similarly driving sentimentality might lay claim to their own immediate revelation as such, and transpose their individuality as universality, thus producing "a universal resistance and struggle of all against one another, in which each claims validity for his own individuality."[262] The law, which transpires at the level of universal, is that which as law in general neglects its own terms of installation by which general law is *in its very name* for everyone, and itself becomes perverted.

> On the one hand, this ordinance proves itself to be a law of all hearts, by the resistance which the law of one individual heart encounters from other individuals. The established laws are defended against the law of an individual, because they are not an unconscious, empty, and dead necessity, but a spiritual universality and Substance, in which those in whom this spiritual substance has its actuality live as individuals, and are conscious of themselves; so that even when they complain about this ordinance as if it went against their own inner law, and maintain against it the opinions of the heart, they cling to it with their hearts, as being their essential being; and, if this ordinance is taken from them, or they place themselves outside it, they lose everything. Since it is precisely in this that the reality and power of public order consist, the latter thus appears as the self-identical essence alive in everyone, and individuality appears as its form. But this ordinance is equally a perversion.[263]

The very nature by which the law maintained its own stability loses itself to the frenzy of all who fight for their individual representation by and

---

262 Ibid., 227.
263 Ibid.

for whom the law is to serve as a universal law of some abstract collective of hearts, which each individual claims as that which flows from their particular heart. Only when we come to find the fall of what was established through the interaction of those who came before us do we come full circle, for now we understand this demand for representation within a totalizing icon as the resistant individual in the face of a totality that has been silent in the face of suffering, is rather one moment of the war amongst plurality as such, whose end is similarly the end of the reproduction of individuality itself.

We see the strict disavowal of an agreement by which standards for conduct had come to be realized as the virtues by which individuals make sense out of the way of the world itself, and by way of compromise, that which mediates the universal and the individual came at the resulting ethical community whose very goal was the happiness and freedom of the citizens that it came to encapsulate: and yet, as Hegel shows us, an ethical community, like that of Ancient Greece, turns out to be not much better, for there is a clash between overriding ethical imperatives that govern the individual and the universal on a much larger scale growing out of the naivete that guided the politics of identity. Hegel writes: "At the centre of the greatest tragedies of Aeschylus and Sophocles we find not a tragic hero but a tragic collision, and that the conflict is not between good and evil but between one-sided positions, each of which embodies some good."[264] What is tragic here is not the fact that there is conflict at all, but rather the ways through which this conflict is generated: the very nature of the conflict within a society which unreflexively adopts positions on either side of this divide, immediately necessitating action. This tragedy is produced through the fact that the very identities and social roles (which the individuals as part of that society understand as expressing their being) are experienced as immediate, determinate,

---

264 "Hegel's Ideas about Tragedy," in *New Studies in Hegel's Philosophy*, ed. Warren E. Steinkraus (New York: Holt, Rinehart and Winston, 1971), 202.

and immutable, and which immediately come into conflict with one another, and yet are constituted by way of a misrepresentation of the authoritative grounds by which the very laws and customs themselves come into being. There is a production of the totality of laws, touchstones, establishments, identities, and the like with an incontestability that constitutes the individual by way of implicit rules and forms of policing which vary from identity to identity, and which overlap in significant ways. To compact the problem, the relationships and practices by which the disagreements about these laws and customs might be rectified are upheld by an authority which is not understood as maintained, shaped, or guided by the actions of those within the community itself, but as a part of the very essence by which the zeitgeist itself has taken shape, and from which the individual as actor has no autonomy within or toward.

This understanding of the self as lacking autonomy is, in part, drawn through a conception of the individuals living in said society understanding themselves *qua* personhood, thus defined in terms of legal status, property, and production. The individual now *has* or *possesses* instead of *being* and *acting*, and thus loses his sense of character when finding his being through this legal conception, for here he is no longer a family member or a citizen of the state through which they maintain positive content, but rather a descriptive container emptied of content which their atomistic legal status alone cannot fill out. This culture of personhood is that by which the individual experiences alienation in every fiber of his 'having'; for in this stage there is no more formal law: no divine or manmade law, but law as law itself wherein equality becomes totalizing and featureless when related to identity and is its very own 'night in which all cows are black.' It may then be that the individual is brought to a higher point of signification while the community is lowered, and yet, due to this, the individual is now capable of receiving a mere formality of recognition: one whose content (that of a legal right) can never satisfy. This becomes the total shape of the individual, whose personal content is emptied and left to the passions and caprice of the individual themselves (which are, in large part, limited to those dictates of the productions of personhood and its rulers) and whose rights are merely maintained, for they are the only matter about which the government is concerned: ownership. This self-conception which actualized itself qua legal recognition in place of the social roles which previously garnered individual recognition, has for itself the defining character of legal property, or the individual's status as a legal entity, which never comes to fruition, and as such finds itself sorely lacking in any semblance of political community.

In this sense, then, the political rulers are in fact the embodiment of the authority of the state: the individuals who make up the state itself are given a way to understand the emptiness of legality. For laypeople there is a contingency seen behind the rulers such that their rule is arbitrary. To those under this rule, might does indeed become right by way of that very arbitrary nature that they understand as having led to the current regime. Yet this is not the endpoint of society, for in fact what "was supposed to be the perversion of the good because it had individuality for its principle" instead finds that "individuality is the principle of the *real* world; for it is precisely individuality that is consciousness, whereby what exists *in itself* exists equally *for an other*; it does pervert the unchangeable, but it perverts it in fact from the *nothing of abstraction into the real of being*."[265] *For* the individual himself manifests principles in all action, and as such maintains a realization of individuality through the interplay of the universal. This compromise between individuality and universality is such that if standards are raised above the individual, then in part the individuality itself is made a sacrifice to maintain the totalizing standards, and yet, if universality (as a disinterested and detached form) is realized, it is only in and through the interaction and detrition of the individuals themselves. Those who live within such a society understand the requirement of the individual

---

265 Hegel, *Phenomenology of Spirit* (trans. Findlay), 233.

to follow a universal law which cannot be formulated *as such*, but must always be particularized in relation to the potential understanding or belief of such an individual (regardless of its relationality). The individual thus understands the laws relating to him as "laws [which] stop short at Ought" and which "have no actuality; they are not laws, but merely commandments."[266] This is because the laws as rules must be qualified in such a particular way such that they lose all definitive content, or at least lose said content within endless obscurity.

With the multiplicity of contradictions arising from the modern age, a new horizon opened upon the world such that the foundation of human study had undergone a radical shift.

This is such that the value systems, the epistemology, and the guide-posts of culture have become so weakened through this disintegration and distrust of the narrative of information in general, there becomes an infinite and yet untenable series of heterogeneous language games, which set themselves up and against each other in a never-ending play of series. However, since from within each game there are innumerable, non-fixed positions which the individual occupies, at the same time there are innumerable positions of subjectivity generating content and contexts for the individual, and yet from this no identity as such may be structured. Many theorists of the postmodern address this issue with a great deal of optimism, looking toward the possibility and potentiality like idealists of yore: however, as we have seen, there is a relegitimation on a micro scale, through which the individual might become universal, and have justification from the subject as universal subjectivity as we saw with identity politics. What's more is that, despite understanding the rise of the age which has just come to prominence against which their identities (as structures of the postmodern) are set in opposition to, and though it has now passed, a great many believe it to still permeate every aspect of their lives, and against which many believe the critiques of this bygone

---

266 Ibid., 256.

era must be maintained. Yet, as is apparent when any of these critiques are restated, without being given a guide that truly understands what our new era demands from a critique, merely wander naked and confused from door to door begging to tell the tale of a lonesome drunkard.

From this bygone era, a great deal many theories represent their found yet full formal expression such as through the conditions which Marx famously criticized as that of the commodity fetish, which saw the subsumption of the individual to the material production of labor, and from which their value to the community is dependent, and is thus reduced to an absurd nothingness itself. Under the relations maintained that produce such a fetish, those persons who succeed in achieving 'realization' through their production subsequently lose any relation to their individuality as it stands through their corporeal being in-and-for-itself. However, in noting this, those who seek to employ Marx's critique fail to see the many steps that have been taken since it was initially conceived; there is a failure to denote the explicit deployment and fetishization of identity, of one's sexuality as a mode of being, and largely of all ideological associations, which often maintain a similar affect. Many who still see themselves in a society of this sort understand this modern 'being' as that which is imposed on man through the technological era, though they fail to see that which Heidegger denoted as 'enframing' as *the* calculated and reductive mode of being. These persons stop short in merely repeating intellectual platitudes which, though perceived as piercing and insightful, only aid in examining a long-dead corpse, and provide little by way of nourishment to the consciousness which seeks to find a way out of the dissonance that limits and exposes its every action as meaningless.

There is a radical failure to understand that, in Heidegger's oblivion of Being, those whose primary mode of sense-making is that of machination have, for example, now shown the individual (non-reflexively) understanding sex as having no value beyond a physical transaction, between knowing and consenting adults. Nor is there any acknowledgment outside of the archaic, one-dimensional, and stale critique of feminists of yesteryear who notice, as if the shadow in Plato's Cave, media works which overload the system as advertisement for more and better bang for their buck. This is simply to say that the foundation of Being (for those beings enthralled in the system of machination) does not inaugurate: it is auto-affection as hetero-affection; it is the libido brought out of its ready-to-hand status, and the guise in which this oblivion is brought forth. However, even should those persons from a bygone era see behind this curtain, they would understand none of this, and simply reduce it to a motto that they believe is the same: "sex sells." Both speak of an economic relation of the 'noble' salesmen (here wealth and power) to those of the base 'consumer,' but the slogan is radically reductive and misses the bare materialist conception of sex which in-and-for-itself is that which undermines every aspect of one's being (i.e., the oblivion of Being). Suddenly children's books, heroes, and our moral and cultural leaders are reduced to mere standing-reserves which not only produce desire for the ineffable content of the simulation, as if a technological erotic transubstantiation, but also this reduction becomes the essential swaying of being, one which is reproduced in the Other by way of communion.

Those persons who invariably miss this information are those who understand this alienation from their libido by means of its status as ready-to-hand (as noted above, it is now mere auto-affection as hetero-affection), as if this amputation was itself progress, as if it were the very means by which liberation of the individual's pure will was somehow achieved. These persons are merely the efficient potentiality within a given system (in this case the machination of the culture industry's spectacle) within which sex is a self-service system: one built on efficiency and repetition through 'progressing' levels of semiotic reprieve, such that the individual may have their libido organized towards maximal satisfaction as utility itself. Within the system of media works, the libido may function at the simulated level of bacchanalian gluttony previously only known to emperors and kings, and yet without asserting the will, self-consciousness as law, or bare function of semiotic power assigned to them: hence as mere utility itself. The individual need not (as a layperson who should have scrapped together enough such that he might find a mate of modest order) cultivate skill, talent, or thought and may simply tumble into the system of media works, without a care or thought in the world, and through which they are promised a habitual simulation of 'more and better bang for their buck.' This mode of Being is such that one can find within media-works as a system of technics that there is in fact "a teleologism in [these] technics linked to the principle of tendency . . . where the technical system develops in ever-growing complication and integration . . . as the phenomenon of concretization, that is, of their tendential path towards perfection."[267] As such, there is a leveling that takes place, wherein the semiotic content of the media works at hand are stripped of meaningful distinctions, such that the highest form of any content may be placed (and becomes readily available) next to the lowest form of any said content, and without the individual relating to said content in a way that can form those distinctions within itself, which are made merely a part of the system as a whole.

Personhood is reduced to a standing reserve of manpower, and the world around him a supply on standby for the use of the modern world's production. Yet against this empty materialist conception there can be no salvation found in the immediacy of the ethical community, for as Hegel showed through his famous section on morality in the *Phenomenology of Spirit*, the morally imperfect individual and that transcendent perfection at which he aims become mere presentation. Both the duplicity which morality fundamentally becomes and the imperfect individual's shifting stance reveals a lack of seriousness in the moral relation. This is exemplified in Hegel's swift reduction of Kantian moral theory to an empty formalism concerned exclusively with the law of noncontradiction and empty universals which have no application toward the particular moments of the

---

267 Stiegler, Bernard, et al., *Technics and Time* (Stanford, Calif.: Stanford University Press, 1998), 54.

real world. This void, which the ethical community represents to our now-worrisome individual, is compacted by Nietzsche's genealogical critique of the moral imperative of responsibility. This is because, as he points out, from that very demand to the adherence of social norms, as well as guilt's radical internalization, the individual himself loses an important sense of identity which is subsumed under the normative identity of "the public" (Kierkegaard), "the herd" (Nietzsche), and "the they" (Heidegger). And yet, this normative identity (and guilt associated with any kind of rule violation therefrom) was shown to be ambiguous, and largely relating to no-thing, nor any person as pointed out by Kierkegaard when he says,

> In the present age, the tendency is towards a mathematical equality . . . In order for leveling really to occur, first it is necessary to bring a phantom into existence, a spirit of leveling, a huge abstraction, an all-embracing something that is nothing, an illusion—the phantom of the public . . . The public is the real Leveling-Master, rather than the leveler itself, for leveling is done by something, and the public is a huge nothing. The public is an idea, which would never have occurred to people in ancient times, for the people themselves *en masse in corpora* took steps in any active situation, and bore responsibility for each individual among them, and each individual had to personally, without fail, present himself and submit his decision immediately to approval or disapproval. When first a clever society makes concrete reality into nothing, then the Media creates that abstraction, "the public," which is filled with unreal individuals, who are never united nor can they ever unite simultaneously in a single situation or organization, yet still stick together as a whole.[268]

---

268 Kierkegaard, Søren, *The Present Age* (New York: Harper Perennial, 1962), 59–61.

Yet, this organization of the individuals from their community to a 'public' is itself simultaneously aimed at policing and flattening the individual, and simultaneously removing the community from the equation.

Nietzsche characterizes this flattening as a result from the exhaustion of religion as a moral compass and overall source of meaning: he states that "God is dead. God remains dead. And we have killed him. Yet his shadow still looms."[269] As but the most famous of many iterations, Nietzsche here warns how, despite the seeming freedom that may come with the removal of the old system of meaning and morality, the movement itself can easily be used by 'the herd' to foolishly plunge themselves, and the rest of the world with them, into chaos and meaninglessness. This is at least in part due to the fact that morality to the herd seems to be nothing more than the will to preservation and nothing more, from which the individual is but a means to an end; thus the propagation of the herd continues and the individual is again reduced to a mere standing-reserve. This is done through the notion of equality from the vantage-point of morality coming from their collective will.

> The problem of 'equality,' while we all thirst after distinction: here, on the contrary, we are supposed to make exactly the same demands on ourselves as we make on others. This is so insipid, so obviously crazy: but—it is felt to be holy, of a higher rank, the conflict with reason is hardly noticed . . . One needed God as an unconditional sanction, with no court of appeal, as a 'categorical imperative'—: or, if one believed in the authority of reason, one needed a metaphysic of unity, by virtue of which this was logical. Now suppose that belief in God has vanished: the question presents itself anew: 'who speaks?'—My answer, taken not from metaphysics but

---

269 Nietzsche, Friedrich, *The Gay Science with a Prelude in Rhyme and an Appendix of Songs,* trans. Walter Kaufmann (New York: Vintage, 1974), §125 (181).

from animal physiology: *the herd instinct speaks.* It wants to be master: hence its 'thou shalt!'—it will allow value to the individual only from the point of view of the whole, for the sake of the whole, it hates those who detach themselves—it turns the hatred of all individuals against them.[270]

The individual is then reduced to sameness for the sake of the herd, and from which the herd attempts to manifest itself through the individual, and thus the individual becomes the site upon which the herd is begotten. The individual, in this abstract public, is maintained as a universal representation of those related to it and is thus able to deploy critique from the standpoint of all and none at the same time.

Hubert Dreyfus remarks that Kierkegaard's critique, while plenty scathing and brilliant for its time, is now ever more pressing when related to our present age, with the internet standing in as a more encompassing manifestation of 'the public':

> The new massive distribution of desituated information was making every sort of information immediately available to anyone, thereby producing a desituated, detached spectator. Thus, the new power of the press to disseminate information to everyone in a nation led its readers to transcend their local, personal involvement . . . Kierkegaard saw that the public sphere was destined to become a detached world in which everyone had an opinion about and commented on all public matters without needing any first-hand experience and without having or wanting any responsibility.[271]

270 Nietzsche, Friedrich, *The Will to Power*, trans. Walter Kaufmann and R. J. Hollingdale (New York: Vintage, 1967), 157.

271 Dreyfus, Hubert, "Kierkegaard & the Information Highway," lecture in *Kierkegaard & the Information Highway*, at UC Berkeley, October 15, 1997; available at www.ieor.berkeley.edu/~goldberg/lecs/kierkegaard.html.

Dreyfus illustrates that the current sphere of discourse is almost incomparable to the past, for 'the public' was seen as that which exists outside of political power proper. It had been seen by many as that which was void of partisan sway, and instead that which allowed for a purely rational reflection: that which held the feet of all institutions to the fire, and allowed critique to function properly as an 'objective' outside source. Dreyfus again reminds us of the parallels through the internet, where unconditional commitments are turned toward a risk-free game, a simulation where risk is forever displaced, as if in a video game or role-playing game, and from which only simulated commitment is worn, and held only as long as simulation plays out before us.

True commitment is inhibited, and the divide before it is spread ever more widely. The internet and the public writ large are iterations of Heidegger's 'they,' which exists as an inauthentic mode of being in stark contrast to Dasein: it is what individuals engage in simply on account of it being 'what one does.' Thus, *das Man* is not an individual or a particularity that can be constituted in and through someone: it is an ambiguous 'they' or 'one' in the sense of an individual universal, as if the particularity and totalizing content flipped from what we saw with identity politics, and now the universal is said to be someone, but as a universal in that *das Man* is the vague authority without a genesis proper ('that's just what one does'), and an epistemology from folk conjecture ('one cannot know that').

Heidegger shows the range of the they when he states that "the 'who' is not this one, not that one, not oneself, not some people, and not the sum of them all. The 'who' is the neuter, the 'they,'"[272] for

> by 'Others' we do not mean everyone else but me—those
> over against whom the "I" stands out. They are rather those
> from whom, for the most part, one does *not* distinguish

---

272 Heidegger, *Being and Time*, 164.

oneself—those among whom one is too . . . By reason of this *with-like* Being-in-the-world, the world is always the one that I share with Others.[273]

There is the condition of always-already being-alongside the Others, although the I and the Other quickly fade into others in general. This is what Heidegger means when he states that "Dasein is for the sake of the 'they' in an everyday manner, and the 'they' itself articulates the referential context of significance."[274] In everyday life Dasein is not necessarily itself, but rather falls back into *das Man* and is, on Heidegger's account, individuated only by nature of its orientation toward its own death. This orientation is that which allows Dasein to stand out from *das Man*, for it pulls Dasein from the everyday conception of time as that which is present and instead orients him toward the future. This shifts him toward a possibility of his lack of being, thus allowing the individual to, looking back at his past, think forward to his specific future-toward-death, and thus reorient his focus.

This is because "anticipation reveals to Dasein its lostness in the they-self and brings it face to face with the possibility of being itself, primarily unsupported by concernful solicitude, but of being itself, rather, in an impassioned freedom towards death: a freedom which has been released from the illusions of the 'they' and which is factical, certain of itself, and anxious."[275] We find Dasein in one of its inauthentic modes of being-with-others (das Man) existing as that which maintains social relations generally, but in a way that hollows these relations or practices out and allows them to be completely disregarded by those who come after. Instead of helping to shape these practices, or to draw out what's best in them and continue to keep alive that which made them worthwhile

---

273 Ibid., 154-55.
274 Ibid., 167.
275 Ibid., 311.

in the first place, mere conformity leads to stagnation, and through this stagnation the original brilliance that once showed through may fade from the grouping altogether. From this decay it becomes harder to carry the attentiveness which we once held with each other, as well as the bond which led us to forge communal practices in the first place. Yet this attentiveness too loses shine through the public's approach to each aspect of society, which it inspects like a prison guard combing the hills for those who have escaped its grasp. You can feel the overt relationship to the Internet and other forms of new media when Dreyfus traces the concern among philosophers already addressing issues with a much smaller and less totalizing form of the "the public" when he states:

> As the Press extended the Public debate to a wider and wider readership of ordinary citizens, Burke exalted that, "in a free country, every man thinks he has a concern in all public matters." Many people including J. S. Mill and Alexis de Tocqueville feared "the tyranny of public opinion" and Mill felt called upon to protect "nonconformists from the grip of the Public itself." According to Habermas, Tocqueville pointed out that "education and powerful citizens were supposed to form an elite public whose critical debate determined public opinion."[276]

Culture once again becomes conflated with pure consumption. In this world of endlessly fresh productions of 'news' which the individual is obliged to have a stance on, thus branding his identity by way of his consumption. Through sheer volume alone, he is prevented from having enough time to form a substantial opinion.

The public holds sway in creating that which is consumed, and on its behalf "the Press speaks for [it] but no one stands behind the views

---

276 Dreyfus, Hubert, and Mark Wrathall, *Background Practices: Essays on the Understanding of Being* (Oxford: Oxford University Press, 2017), 220.

the Public holds. Kierkegaard wrote in his Journal: 'Here . . . are the two most dreadful calamities which really are the principle powers of impersonality--the Press and anonymity.'"[277] We need not here read 'anonymous' in the sense in which we are unable to place a face or name to the individual whose views are espoused, but rather that these are persons whose contribution to that which is larger than them disregards their voice as a particular, for

> the public is a body, more numerous than the people which compose it, but this body can never be shown, indeed it can never have only a single representation, because it is an abstraction. Yet this public becomes larger, the more the times become passionless and reflective and destroy concrete reality; this whole, the public, soon embraces everything . . . . The public is not a people, it is not a generation, it is not a simultaneity, it is not a community, it is not a society, it is not an association, it is not those particular men over there, because all these exist because they are concrete and real; however, no single individual who belongs to the public has any real commitment; some times during the day he belongs to the public, namely, in those times in which he is nothing; in those times that he is a particular person, he does not belong to the public.[278]

'The public' is an excess which supersedes the individuals who compose it similar to the same abstracted space where we found the universal particular occupying the relation to followers of identity politics. As Kierkegaard shows, the individual occupies multiple spaces at once, being both particular and universal: being abstract and concrete, and thus upon

277 Ibid., 222.
278 Kierkegaard, *The Present Age* (New York: Harper Perennial, 1962), 59–61.

trying to respond to the views, commentary, or critique employed by 'the public,' one can only ever sever a singular head of this our modern hydra, and yet from the chasm of the abyss it draws two more disposable identities in place of that which was freshly slain. This is because 'the public'

> consist[s] of such individuals, who as individuals are nothing, [and from which] the public becomes a huge something, a nothing, an abstract desert and emptiness, which is everything and nothing . . . More and more individuals will, because of their indolent bloodlessness, aspire to become nothing, in order to become the public, this abstract whole, which forms in this ridiculous manner: the public comes into existence because all its participants become third parties. This lazy mass, which understands nothing and does nothing, this public gallery seeks some distraction, and soon gives itself over to the idea that everything which someone does, or achieves, has been done to provide the public something to gossip about.[279]

As we saw, through the notion of machination, individuals *as such* are reduced to a mere standing reserve. When adopted under the totalizing view of that which stands in as a universal (for neither mere abstraction nor a particularized identity can fill out its identity, and as such are merely the equivalent of dense minds set about unraveling the mystery of a child's joke) they

merely desire the reproduction of their subsumption. And as the individual finds himself reprieved of the need to understand or act, they find their last expression of their individuality through the stimulation of their libido, which is often shared through community activities. This is the collective eroticization of figures from children's books, religious heroes, and our moral and cultural leaders which have become normative

---

279 Ibid.

and thus expressed beyond their conception in fan clubs, subcultures, and the like, and now often support the most mainstream of media works as if reflecting a fundamental of life itself. Here we can understand when Kierkegaard states that

> the public has a dog for its amusement. That dog is the Media. If there is someone better than the public, someone who distinguishes himself, the public sets the dog on him and all the amusement begins. This biting dog tears up his coat-tails, and takes all sort of vulgar liberties with his leg—until the public bores of it all and calls the dog off. That is how the public levels.[280]

This need not apply simply to the spectacle, which defines the society of these media works, but rather the commanding head of this dog, our Cerberus 'eroticization.' This is because eroticization extends beyond media and into daily life where one would find it near impossible to seek out any distinguished individual who does not have hordes turning their every action into that which makes them more desirable as a toy for others' libidinal pleasure. No matter how earnest, humble, serious, or otherwise decent the act or action taken by the individual himself, it will, without effort, find itself perverted and repeated through an infinite variety of means until its valuable content is drained and replaced with a doppelganger whose pure function is that of sexual stimulation.

The ultimate critique which results from the language games of postmodernism and is leveled against the hierarchy of the modern (that of the multiplicity of meaning resulting from various communities, and the incompatibility of the rules and formulation of these separate systems of meaning) nevertheless merely distilled and fermented its content to produce one's truth, one's morality, one's values, etc. Notwithstanding

---

280 Ibid.

keeping alive the aim of a focus on the differend as Lyotard sought to do (as that by which universalized ethical content is denied by way of a lack of agency, possibility, and language to articulate particular wrongs that exist exterior to the universal itself) there are erected instead particular universals. Despite the lack of and inability to formulate a proper ontology or epistemology, while still claiming that the localized language-games being played have ended the grand narratives of the modern, theirs is instead the formulation of a grand narrative itself which finds expression in the universal individual. This mode of tolerance as a political category proper has indeed turned toward rejection of difference, including any attempt to overcome the fissure through rational means, but rather through polemics of identity and their concretization within the popular to which the theoretical aspects of accepting difference and the use of language-games have become tertiary. By means of the popular, individuals were introduced to

> a comprehensive view of how hypocritically the U.S.A. saw itself circa 1960, [through which] early television helped legitimize absurdism and irony as not just literary devises but sensible responses to an unrealistic world. For irony— exploiting gaps between what's said and what's meant, between how things try to appear and how they really are—is the time-honored way artists seek to illuminate and explode hypocrisy.[281]

Here apathy became the primary mode informing the politics of those educated by this new wave of popular media. And yet where postmodernism founded its particular individuals through their unique standpoints as they were in-and-for-themselves (unlike modernism which sought to transcend those boundaries towards a true universal citizen), we find the

---

281 Wallace, David Foster, "E Unibus Pluram: Television and U.S. Fiction," *Review of Contemporary Fiction* 13, no. 2 (Summer 1993), 182.

imposition of the universal individual as the very bound itself, rejecting explicitly the transcendent goals of the modern, and instead blowing up the individual icon as that which now delimits the individual qua their very own representation. There is no longer any epistemic humility (which was postmodernism's original saving grace in the face of the absurd certainty which was its evidence against modernism on trial) but in its stead stood a bleak apathy which announced that truth is no longer that which the individual strives to achieve, but that which is inborn, and as such that which is disregarded outside of its 'natural' state.

Yet criticism with just as much weight began to surface undermining the more reasonable and predominant tools which presented a possibility for such a universalist individuality to take hold, such as that put forward by lawyer Suzanna Sherry and historian Daniel A. Farber who together claim that

> if the modern era begins with the European Enlightenment, the postmodern era that captivates the radical multiculturalists begins with its rejection. According to the new radicals, the Enlightenment-inspired ideas that have previously structured our world, especially the legal and academic parts of it, are a fraud perpetrated and perpetuated by white males to consolidate their own power. Those who disagree are not only blind but bigoted. The Enlightenment's goal of an objective and reasoned basis for knowledge, merit, truth, justice, and the like is an impossibility: "objectivity," in the sense of standards of judgment that transcend individual perspectives, does not exist. Reason is just another code word for the views of the privileged. The Enlightenment itself merely replaced one socially constructed view of reality with another, mistaking power for knowledge. There is naught but power.[282]

282 Farber, Daniel A., and Suzanna Sherry, *Beyond All Reason: The Radical Assault on Truth in American Law* (Oxford: Oxford University Press, 1998).

These critiques, in tandem with "material events like climate change, financial crises, terror attacks and digital revolutions," pushed post-modernism as the dominating influence of culture to a breaking point wherein it more or less gradually faded into a shared space of dualism with modernism. It has by "the appropriation of critique by the market and the integration of *difference* into mass culture" and "the diverging models of identity politics, ranging from global postcolonialism to queer theory"[283] fallen to the modality of provider of supplemental tools, rather than of dominant theoretical success; or, in what is to say the same thing, "the postmodern moment has passed, even if its discursive strategies and its ideological critique continue to live on—as do those of modernism—in our contemporary twenty-first-century world."[284]

It is from the sustained presence of both movements that a nuanced understanding of the purposeful tension of each side might provide a modified take on their channels so as to not fall into the trap of totaliza-tion. One might maintain a strong dose of cynicism which is founded in desire rather than an apathetically informed sense of irony as given by the postmodern.[285] Supplementing the tools of the postmodern are pillars of modernity like optimism and sincerity, which thus help to enable a way of being which seeks "to collapse distances, especially the distance between things that seem to be opposites, to recreate a sense of wholeness that allows us to—in the lay sense—transcend our environment and move forward with the aim of creating positive change in our communi-ties and the world."[286] To put it another way, there is a growing resolve between the two approaches, which do not necessarily culminate in a singular response, but rather into a time in which there is a demand for

283 Vermeulen, Timotheus, and Robin Van Den Akker, "Notes on Metamodernism," *Journal of Aesthetics & Culture* 2, no. 1 (2010).
284 Hucheon, L., *The Politics of Postmodernism* (London: Routledge, 2002), 165.
285 Vermeulen and Akker, "Notes on Metamodernism."
286 Abramson, Seth, "Metamodernism: The Basics," *The Huffington Post* (October 12, 2014).

the end to "the inertia resulting from a century of modernist ideological naivety and the cynical insincerity of its autonomous bastard child."[287]

There may in fact be an innumerable multiplicity of responses whose end reports the same resounding demand, for history has procured such intensive critique that the 'inertia' created permeates the totality of authentically singular positions thereby provided. The new tools of critique are available to all, whether they be local news reporters, musicians, or carpenters, for as we have seen throughout the history of consciousness (which Hegel documented in his *Phenomenology*), this dialectical deadlock generates intolerable tension for its historical citizens. The way forward seems as if it is taking shape by "treat[ing] history's grand narratives with just as much skepticism and mistrust as postmodernism does, but it simultaneously act *as if* these narratives can be known," thus "neither neglect[ing] the movements that preceded it, nor extend[ing] them; it oscillates between, forging ahead to form something entirely new and downright daring."[288]

What seems to be new here is born from the openness present where the two elements overlap, rather than being a gap from which something concrete forges its path directly in opposition to each side; as an alternate position it attends to both modalities and yet neither does it share in their condition of total identity. It is a multiplicity that is the unifying term of the set of multiplicity and singularity in the first place. This is then a moment from which it is challenging to say exactly what is dead and what is alive: it could simply be so late in the struggle that both positions have made compromises that leave open the range of potentialities for all points of view that there can no longer be any clear

---

287 Turner, Luke, "The Metamodernist Manifesto" (2011); available at www.metamodernism.org.extend[ing] them; it oscillates between, forging ahead to form something entirely new and downright daring."288

288 Bunnell, Noah, "Oscillating from a Distance: A Study of Metamodernism In Theory and Practice," *Undergraduate Journal of Humanistic Studies* 1 (Spring 2015).

differentiation among one side or the other. It seems that the beliefs and hopes long suppressed by the infinite skepticism of postmodernism, as well as the disappearing center (be that in terms of politics, the middle class, etc.) provoked a change of some sort or another. This change seems to be based around "the structure of the In-Between, of the Platonic *metaxy*, and if anything is constant in the history of mankind it is the language of tension between life and death, immortality and mortality, perfection and imperfection, time and timelessness, between order and disorder, truth and untruth, sense and senselessness."[289] It is from the phenomenological understanding of man as being neither fully interior or exterior (as Merleau-Ponty sought to show through the status of the body), through the historical understanding of being both/neither fully free nor conditioned, through the cultural understanding of being neither purely individual nor communal: we can see, from this vantage point, that we begin to understand what this both/neither potential is.

We can find its historical image when

> Hegel envisions a holistic form of conscientiously guided thought and expression, guided normatively by shared convictions and communal recognition, which preserve and embrace the contradictions within a holistically unifying attitude. When viewed against a background of shared convictions, a restorative unity is achieved within agents by virtue of their knowing that their convictions are shared by like-minded individuals. Admittedly, [this] is not a position which Hegel unqualifiedly endorses, or presents as a terminal solution, if by 'solution' you mean a criterion that eliminates the appearance of contradiction altogether in every rare, borderline case. In an imperfect world, good

---

289 Voegelin, E., "Equivalences of Experience and Symbolization in History," ed. E. Sandoz, in *The Collected Works of Eric Voegelin* (Baton Rouge: Louisiana State University Press, 1989), 12:119-20.

intentions come uncoupled from consequences, and when they do, they inevitably enable us in messy contradictions, ruptures, and errors. But conscience gives us a holistic way of understanding moral actions, as they appear unified through contradictory appearances in a way that doesn't eliminate, suppress, or deny the contradictions even at the highest levels. By accommodating the contradictory aspects of action in an organic unity, the ontic conflict in the act doesn't vanish. Conscientious identification and recognition remove the epistemic conflict within the agent (PhG 596). Moral conflict is just the local appearance of contradiction to be understood against the background of this deeper, organic self-unity.[290]

Ultimately, then, what is sought after is not a blind ignorance to the disruption of Being caused by contradiction in the self-conscious individual faced with opposing viewpoints, nor is it complacency with that which is destructive, epistemologically unsound, or that which is ontologically ouroboric. Instead, as we have been pursuing it, what is sought is rather that which itself is open to the possibility of difference through an "epistemology (*as if*) and its ontology (*between*) [which] should thus be conceived of as a 'both-neither' dynamic."[291] This also does not mean that the openness which the discourse itself is disposed to is that of the 'uncommitted' or that which by its nature flips between two pages of the text of Being without taking a stance. This is essentially the position of an ivory tower centrist taunting the world by claiming the most radical intelligence without ever taking an intellectual position.

Rather this is the potential which understands itself in relation to becoming as well as the self-cultivation which is metonymic of the culture

290 Hahn, Songsuk Susan "Hegel's Final Synthesis," in *Contradiction in Motion: Hegel's Organic Concept of Life and Value* (Ithaca, N.Y.: Cornell University Press, 2007), 195.

291 Vermeulen and Akker, "Notes on Metamodernism."

that it seeks to establish in its totality. Fundamental to this discourse is seeking "conscientiously guided thought and expression, guided normatively by shared convictions and communal recognition."[292] This of course is not the recognition of the individual as universal, as was the case of identity politics proper, nor is it a tolerance of a multiplicity of convictions, as was the case in postmodern discourse, but a genuine understanding of normativity, which is formulated by conscience and collectively shaped by the community that commands it. Thus it can in fact be an "attempt to turn the finite into the infinite, while recognizing that it can never be realized . . . 'that it should forever be becoming and never be perfected.'"[293] However, this should at the same time not confuse "this oscillating tension (a both-neither) with some kind of postmodern in-between (a neither-nor)."[294] This is to say that, while the critique of the postmodern has been to expose the failures of modernism (to transcend or to properly call upon the mysterious or sublime) through means of the negating neither-nor (and yet to subsequently open the doors for all possibility as its both-and ontological/epistemological position would encourage) the both-neither maintains a possibility, an openness that allows for a conception of function and limitation—an ability to call upon the frame itself and where the process of framing falls short, but also to see the purpose of what's framed, and the need of unification—a holistic understanding of what neither calls upon the heartbreak of the modern in failing to achieve, nor the mockery of the postmodern in their apathy, but one which seeks to find "the re-signification of 'the commonplace with significance, the ordinary with mystery, the familiar with the seemliness of the unfamiliar, and the finite with the semblance of the infinite.' Indeed, it should be interpreted as *Novalis,* as the opening up of new lands in situ of the old ones."[295]

---

292 Hahn, *Contradiction in Motion*, 195.

293 Ibid.

294 Ibid.

295 Ibid.

What's being situated here is the condition whereupon one is forced by nature of one's being as a human to take in and judge content, not merely to stand passively before the world as if in some sort of fanatic ecstasy. This is because such a thing is not possible (at least most of the time for most of us) and as such judgment is found pressing ever onward, as if in parallel canter with our breath. This is often given in deferment to those 'experts' whose treatment, so long as it doesn't conflict with one's first ideological commitments, is uncritically valued by name alone. As one comes to find the groundlessness situating the content of their judgments, the faculty procuring them becomes weaponized as pure skeptic negation or ignorant affirmation. What's worse is that the collective nature of either judgment is characterized under the dominant societal condition as legislative politicizing, from which hordes wage war against one another, as if conglomerates proved individuals: their warfare might be literally conducted at the level of legislation, and yet it is always-already in deferred reference to one's status as a fractal member of said group-identity, the nature of which is a mystery as challenging as can be found among the most obscure of mystics, and yet asserted in the self-confident rational terms of the Enlightenment. There must exist a network of relations vested as legal benefits to the individuals comprising each group, and yet each identity, by way of its failure to relate stature and personhood toward the individual fractures or hyphenates, thus loses power. In order to be understood as seriously engaging in an identity-sourced cultural battle, one must lose one's grip on the certitude from which one's identity is constituted, unless one is able to find their situated content within that of the both-neither paradigm from which function and limitation are understood as a positive construction allowing for the signification of Hegel's spatiotemporal dimension of the particular and the universal—the one and the many—and speaks to the virtual nature whereby the two are understood as inseparable. "This is what we might call the speculative dimension of the one and many, to distinguish it from the existential or rhetorical dimension. To it applies all the issues of determinacy, temporality, and logic that relate to the power of language to signify."[296] The nature whereby the rhetoric of meaning manifests as

> moving from a faith in the absolute to an acceptance of the inexactness of language, the privileging of the particular and the contingent, the metaphoricity of concept formation and the occasionality of speech . . . [we] . . . ultimately find [ourselves] back in the classical rhetorical polis, although certainly transformed by the journey. My cautionary claim about this return is that the circling back is not a *destruktion.* Whatever direction [we go] in, it is always tracking with a sympathetic resonance that picks up the harmonics of the tradition, in the same way that the notes of a stringed instrument in its lowest registers contain all of the overtones.[297]

The nature of language is situated in a both-neither framework with 'speculative reflection' which grants the truth of our being the possibility to illuminate the standing we maintain between the particular and the universal. This is what Gadamer's invaluable contribution to our current understanding shows us. In part, then, to understand the hermeneutic experience that he illuminates the path toward, we must look to the way that Gadamer "reinterprets Bildung's relation to the past (tradition and language) and the future (possibility and invention) through Heidegger's temporal ecstatic being of Dasein."[298] In explication: the experience of Dasein is given as fundamentally oscillating in the position of both-neither.

---

296 Arthos, John, "Introduction," in *The Inner Word in Gadamer's Hermeneutics* (Notre Dame, Ind.: University of Notre Dame Press, 2009), 10.

297 Ibid., 13.

298 Ibid., 18.

In contrast, those who long for the comfort of a singular concept as a monolithic identity find neither openness nor a position facing reality to be sculpted in reciprocity: rather this concept-identity is often the binds of a reductive grounding, from which one cannot avert one's gaze, lest one fail to maintain security. Otherwise such a stance may instead be the absolutely open frame, which allows all nondeterminate content to pass through, yet thereby remaining empty. This is the space of singularity either caught in the past as dead and gone, or dwelling ever within the future, a fantasy detached from reality and never allowing for the lived experience of man. It is rebellion against this modality of identity which is founded by the habitual work of living authentically within

> the reciprocating structure of being-in-the-world. Our informing form, which is "consciousness at work" working the world through works, [a]s simultaneously a coming to terms with the world and a self-forming human being is such that, "by forming the thing it forms itself" the distance between the agencies of the self and thing are actually generative, since, in a Hegelian sense, the alienation of spirit in time motivates the movement of the understanding. The basic character of Bildung is "to reconcile itself with itself, to recognize oneself in other being." The felt absence of what has been lost of us to ourselves through time, quoting Hegel, "contains at the same time all the exit points and threads of the return to oneself, for becoming acquainted with it and for finding oneself again."[299]

The empty platitudes of endlessly reproduced mantras and re-expressed facts become nothing more than the reflexive bark of the master who, despite knowing nothing of the work done under him, nor of how the material processes take their shape, nevertheless takes great pride

299 Ibid.

in announcing his position and the benefits and conditions resulting from his having taken possession of it. His understanding of his identity is constituted on and by the ink of the word itself, as if the text held within the atoms which constitute the form of the word were somehow constitutive of some discrete meaning capable of being extracted in isolation as a brute fact of the world.

This view fails to see that "language is not on the outside of the constitution of social meanings, but [is] its living meaning."[300] Part of the reason that these confusions of the everyday understanding of nonreflexive being (found in such notions as identity and group identity) arise is due to the difficulty in even coming to terms with the both-neither concept or its explication. For Gadamer, this difficulty is expressed through a type of language, the expression of which is

> *wirkungsgeschichliches Bewusstsein* [which is] an idea that . . . is untranslatable partly because it uses the particular resources of German to express a doubled over, folding back structure that is neither completely subjective understanding nor the anonymous intentionality of history, but something 'in-between' . . .
>
> [of which] . . . Weinsheimer offers an admirable précis [as] *wirkung* is related to *wirken* (knit, weave, integrate), to *verwirklichen* (realize, make real), and to *wirklichkeit* (reality, actuality). *Wirkungsgeschichte* is the reality of history in that it is the history of realization. What is real works in its working out, is *wirkungsgeschichte*. *Wirkung*, then, means work in the transitive sense. History is *wirkungsgeschichte* in that it works something or works on something: it effects and has an effect. The effect of history—its realization, its reality—is history itself. Precisely for this reason history always exists in relation:

---

300 Ibid., 21.

to its effects and hence to subsequent history, the course of events. The history of an event's consequence and effects is not something different from the history of the event but is rather the history of the event itself, its own history.'[301]

We shall see the concept itself teased out through the remainder of this present work, such that true understanding of the failures of recent conceptions of identity, community, and attempts at communication in general might make themselves clear, and these concepts thus might find their expression through the concrete and practical being found within the social and political community.

That is, we will find that

> understanding is to be thought off less as a subjective act than as involvement in the event-happening of what is passed down ... [thus] ... subjectivity is not the end-all, but only part of a participatory structure in which destiny plays an equal role .. . on the one hand "we are always already affected by history," but on the other hand, we are conscious of the hermeneutical situation in which we are surrounded. This is the positive case for the dog that chases its tail: "understanding proves to be a kind of effect that knows itself as such."[302]

However, Gadamer does seek to demarcate the limits of the reflexivity central to human intuition so as to keep the both-neither paradigm from relapsing into a singular moment or its other. This is because "we are concerned with understanding historically effected consciousness in such a way that the immediacy and superiority of the work does not dissolve into a mere reflective reality in the consciousness of the effect—

---

301 Ibid., 24.
302 Ibid., 25.

i.e., we are concerned to conceive a reality that limits and exceeds the omnipotence of reflection."[303] And yet, the immediacy of experience is tied up in the intuitive status of being as that fundamental element that neither identity, language, nor thought itself can exist without. This is somewhat the inverse of Avicenna's incomprehensible floating man argument whereby the existence of the individual as soul is inferred by way of something that is supposed to be pure reflexivity (embodied as it is in a more limited case of conventionally understood experiential perspectives). This notion demarcates all that is as personal possession and immediately relates experience beyond sensory fields to that which is abstractly defined as innate.

However, the experience of which Gadamer speaks is "a shared possession, the incursion of history into the person, the imprint of common human finitude, [and thus] experience is the learning of one's own finitude: 'the nature of experience is conceived in terms of something that surpasses it.'"[304] Following Hegel and Heidegger, Gadamer states, "What makes a limit a limit always also includes knowledge of what is on both sides of it."[305] This notion, as dull an insight as it may seem, is that which the common world of ignorant ideology and masturbatory identity, no matter how loudly they proclaim their transcendence, nevertheless remains severed from. Rather than operating from "the Socratic docta ignorantia, which is paradoxically both a vigilant humility and the wisdom that arises out of their humility, thus operating from both sides of the limit,"[306] the common ignorant belief seems content with pretend sutures, proclaiming divine wisdom regarding the totality of information around the limit and its supposed source of being, as well as the equally divined 'purely humanistic insight' that denies the limit

---

303 Ibid.
304 Ibid., 26.
305 Ibid.
306 Ibid.

at all, and seeks rather through various oppositions of the 'normative' to delimit all that is.

Thus in opposition to this perspective, the Socratic *docta* as well as Aristotle's *Phronimos* find their expression in "the basis of prior hard experience and knowledge of the constitutive indeterminacy of the future," and thus maintains a relation toward

> a cultivated openness to what is probable. This means that the *Phronimos* has both "a sense of direction" about the question in hand—i.e., what direction to face in addressing the question—and a deeply internalized sense of inadequacy before the question. The combination of two sides of the limit is expressed in a comportment that we recognize in the wise person what Gadamer calls a "readiness for experience." [We find then that] this comportment is formed under the pressure of awareness that we are less directing our own destinies than responsive to the questions that present themselves to us, and that these questions typically will remain "unsettled."[307]

In facing the requisites of intellectual humility and being at peace with the "unsettled" nature of the questions in pursuit, one divests themselves of blind devotion and pursuit of the explication of any resolution, be it positive (of the limit) or negative (without limit). Situated then as one possessing *phronesis*, there is a multiplicity in one's being-toward-language which opens (or rather holds open in the Heideggerian sense) language as the very site from which history and understanding may in fact find their concrete expression.

This understanding of language, it is important to highlight once more, does not consist in a radical, subjective, and private relationship toward text/sound/symbols against which all semblance of meaning

---

307 Ibid.

is constructed. Nor is it the simple-minded, direct, and immediate one-to-one relation of concrete meaning, affixed toward the real world, imparting meaning to those looking upon it with greedy eyes and inborn, innate relations toward said language. Gadamer states that "All this misses the point that the truth of things resides in discourse—which means, ultimately, in intending a unitary meaning concerning things—and not in the individual words, not even in a language's entire stock of words."[308] Unity, then, is yet eternally manifest through discourse, that is, through the transcendental act which is the meeting point of the many and the one, the historical and reactive, the universal and the particular. Understanding is this meeting place—it is the both-neither of discourse, of *logos*. Part of the way this mode of being operates is through the function of tradition in Gadamer's account of understanding. In one aspect,

> Tradition sets the normative context of inquiry for a community of learners. In this sense 'tradition' determines things such as which questions are most important, which have priority for a particular research community at a particular time, and it sets at least *prima facie* boundaries of what conceptual tools are acceptable in attempting to answer these questions . . . Such traditions are normative in that they guide communities or inquiry toward an epistemic ideal, an ideal that is historically grounded.[309]

Despite the perspective that many 'radicals' have of their operating over-and-against isolated and ignorant communities of traditions whose normative standards repress or oppress the 'pure and total'

---

308 Ibid., 27

309 Wachterhauser, Brice, "Getting It Right: Relativism, Realism, and Truth,"
    in *The Cambridge Companion to Gadamer*, ed. Robert J. Dostal (Cambridge:
    Cambridge University Press, 2010), 58.

freedom of being that they and whatever community of individuals possess by standing in opposition, they fail to note that their normative or interpretive standards are also conditioned in part by the very tradition they are reacting to, and as such they are prescribed either with accepting the concrete determination that guide their answers and continue to seek validation therein, or risk absolute incomprehensibility. Thus, while

> the space of reasons within which we offer justification for our beliefs is intentional in nature . . . [which] can only be understood as a product of extended rational reflection on experience, which presupposes that we can disengage from the push and pull of nature, and freely survey at least a part of that same causal network . . . [it must simultaneously be noted that] . . . such reflection is engaged in by humans over generations of inquirers and passed on explicitly and implicitly as the norms of a community of inquiry [and that] our understanding of such norms evolves historically within communities into which we are socialized and shaped through a matrix of language, practice, and individual and corporate experience.[310]

Many are quick to conflate social and absolute causation, for very few meditate on the notion that the social itself is largely within the sphere of human freedom, and abysmally less still (by even the small but radical margin of thinkers such as Judith Butler) that "these standards are 'recommended' to us; we are encouraged to 'freely' appropriate them, to make them our own, by demonstrating that we can 'apply' them intelligently. 'Intelligently' means that we do not ape them blindly, but apply them in new ways, which, despite their novelty, attain readily

---

310 Ibid., 59-60.

recognizable 'family resemblances' to the previous applications of such norms."[311] The suggestion to do away with the intentional "products of the reflective conscious experience of a community of researchers"[312] has been historically compounded by the mere whims of pure abstraction the likes of which, like Avicenna or Butler, arbitrarily subtract properties from material in a flight of metaphysical dissociation.

These fantastical thought experiments lead the learned to turn from history and language toward the use of cognition free from comprehensive grounding to dismiss norms as

> the result of a causal process that simply implanted [them] in us, which then continue to exercise their effects independently of our conscious reflection on them. Instead, it must be stressed that whatever causal imposition of these norms may have occurred in the course of our social formation as members of a community of inquiry, these same norms evolve in the space of free reflexivity that is generated whenever we think about our own thinking.[313]

The difference emerges between one who understands the authority of norms as that which "a tradition earns by demonstrating its value in the pursuit of knowledge"[314] and the other who fails to recognize that "we can say that authority is normative because it has the capacity to operate within our freedom and should not be conceived as simply imposed on us from a point beyond our freedom."[315] We find the same metaphysical ghost which the authoritarian writes into being (and thus which both he and the reactionary/revolutionary both impose, either positively or

311 Ibid., 60.
312 Ibid.
313 Ibid., 60-61.
314 Ibid.
315 Ibid.

negatively) as restrictive on both human freedom and knowledge. One states that there is no such thing as normative content—that norms are as arbitrary as the spoon chosen for supper—while the other reduces all of one's being to an essential and causally determined effect (similar to the corporatist who reduces all of one's being to mere production related to capital).

The hard opposition of the either-or dichotomy requires of us to make the norms to which we submit "fully transparent to our own reason and thus control the conditions of our own submission to them."[316] This hard opposition requires far too much and becomes like that which it opposes, for both sides (which radicalize human freedom and knowledge) fail to understand the finitude of which Gadamer speaks, for the true freedom of humanity cannot be that which knows "exhaustively the grounding of such norms, nor [can be demanded of it] that we be able to see in advance all the implications of such norms."[317] To do so would be to clearly grasp the totality of being from the vantage point of God, and thus would also preclude what is normally understood by freedom or autonomy. This naive view misses entirely that such conditions situate our freedom and autonomy "within an ongoing dialogue, which is the driving force of any historical condition."[318] When we speak of a both-neither paradigm, we are speaking in part to the reciprocal nature whereby we turn our gaze toward history and its tradition only after its gaze has been set upon us.

Hence, while our gaze does in fact speak to our freedom, it is not an absolute freedom, for

> even in critically revising the norm, its authority is acknowledged, even though we have freely modified it to fit the context of inquiry. The need to "tweak" the norm is not

---

316 Ibid., 62.
317 Ibid.
318 Ibid., 63.

necessarily evidence for its inadequacy, but may in fact provide evidence for its normative strength in the sense that such a norm demonstrates it is normative by its flexible applicability to diverse situations . . . [they are] . . . open, but binding.[319]

Rather than operating from the outside perspective of Gods, we argue from within the complex matrix of historical relations, and thus tend to see those voices which shape and change norms as those not external and alien to said matrix (for to truly be so would be to be incomprehensible) but rather as

demonstrating a deeper understanding of them. Otherwise we simply opt out of this conversation, which of course we can attempt, although it is not clear what space there is completely outside these norms. Be that as it may, if we seek the required, deeper grasp of these norms, we tacitly admit their normative authority over use; they have, as it were, a "grip" on us and their grip exceeds our grasp.[320]

Comprehensibility presupposes a link between understandings such that difference may be demarcated in its relationship to normativity. Thus "disagreements presuppose deeper agreements of a more general kind."[321] It is from this vantage point that we may understand the difficulty underlying the issue of the one and the many, for difference is that whereby perspective and cognition in free form abstraction take flight relying on a half-truth of sorts, observing the "sense in which all traditions occupy the same normative ground," yet ignoring that "they may very well occupy different pieces of it at different points in time."[322]

319 Ibid.
320 Ibid., 64.
321 Ibid., 65.
322 Ibid.

From the isolation of either perspective from its other, each is convinced either by its own assertion as to the direct access of man to reality, or the absolute relativity maintained by the use of language and the constitution of being that they understand themselves to have through it. They believe themselves to grasp the totality of their language, either in its relation to the outside world, or as it stands as 'their truth.' The essentialist speaks as if language were but a mighty tool, clasped firmly in one's hands, toward which they possess as little bias as a mechanic toward any singular wrench. This is a conception of language which can allow no otherness, not even that which dwells in the same. It can neither listen nor be heard, for it asserts language is a dead thing, and that we are separated from its meaning. It can in no way understand that "we are always already biased in our thinking and our knowing by our linguistic interpretation of the world. To grow into this linguistic interpretation means to grow up in the world. To this extent, language is the real mark of our finitude. It is always out beyond us."[323] In this sense, even those who attempt to turn over their identity through language fail to come to terms with their finitude at an even more fundamental level, whereby they misplace distrust on the relation to language itself, and engage in a theater of shapeshifting meanings.

This is the position opposite the essentialist, whereupon their use of language becomes so far removed from any joint agreement that their display is not only incomprehensible as to its signification, but also as to any positive social or moral character that guided the language to begin with. A lengthy example here is of help not only due to the fact that it shows the issue we seek to interrogate, but also the radical degree to which distinction and the multiplicity of branches that stem from such monological language go unnoticed. Our example watches the notions of racism and sexism devolve from near-universal agreement and discursive moral argumentation to mere equation which reduces

---

323 Ibid., 64.

282   IDEOLOGY AND UNDERSTANDING

the abuse of an individual to a stale economic relation. The initial character of these terms was centered around prejudice, discrimination, or otherwise maltreatment of some kind which arises and is directed on the basis of the immutable characteristics of one's racial or gendered character. At this stage, the characterization of the words is then seen as a phenomenon which is a collective issue facing society at large, and which each individual poses the possibility of falling into. These definitions date back to their origin, and might be understood as wrong or evil without appeal to anything beyond the shared understanding of the linguistic tradition which birthed its terms. This set of definitions does not seek to find an end through which all occasions of the term may be concluded, but rather the closest central issues at task in the terms of which many definitions may come to be at play. However, the terms begin to take on meaning as many sought to speak to the ways in which power and one's 'perceived group identity' worked to distribute benefits within racial or gendered application.

The National Education Association, for example, found their expression of this form of the term 'racism' in 1973 when they stated that

> in the United States at present, only whites can be racists, since blacks and other Third World peoples do not have access to the power to enforce any prejudices they may have, so they cannot, by definition, be racists. All white individuals in our society are racists. Even if a white is totally free from all conscious racial prejudices, he remains a racist, for he receives benefits distributed by a white racist society through its institutions. Our institutional and cultural processes are so arranged as to automatically benefit whites, just because they are white.[324]

---

324 National Education Association, "Education and Racism" (Washington, D.C., 1973).

In addition to this being an instance of an incredibly powerful institution (the largest labor union in the U.S.) dictating the moral character of individuals based on their immutable characteristics, at the time groups were in large part separated exclusively into the categories of blacks, whites, and Hispanics with 'whites' absorbing a great deal of other races and ethnicities (equating disparate cultures into a single category). In addition, this reduces all instances of varied racism to a

> singular cause and type of racism . . . [which] dangerously implies that there is a single solution to the phenomenon. The view that racism is an attribute of the monolithic category of people termed "white" who hold all the power in society is equally confused and confusing . . . The approaches [of this theory of race] are theoretical and thus closed to the canons of scientific evaluation . . . the discourse itself prohibits the open, rigorous, and critical interrogation which is essential to theoretical, professional and personal development.[325]

This notion of prejudice mixed with power as the true notion of racism, or sexism, depends on the historical stagnation and monolithic production of the present as totalizing and absolute. This unilaterally relates power in discrete transactions from the sole whim of unconscious bias, which cannot be corrected, and can hardly be tracked outside the realms of pure speculation. It also depicts a scenario for those it claims as whites where even at their best they are capable of mere mute penitence, despite the necessity of change apparently falling into their white hands.

Even still, should this notion transpose fantasy to reality, such a closed discourse, the dead *logos* of dispensation, seems ultimately to engender

---

325 Macey, M., and Eileen Moxon, "An Examination of Anti-Racist and Anti-Oppressive Theory and Practice in Social Work Education," *The British Journal of Social Work* 26, no. 3 (June 1996): 297–314.

further resentment and prejudice in whites, and maintains only a passive position for blacks. This can also be seen to malfunction as it becomes necessary to reduce individuals to a singular term, despite the obvious antagonisms alive in said terms, as Lindsay Johns states:

> It would . . . be disingenuous to deny that much racial tension can and does exist between various peoples of colour. For example, many African nations do not like each other very much, as is sadly the case with many African and Caribbean people. Likewise, many Asians are very prejudiced against black people, and vice versa. Many of these attitudes have come about as a result of European "divide and rule" colonial politics. Many of them, equally, have not.[326]

Thus, instead of opening the discourse of expressions of prejudice to examine which have bigger and more direct impact, there is instead a reduction of responsibility to an ambiguous group, of which there are no leaders, and up until recently, very little consciousness of/for. Cathy Young makes this point when stating that this secondary definition

> has legitimized overt race- and gender-based hate speech; if it's okay to say hateful things about white men, the claim that it's not okay to say them about other groups becomes tenuous. It has lent credibility to claims that whites, especially straight white men, are under attack. It has subverted the moral authority of anti-racism—and of liberalism (in the classic sense), dismissed in current progressive discourse as "a philosophy of white male domination." And it has so

---

326 Lindsay Johns, "Why Lee Jasper Is Wrong: White People Don't Have a Monopoly on Racism," *Daily Mail Online* (May 1, 2012); available at www.dailymail.co.uk/debate/article-2137787/Why-Lee-Jasper-wrong-White-people-dont-monopoly-racism.html.

trivialized the concepts of bigotry and racism that they have
lost much of their stigma.[327]

The maintaining of two definitions with no discernible difference in
application (especially with terms whose use is meant to carry a heaviness
with it) ultimately only succeeds in holding space for the terms to be
applied ideologically, and thus retroactively relates ideological motiva-
tions. Despite language being a vehicle for history to affect us, which
Gadamer calls a 'history of effects' that speak to the causal conditions
of this relation, man too must be open to receive the "being that can
be understood [as] language," for "Gadamer does not think that our
words produce the intelligibility of reality in some strong sense. It's
not as if our words project an intelligibility onto reality, which would
then stand between us and the real world like a shroud. No, Gadamer
says that growing into a linguistic interpretation means "grow[ing] up
in *the* world."[328] This transpires because language itself is that which
enriches all intelligible reality, and thus these words take a stance on
the intelligibility of the world. There is then "a sense for Gadamer in
which words 'complete' and 'complement' the intelligibility of the world.
Words do not create the intelligibility of the world, but they do more
than simply mirror it in a representation. Words make the world more
intelligible and accessible than it would be without words."[329] Alongside
this enhancement, language is also the means of disclosure of the world,
and hence when language is changed unnaturally at the hands of abstract
theory in this way, language instead discloses the ideology behind it, and
instead of reifying the content in said ideology, the inversion of language
instead designates the originary language, which was understood as

---

327 Young, Cathy, "You Can't Whitewash the Alt-Right's Bigotry," *The Federalist*
      (April 20, 2016); available at thefederalist.com/2016/04/14/you-cant-
      whitewash-the-alt-rights-bigotry/.
328 Wachterhauser, "Getting It Right," 66.
329 Ibid., 67.

universally functioning, to a signifier or call to an ideologically charged notion, one which in application alone attempts to co-opt the totality of the dialogue to the service of the matrix of interconnected buy-ins.

This is often because the ideological grip upon words functions as a limit to the freedom of the *logos* to speak itself and of the relation of the dialogue itself through placing walls on the infinite extendibility inherent to it. This is not the same as the finitude imparted by the historical particularity of language in general, nor is it the echoed effect influenced in language by those specialized or technical terms of the philosophers or other such scientific minds. For instead of being open to revision or emendation, it is rather the restriction on language itself: inflecting neither history nor tradition, but a sort of revolutionary authoritarianism that holds shut the window otherwise open unto the world by language itself. We can see more how this plays out when we see at the ways in which

> Gadamer argues that the development of our linguistic heritage involves "application" in that the seemingly infinite variability with which we can project and extend the use of a word is part of the reason inherent in language itself. Language is not fixed by or reducible to a set of rules. Of course, there are rules of language, but like the rules of chess they allow for and even seem to require an open variability that cannot be delimited a priori on all fronts. Our intelligence as speakers is not reducible to these. Because intelligent use of language requires a kind of unconscious creation. I am tempted to speak here of linguistic "genius," but the point is that such creativity is a regular occurrence that transpires every time we extend or "apply" a familiar term in a new way. Such ability is something every competent speaker possesses at least to some degree. Hence, Gadamer insists that "application" is a kind of interpretation that presupposes the *authority* of a

linguistic tradition and a *freedom* to extend that tradition, neither of which can be surveyed and made transparently available to use.[330]

The only certainty that extends from the ideological language mentioned earlier is its formulaic outcome, whose teleological foundation relies on the totalizing and closed epistemology informing the ideology that structured it. In this way, both certainty and truth rely on the success in and authority of the ideology itself. Once again the good, the true, and the beautiful become situated through an 'anything goes' relativism that is secured through power. Yet the status of ideologically grounded epistemology is such that it does not allow for the "ever-present possibility of having to change our minds when the weight of evidence against us makes it preposterous to stick to some belief or set of beliefs we once thought true."[331] This is because the epistemology of ideology, in order to establish and transmit a hierarchy of domination, blindly asserts both truth and certainty as its own. However, the regular status of knowledge in the hermeneutic state of inquiry (as in both Plato's *docta ignorantia* and Aristotle's state of *phronesis*) finds that

> our epistemic self-confidence is not a matter of luck and the truth or probability, that in any case where we must choose between two conflicting knowledge-claims we have a 50 percent chance of guessing the right one. Even this would provide a rational warrant of sorts, albeit a very thin one . . . While our justifications are qualified by the fallibilistic awareness that we may be wrong, they are far from arbitrary and even further from an "anything goes" relativism. We can develop, apply, and retest criteria of knowledge that can give

---

330 Ibid., 68.
331 Ibid., 70.

us enough reliable evidence or rational assurance to claim in multiple cases that we in fact know something and do not just surmise or opine that it is the case.[332]

This is far from the bald assertions of ideology, which would not even permit the paper-thin warrant of the first case, for to do so would be to allow a query not simply into the moment of assertion but also into the foundation of the epistemological matrix, which makes a necessity of the assertion as well as the moment of knowledge established in it. Thus, both the skeptic who *demands* absolute knowledge and certainty as well as the ideologue who *asserts* absolute knowledge and certainty stand in the position of dictating conditions of knowledge, where the burden of proof is built already within said conditions. However it is by nature of the need for monopoly and totality to sustain the absolute condition of ideology where it misses the bedrock of knowledge. That is, "the fact that knowledge is always dependent on historical, linguistic and normative conditions, which constitute a relative stand point, is not an inherent danger to knowledge, but a condition of its possibility."[333]

All of this is not to say that historical, linguistic, and normative conditions are themselves authoritative in the sense of being the absolute source of knowledge or certainty, or both, nor is it to say that they are always the irrational arbitrary and blind conditions that many young revolutionaries tend to cast them as. One can see that

> What needs to be emphasized here is that a standpoint is precisely a point from which we see and not a point from which we are necessarily blinded. Gadamer makes this point by saying that the linguistic preconditions of knowledge are not barriers between us and the world, but they encompass everything that

---

332 Ibid., 71.
333 Ibid., 72.

is humanly knowable. As such language is like a light; it is a "medium" in which the world discloses itself to us: it is the vehicle that delivers the intelligible world to us, "the verbal world in which we live, is not a barrier that prevents knowledge of being in itself, but fundamentally embraces everything in which our insight can be enlarged and deepened."[334]

This reveals that the formula of ideological conviction is at odds with the root of knowledge, for the insight itself functions always-already from the relativist epistemology grounding it and therefore is a reflection rather of those who sought to establish the notion, without appealing to concrete relations growing from the world itself, which such a formula renders 'independent.' This perspective is not, however, one that can see "that concepts and objects, or language and the world, constitute spaces of overlapping or interpenetrating intelligibility or meaning. Neither side is reducible to the other; neither side is the product of the other."[335]

This is not to say that intelligibility is transmitted from language, for normative experience is always-already caught up in intelligibility which would otherwise be impossible.

This is because the epistemological perspective that only holds its gaze upon belief, and sees belief as the totalizing constitutional atom of all intelligibility, thus maintains a position of arbitrary subtraction which is just as steadfast and dogmatic as those spoken of earlier. An artificial totality constructed therefrom is such that gaps are opened like sores in its ontology, which cannot know any function of relationality outside of form-mirrored replication of belief itself. There is then no difference between gnosis, mental life, or even a naturalized empiricism: this itself is not the same as "the explicitly Gadamerian theses that all understanding is in terms of some language, situated in a normatively charged history . . . [which] has

---

334 Ibid., 72-73.
335 Ibid., 74.

incorporated Hegel's insight into the historically mediated nature of human knowing with Hegel's (and Plato's) conviction that the world is inherently intelligible."[336] It is not difficult to see how the ontological predicament of those who embrace this form of identitarianism produces a belief about all possible intelligibility which not only creates artificial gaps that destabilize meaning in a real sense, but also fills in gaps from which meaning arises.

In the moment of this belief about intelligibility we can recognize its inverse as the perspective of Gadamer, one which keeps both the finite participation of the individual and its overall relation to the absolute intact: for rather than belief being the moment of infinite regress, intelligibility itself holds open the possibility of a regress for the moment of infinity in its stead. Our historical existence is therefore among the wide variety of reflections of this infinity of Being, which an identitarian ontology cannot make sense of. This is because

> "to exist historically," writes Gadamer, mean "that knowledge of oneself can never be complete," because "all knowledge of oneself" proceeds from "what is historically pre-given," out of a "substance" that is the basis for "every subjective meaning and attitude." Thus, philosophical hermeneutics must "move back along the path of Hegel's phenomenology until we discover in all that is subjective the substantiality that determines it" (Truth and Method 269). This is just what the "ontological turn" to language should accomplish. With it the "substantiality" of historical life should find its validity.[337]

The notions of identity and determination which have been tossed about by identitarians, then, have been dead from the start. This is

---

336 Ibid., 77.

337 Figal, Gunter, "The Doing of the Thing Itself," in *The Cambridge Companion to Gadamer*, ed. Robert J. Dostal (Cambridge: Cambridge University Press, 2010), 104-5.

because, despite the limitations of Gadamer's finite being, it possesses a historical consciousness that thus distinguishes the elements of tradition through a projected historical horizon, simultaneously laying them over its living tradition, such that a suture might appear to recombine the two. "This process of fusion is continually going on, for there old and new continually grow together to make something of living value,"[338] by its very nature *dynamically*. This is the lifeblood of language: of not only tradition as previously defined, but also of self-understanding. Language is "the universal medium in which understanding itself is realized."[339] This is in contrast to claims of definitive knowledge, of which identitarian statements wind up being, regardless of their appearance as denying truth-value altogether. In understanding proper, truth remains a possibility in direct contrast to 'definite knowledge' which itself is static and impotent. Identitarian ontology denies the essential finitude of understanding, thus rejecting philosophical thought altogether, and by this move denies experience itself. For "the truth of experience always contains an orientation towards new experience . . . The dialectic of experience has its own fulfilment not in definitive knowledge, but in that openness to experience that is encouraged by experience itself."[340] It is through an *expérientialisme morale*, which retains being-in-the-world, that truth may become lived. This is perhaps why Ricoeur states that "verification is therefore a question of our whole life. No one can escape this . . . I do not see how we can say that our values are better than all others except that by risking our whole life on them we expect to achieve a better life, to see and to understand things better than others."[341]

---

338 Gadamer, *Truth and Method*, 273.

339 Ibid., 350.

340 Ibid., 319.

341 Ricoeur, Paul, and George Taylor, *Lectures on Ideology and Utopia* (New York: Columbia University Press, 1986), 312.

DEBILITATING
ENLIGHTENMENT

E ven today, dialogue is made subservient to the hypnotic spell still being cast from a generation of thought from centuries past. The Enlightenment asserted that it had no father or mother, acting as if there were no record of its ancestors. It should like us to believe that it was never born, and never died, as if an ideology were eternal. In speaking of the 'Enlightenment,' I do not intend to bring to mind its assertion of an ahistorical and singular moment of development whereupon man stepped more fully into the light of reason, now grasping the tools of a redefined yet ultimately artificial science, which sets about carving out the path of truth for the world. Instead, I speak of a mode of being which believes itself to possess Hegel's 'pure insight,' which admits nothing beyond itself, and creates an unreal distance between all that is other to it. This is most obvious first and foremost in relation to religion, where pure insight

> falsely charges religious belief with basing its certainty on some *particular historical evidences* which, considered as historical evidences, would certainly not guarantee the degree of certainty about their content which is given by newspaper accounts of any happening—further, that its certainty rests on the accidental *preservation* of these evidences; on the one hand, the preservation by means of paper, and on the other hand, by the skill and honesty of their transference from one piece of paper to another, and lastly, on the *correct interpretation* of

the meaning of dead words and letters. In fact, however, it does not occur to faith to fasten its certainty to such evidences and such fortuitous circumstances. Faith, in its certainty, is an unsophisticated relationship to its absolute object, a pure knowing of it which does not mix up letters, paper, and copyists, in its consciousness of absolute Being, and does not bring itself into relation with it by means of things of that kind. On the contrary, this consciousness is the self-mediating ground of its knowledge; it is Spirit itself which bears witness to itself, both in the *inwardness* of the *individual* consciousness and through the *universal presence* in everyone of faith in it. If faith wants to appeal to historical evidences in order to get that kind of foundation, or at least confirmation, of its content that Enlightenment talks about, and seriously thinks and acts as if that were a matter of importance, then it has already let itself be corrupted by the Enlightenment; and its efforts to establish and consolidate itself in such a way are merely evidence it gives of its corruption by the Enlightenment.[342]

Here, Hegel speaks to what has become the faith of the modern in general, provoked by a critique that was understood inadequately, if it can have been said to understand anything at all. This is the moment of biblical literalism, which itself inverted all that bore fruit within the Christian faith, and returned to the stale atoms comprising the words themselves, as if they bore thunderous revelation by mere relation of ink to paper. They found a search for factual instantiation and the bare materialism that gave rise to them to be of more worth than any instance of the lifeblood of the living *Logos*, which they saw to be at work no longer within what was proper to the faith, but rather, upon hearing the assertions of the Enlightenment, sought to restructure the Christian

342 Hegel, *Phenomenology of Spirit* (trans. Findlay), 338.

faith such that it may claim the hegemonic victory otherwise given to the Enlightenment.

This victory was sought on the behalf of the Christians by informally disregarding Origen's threefold division of scripture into the literal (bodily), moral (psychic), and symbolic (spiritual), which themselves engage in free play such that certain passages might contain two or more meanings. By doing away with this division, there was a reduction of man's consciousness within Christianity to a flat sense-certainty which neglects the collective and universal meaning of the text. Christianity came necessarily into direct conflict with Origen's guiding words regarding scripture, which invite us

> to transform the Gospel known to sense-perception into one intellectual and spiritual. For what would the narrative of the Gospel known to sense-perception amount to, if it were not developed into a spiritual one? It would be of little account or none. Anyone can read it and assure himself of the facts it tells— nothing more. But our whole energy is now to be directed to the effort to penetrate to the depths of the meaning of the Gospel and to search out the truth that is in it when it is divested of its prefigurations.[343]

The faith of these Christians became simply 'the facts' as they relate directly to our sense experience, and which can be understood head on without labor. As if by the nose of a dog leading it from scrap to scrap, the Christian became reduced to reading from word to word, only capable of organizing facts. Origen's approach to scripture, much like Plato's *docta* and Aristotle's *Phronimos*, was one based entirely in a tradition of

---

343 Origen, *Commentary on John*, cited in Athanasios Papanikolaou, "The Allegorical Exegetical Method of Origen," in *Theology: Quarterly Edition of the Holy Synod of the Church of Greece* 45, no. 2 (1974): 349.

intellectual humility, which itself was what literalism presumed to be, the condition crippling Christianity in the face of the Enlightenment's brash account of truth. This is because the hermeneutic and epistemological grounding of Origen was seated in a belief that any understanding of scripture was a gift of grace. This is not to say that Origen imagined that all who were saved under the grace of Christ were to submit to a radical devotion to one's own development therein, for he states that "those who follow the letter of the Gospel are saved, because even the bare literal narration of the Gospel is adequate for salvation of the simpler fold."[344]

However, even here the 'simpler' followers were not what Origen perceived to be those ordinary to the faith, and to them Origen considered the Gospel itself veiled. In fact, in his later expounding of scripture, Origen saw both the realm of the soul and the realm of the spirit bleeding together to such an extent that he came to speak of the two as one unified 'spiritual' level of understanding which he identified with the allegorical, which "for Origen [is] something distinct. It is not an ingenious play with words or thoughts, nor is it an exegetical method aside from other methods. 'In his eyes it is the only method of interpretation which is worthy of the Holy Scriptures. It is the conditio sine qua non for understanding the Scriptures, and those who do not accept it, are excluded from grasping the contents the divine sayings.'"[345] For Origen, what is crucial about understanding when it comes to scripture is a sense of dialogue with the *Logos* from which, with his hands lifted in prayer, truth may be revealed. It is this sense of understanding, one resulting from a metamodern relation to the matter-at-hand which is the result of a living engagement, that one can, as Heraclitus wrote, "follow what's common" while yet seeing that "although the Logos is common, most people live as if they had their own private understanding."[346]

---

344 Ibid. 352
345 Ibid.
346 Diels-Kranz 22B2.

This private understanding, for Heraclitus as it would have been for Origen, was that which ignored the very form, function, and relations which language in transient autopoiesis would itself garner, instead attending to the bare senseless moment of letters set beside one another. This is why, when N. T. Wright speaks to the Enlightenment mode of literalist investigation of scripture, he states that such an interrogation "doesn't settle ahead of time the question of what it actually refers to."[347] He situates authentic, literal, and allegorical approaches to language as semiotic relations opposed to concrete and abstract approaches to meaning. This effect is such that the authentic literal meaning of Genesis, the one presumably grasped by Origen's 'simpler fold,' is itself beyond the comprehension of literalist interpretation, for their rendering is the pure materialism of the Enlightenment. The authentic literal interpretation of Genesis however finds that it is

> a story about someone who constructs something in six days—it's a temple story, it's about God making a place for himself to dwell, and this is Heaven and Earth, and what you do with that is, the last thing is you put an image of God into this temple. And suddenly, Genesis 1, instead of it being 'were there six days, or were there five or were there seven or were they twenty-four hours?,' it's actually about God making the heavens and the Earth as the place where he wants to dwell, and putting humans into that construct as a way of both reflecting his own love into the world, and drawing out the praise and glory from the world back to himself.[348]

Where the Enlightenment sought to establish the 'scientific' grasp of understanding in general, based on a narrow and immodest understand-

347 Wright, N. T., "What Do You Mean by Literal?," *BioLogos*, September 8, 2010; available at www.youtube.com/watch?v=fxQpFosrTUk.
348 Ibid.

ing of science as such, we find a *telos* which seeks to establish a static key to knowledge, itself exclusive of life and historical movement, and as such obliterating all before its gaze. This Enlightenment-based scientific knowledge, when applied to human affairs, is opposed to an understanding that results from engagement with an interlocutor, from which

> some differences are obvious. The first is unilateral, the second bilateral. I know the rock, the solar system; I don't have to deal with its view of me, or of my knowing activity. But beyond this, the goal is different. I conceive the goal of knowledge as attaining some finally adequate explanatory language, which can make sense of the object, and will exclude all future surprises. However much this may elude us in practice, it is what we often seek in science; e.g., we look for the ultimate theory in microphysics, where we will finally have charted all the particles and forces, and don't have to face future revisions. But coming to an understanding can never have this finality. For one thing, we come to understandings with certain definite interlocutors. These will not necessarily serve when we come to deal with others. Understandings are party-dependent. And then, frequently more worrying, even our present partners may not remain the same. Their life situation or goals may change, and the understanding may be put in question. True, we try to control for this by binding agreements, contracts, but this is precisely because we see that what constitutes perfect and unconstrained mutual understanding at one time may no longer hold good later.[349]

The proto-Enlightenment operation is consistent with the formal movement of Levinas's conception of a totality, presenting nothing as exterior

349 Taylor, Charles, "Gadamer on the Human Sciences," in *The Cambridge Companion to Gadamer*, ed. Robert J. Dostal (Cambridge: Cambridge University Press, 2010), 127.

to its employment such that both what is contained within the other and exteriority proper are barred from attending to their manifestation. This denial of alterity is what characterizes Enlightenment knowing *as such,* for its ideal is this total knowledge. This search for total knowledge, in the instance of human affairs, is made manifest through ontology in an attempt to grasp being qua being in its totality.

This mode of ontological investigation can only happen by way of the generalities of concepts, for as Levinas states, "For the things the work of ontology consists in apprehending the individual (which alone exists) not in its individuality but in its generality (of which alone there is science). The relation with the other is here accomplished through a third term, which I find in myself."[350] This third term is the concept through which individuals are reduced to the content represented by generalities. This is what all is meant when we state that

> the unilateral nature of knowing emerges in the fact that my goal is to attain a full intellectual control over the object, such that it can no longer "talk back" and surprise me. Now this may require that I make some quite considerable changes in my outlook. My whole conceptual scheme may be very inadequate when I begin my enquiry. I may have to undergo the destruction and remaking of my framework of understanding in order to attain the knowledge that I seek. But all this serves the aim of full intellectual control. What does not alter in this process is my goal. I define my aims throughout in the same way.[351]

'Knowledge' in human sciences seeks to absorb and to dominate the other such that it may be pulled into the moment of the same, and may thus lie to rest in its concurring establishment of totalizing order. This

350 Levinas, *Totality and Infinity*, 44.
351 Taylor, "Gadamer on the Human Sciences," 127-28.

knowledge is that which "rest[s] on the essential self-sufficiency of the same, its identification in ipseity, its egoism."[352] Here we find that "the correlation between knowledge and being . . . indicates both a difference [between the two] and a difference that is overcome in the true. Here the understood is known and so appropriated by knowledge."[353] It becomes the known as grasped by the same alone, such that its appropriation is founded by knowledge comprised of our concepts.

The reduction of Being in general, which is the subsumption of the Other under the totalizing order of the same, occurs when "the meaning of individuals (invisible outside this totality) is derived from the totality."[354] This totality is known by way of the imposition of concepts which neglect the particularities of the individual. As such, the concepts involve us in a situation whereby individuals are lost to being in general, or what is to say the same thing, the impersonality of totality is such that the individual is barred from the field of disclosure, and the ethical relation which itself founds said barring is itself hidden from this viewpoint. Levinas here is establishing a third way beyond Heidegger's ultimate ontology and Hegel's eschatological absolute idealism by revealing that an "infinity is produced in the relationship of the same with the other."[355] This infinity is that signification of surplus which implies both limits and the exceeding of those limits. This is because its mode of being, that of infinition, "is produced in the improbable fact whereby a separated being fixed in its identity, the same, the I, nonetheless contains in itself what it can neither contain nor receive solely by virtue of its identity . . . [Thus, understanding is that] . . . knowing qua intentionality [which] already presupposes the idea of

---

352 Levinas, *Totality and Infinity*, 44.

353 Levinas, Emmanuel, "Ethics as First Philosophy," in *The Continental Philosophy Reader*, ed. Richard Kearney and Mara Rainwater (London: Routledge, 1996), 124.

354 Levinas, *Totality and Infinity*, 22.

355 Ibid., 26.

infinity, which is pre-eminently non-adequation."[356] In the movement of understanding there is a vast multiplicity of movements which first contain an intentionality as that which speaks to consciousness of an excess contained fundamentally within a relation to an other as other. Secondarily, in order that objective knowledge itself be sustained, it must do so in and by external verification, which must take place through the confirmation of an other, who must remain other for the possibility of confirmation, and therefore objective knowledge presupposes the necessary relation toward an other, who by the very nature of his status as other exceeds both the knowing relation and the intentionality that sought it out. This is because the other contains anticipations, interpretations, and memories tied to an individual historical being which escape the grasp of the same in an essential dimension which cannot be extracted or subsumed under a totality in any way.

Understanding, then, as a result from the transcendental relation of dialogue, presents the fusion of horizons in a *face to face* production of conversation: one which utilizes the semiotic relationality of the face itself to transcend the mere spoken word, which itself is irreducible to the written word, which is further irreducible to the mere material constituents of its visible manifestation. This dialogue, which gives way to the possibility of understanding, is always-already the result of an intention that intends its own sublation, its own transcendence, which maintains distance between the same and the other. A true dialogue maintains all of these relations, and as such it admits the right of each to call the other into question, and it admits the response of each to this question as such. This is the site of Levinas's ethics, where he states that "a calling into question of the same . . . is brought about by the other. We name this calling into question of my spontaneity by the presence of the other 'ethics.'"[357] Ethics, then, stems from self-restriction, whose basis

---

356 Ibid., 27.
357 Ibid., 43.

is in the foundational understanding that permeates all areas of human affairs, manifested first and foremost in the relation of dialogue rather than of pure reason. It is through this dialogical primacy that newness finds its way into the common world. It is itself verified and animated by this fundamental relationality that always-already includes in its conception of being the other as Other. Central to this relationality is the Hegelian notion of negation, which involves beliefs being threatened by the refutation of the other, and the justification of belief beyond the basis of experience. Rather than Enlightenment 'knowing,' however, understandings "are bilateral, they are party-dependent, and they involve revising goals,"[358] whereas "the content of knowledge shouldn't vary with the person who is seeking it; it can't be party-dependent. And the true seeker of knowledge never varies in [his] goal; there is no question of compromise here."[359] Yet on this idealistic image of 'scientific man,' it is worth noting that the 'crisis of European sciences' revealed itself as early as 1928 where Max Scheler noted "man is more a problem to himself at the present time than ever before in all recorded history . . . we do not have a unified idea of man. The increasing multiplicity of the special sciences, valuable as they are, tend to hide man's nature more than reveal it."[360]

It is from the split of Enlightenment approaches to science proper that a grave problematic has resulted, for Enlightenment-based knowledge cannot step outside of its bounds as a methodological approach to anything but bare objects unresistant to the totalizing account of knowledge that the method offers. Yet neither can there be a true understanding while holding to the Enlightenment approach to *gnôsis*, for even though one may wear the mask of understanding, if underneath they bear the

358 Taylor, "Gadamer on the Human Sciences," 128.

359 Ibid.

360 Scheler, Max, and Hans Meyerhoff, *Man's Place in Nature* (New York: Farrar, Straus and Cudahy, 1961), 4-6.

Enlightenment's ontological aim, they nevertheless will always-already reduce content to an object of knowledge, and thus will transmogrify the other into the same. This is to say that the Enlightenment's concept-oriented ontology seeks to dismiss every type of independence other than that of this modality of self-consciousness. Hegel outlines the foundation of this concept-oriented ontology which he understands as the 'pure insight' of the Enlightenment. He states:

> The form in which the Notion of pure insight first makes its appearance [is not] yet realized. Accordingly, its consciousness still appears as contingent, as single and separate, and its essence appears for it in the form of an end which it has to realize. It has, to begin with, the intention of making pure insight universal, i.e. of making everything that is actual into a Notion, and into one and the same Notion in every self-consciousness. The intention is pure, for it has pure insight for its content; and this insight is likewise pure, for its content is solely the absolute Notion, which meets with no opposition in an object, nor is it restricted in its own self. In the unrestricted Notion there are directly found the two aspects: that everything objective has only the significance of being-for-self, of self-consciousness, and that this has the significance of a universal, that pure insight is to become the property of every self-consciousness. This second aspect of the intention is a result of culture in so far as in this culture, the difference of objective Spirit, the parts and the determinations which its judgment imposed on the world, as well as the differences which appear as natural predispositions, have all been upset. Genius, talent, special capacities generally, belong to the world of actuality, in so far as this world still contains the aspect of being a spiritual animal kingdom in which individuals, amid confusion and mutual violence, cheat and struggle over the

essence of the actual world. These differences, this truth, have no place in this world as honest species; individuality neither is contented with the unreal 'matter in hand' itself nor has it a particular content and ends of its own. On the contrary, it counts merely as something universally acknowledged, viz. as an educated individuality; and the difference is reduced to one of less or more energy, a quantitative difference, i.e. a non-essential difference. This last difference, however, has been effaced by the fact that in the completely disrupted state of consciousness difference changed round into an absolutely qualitative difference. There, what is for the 'I' an 'other' is only the 'I' itself. In this infinite judgment all one-sidedness and peculiarity of the original being-for-self has been eradicated; the self knows itself qua pure self to be its own object; and this absolute identity of the two sides is the element of pure insight. Pure insight is, therefore, the simple, immanently differentiated essence, and equally the universal work or achievement and a universal possession. In this simple spiritual substance, self-consciousness gives itself and preserves for itself in every object the consciousness of this its own particular being or of its own action, just as conversely, the individuality of self-consciousness is therein self-identical and universal. This pure insight is thus the Spirit that calls to every consciousness: be for yourselves what you all are in yourselves-reasonable.[361]

However, rather than the negating critique of pure insight being a moment of man's liberation, it is in fact a mere replication of its self-generated critical image of faith refusing space for the subjective activity of human freedom. In the first moment (pure insight's constructed image of faith) we see that to the Absolute belongs every moment of

---

361 Hegel, *Phenomenology of Spirit* (trans. Findlay), 326-28.

the entire movement of social relations. The reason that the Enlightenment's object-oriented ontology so easily displaced the robes of the king it critiques is that the king is itself already falsely attributed to faith as a modality of the Enlightenment's critique. That is the state of affairs that the Enlightenment sought to critique which is always-already emanating from the Enlightenment itself.

This shift to the rational command of materialism in place of 'superstition' itself leaves social relations to the laws of nature, which the Enlightenment boasts as a product adopting the cold blade of rationality. In the end, this sequence of concept-oriented ontology's production is one that finds the Enlightenment in agreement with the superstition that it had constructed as its opponent: an agreement which can be found exemplified in Spinoza's synthetic monism which understands God's will and the laws of nature to be one in the same thing. Paradoxically however, through the Enlightenment's dependence on conceptual knowledge, its ontology, which forces the totalizing concept to bear the mediation of the concrete, has become abstract intelligence which itself is detached from the actual particulars of lived experience, and to the personhood or self-identity which was adopted by many. Thus, conceptual overreach is the disrupted mode of knowledge which now bears the historical legacy of the Enlightenment as that which misunderstands even the most transparent knowledge that it seeks, for this knowledge is not only historically situated as such, but it is also limited by the finitude of the very humans who seek it out. Even when Enlightenment's concept-oriented ontology is adapted to this critique, the resulting epistemological movement becomes the Marxist material laws of history, which merely augment their representation by solidifying the inherent utilitarian aim of this ontology such that the dignity it was supposed to find for humanity is undercut by their use as a means to its end.

Yet the mere reactive stance of the postmoderns who stand in stark opposition to the Enlightenment object-oriented ontology adopts a negating stance toward the movement of the modern, celebrating "a radical historicism in the wake of a jettisoning of the transcendental unities of modern thought."[362] A wholesale direct opposition to the overreaching exuberance of this ontology is but a discarding of the champagne after popping its cork: both moments do away with the "approach [toward] the other in conversation [which] is to welcome his expression, in which at each instant he overflows the idea [that] a thought would carry away from it."[363] There is an inability to cope by way of this overflowing for both the Enlightenment object-oriented ontology and postmodernism's radical historicism, as their ontologies demand either absolute exteriority or interiority against which teaching or understanding as a comprehensive account become unintelligible. Both are formal manifestations of a radical and intellectually fetishized egology, against which stands the possibility of understanding and open conversation. For "Teaching is not reducible to maieutics; it comes from the exterior and brings me more than I contain."[364] Through welcoming open conversation, then, we are made vulnerable and are called into question by the exterior interpretation of the matter-at-hand which "puts the spontaneous freedom within us into question. It commands and judges it and brings it to its truth."[365] This relationship then is the bedrock of metamodern rationality, which is understood as "interpretive narration and praxial critique"[366] that acts as a special sort of social/communicative practice, which is

at once performances of discernment and articulation . . . [which] articulate[s] the sense of lived-through historical experience as we attempt to achieve both a measure of self-

---

362 Schrag, Calvin O., "Rationality Between Modernity and Postmodernity," in *Philosophical Papers: Betwixt and Between* (Albany: State University of New York Press, 1994), 260.

363 Levinas, *Totality and Infinity*, 51.

364 Ibid.

365 Ibid.

366 Schrag, *Philosophical Papers*, 261.

identity and a comprehension of our social and natural world
. . .

> Their sense-giving performance is fulfilled through reference [for they] articulate, disclose, make manifest, intimate, reveal and thus comport their own agency of reference.[367]

This image of the foundational possibility of the metamodern is found also in Levinas, where he states that

> psychic life, which makes birth and death possible, is a dimension in being, a dimension of non-essence, beyond the possible and the impossible. It does not exhibit itself in history; the discontinuity of the inner life interrupts historical time. The thesis of the primacy of history constitutes an option for the comprehension of being in which interiority is sacrificed. The real must not only be determined in its historical objectivity, but also from interior intentions, from the *secrecy* that interrupts the continuity of historical time. Only on the basis of this secrecy is the pluralism of society possible. It attests this secrecy. The way of access to social reality starting with the separation of the I is not engulfed in "universal history," in which only totalities appear. The experience of the other starting from a separated I remains a source of meaning for the comprehension of totalities, just as concrete perception remains determinative for the signification of scientific universes. Cronos, thinking he swallows a god, swallows but a stone.[368]

---

367 Ibid., 263.
368 Levinas, *Totality and Infinity*, 57-58.

PHENOMENON OF UNDERSTANDING

G adamer's introduction to *Truth and Method* humbly lays out the problem of scientific knowledge-claims against understanding as *the* mode of Being for man as shown by Heidegger's temporal analytics (a point Gadamer himself makes in the introduction). He specifically mentions the experience of art, philosophy, and history as being chief causes for concern, for their commonalities with science are revealed as both the set of experiences which are categorized beyond the everyday march of life, being considered in most societies as fundamental modes of experience specific to man, and yet universally present in some manner or another. Gadamer makes clear that these modes of experience communicate a truth, yet this truth is unverifiable to the methodological utility of the scientific knowledge, and what's more that the truth-experience of these modes of understanding reveal the limitations of a scientific conception of truth:

> The scholarly research pursued by the "science of art" is aware from the start that it can neither replace nor surpass the experience of art. The fact that through a work of art a truth is experienced that we cannot attain in any other way constitutes the philosophic importance of art, which asserts itself against all attempts to rationalize it away. Hence, together with the experience of philosophy, the experience of art is the most insistent admonition to scientific consciousness to acknowledge its own limits.[369]

---

369 Gadamer, *Truth and Method*, xxi-xxii.

This is not to say that explication, critique, and commentary related to a work of art have no place, and that in the face of art we are to adopt a position of quietus, but rather that our attempts to speak methodologically of the truth of art is itself always-already surpassed by the truth of the art as it is in-and-for-itself. Thus aesthetic theories of art which are themselves a mode of scientific methodology directed at 'knowing' art rather than understanding it are to be disregarded in order to have an authentic relationship to art, and in order to attempt a pursuit of truth that is beyond the mere possessive totalizing of these modes of 'knowing.' For it is by this possessive demand of the aesthetic methodology which is but a mere reflection of itself that it relates itself to the work of art, as if by way of the art the methodology of science is to be made more beautiful. Like the obsessive synergistic mergers between multi-billion-dollar corporations, this methodology maintains no care for the radically Other save for its utility in promoting a horizontal growth of power and naturalized metonymic domination of the sphere of intellectual thought. This methodological greed is however fundamentally opposed within the nature of the work of art itself, for

> the act of understanding, including the experience of the work of art, surpasses all historicism in the sphere of aesthetic experience. Admittedly, there appears to be an obvious distinction between the original world structure established by a work of art and its survival in the changed circumstances of the world thereafter. But where exactly is the dividing line between the present world and the world that comes to be? How is the original life significance transformed into the reflected experience that is cultural significance? It seems to me that the concept of aesthetic non-differentiation that I have coined in this connection is wholly valid; here there are no clear divisions, and the movement of understanding cannot be restricted to the reflective pleasure prescribed by aesthetic differentiation. It should be admitted that, say, an

ancient image of the gods that was not displayed in a temple as a work of art in order to give aesthetic, reflective pleasure, and is now on show in a museum, retains, even as it stands before us today, the world of religious experience from which it came; the important consequence is that its world still belongs to ours. What embraces both is the hermeneutic universe.[370]

The necessity in the rejection of the wholly subjective experience of the beautiful is such that its ability to disclose truth is kept intact, and furthermore keeps it from losing its historical connection. This is because the wholly subjective experience of art reduces its appreciation to the merely formal which collapses content upon itself. It is thus against the concept of aesthetic differentiation, which maintains the formal categories of the subject-object distinction which aims at procuring 'knowledge' from a work of art, that Gadamer formulates the category of aesthetic non-differentiation. That is to say, within aesthetic differentiation the work of art and its subject matter or the work of art and its performance are split, and those formal qualities which are given as objects of study by what Gadamer saw to be followers of Kant—the mechanical and technical execution of the work—take on primacy as the sole element for appreciation of the work of art, which wholly neglects the subject matter and more fundamentally the truth-revealing nature that it elicits in the percipient. This relationship which maintains the subject-object distinction highlights the subject by way of the Kantian genius in relation to the creation of the work, and forever opposed to it is the 'objective' world of the ahistorical work of art, which, if it maintains truth, can never be imparted due to this infinite distance.

Against this arbitrary set of distinctions, whose lines blur upon investigation, Gadamer seeks to explain how the disclosure of the particular presentation of the work of art allows for the loss of the percipient therein,

---

370 Ibid., xxvii-xxviii.

where the work of art may make a claim upon him. Here, in pursuit of the neglected middle term which emphasizes the dialogue between the percipient and the work of art, which as an experience of understanding is capable of disclosing truth, Gadamer states:

> What I described as aesthetic nondifferentiation clearly constitutes the real meaning of that cooperative play between imagination and understanding which Kant discovered in the "judgment of taste." It is invariably true that when we see something, we must think something in order to see anything. But here it is a *free* play and not directed towards a concept. This cooperative interaction forces us to face the question about what is actually built up in this process of free play between the faculties of imagination and conceptual understanding. What is the nature of this significance whereby something can be experienced meaningfully and is so experienced?[371]

This notion of a free play at work within the individual is also reflected in the nature of play between the individual and the work of art, which itself acts as a mode of dialogical interaction with art such that the 'subject' previously named as the subjectivity of the percipient now falls under the experience of the artwork itself. This play, much like the dialogue with the Other, must be one which the individual loses himself within, such that the seriousness with which the understanding between the two is approached is one whereby, much as Heidegger described the rules of interacting with a tool, the rules of engagement which dictate the entry of said relation fade to the background.

This does not mean that the rules cease to exist, or that the seriousness with which one approaches the game is made moot, but rather that

---

371 Gadamer, Hans-Georg, and Robert Bernasconi, *The Relevance of the Beautiful and Other Essays* (Cambridge: Cambridge University Press, 2002), 29.

the establishment of movement within the game itself, the "to-and-fro" which characterizes that response of the engaged individual, is itself part of the establishing conditions of play, whose spontaneity provides the very possibility of a game at all. For, as Gadamer says, "in order for there to be a game, there always has to be, not necessarily literally another player, but something else with which the player plays and which automatically responds to his move with a countermove."[372] Thus, this metamodern relation to art is one which involves the subjective consciousness of the percipient, but is not limited to it. For as it is a modality of dialogical understanding, it requires something that supersedes its own limitations: something that is always-already incapable of reduction to the same. Art then is itself neither the copycat that Plato asserted it to be, nor the inferior mode of pure conceptual expression which Hegel thought it to be, for as Gadamer says "it is obvious that any pure theory of imitation or reproduction, any naturalistic copy theory, completely misses the point. The essence of a great work of art has certainly never consisted in the accurate and total imitation or counterfeit of 'Nature,'"[373] and this is because "the presentation of the essence, far from being a mere imitation, is necessarily revelatory."[374] It is revelatory, again, in the Heideggerian sense of disclosing and concealing moments of the truth of Being itself, which, as neither reducible to the subject matter, nor the aesthetic characteristics discernible by the aesthetic consciousness, is part of the presentation of the work of art as its mode of being. Gadamer addresses this issue within the realm of multiple mediums when he states that

> when a distinction is made, it is between the material and what
> the poet makes of it, between the poem and the "conception."
> But these distinctions are of a secondary nature. What the

372 Gadamer, *Truth and Method*, 106.
373 Gadamer and Bernasconi, *The Relevance of the Beautiful*, 29.
374 Gadamer, *Truth and Method*, 114.

actor plays and the spectator recognizes are the forms and the action itself, as they are formed by the poet. Thus we have a *double mimesis:* the writer represents and the actor represents. But even this double mimesis is *one*: it is the same thing that comes into existence in each case. More exactly, one can say that the mimetic representation, the performance, brings into existence what the play itself requires. The double distinction between a play and its subject matter and a play and its performance corresponds to a double non-distinction as the unity of truth which one recognizes in the play of art. To investigate the origin of the plot on which it is based is to move out of the real experience of a piece of literature, and likewise it is to move out of the real experience of the play if the spectator reflects about the conception behind a performance or about the proficiency of the actors. Already implicit in this kind of reflection is the aesthetic differentiation of the work itself from its representation. But for the content of the experience as such, as we have seen, it is not even important whether the tragic or comic scene plaything before one is taking place on the stage or in life—when one is only a spectator. What we have called a structure is one insofar as it presents itself as a meaningful whole. It does not exist in itself, nor is it encountered in a mediation accidental to it; rather, it acquires its proper being in being mediated.[375]

he experience of the work of art is thus 'non-differentiated' between the subject matter of which the art discloses, and the presentation which itself makes available the same disclosure for the percipient to lose themselves within. There is an inseparability of the movement such that the focus on the particularities which aesthetic conscious-

---

375 Ibid., 116-17.

ness analyzes is made to speak on a different matter entirely, namely itself. The temporality of the relation itself is overcome in the fusion of horizons from which the experience of art can be said to mediate the historicity of both the percipient and the work of art, rather than the Kantian ahistorical self-understanding involved in the development of formal taste. This solipsism is avoided in Gadamer's conception by the temporal process of understanding that the percipient is always-already engaged in. This conception holds the movement together from art's role within Heidegger's *alētheiatic* truth as uncovering, to its intelligibility found through the performance and play of the work of art itself, which is always-already processed by way of interpretation.

However, it is important to take note that this interpretation is not a boundless freedom which prances about as it wills, flattening all before its gaze into an undifferentiated gray primordial content whose meaning is arbitrarily endorsed. Rather, as the notion of the playing of a game should indicate, there are in fact a set of 'rules' that bind the 'tradition' of the performative, which Gadamer describes by stating:

> Although the tradition created by a great actor, director, or musician remains effective as a model, it is not a brake on free creation, but has become so fused with the work that concern with this model stimulates an artist's creative interpretative powers no less than does concern with the work itself. The performing arts have this special quality: that the works they deal with are explicitly left open to such re-creation and thus visibly hold the identity and continuity of the work of art open towards its future. Perhaps in such a case the criterion that determines whether something is "a correct presentation" (*Darstellung*) is a highly flexible and relative one. But the fact that the representation is bound to the work is not lessened by the fact that this bond can have no fixed criterion. Thus we do not allow the interpretation of a piece of music or a drama the

freedom to take the fixed "text" as a basis for arbitrary, ad-lib effects, and yet we would regard the canonization of a particular interpretation —e.g., in a recorded performance conducted by the composer, or the detailed notes on performance which come from the canonized first performance—as a failure to appreciate the real task of interpretation. A "correctness" striven for in this way would not do justice to the true binding nature of the work, which imposes itself on every interpreter immediately, in its own way, and does not allow him to make things easy for himself by simply imitating a model.[376]

We find here a sober medium between which freedom and determination grant temperance that keeps understanding from falling into something like a mere formalism or radical poststructuralism which mediates authentic content, but fails to understand the relation presupposing their opposites within the moment of *experience itself*. Here it is important to note that "obviously there is an essential difference between a spectator who gives himself entirely to the play of art and someone who merely gapes at something out of curiosity."[377] That is, the object of the curious is of no concern and does not cause a significant relation or experience that lasts beyond the moment of radiant novelty.

For this individual, the moment of 'being present' with the work of art which constitutes the possibility of understanding itself finds that there is a lack whereby the openness which constitutes the authentic fundamental disposition toward the work of art is instead simply that disposition whereby "several objects of aesthetic experience [*Erlebnis*] are all held in consciousness at the same time—all indifferently, with the same claim to validity."[378] This disposition, rather than achieving unity in multiplicity

---

376 Ibid., 117-18.
377 Ibid., 122.
378 Ibid., 123.

which is itself the serious task of understanding, presents a destruction of multiplicity through the apathetic identity of the singular (mistaken as a unity). This neglects the differentiation that the existence of a work of art maintains through each iteration of its presentation, and as such the mediated essence which arrives from participation (that mode of being wherefrom 'full presence' is achieved) is itself entirely absent. Thus, the essence of a work of art, which goes beyond the common accounts of events or persons, is neglected by this second individual, where the danger of equating this art with mere signs or mementos becomes a reality.

Gadamer makes a great distinction between the two, stating that the memento exists only to relate a person in the present back to a reality that they *were* present for, and the sign exists to become invisible such that it may draw the user's eye away from it and toward the object signified. The work of art however has its own presence, and by way of this fine distinction we come to see that Gadamer's discussion of the work of art and its audience helps to showcase the unsatisfactory nature of aesthetic theories of art. For these theories seek to make the definition of art that which expresses individual experiences or on the opposite end merely any object which has been interacted with by humans. However,

> the "ideality" of the work of art does not consist in its imitating and reproducing an idea but, as with Hegel, in the "appearing" of the idea itself. On the basis of such an ontology of the picture, the primacy which aesthetic consciousness accords the framed picture that belongs in a collection of paintings can be shown to fail. The picture contains an indissoluble connection with its world.[379]

This speaks again to the ontological structure of the work of art beginning phenomenologically with presentation, which "is an event of

---

379 Ibid., 138.

being—in it being appears, meaningfully and visibly."[380] For already included within presentation are the notions of play, communion, and representation such that the transition from aesthetic consciousness to a necessary concern with hermeneutics proper becomes apparent. This necessity is due to evidence of the disclosure of being found within works of art, and whose adoption resolves a great many problematics of the art world in total by focusing on shifting toward "the original characteristic of the being of human life"[381] which is itself *understanding*. Following Heidegger's ontological clarification of the structure of Being, we come to find both "the projective character of all understanding" as well as "the act of understanding itself [which is conceived of] as the movement of transcendence, of moving beyond the existent."[382] Understanding, then, is the fundamental character which allows for transcendental disclosure of the truth of a relation, and as such, the result of our investigation into the work of art radically reveals the character with which we, in the pursuit of the disclosure of said truth, are to maintain.

In order to procure understanding one must retain an openness toward the meaning of a text or an Other such that

> this openness always includes our situating the other meaning in relation to the whole of our meanings or ourselves in relation to it. Now, the fact is that meanings represent a fluid multiplicity of possibilities, but within this multiplicity of what can be thought . . . not everything is possible; and if a person fails to hear what the other person is really saying, he will not be able to fit what he has misunderstood into the range of his own various expectations of meaning. Thus there

---

380 Ibid.
381 Ibid., 250.
382 Ibid.

is a criterion here also. *The hermeneutical task becomes of itself a questioning of things* and is always in part so defined.[383]

What this ultimately means is that there is constant revision in the fore-meaning of the interpretation process: in every new moment, each person engaged in the act of understanding must form a new fore-meaning when there is dissonance in the unconscious use of language.[384] However, what we have seen in lieu of such questioning is the mere unthinking repetition of Enlightenment and Romanticist assumptions that we find in historicist readings. The repetition of Enlightenment assumptions condemn by way of the designation of 'prejudiced' interpretations of tradition and other 'dogmatic' influences, which become objects of suspicion, and are demarcated polemically through naturalization. This is the Enlightenment's radical move to 'empower' the individual such that authority and the objects of which it speaks fall before the judgment seat of reason alone which will inevitably reject them. This is seen most purely by the arch-Enlightenment figure of Kant who states, at the beginning of his essay "What is Enlightenment?":

> Enlightenment is man's emergence from his self-imposed immaturity. Immaturity is the inability to use one's own understanding without another's guidance. This immaturity is self-imposed if its cause lies not in lack of understanding but in indecision and lack of courage to use one's own mind without another's guidance. *Dare to know! (Sapere aude.)* "Have the courage to use your own understanding," is therefore the motto of the enlightenment.[385]

---

383 Ibid., 271.

384 Ibid., 270.

385 Kant, Immanuel, "What Is Enlightenment?," trans. Mary C. Smith; available at www.columbia.edu/acis/ets/CCREAD/etscc/kant.html.

However, this 'prejudice against prejudices' wasn't equal in its application across the board—one can easily look to the German Enlightenment which "recognized the 'true prejudices' of the Christian religion. [For s]ince the human intellect is too weak to manage without prejudices, it is at least fortunate to have been educated with true prejudices."[386] However, the naturalization of the Enlightenment did not really set in until the second half of its march through the annals of history were complete, with the hand of the Enlightenment savagely flinging texts from its shelves, while its twin brother Romanticism desperately grasped at those whose ancient robes presuppose value for it. This is the "curious refraction caused by romanticism"[387] of which Gadamer speaks. Through the false dualism of the two, what is properly naturalized is a philosophy of history which contains within it an "abstract contrast between myth and reason."[388]

In the space of presupposed 'opposites,' we find the assumption that poetry, theology, art, and the like do not relate 'truth' in the way that science does, and thus these endeavors are rendered 'historical' in their address. This means that they speak to someone 'other than the reader' so that within the very ontological presuppositions before these endeavors, there is the pure impossibility of 'truth' in the way that science is believed to 'possess it.' In this Enlightenment-oriented 'prejudice against prejudice' we note then that it is the result of a belief in progressive 'perfection' whereupon today's citizens have access to perfected resources of reason whereby not only are those who hold fast to 'traditional' positions seen as retrograde, but also lacking the intelligence to grasp what 'reason' presents to them (as a transcendental 'good' which is supposedly self-canceling) and as such are 'on the wrong side of history,' which those 'heirs of reason' themselves unfold against/from, as if the others are but a

---

386 Gadamer, *Truth and Method*, 275.
387 Ibid.
388 Ibid.

shell to be shed, and towards which a progressive unfolding of 'universal reason' might therefrom bloom. Gadamer shows us that

> In contrast to the Enlightenment's faith in perfection, which thinks in terms of complete freedom from "superstition" and the prejudices of the past, we now find that olden times—the world of myth, unreflective life, not yet analyzed away by consciousness, in a "society close to nature," the world of Christian chivalry—all these acquire a romantic magic, even apriority over truth. Reversing the Enlightenment's presupposition results in the paradoxical tendency toward restoration—i.e., the tendency to reconstruct the old because it is old, the conscious return to the unconscious, culminating in the recognition of the superior wisdom of the primeval age of myth. But the romantic reversal of the Enlightenment's criteria of value actually perpetuates the abstract contrast between myth and reason. All criticism of the Enlightenment now proceeds via this romantic mirror image of the Enlightenment. Belief in the perfectibility of reason suddenly changes into the perfection of the "mythical" consciousness and finds itself reflected in a paradisiacal primal state before the "fall" of thought.[389]

The generation of the Romanticist's own reactionary 'tradition' fundamentally accepts and naturalizes the ontology of the Enlightenment and its consequences. Its very creation is but a subtle sideroad toward the Enlightenment itself whereby those who seek solace from its demands blindly and superstitiously conjure an idealized bygone era which by its foundation always-already gives rise to the Enlightenment. The fantastical ideals of Romanticism on every front seem to fall back into the traps

---

389 Ibid., 275-76.

of the Enlightenment: their mythical collective consciousness is "just as dogmatic and abstract as that of a state of perfect enlightenment," and ultimately

> the fact that the restorative tendency of romanticism could combine with the fundamental concerns of the Enlightenment to create the historical sciences simply indicates that the same break with the continuity of meaning in tradition lies behind both. If the Enlightenment considers it an established fact that all tradition that reason shows to be impossible (i.e., nonsense) can only be understood historically—i.e., by going back to the past's way of looking at things —then the historical consciousness that emerges in romanticism involves a radicalization of the Enlightenment. For nonsensical tradition, which had been the exception, has become the general rule for historical consciousness. Meaning that is generally accessible through reason is so little believed that the whole of the past— even, ultimately, all the thinking of one's contemporaries—is understood only "historically." Thus the romantic critique of the Enlightenment itself ends in Enlightenment, for it evolves as historical science and draws everything into the orbit of historicism. The basic discreditation of all prejudices, which unites the experimental fervor of the new natural sciences during the Enlightenment, is universalized and radicalized in the historical Enlightenment.[390]

The belief that Romanticism maintains—that tradition stands in opposition to the 'freedom of reason'—naturalizes tradition in explicitly oppositional terms, failing to see that tradition is itself an element of freedom and history which

---

390 Ibid., 276-77.

needs to be affirmed, embraced, cultivated. It is, essentially, preservation, and it is active in all historical change. But preservation is an act of reason, though an inconspicuous one. For this reason, only innovation and planning appear to be the result of reason. But this is an illusion. Even where life changes violently, as in ages of revolution far more is preserved in the supposed transformation of everything than anyone knows, and it combines with the new to create a new value. At any rate, preservation is as much a freely chosen action as are revolution and renewal. That is why both the Enlightenment's critique of tradition and the romantic rehabilitation of it lag behind their true historical being.[391]

Significantly, this also speaks to both the Heideggerian notions of being-in-the-world, projection and thrownness, for in Gadamer's formulation "history does not belong to us: we belong to it."[392] For we are always-already situated within traditions, and these traditions are themselves outgrowths of and reactions toward other traditions that they are situated within. There is no objectifying process: our faculty of reason is delivered to us by way of its situatedness within the concrete historical terms that depends upon the conditions which give rise to any and all of its operations. This does not mean, however, that understanding maintains some pure and simple unity with the past, for its mediation is not some unquestionable and undifferentiated moment of the phenomenon itself, but rather the relation of tradition which itself always maintains a moment of strangeness in its historical distance from us.

As such, all understanding has a "strangeness and familiarity to us, between being a historically intended, distanced object and belonging

---

391 Ibid., 282-83.
392 Ibid., 278.

to a tradition. *The true locus of hermeneutics is this in-between.*[393] *It* is through a historical awareness which acknowledges the deliberation and experiences of previous generations, which sees the reasoning of any historical moment possessing the possibility of being dominated by its bad ideas, that the positive potentiality of tradition and its authority find their place among our reasoning as it is in-itself. The in-between nature, then, of understanding is that which finds the truth of reason encompassing both the 'revolutionary' Enlightenment and its 'reactionary' offshoot in the Romantic as moments (both innovation and conservation) within the larger constellation of phenomena which is *reason itself.* It follows, then, that *all* of human inquiry maintains tradition and innovation in that they are functions necessitated by our existence as temporal beings. Time is not a yawning abyss by which previous and present understandings are forever divided, but rather it is the very constitution where one spills forth into the other! Significantly, "temporal distance can solve . . . how to distinguish the true prejudices, by which we *misunderstand,* from the *false* ones by which we *understand.*"[394] Thus we see that maintaining fidelity to either moment is itself a construction of false consciousness—one which covers up the necessary moments of openness wherefrom authentic understanding may occur—doing away with the expectation of the knowledge of the other, anticipation of the closed nature of ideology, an openness to being wrong, and a sensitivity to alterity. These foundational axes of understanding are often incriminated as necessitating an unwanted position of openness toward wrongfulness or misunderstanding whereby ideology may take hold. They state that these kinds of sensitivities are neutral in the face of real and true evils, as such individuals fall prey to.

However, these accusations overlook the fundamental possibility of understanding which necessitates these sensitives as the "foregrounding

---

393 Ibid., 295.
394 Ibid., 298.

and appropriation of one's own fore-meanings and prejudices."[395] This foregrounding

> clearly requires suspending its validity for us. For as long as our mind is influenced by a prejudice, we do not consider it a judgment. How then can we foreground it? It is impossible to make ourselves aware of a prejudice while it is constantly operating unnoticed, but only when it is, so to speak, provoked . . . For what leads to understanding must be something that has already asserted itself in its own separate validity. Understanding begins . . . when something addresses us . . . But all suspension of judgments and hence . . . of prejudices, has the logical structure of a *question*.[396]

It is with our arrival to the privileged status of the question that we can begin to understand the phenomenological nature of understanding as it seeks to "open up possibilities and keep them open."[397] It is important to note again however that the opening is not itself the neutrality, its critics are quick to label it, for

> if a prejudice becomes questionable in view of what another person or a text says to us, this does not mean that it is simply set aside and the text or the other person accepted as valid in its place [for] . . . our own prejudice is properly brought into play by being put at risk. Only by being given full play is it able to experience the other's claim to truth and make it possible for him to have full play himself.[398]

---

395 Ibid., 271.
396 Ibid., 298.
397 Ibid.
398 Ibid.

It is this non-neutral openness which is foundational to the metamodern paradigm which is established by the sublation of epochs that came before it (modernity and postmodernity), and through which we see that "understanding is, essentially, a historically effected event."[399]

This returns us to the original notion of understanding that we have begun with, which speaks of the horizon from which understanding is founded, yet makes explicit that this foundation is not itself a prison, for understanding is by definition neither static nor unchanging. Our understanding, just like the prejudices that form all experience *as such* is itself brought into question during its own founding process. In other words, in the encounter with an other, our own horizon (which is foundational to understanding) is, as its status of non-neutral openness demands, truly susceptible to the tides of change. These tides of change are the positive instability of negotiation, whereby the dialogue between oneself and one's partner produces *agreement* which itself is the moment of understanding related to the matter at hand. We encounter the interrelated flow of understanding, interpretation, and application as but moments comprising a unified process, for "interpretation is not an occasional, post facto supplement to understanding: rather, understanding is always interpretation, and hence interpretation is the explicit form of understanding."[400] The interpretation serves as species of prejudgment of understanding whereby the concerns of the present are the very means which we can truly engage with the matter at hand. We can then already see the flow from interpretation and understanding to application by the very determination of the two as extending from a practical teleology that concerns the middle ground which interpretation, understanding, and application all hold. This is why "an interpreter's task is not simply to repeat what one of the partners says in the discussion he is translating, but to express what is said in the way that seems

399 Ibid., 299.
400 Ibid., 306.

most appropriate to him, considering the real situation of the dialogue, which only he knows, since he alone knows both languages being used in the discussion."[401] This is how understanding which has not only enabled us to move beyond restrictive and totalizing knowledge as it is in-and-for-itself, but one which encompasses the truth of art, and even more shockingly, one which finds philological, legal, and theological truth kept intact. For example,

> a law does not exist in order to be understood historically, but to be concretized in its legal validity by being interpreted. Similarly, the gospel does not exist in order to be understood as a merely historical document, but to be taken in such a way that it exercises its saving effect. This implies that the text, whether law or gospel, if it is to be understood properly—i.e., according to the claim it makes—must be understood at every moment, in every concrete situation, in a new and different way. Understanding here is always application.[402]

This concreteness relates meaning to the individual's situation: it is the very meaning of the tripartite movement of the process itself. This is the middle ground, once again, whereby the pretensions of absolute objectivity and absurdity of radical subjectivity are sublated within the purview of the understanding of man as he is in the world, favoring neither the objectivity of the historically defined text nor the subjectivity of psychology or individuating perspective but rather the dialogical meaning procured therefrom which is irreducible to one or the other, but is rather itself differentiated *as meaning*. This meaning is "the miracle of understanding [which] consists in the fact that no like-mindedness is necessary to recognize what is really significant and fundamentally

---

401 Ibid., 307.
402 Ibid., 307-8.

meaningful in tradition. We have the ability to open ourselves to the superior claim the text makes and to respond to what it has to tell us."[403] It is important to note that "in many respects, the discussion here is much too restricted to the special situation of the historical human sciences and 'being that is oriented to a text,'"[404] and as such, even though we have spoken briefly of language and dialogue with otherness and distance, they are topics for a later chapter, as is the issue of morality which undulates below the surface of the words in use here.

For here it is enough to remind ourselves that the act of understanding is not

> an appropriation as taking possession; rather, it consists in subordinating ourselves to the text's claim to dominate our minds . . . [and that to do so is rather] . . . clearly not a form of domination but of service. They are interpretations— which includes application—in the service of what is considered valid. Our thesis is that historical hermeneutics too has a task of application to perform, because it too serves applicable meaning, in that it explicitly and consciously bridges the temporal distance that separates the interpreter from the text and overcomes the alienation of meaning that the text has undergone.[405]

Yet this process by which meaning unfolds does not obliterate this alienation as it subsists in the other as *alterity itself*, for to do so would in fact be tantamount to the totalizing reduction of the other to the same, and as such would not be fueled by the metaphysical desire that constitutes it.

---

403 Ibid., 309-10.
404 Ibid., 367.
405 Ibid., 310.

Hermeneutics and Morality

Contrary to what many want of the ethical, it must retain the state of habitual refreshment so that non-neutral openness is necessary to its ground. This is because, as a living relation, it can be neither realized through methodological exactitude nor relegated to alien grounds of radical subjectivity conjured in an attempt to keep culpability differed. For even if an individual should attempt to utilize either extreme grounding of morality as an alibi, it is intrinsic to moral phenomena as they are in-and-of-themselves that the action and the person acting must be the site of decision and responsibility. This is the background against which "it is essential that philosophical ethics have the right approach, so that it does not usurp the place of moral consciousness and yet does not seek out purely theoretical and 'historical' knowledge either but, by outlining phenomena, helps moral consciousness to attain clarity concerning itself."[406] As moral knowledge is eminent within the temporal moment that it can be conceived, it necessitates action therein, and thus the individual who seeks the moral aid of philosophical knowledge must "be mature enough not to ask that his instruction provide anything other than it can and may give."[407] This is consistent with the practical nature with which hermeneutics is concerned: one which is concretized through lived experience rather than generated by mere abstract theory/methodology. Just as one does not engage in hermeneutics over and above the experience of life which is

---

406 Ibid., 311.
407 Ibid.

always-already alongside-the-world, neither does he engage in philosophical ethics as absolute and divorced from revision and interpretation, for this is always-already inherent in application, without which morality is utterly meaningless. Thus, the atomistic subject which has dominated the moral world since the ancients has merely shifted in terminology since its conception, which save through the critical lens of radical subjectivity, has consistently ignored the community and tradition from which the individual always-already inherits prejudices. With the process of understanding as a historically conditioned event, and recognizing that this includes the processes of interpretation and application, we discover the moral individual is an *acting individual* and also come to see that "an active being . . . is concerned with what is not always the same but can also be different. In it he can discover the point at which he has to act. The purpose of his knowledge is to govern his *action.*"[408]

When people ask philosophical ethics to survey the possibilities of life and supply determinate rules wherefrom all shifting axes are considered, alongside a complete response of what one ought to do, they ignore all context and aspects of one's situation, whose understanding as such is only manifest within the moral life itself. Yet the ethical path is one which obviously fails to be relative as it is concretely determined by one's being-in-the-world. As such the world, which we as individuals within a community and network of others constitute, gives forth this dialogical reason whereby non-neutral openness situates our relationality with others such that radical relativity is itself demarcated as an impossibility. In addition, "the most basic of all hermeneutic preconditions remains one's own fore-understanding, which comes from being concerned with the same subject. This is what determines what can be realized as unified meaning and thus determines how the fore-conception of completeness is applied."[409] This is to say that the "immanent unity" of meaning is

---

408 Ibid., 312.
409 Ibid., 294.

assumed by the very guidance of the "constant transcendent expectations of meaning" which grounds his relation to the "truth of what is being said" such that the anticipation of meaning is the anchor to and derived from the "commonality that binds one to the tradition."[410] This is why 'moral knowledge' is different from *techne*, for "we learn a techne and can also forget it. But we do not learn moral knowledge, nor can we forget it. We do not stand over against it as if it were something that we can acquire or not, as we can choose to acquire an objective skill, a techne. Rather, we are always already in the situation of having to act . . . and hence we must already possess and be able to apply moral knowledge."[411]

Here it is important to note the necessary origin of Gadamer's hermeneutical approach to morality as generated, following Heidegger, by our fundamental facticity, temporality, and finitude. This not only demands that we seek behind the categories of man's rationality and consciousness, but also do away with the methodological approach and neglect of historical situatedness which are symptomatic issues stemming from the assumptions of modernism. From here we look to the ways in which we are caught up in meaning as such, for within it perception is cast twice in a single moment; the first time as perception, the second as interpretation. Heidegger makes this clear when he shows that "in interpreting, we do not, so to speak, throw a 'signification' over some naked thing which is present-at-hand, we do not stick a value on it; but when something within-the-world is encountered as such, the thing in question already has an involvement which is disclosed in our understanding of the world, and this involvement is one which gets laid out by the interpretation."[412] Contained already within the moment of perception is also the recognition of a relation to meaning, such that learning itself is an act of world interpretation. In so doing it distinguishes between

---

410 Ibid., 295.

411 Ibid., 315.

412 Heidegger, *Being and Time*, 190-91.

that which presents itself to us as something we do not recognize and that which has already constituted familiarity through our initial learning process. The moment of familiarity implies an *a priori* intelligibility such that the conditions for the possibility of understanding can be seen to function in three moments of a unified phenomenon.

This unified phenomenon finds that we grasp, have, and see in advance—what are respectively termed fore-conception, fore-having, and foresight—for already within the concept of meaning is "the formal existential framework of what necessarily belongs to that which an understanding interpretation articulates. *Meaning is the 'upon-which' of a projection in terms of which something becomes intelligible as something; it gets its structure from a fore-having, a fore-sight, and a fore-conception.*"[413] *For* Heidegger, then, this existential framework is already enclosed within the structure of man himself, rather than merely a property added to it later on. It is due to the facticity of existence then, of a concrete experience with a determinate time and place, that options are open to us from an almost indefinite amount of dimensions, and yet the primary mode of determinate sense-making of the world is through language which is understood as fore-having: the prejudices and preconceptions which a particular tradition of language itself always-already brings with it. Secondarily, we find that fore-sight is the application of understanding such that its object is given categorically implicit determination that casts it within a certain light—that is to say, the guiding claim of interpretation is the 'as' with which the object before it is angled. Lastly then we see that the fore-conception is the part of the process which opens the conceptual framework to forge a link in the web of intelligibility available to it in its time and space, and imposed through discourse itself—thus giving understanding over to the movement of dialogical reasoning—although it is important to note that the fore-conception is generally the governing intelligibility

413 Ibid., 193.

of understanding regardless of its expression. The facticity of being-in-the-world denotes that interpretation is always-already guided by this unified fore-structure in its totality and as such recognizing our finitude therein precludes somehow divorcing ourselves from this being-in-the-world such that we may take on an absolute god's-eye view of any particular matter at hand.

It is important, then, to see that the finitude of man makes explicit the impossibility of understanding's completion, and hence contained within this description is the habitual ongoing nature of the process of understanding which precludes absolute determinacy. The search for truth is already contained within the desire that propels the individual toward the fore-conception of completeness which is "obviously a formal condition of all understanding. It states that only what really constitutes a unity of meaning is intelligible. So when we read a text we always assume its completeness . . . The fore-conception of completeness that guides all our understanding is, then, always determined by the specific content."[414] The fore-conception of completeness is an enabling and productive condition such that understanding "means, primarily, to understand the content of what is said, and only secondarily to isolate and understand another's meaning as such."[415] We here again find that this truth of the content inherent to the fore-conception of completeness can profoundly affect our prejudices, and thus can impart itself to our understanding rather than merely recognizing the content itself as *the truth*. For again, this type of correspondence theory is unsubstantiated and amounts to sophistry. Instead it is the non-neutral openness to the truth of what is being said that draws us close to its transcendental nature by way of dialogical reason. It is in this sense that we bring images to bear on deciding what action ought to be taken when faced with a moral decision. This is why

---

414 Gadamer, *Truth and Method*, 295.
415 Ibid., 294.

the concept of application is highly problematical. For we can only apply something that we already have; but we do not possess moral knowledge in such a way that we already have it and then apply it to specific situations. The image that a man has of what he ought to be—i.e., his ideas of right and wrong, of decency, courage, dignity, loyalty, and so forth . . . —are certainly in some sense images that he uses to guide his conduct.[416]

These images, however, do not constitute a Kantian categorical imperative, nor a Platonic form of justice, and are themselves aspirational horizons of dialogical reason rather than a universalized and absolute judgment on behalf of the Enlightenment's all-seeing reason. Or what is the same thing, "What is right . . . cannot be fully determined independently of the situation that requires a right action from me."[417] It's not the matter of determining a specific end through which ideas of right and wrong, of decency, courage, dignity, loyalty, and so forth maintain a concrete relation, for it is obvious enough that the meaning of any specific trait might come to find opposite and equal employment in separate particular instances across ever-changing contexts.

It is the background principles that incite application in concrete situations and which only become clear and relevant therein, and yet simultaneously what this incitement demands of the situation is irreducible to the specific instantiation of its experience. This is made explicit by Gadamer, salvaging the true insight of Aristotelean natural law:

Certainly he accepts the idea of an absolutely unchangeable law, but he limits it explicitly to the gods and says that among men not only statutory law but also natural law is changeable.

416 Ibid., 315.
417 Ibid.

For Aristotle, this changeability is wholly compatible with the fact that it is "natural law." The sense of this assertion seems to me to be the following: some laws are entirely a matter of mere agreement (e.g. traffic regulations), but there are also things that do not admit of regulation by mere human convention because the "nature of the thing" constantly asserts itself . . . Rather, Aristotle affirms as true of the teacher of ethics precisely what is true, in his view, of all men: that he too is always already involved in a moral and political content and acquires his image of the thing from that standpoint. He does not himself regard the guiding principles that he describes as knowledge that can be taught. They are valid only as schemata . . . Thus they are not norms to be found in the stars, nor do they have an unchanging place in a natural moral universe, so that all that would be necessary would be to perceive them. Nor are they mere conventions, but really do correspond to the nature of the thing—except that the latter is always itself determined in each case by the use the moral consciousness makes of them.[418]

Just as the way in which understanding is the dialectical product of the truth of a subject matter standing in provocation to those engaged in dialogical reason and transcending the subjective aims of each interlocutor, so too is the foundation of law this interplay between general principles and the particular case of the matter at hand. Prereflective understanding of general principles relates to the individual experience such that a unified application of this prior direction and specific instantiation of a demand may make sense out of moral action, and at the same time, the concrete itself *clarifies the schemata.*

Methodological approaches to morality which seek to define moral principles *a priori* such that the specific expressions can be measured up

---

418 Ibid., 317-18.

against them reveal a perspective on human rationality which fails to accurately relate to the finite, historically-affected consciousness that is foundational to man. All of this simultaneously shows that the conditions of objectivity which any such correspondence theory of morality assumes to uphold are in fact inherited from a preexisting framework of tradition, and are thus projections and judgments that form the various moral 'philosophies.' What this shows us is that

> ...we are dealing here with a fundamental relationship. It is not the case that extending technical knowledge would obviate the need for moral knowledge, this deliberating with oneself. Moral knowledge can never be knowable in advance like knowledge that can be taught. The relation between means and ends here is not such that one can know the right means in advance, and that is because the right end is not a mere object of knowledge either.[419]

This is because practical wisdom is the instrument of moral ability: the substantive content of morality begins in life. What's at stake is the concrete good of factic life itself, for the never-ending engagement of praxis denies the sufficiency of theoretical knowledge thereof. Flexibility and improvisation are rather more helpful to ethical action than rules and principles which are subsidiary at best. What this means is that, like "Aristotle's definitions of phronesis," our moral knowledge has "a marked uncertainty about them in that this knowledge is sometimes related more to the end, and sometimes more to the means to the end."[420] The formation of virtue wherefrom we can reflect upon moral knowledge is molded within the character of the individual in relation to the community, tradition, and sets of authorities which they grow

---

419 Ibid., 318.
420 Ibid.

up within such that at all times we, as individuals, can be seen to be engaging in moral action.

Again following Gadamer's reading of Aristotle, this is because "Phronesis is not simply the capacity to make the right choice of means, but is itself a moral hexis that also sees the telos towards which the person acting is aiming with his moral being."[421] With *hexis* itself being roughly translated as a relatively stable disposition, we can understand that moral action as that which is always-already involved with the concrete practical world is that which is expressed in each moment of our lives as a whole, rather than being a conscious choice which the individual gives themselves over to or denies from one moment to the next. The challenging underlying condition here is that

> This means that the end toward which our life as a whole tends and its elaboration in the moral principles of action described in Aristotle's *Ethics* cannot be the object of a knowledge that can be taught. No more can ethics be used dogmatically than can natural law. Rather, Aristotle's theory of virtue describes typical forms of the true mean to be observed in human life and behavior; but the moral knowledge that is oriented by these guiding images is the same knowledge that has to respond to the demands of the situation of the moment.[422]

It seems as though 'moral character' is brought about more by imitation than through the moral teachers of each age. This is because ethical or moral teachings, descriptions, and theories are always unelaborated without concrete practical action; and this is because we, in Aristotle's view, neither learn nor forget 'moral knowledge.' We are habituated into virtue by way of that fundamental irreversible transcendental

421 Ibid., 377-78.
422 Ibid., 318-19.

relation whereby the I leaves itself, which is "primordially enacted as conversation."[423] This is "[a] relation whose terms do not form a totality [which] can hence be produced within the general economy of being only as proceeding from the I to the other, *as a face to face* as delineating a distance in depth – of conversation, of goodness, of desire."[424] Once again, at the center of this relation stands interpretation, which not only founds the actions of the other, but so too is our projected anticipation of present events based on interpretation in light of the events of the past. Yet, because the other is truly other, his memories and anticipations preclude my access. His interpretations and actions are, at their genesis, unavailable to me, thus retaining an unpredictability which is defined by the other's status as Other. Levinas points out that the title 'stranger' also means 'free one' which by way of this unpredictability retains the status of personhood for the other. For it is speech with an other whereby we find not only that the truth of the conversation is the transcendent principle through which a fusion of horizons may take place, but so too does face to face conversation find the speaking face as the site which exceeds that which is said. It is this transcendental character of excess that holds open "the distance between me and the other, the radical separation asserted in transcendence which prevents the reconstitution of the totality."[425] This tension is sustained by "[a] calling into question of the same . . . brought about by the other. We name this calling into question of my spontaneity by the presence of the other 'ethics.'"[426] This 'calling into question' that demands our response is the interpretation of the other such that our justification within the framework of the ethical is "not contrary to truth; it goes to being in its absolute exteriority, and accomplishes the very intention that animates

---

423 Levinas, *Totality and Infinity*, 39.
424 Ibid.
425 Ibid., 40.
426 Ibid., 43.

the movement unto truth."[427] The obvious ontic sense of being whereby man is always-already caught alongside the other in society writ large is animated by man's relation to Otherness as such (the very nature of an authentic transcendental subject). This is to say that the embodied excess toward which 'saying' is directed is already included within the notion of being itself; it is the anticipation toward which the openness of being is invited. This is "the way in which the other presents himself, exceeding the idea of the other in me, [which] we here name [the] face."[428] This is because it expresses itself immediately against that which is said, and in so doing reflects the excess which is the very potency of the transference of teaching; it carries the heritage of its exteriority beyond the contents of the same. This relation to the other is that by which his speech is the external interpretation which "puts the spontaneous freedom within us to question. It commands and judges it and brings it to its truth." It is within the face that we find "philosophical priority" that is "extant over Being."[429] Being here refers to Heidegger's standard of disclosure which would never be called into question by the existent, for "to say that the existent is disclosed only on the openness of Being is to say that we are never directly with the existent as such."[430]

This is the corrective that Levinas found whereby to be disclosed by Being alone is to do so by way of its standards without question. Levinas puts this by stating that "without separation, there would not have been truth: there would have been only being."[431] By showing the necessary condition of the existent in relation to truth we can see the intimate unity of thought and speech as caught up in the inseparability of the finite and infinite of Gadamer's notion of historically affected consciousness, which retroactively establishes the necessity of the existent for truth which "in

427 Ibid., 47.
428 Ibid., 50.
429 Ibid., 51.
430 Ibid., 52.
431 Ibid., 58.

the risk of ignorance, illusion and error, does not undo 'distance,' does no result in the union of the knower and the known, does not issue in totality."[432] This is what it means then to say that interpretation is never complete, for it is by our living in the world by which our dialogue as it is related to Being is only resolutely integrated and complete upon death. Thus, as is obvious, our ethical life is one of engagement with the world and as such a virtuous life stems from one's horizon wherefrom engagement is made possible.

The marriage of dialectic and language as they relate to Being in Gadamer's hermeneutic is that which "exists as a kind of double loop, cycling through the human capacity to reflect, which is both a capacity that language confers and creative of the reality by which it continues to evolve."[433] Ethical knowledge as *phronesis* relates our finitude to the challenge of dialogue with the fore-completeness of knowledge such that understanding may relate these novel truths beyond any resemblance of methodology, and toward the transcendental identity of the infinite relation of mind and world. And yet, it is important to note that "virtue is behaving *with* Logos . . . [which] means that this behavior . . . does not just correspond to thought but has thought in the very midst of it."[434] Here, thinking and doing are caught up in the movement of seeking truth, which is this "going towards the other in Desire . . . [such that] the idea of exteriority guides the quest for truth is possible only as the idea of infinity."[435] It is by our relation to the infinite that we see that despite the conditionedness of our experience, *phronesis* is always-already striving for the good, yet we should remember to subject our own prejudices and preferences to critique, such that we may not fall victim to the "dialectic of the exception that at once considers something valid

---

432 Ibid., 60.

433 Arthos, *The Inner Word*, 165.

434 Gadamer, Hans-Georg, *Hermeneutics, Religion, and Ethics* (New Haven, Conn.: Yale University Press, 2012), 155.

435 Levinas, *Totality and Infinity*, 61.

yet excepts itself from it."[436] Such subjection to critique aims also to keep from subverting an ought to an inclination.

From here it is significant to see that, *contra* Heidegger, Levinas seeks to establish man's relation to truth as beyond mere disclosure, which is the relation of Being and objects in the world for Heidegger. This relation is truth without risk, and as such ignores the leading nature of the world which results from our conversational relation to it. Disclosure in this prior sense rejects the necessity of transcendence implicit in the notion of infinity. For Levinas, the search for truth is fundamentally a moral relation whereby the desire that animates it "marks a sort of inversion . . . in it being becomes goodness: at the apogee of its being, expanded into happiness, in egoism, positing itself as *ego*, here it is, beating its own record, preoccupied with another being! This represents a fundamental inversion not of some one of the functions of being, a function turned from its goal, but an inversion of its very exercise of being..."[437] Truth then actively reveals itself through the relation to the Other, exposes itself through the transformation of our horizons by non-neutral openness, and affects our understanding such that attention and response to the Other may act as a moral foundation for truth, one which denies instrumental or dehumanizing objectification through refusing to overestimate our capacity to judge the true being of an Other. This is because through attentiveness an other may express themselves "independently of every position we have taken in its regard . . . [I]t is present as directing this very manifestation—present before manifestation which only manifests it."[438] With an other, the saying always surpasses the said such that the categories with which we are present in relation to an other are simultaneously modified. Yet this is at the same time irreducible to the whole of the dialogue, for "discourse is not simply a modification of intuition

---

436 Gadamer, *Hermeneutics, Religion, and Ethics*, 158.
437 Levinas, *Totality and Infinity*, 63.
438 Ibid., 65.

(or of thought), but an original relation with exterior being."[439] It is the excess manifest in the face which denotes interiority. This interiority is related through the eyes which see in addition to being seen and thus we find that "the eye does not shine, it speaks."[440] And thus it is the face-to-face encounter with an other whereby language erupts, for language presupposes the exteriority of others, an interlocutor, a plurality.[441]

And as such, discourse (contrasted to rhetoric, its opposite, which is corrupting and manipulative) requires not only freedom of each to his own interpretation, but the generosity with which a response moves beyond the world as it is *for-me* into discourse where the world is there for us. Thus it is listening which allows us first to participate in that which is greater than us: we see this in the implicit necessity to receive, which is ontologically established as prior to our response. The ethical relation extends from non-neutral openness, spilling over into language which "lays the foundation for a world in common," and so "To speak is to make the world common."[442] On this, Levinas and Heidegger are in supreme agreement, for Heidegger states that "To think is before all else to listen, to let ourselves be told something . . . Language must, in its own way, avow to us itself—its nature. Language persists as this avowal."[443] We can see that in Heidegger's temporal circle, the concept of *logos* brings about understanding which allows past and future to be present, and as such grounds thinking as that which language anticipates.

This means that it is through the attempt to learn from an other's perspective, where shared investigation may occur which is not only aimed at the matter-at-hand but also the proposition that extends from the other, who is himself promised through speech to "clarify what is

439 Ibid., 66.
440 Ibid.
441 Cf. ibid., 72.
442 Ibid., 76.
443 Heidegger, Martin, *On the Way to Language*, trans. Peter D. Hertz (New York: Harper and Row, 1982), 74.

obscure in the utterance."[444] It is through this promise that discourse is maintained, which in truth relates alterity proper to what is shared, for without this alterity sign and signified would remain identical. Rather because the Other remains external to one's own ideological system, he is able to bring it into question, and as such call me to attend to the world. We find that "our relations are never reversible."[445]

As Heidegger says, "If man is to find his way once again into the nearness of Being he must first learn to exist in the nameless . . . Before he speaks man must let himself be claimed again by Being, taking the risk that under this claim he will seldom have much to say. Only thus will the preciousness of its essence be once more bestowed upon the word."[446] The nameless is that which philosophy presses us toward and which like Lacan's real always eludes that which is named. The Word then finds its non-totalizable nature expressed in the social relation through which it is clarified and before which it is anticipated. This is why, when observing Aristotle's comments on morality, we should take careful note in finding that it is perfect application rather than perfect knowledge which allows employment of any understanding within the field of immediate concrete experience. Yet this does not necessarily mean there is a clear differentiation of experience and knowledge as such, for

> Moral knowledge is really knowledge of a special kind. In a curious way it embraces both means and end, and hence differs from technical knowledge. That is why it is pointless to distinguish here between knowledge and experience, as can be done in the case of a techne. For moral knowledge contains

---

444 Levinas, *Totality and Infinity*, 97.

445 Ibid., 101.

446 Heidegger, Martin, *Basic Writings*, trans. David F. Krell (New York: Harper and Row, 1977), 199.

a kind of experience in itself, and in fact we shall see that this
is perhaps the fundamental form of experience.[447]

We have come full circle in noting that the virtuous life is that which
requires not only theoretical knowledge, but action within the specific
situations we find ourselves. It thus makes clear that it is not the reflecting
individual who acts in an ethically demanding situation, but rather the
deliberative skills of *phronesis* which affect an Other. Hence when we see
that "self-knowledge of moral reflection has, in fact, a unique relation
to itself . . . [for] besides phronesis, the virtue of thoughtful reflection,
stands 'sympathetic understanding.'"[448] Hence, judgment from *phronesis*
is modified (by the term *synesis*) so that its judgment now includes a
relation to the infinite (represented by the Other). This means that the
perspective of the Other, inasmuch as it can be conceptually reflected
in an authentic action of the individual, now restricts the selfish and
detrimental ends of deliberation. Gadamer states that

> This becomes fully clear when we consider other varieties of
> moral reflection listed by Aristotle, namely insight and fellow
> feeling. Insight here means a quality. We say that someone
> is insightful when they make a fair, correct judgment. An
> insightful person is prepared to consider the particular
> situation of the other person, and hence he is also most
> inclined to be forbearing or to forgive. Here again it is clear
> that this is not technical knowledge.[449]

Insight, then, is evidenced by the affected individual retroactively, the
knowledge thereof is procured through authentic empathy, and an eye on

---

447 Gadamer, *Truth and Method*, 319.
448 Ibid.
449 Ibid., 320.

a universalized good to be brought about within the particular situation itself. Thus, Gadamer summarizes for us:

> If we relate Aristotle's description of the ethical phenomenon and especially the virtue of moral knowledge to our investigation, we find that his analysis in fact offers a kind of *model of the problem of hermeneutics*. We too determined that application is neither a subsequent nor merely an occasional part of the phenomenon of understanding, but co-determines it as a whole from the beginning. Here too application did not consist in relating some pregiven universal to the particular situation. The interpreter dealing with a traditionary text tries to apply it to himself. But this does not mean that the text is given for him as something universal, that he first understands it per se, and then afterward uses it for particular applications. Rather, the interpreter seeks no more than to understand this universal, the text—i.e., to understand what it says, what constitutes the test's meaning and significance. In order to understand that, he must not try to disregard himself and his particular hermeneutical situation. He must relate the text to this situation if he wants to understand at all.[450]

Application and understanding are linked within experience itself, with application as something of the core relation of understanding to itself: as essential to understanding. The constitution of experience in relation to both is undeniable, and we find at the same time the relation of the application and understanding to mirror the relation of the body to the world. This is because, as Levinas says, "the body naked and indigent identifies the *center* of the world it perceives," and its representation there-

---

450 Ibid., 320-21.

fore is "as it were, torn up from the center from which it proceeded."[451] It is our being-in-the-world that is itself representational *within us,* such that the experience of the concrete world, in relation to our position of non-neutral openness, relates a mutual determination such that "to posit oneself corporeally is to touch an earth, but to do so in such a way that the touching finds itself already conditioned by the position, the foot settles into a real which this very action outlines or constitutes, as though a painter would notice that he is descending from the picture he is painting."[452]

The unrepresentable nature of being-in-the-world is for Levinas the surplus of the living body over and against the representation of it. Irreplaceable singularity (founded by enjoyment as a subjectivized experience) of this must go about its functions for itself (this is the bodily sensible qua bodily sensible,) and yet it also possesses an equally unique particular interiority which must be transcended by way of the ethical relation. As such, the body then is the condition of dependence upon which the ethical relation is established towards the unique Other. What this simultaneously means is that the other exceeds our representation of them by way of the non-representable singularity—an immeasurable interiority which is irreplaceable by way of the horizon which is unique to it—in a way already understood by our paradoxical relationship to our own body. This is why

> the interiority that ensures separation . . . must produce
> a being absolutely close over upon itself, not deriving its
> isolation dialectically from its opposition to the Other. And
> this closedness must not prevent egress from interiority, so
> that exteriority could speak to it, reveal itself to it, in an
> unforeseeable movement which the isolation of the separated

---

451 Levinas, *Totality and Infinity,* 127.
452 Ibid., 128.

being could not provoke by simple contrast. In the separated being the door to the outside must hence be at the same time open and closed.[453]

The rigid categories of interiority and exteriority are rather like the relation of the *logos* and Augustine's verbum such that the variety of languages never reveal the true being of the verbum (despite having its being in revealing). This investigation into language as the medium of hermeneutic experience will be explored in the next chapter, but perhaps for now it is enough to realize that "In interiority a dimension opens through which it will be able to await and welcome the revelation of transcendence."[454]

---

453 Ibid., 148.
454 Ibid., 150.

LIVING AMBIGUITY

As modernism was canonized, many imagined that the diversification of its reproduction was presenting modernism with the subversion that it itself once carried against the hegemony that birthed it. However, many years after the fact, it is clear that the ever-novel combinations of postmodernity, the mediated simultaneity of "the universality of modernization and of particular lifeworlds,"[455] merely grants many masks to the hegemonic figure. Those who believe that postmodernity carries with it the potentiality for true multiplicity, beyond the totalizing nature of modernity, see only that "in the postmodern universe, pre-modern 'leftovers' are no longer experienced as obstacles to be overcome by progress towards a fully secularized modernization"; however, what this fully means is that while, yes, "all traditions survive," they do so in "mediated 'de-naturalized' form, that is, no longer as authentic ways of life, but as freely chosen 'life-styles.'"[456] While in the metamodern episteme, the reflexivity with which the tensions between the particular and the universal are maintained is kept alive, in postmodernity these tensions are 'dissolved' by falsely generating the tautology of hegemony that 'sides with the resistance' by reproducing its dominant images. It is important to observe this "cunning of postmodernity" should it be avoided, for it is that whereby the particular lifeworld is said to be alive and well in the 'connection' that the postmodern subject maintains.

Yet it is this same relation which finds that the particular lifeworld in all of its discrete parts have already been "'mediatized' and incorporated

---

455 Žižek, Slavoj, *Living in the End Times* (London: Verso, 2010), 283.
456 Ibid.

into global capitalism, rendering possible its smooth functioning."[457] It is not a resolution of antagonisms but rather an emptying of content so as to grant hegemony the image of multiplicity in a unified synthetic whole which consumes all of the space save for the image itself. The sustained totality of postmodernity is that whereby "elements of pre-existing lifeworlds and economics (including money) are gradually re-articulated as its own moments, 'exapted' with a different function."[458] With the shift from national to global we find that the veil covering over gaps and antagonisms is named universality. The network whereby the particular ritual is enacted by the global citizen is the suture which divorces the moment from its living foundation within the lifeworld from whence it came toward a falsely 'multicultural' hegemony. The reason that this falsity exists is by way of a grand misunderstanding of the way that culture works in general. Multiculturalism engages in a struggle that's not really there when it engages with the assertions of colonial notions of modern nationalism whereby culture is seen as a self-contained whole. It is under the acceptance of this false premise that multiculturalism tries to erect the impossible, and seeks to establish a unified synthetic whole that contains already within it the distinct differentiated and self-contained varieties of culture. It does this by utilizing a naive 'pure' *image* of a culture, which is isolated from the living mass of culture itself, and is set apart as a privileged and protected icon to which the individual attempts to conform.

In this way it follows the route walked by the Enlightenment which sought to establish a world citizen as a universal subject whose works belong to all ages, and who, as such, ultimately sought to cover the self and privilege the 'universal.' Much like Christianity sold itself short by being all too ready to rebut the 'pure insight' of the Enlightenment, here multiculturalism acts as an elaboration of the totalizing power pursued from

457 Ibid.
458 Ibid., 284.

the liberal perspective. It falsely grounds itself by ignoring what it secretly cedes through engaging in the debate placed before it, for as Žižek states:

> Whatever else one can accuse liberal multiculturalism of, one should at least admit that it is profoundly anti-"essentialist": it is its barbarian Other which is perceived as essentialist *and thereby false.* Fundamentalism "naturalises" or "essentialises" historically conditioned contingent traits. To modern Europeans, other civilizations are caught in their specific culture, while modern Europeans are flexible, constantly changing their presuppositions.[459]

There is a dual movement through which the assertion of these universal cultures is made. One is generated from a supreme inability to engage with the complexity of tradition in any sensible way: and as if in response to the question of the relativity of ethics, there is a faux-veneration of the Other such that one refrains from judgment, yet retains the superiority of their vision for their society which they clearly articulate in political terms. These political beliefs will cast severe judgment on one's fellow man so long as they are directly 'culturally related,' and despite the family resemblance of their 'crime' (in relation to the Other) for which they are judged, the Other is, by nature of this 'respect,' kept from judgment.

The relativity in relation to the Other is shown to be something other than respect when placed against the backdrop of the 'true seat of judgment' of universality. However, at the same time the movement itself redacts the cultural freedom which gave birth to it in the first place, and denies the possibility of culture in its homeland. "What this means is that the 'subject of free choice' in the Western 'tolerant' multicultural sense can emerge only as the result of an extremely *violent* process of being torn out of a particular lifeworld, of being cut off from one's

---

459 Žižek, *Violence: Six Sideways Reflections*, 147.

roots."[460] Tolerance in multicultural societies is this 'preservation' of the *image* of a culture, whereby those who share its family resemblance are subsumed, stripped of substantiality, and artificially crippled from their natural adaptive relation to their tradition. Application or interpretation, the two most fundamental relations one can have toward any tradition (from which all understanding is in some form in relation to) are seen as fundamentalist relations to a lifeworld, and thus antagonistic to the universality of multiculturalism. The cunning of postmodernity is once again the bearer of images and a brief description of those who 'subscribe' to this 'lifestyle,' believed to be as natural as animals captured in a zoo. Multiculturalism is this zoo that declares its love for the animals it harbors. The moment whereupon there can be a 'pure' performance of a cultural artifact is the moment which that tradition is dead in-and-for-itself. The culture has been mutilated, stripped bare of its interaction with and influence from/on other living traditions. It is no longer engaged, as cultures are themselves, in relation to the world around it; and its adoption within the enframed modality of 'universal' capitalism is not, as it claims, cultural hybridity, but rather a 'museum of natural history' whereby dead objects are neutrally observed with passive bemusement.

To express the same failure of understanding in relation to culture, both the idolization of the premodern inspired by the right in reaction to this universalism, and the 'multiculturalism' which liberal-minded critics have pursued as a modification of this universalism stand in opposition to "the interactive structure (*Gebilde*) of a world not captive to the fixed binary of subject and object . . . [This structure is] at work on the scale of history, that is, the contact of consciousness with its own history exhibiting the same emergent, reciprocating structure . . .

[with] *sprachlichkeit*, linguality or living speech, [as] the fundamental idiom of this interaction."[461] The experience of either can be considered

---

460 Ibid., 146.
461 Arthos, *The Inner Word*, 219.

in no real sense authentic, for "genuine experience is experience of one's own historicity."[462] The genuine experience, then, is one stemming from intellectual humility and a willingness to learn; one which understands the situatedness of oneself always already involved with tradition as the means by which one experiences the world. But, perhaps just as importantly, the genuine experience is one which possesses an inner historicity. As historically effected, consciousness is structured like experience, and so too is history structured like inner historicity which is its analogous foundation. If we are to have an authentic experience, it is important for us to see the ways in which we may stray from the pitfalls of our contemporaries. This is partly because the hegemonic culture has created a monopolized vision of experience informed by modern science, which, "in its methodology . . . simply proceeds further toward a goal that experience has always striven after. Experience is valid only if it is confirmed: hence its dignity depends on its being in principle repeatable. But this means that by its very nature, experience abolishes its history and thus itself."[463] The methodological approach to experience reduces and isolates it from its position as a process in itself - seeking neither to keep intact its negativity mounted from within its diachronic relationality, nor its reciprocity that unites both future (expectation) and past. Yet Gadamer notes that many, in reaction to this one-sidedness, critically assess the problems therefrom by taking the opposing view, which is itself dictated again by one-sidedness. For instance, Husserl makes an

> attempt to go back genetically to the origin of experience, and to overcome its idealization by science, [which] obviously has to struggle especially with the difficulty that the pure transcendental subjectivity of the ego is not really given as such but always given in the idealization of language; moreover,

---

462 Gadamer, *Truth and Method*, 351.
463 Ibid., 342.

language is already present in any acquisition of experience, and in it the individual ego comes to belong to a particular linguistic community.[464]

From here, Gadamer leads us on a historical investigation starting with Francis Bacon, going back to Aristotle, and then concluding with Hegel in order to show us the variety of failures in approaching experience that have resulted in our current bankrupt understanding. In so doing we are explicitly tracing the lineage of pure reason's methodological exclusion of language as the positive condition and guide for experience as such.

This set of principles ignores the predispositions and prejudices of all sorts in an attempt to attain greater 'purity' where 'verbalistic' prejudice is ignored (as contrasted to purged). The teleological approach, while granted its perception of a true element proper to the structure of experience ("the fact that experience is valid so long as it is not contradicted by new experience"[465]) is by its very nature aimed only at experience that results in knowledge. By this we can note how its one-sided nature restricts the very possibility of understanding outside of the invariable methodological principles that it began with. In Aristotle's description of induction, we note that "various perceptions unite to form the unity of experience when many individual perceptions are retained."[466] The singular nature of experience which allows it to be open to new experiences is not accounted for by universals, and are considered only corrective thereof. The fact that "experience is essentially dependent on constant confirmation"[467] becomes thrown away for the certainty provided by the universal methodology, and as such we find that the universality of which Aristotle speaks is clearly something different from

---

464 Ibid., 342-43.
465 Ibid., 345.
466 Ibid.
467 Ibid., 346.

that which science takes for itself, and is in fact closer to our common concept of knowledge.

However, even if we arrive at this point, it is the result of oversimplification and has thus completely missed the process of experience itself, which is the commonality that knowledge claims as its foundation. The generation of universals are rather brought about through the negation of false generalizations, for "language shows this when we use the word 'experience' in two different senses: the experiences that conform to our expectation and confirm it and the new experiences that occur to us. This latter—'experience' in the genuine sense—is always negative. If a new experience of an object occurs to us, this means that hitherto we have not seen the thing correctly and now know it better."[468] This kind of experience does not merely rub the web from our eyes; it is the reversal of an earlier experience as such which gives us greater knowledge than we had before, and therefore it is fundamentally dialectical in that it is through determinate negation that we arrive at the different and unexpected which provoke new experiences.

What we find, then, is that through negation one becomes aware of one's experience, acquiring a new horizon of possibilities which up until this achievement of awareness was closed off from them. It is with the dialectic that we approach the proper element of historicity as it is presented by Hegel who, following Heraclitus, shows us that "we cannot have the same experience twice."[469] And it is from this position that we see consciousness experiencing the in-itself of objects as an in-itself *for us*, for "Hegel is not interpreting experience dialectically but rather conceiving what is dialectical in terms of the nature of experience."[470] Experience, for Hegel, is then a dialectical reflection of consciousness—it is structured dialectically as the reversal of consciousness such that in

---

468 Ibid., 347.
469 Ibid., 348.
470 Ibid., 349.

experience new knowledge, and a new object (which contains the truth of the old object) becomes compiled within the experience, which is really that which consciousness has of itself. For Hegel, then, experience teleologically results in consciousness certain of the truth of itself, what is to Hegel called absolute spirit (consciousness recognizing itself in both itself and that which is alien). Because of this it is clear that self-consciousness is the whole of Hegel's concept of experience, and as it necessarily relates to his notion of absolute spirit it cannot do justice to hermeneutic self-consciousness which we have been seeking. Thus, contra Hegel, Gadamer posits that

> the experienced person proves to be . . . someone who is radically undogmatic: who, because of the many experiences he has had and the knowledge he has drawn from them, is particularly well equipped to have new experiences and to learn from them. The dialectic of experience has its proper fulfillment notion definitive knowledge but in the openness to experience that is made possible by experience itself.[471]

Hegel's equation of substance with subject is beyond the scope of experience which belongs to our historical nature as that which negates, for "every experience worthy of its name thwarts an expectation. Thus the historical nature of man essentially implies a fundamental negativity that emerges in the relation between experience and insight."[472] This insight then is a part of self-knowledge whereby one recognizes the limits of human finitude. Gadamer tells us that

> The truly experienced person is one who has taken this to heart, who knows that he is master neither of time nor the

---

471 Ibid.
472 Ibid.

future. The experienced man knows that all insight is limited and all plans uncertain. In him is realized the truth value of experience. If it is characteristic of every phase of the process of experience that the experienced person acquires a new openness to new experiences, this is certainly true of the idea of being perfectly experienced. It does not mean that experience has ceased and a higher form of knowledge is reached (Hegel), but that of the first time experience fully and truly is. In it all dogmatism, which proceeds from the soaring desires of the human heart, reaches an absolute barrier. Experience teaches us to acknowledge the real. The genuine result of experience, then—as of all desire to know—is to know what is. But "what is," here, is not this or that thing, but "what cannot be destroyed" (Ranke).[473]

It is through the concrete actions of the individual whereby we come to understand that our power and planning are determinately related to our historicity, which is to make obvious the limits not only of ourselves as temporal beings, but so too of our relation as being-in-the-world. This is why "genuine experience is experience of one's own historicity."[474] This is to say that it is within the limits of irreversibility, the limitations of time, and limited return that we are given over to tradition as that which is experienced. It is that which is caught between a past that has been utterly revolutionized by understanding (and therefore barred from our access) and the transformations that we have yet to achieve. We are in a state projected through experience into openness which receives more readily new experiences. This is why Gadamer states that

> Hermeneutical experience is concerned with tradition. This is what is to be experienced. But tradition is not simply a

---

473 Ibid., 351.
474 Ibid.

process that experience teaches us to know and govern; it is language—i.e., it expresses itself like a Thou. A Thou is not an object; it relates itself to us. It would be wrong to think that this means that what is experienced in tradition is to be taken as the opinion of another person, a Thou. Rather, I maintain that the understanding of tradition does not take the traditionary text as an expression of another person's life, but as meaning that is detached from the person who means it, from an I or a Thou. Still, the relationship to the Thou and the meaning of experience implicit in that relation must be capable of teaching us something about hermeneutical experience. For tradition is a genuine partner in dialogue, and we belong to it, as does the I with a Thou.[475]

Through a genuine openness to the infinite, dialogical reason allows us to be put into question by tradition which is, perhaps more reasonably, an Other to us, which allows us to understand the necessity of reciprocity therein. This reciprocity refers to the openness and attentiveness with which one regards the other such that a true response and understanding may result in an ethical relation. This ethical relation avoids firstly the pitfalls of seeing the Other as that about which we already possess enough knowledge, and which is therefore determinately predictable; and secondly, the view of the Other as locked in competition for a superior claim to recognition. Both seem to result from a false claim to absolute (unconditioned) knowledge, which destroys the meaning of the relation and kills that which lives, producing dead knowledge to the world around us. One can see how

A person who does not admit that he is dominated by prejudices will fail to see what manifests itself by their light. It is like the relation between I and Thou. A person who reflects

475 Ibid., 352.

himself out of the mutuality of such a relation changes this relationship and destroys its moral bond. *A person who reflects himself out of a living relationship to tradition destroys the true meaning of this tradition in exactly the same way.* In seeking to understand tradition historical consciousness must not rely on the critical method with which it approaches its sources, as if this preserved it from mixing in its own judgments and prejudices. It must, in fact, think within its own historicity. To be situated within a tradition does not limit the freedom of knowledge but makes it possible.[476]

An authentic relation towards tradition, such as the I to its Other, is found in the openness of the hermeneutic sphere known by the name *historical consciousness.* Like the relation of the I to the Thou, it is significant that we hold back this false claim to absolute knowledge and truly listen to the Other, such that we enter together into an understanding which is by its very nature mutual. In this understanding there is no blind obedience to the claim of the Other, but openness which by its very nature means accepting that the Other has something to say to me, which ultimately must involve things which are in some sense against me. And yet, in relation to tradition, it is not merely to acknowledge its otherness by recognizing it as the past *in-itself* as both methodological and historical approaches to tradition do, for such a relation is

> not really open at all, but rather, when it reads its texts "historically," it has always thoroughly smoothed them out beforehand, so that the criteria of the historian's own knowledge can never be called into question by tradition. Recall the naive mode of comparison that the historical approach generally engages in. The 25th "Lyceum Fragment" by Friedrich

---

476 Ibid., 354.

Schlegel reads: "The two basic principles of so-called historical criticism are the postulate of the commonplace and the axiom of familiarity. The postulate of the common-place is that everything that is really great, good, and beautiful is improbable, for it is extraordinary or at least suspicious. The axiom of familiarity is that things must always have been just as they are for us, for things are naturally like this." By contrast, historically affected consciousness rises above such naive comparisons and assimilations by letting itself experience tradition and by keeping itself open to the truth claim encountered in it. The hermeneutical consciousness culminates not in methodological sureness of itself, but in the same readiness for experience that distinguishes the experienced man from the man captivated by dogma.[477]

We arrive then at historically affected consciousness which is authentically open to the truth-claims of tradition and maintains an openness thereto by refusing dogmatism which seeks to radically limit the freedom of understanding at which an individual and its Other may arrive. We must maintain the openness to resist our presuppositions, for to otherwise blindly listen to them is likewise slavish. It is only by acknowledging the possibility of a superior knowledge to our own within the truth claim of the Other that the relation to the transformative effects of truth may be encountered. It is then an ongoing process, one which keeps intact the alien nature of alterity without fully resolving the tension. It is only by this ongoing tension-filled relation to the Other that an authentic fusion of horizons may occur.

It is thus between self-possession and that which calls our position into question that this hermeneutical space is positioned. The attendance to understanding finds, as central to its production, the criterion for

---

477 Ibid., 355.

questioning, that its task may become "*of itself a questioning of things and is always in part so defined*"[478] which, put another way, is to say that "the real power of hermeneutical consciousness is our ability to see what is questionable."[479] Thus, the foundation of a hermeneutic recognition of the other is

> entailed as a contextually sensitive, potentially self-transformative, and mutually respectful undertaking. The alterity of the other is indeed recognized as a strong voice, as the cognitive expression of someone about something of shared interest. The reconstruction of the unavoidable investment of one's prejudgments into the process, which nonetheless assails the other a space in-between in which alternative views and perspectives are able to be articulated, leads to a form of recognition that avoids abstract respect or individualized empathy; rather, the other appears as a partner, a mutual co-self, an Other who is both different and close enough to be understood, to be taken seriously, to be taken into account.[480]

This is where existential thought, in its less excessive moments, aims at an ambiguous relation to phenomenology such that we find the very in-betweenness processed as a desirable status to retain for oneself (as in Simone de Beauvoir's work *The Ethics of Ambiguity*), seeking to refute the oversimplification of our existence, and hence preserving its place as ambiguous. Here de Beauvoir took up the existential focus on the freedom of the individual as Jean-Paul Sartre did, yet related it to Husserl (and

---

478 Ibid., 271.

479 Gadamer, Hans-Georg, "The Universality of the Hermeneutical Problem," in *The Gadamer Reader: A Bouquet of the Later Writings* (Evanston, Ill.: Northwestern University Press, 2007), 85.

480 Kögler, Hans-Herbert, "The Crisis of a Hermeneutic Ethic," *Philosophy Today* 58, no. 1 (2014): 9.

perhaps somewhat less convincingly to the resolutions of mutual recognition in Hegel's dialectic) where she seeks to avoid the solipsistic excesses that existentialism fell into numerous times during its initial success (as well as the ethical egoism that predated it). She starts the book with an examination of intentionality that relates the circle of meaning as both insistent and ambiguous, such that it always already precludes the possibility of absolute consummation, as well as the fact that the individual is always already spontaneously caught up in this circle. In approaching an ethics of ambiguity, de Beauvoir seeks to keep at the forefront our acknowledgment of limitations, and that our relation to meaning is always already open; for it is related to the openness of the future, which speaks to the very nature of our living production of said meaning.

She does, however, seem to fall into the existentialist's common error in overprivileging the individual seeking to do away with more determinate relations, which she believes allows us to flee from the responsibilities of our existence and do away with the tensions and anxieties of ambiguity. However, in so doing, she misses the very means whereby meaning is produced as a transcendental relation between the individual and the Other who appears as a partner, a mutual co-self, an Other who is both different and close enough to be understood, to be taken seriously, to be taken into account. She seeks to do away with these absolutes in that she sees them as directly leading to a utopian teleology that sacrifices the now to the future, whereby ends justify brutal means. Such is the perversion of temporality, the individual *and* the Other. From here, de Beauvoir outlines somewhat unsystematically what she takes as the shapes of individuals that somewhat progress from each stage in relation to freedom. The first is that stage where we emerge into this world as children, which de Beauvoir calls the 'serious world.' It is this stage where we are dependent on others, and the already meaningful readymade values and authorities, from the conglomeration of which we assume the world to be secure, given, and unchanging. This is a state without freedom in any capacity which de Beauvoir says predisposes the individual to assume the lures of bad faith.

If the individual, upon leaving childhood, should maintain this relation, he is a 'serious man,' who, by passively assuming the dogma of their environment, avoids all things that may call him into question. This state then is related to a fantasy: it is upon entrance into the symbolic realm that we imagine (create) the loss of an idealized relation to objectivity, for as we enter adulthood and recognize our limitations, we retroactively produce that which they limit. Our being drawn to the past produces a pure security in relation to the real objective conditions of our existence, and is sought by the 'serious man' in unquestioning obedience to the law around him. This is the individual who wholeheartedly submits himself to a lifelong ideological label, whereby all contradictory experiences and understandings are negated so as to preserve the relation to dogma. This is the state whereby the individual believes he has found a relation to that which fulfills the lack within himself. The inverse of this position is what de Beauvoir calls the "sub-man," who retains an ambivalence in relation to the infinite in what amounts to being overwhelmed by the demand of sheer possibility, and thus they believe themselves to be closed off from its relation by denying choice. They are either unaware of or deny this tension or lack within themselves by choosing nothing, and thereby purely identifying with the 'they.'

Hence, both the serious man and the sub-man are portraits of the refusal to recognize the relation to the infinite (be it through dialogue with the Other, tradition, etc.). From their inability to reconcile the world of the for-itself and the in-itself—from his unconsummated desire to ground objectivity as his will, and unify the world with himself—this man eventually decides to be nothing rather than something. He denies the attempt of anything at all, and, as such, de Beauvoir denotes this position as that of the nihilist. It is the "disappointed seriousness which has turned back upon itself . . . [It] feels the lack which is in his heart."[481] The nihilist in de Beauvoir's examination is merely the frustrated sub-man or serious man

---

481 De Beauvoir, Simone, "II Personal Freedom and Others," in *The Ethics of Ambiguity*, trans. Bernard Frechtman (Citadel Press, 1975), 52–53.

who, upon failing to run from his freedom, seeks to reject existence, yet without eliminating it. He realizes the lack within himself and recognizes the impossibility of absolutely fulfilling this lack. He, by systematically rejecting the world, becomes the very positive desire for destruction such that, despite denying meaning in relation to his transcendental relation to himself, it nevertheless persists. He denies existence, and yet he exists *and he knows it.* He understands truly the ambiguity of existence, and yet in challenging all given values he does not find an absolute universality: he is a means without an end which is to say he relates the same complete nature to himself as regards a lack of absolute universality. It is the radical skepticism which, in recognizing foolhardy blind devotion to an ideology, maintains the relation of a fool, shifting only the vision of their relation as such. Instead of proclaiming the meaning as a granted vision, here it is the proclamation of meaning as a denied vision, but both are still positive relations to the meaning of the world. Both positions are embodied in the pseudo-theoretical and pseudo-praxiomatic necessary moments of one's life. The second individual who misreads the ambiguity of existence is the adventurer who privileges means without end, and likewise holds a contempt for others. He vigorously endorses himself in relation to experience of conquest: a celebration of action and movement for its own sake. Thus de Beauvoir tells us that

> the adventurer devises a sort of moral behavior because he assumes his subjectivity positively. But if he dishonestly refuses to recognize that this subjectivity necessarily transcends itself toward others, he will enclose himself in a false independence which will indeed be servitude. To the free man he will be only a chance ally in whom one can have no confidence; he will easily become an enemy. His fault is believing that one can do something for oneself without other and even against them.[482]

---

482 Ibid., 63.

The adventurer, then, comes very close to becoming free, and as such is in perhaps the most dangerous position, for he recognizes many ways of denying or running from one's freedom, but in asserting privilege of the action as it is in-and-for-itself, he denies the possibility of anything but the action itself. He denies that the tradition that gave rise to the possibility of the freedom to pursue this action is the direct result of the freedom of the Other, whose action in relation to itself is also part of the constitution of this tradition. Lastly, there is the maniacally passionate man who asserts his subjectivity only in relation to the object of his desire, where through his passion he believes he can manifest true Being and that, once he attains it, it will complete him in turn. He cares for nothing save this object (or project of his) and as such will not hesitate to treat all Others as things. True communication with him is impossible, as he is an isolated individual who through seeking to unite himself with his desired object finds his totalizing adoration becoming all consuming. This totalizing adoration is itself a partially nihilistic relation that cannot allow for a love toward a free subject *as such*.

The nihilist, adventurer, and passionate man all seek to make the alien into the same, and all seek to reduce the Other to a status of an object of their will, denying as they do the bonds that one has to the Other; thus their being results in a misuse of freedom rather than strictly an avoidance of it. From here, de Beauvoir believes that she has made it clear why willing the freedom of Others is significant, and has also clarified the many pitfalls the individual can meet upon attempting to approach freedom for themselves without this understanding. She believes that, in transitioning to a state of authentic freedom, one brings the excitement of the adventurer and the passion of the passionate man and unites them with a concern for the Other. However, once one achieves this understanding, one is not safe from pitfalls, for perhaps one of the greatest traps available for an individual lies in wait. This mistaken way of looking at the world is the aesthetic attitude. As we have seen the failures of this attitude through Gadamer's hermeneutical relation to art, this relation is a separate and detached 'universal' relation that pretends the subjectivity of the individual can be shed in order for the individual to relate a 'pure' methodological approach to art and extrapolate the entire being of the individual. It is perhaps the most dangerous individual, then, who adopts Enlightenment reason, which seeks to make its methodological observations of the world 'objective' and 'unbiased' such that the individual is repositioned as the absolute. This position supposes that, by 'subtracting the self,' they are now standing over-and-against history and that their actions, thought, freedom, interpretation, relation, and so on are now no longer caught within the process of history unfolding around them — they believe themselves to be divorced from the very situated position of being-in-the-world despite actively contributing to the unfolding of the historical moment itself.

In concluding, de Beauvoir puts forth a relationship of the individual to the concrete moment of their temporal space, which is readily available for augmentation, that reflects the non-neutral openness and intellectual humility which were requirements of ethics in Gadamer and Levinas. De Beauvoir tells us that in order for the one and the Other to remain free we are called to invent an original solution for every moment of our being-in-the-world. As such, she closes her work by remarking that "we are absolutely free today if we choose to will our existence in its finiteness, a finiteness which is open on the infinite."[483] From here, it will prove useful to follow Gadamer in his examination of the logical structure of openness such that we might find, by way of the privileged position of the question in the center of its ontological picture, a way in which to properly understand this will of our existence. Gadamer tells us in one sweeping sequence that "we cannot have experiences without asking questions," which he then proceeds to expound upon by stating,

It is clear that the structure of the question is implicit in all experience. We cannot have experiences without asking

---

483 Ibid., 159.

questions. Recognizing that an object is different, and not as we first thought, obviously presupposes the question whether it was this or that. From a logical point of view, the openness essential to experience is precisely the openness of being either this or that. It has the structure of a question. And just as the dialectical negativity of experience culminates in the idea of being perfectly experienced—i.e., being aware of our finitude and limitedness—so also the logical form of the question and the negativity that is part of it culminate in a radical negativity: the knowledge of not knowing. This is the famous Socratic *docta ignorantia* which, amid the most extreme negativity of doubt, opens up the way to the true superiority of questioning.[484]

By returning to a (pre-Platonic) Socrates, Gadamer is making a turn which finds attentive listening akin to that of a discipline, or an ascetic path whereby, rather than the will-to-power (where all is made questionable at once), the questioner and that which is questioned are both by nature of the activity itself called into question, which need not will closure but rather through a more refined and truthful understanding of that which is questioned brings about yet another question. It is an insight which Socrates himself made clear that, contrary to common sense, the posing of correct questions is more significant and challenging than is answering them. This is because

> when the partners in the Socratic dialogue are unable to answer Socrates' awkward questions and try to turn the tables by assuming what they suppose is the preferable role of the questioner, they come to grief. Behind this comic motif in the Platonic dialogues there is the critical distinction between authentic and inauthentic dialogue. To someone who engages

---

484 Gadamer, *Truth and Method*, 356.

in dialogue only to prove himself right and not to gain insight, asking questions will indeed seem easier than answering them. There is no risk that he will be unable to answer a question. In fact, however, the continual failure of the interlocutor shows that people who think they know better cannot even ask the right questions. In order to be able to ask, one must want to know, and that means knowing that one does not know.[485]

By opting for a dynamic relation to the question in place of the desire for a totalizing schematization we find every desire to understand as starting with the jolting of the individual to a standstill by way of that which calls previous understanding into question.

Gadamer asserts that the Greek word *atopon* is this very moment, which he takes to literally mean "the place-less" and says that it denotes "that which is not to be brought under the schematisms of our intelligent expectations, and which therefore leaves us startled. The renowned Platonic doctrine that philosophizing begins with wonder means this becoming startled, this not getting any further on the basis of the preschematized expectations of our world-orientation, which calls us to take thought."[486] It is against this background that Gadamer allows us to see that the question is that by which openness is encouraged against the indeterminacy of the answer. It is interpretation in the face of a recognition of the alien *as such*. It makes sense then that Gadamer finds in Plato the recognition of "the *priority of the question* in all knowledge and discourse [as] that [which] really reveals something of an object. Discourse that is intended to reveal something requires that the thing be broken open by the question."[487] It is a good question

---

485 Ibid., 356-57.

486 Gadamer, Hans-Georg, "Language and Understanding," *Theory, Culture & Society* 23, no. 1 (2006): 13–27; available at 6.

487 Gadamer, *Truth and Method*, 357.

that puts the understanding held prior to dialogue in a questionable state, or what is to say the same thing, a good question will not only showcase the irreducibility of that which is questioned by my previous understanding, but it will *also* situate my previous understanding as puzzling to me.

The resulting authentic dialogue is that by which those engaged try to work out an interpretation related to the horizon against which the question itself is provided. It is here that Gadamer makes references to the *logos*, stating that "the logos that explicates this opened-up being is an answer. Its sense lies in the sense of the question."[488] For Gadamer it is not only true that "the path of all knowledge leads through the question," but also that fundamentally what it means to ask a question is "to bring into the open."[489] However, this does not mean that Gadamer allows for all questions to retain this privileged position, for it may be the case that a bad question has been posed, one that precludes openness by "retaining false presuppositions," which we can see in the case of the 'slanted question,' whereby "there can be no answer . . . because it leads us only apparently, and not really, through the open state of indeterminacy in which a decision is made."[490] This is because slanted questions are either somewhere between a statement, which by its very nature smuggles in unarticulated presuppositions, or that of a question. They thus either fail to give a proper direction and sense from which the investigation of the question can continue, or show that counter-instances and counterarguments are kept intact through the smuggled, motivated statement, and, as such, permanently in any authentic sense of the word. This is not to say that questions exclude presuppositions, for all questions both highlight through positivity and discard with negativity, but it is rather the regard of possibilities *as* possibilities.

---

488 Ibid., 356.
489 Ibid.
490 Ibid., 357.

This is what the example of Socrates teaches: "that the important thing is the knowledge that one does not know. Hence the Socratic dialectic—which leads, through its art of confusing the interlocutor, to this knowledge—creates the conditions for the question. All questioning and desire to know presuppose a knowledge that one does not know; so much so, indeed, that a particular lack of knowledge leads to a particular question."[491] It is not only a desire to know that finds and sustains openness, but so too is the awareness of our ignorance vital in this process. Instrumental theories of language (by the implication of the unconscious production according to the intention of some reading of the conceptual, and the dictates of the causality of meaning,) rather than merely exteriorize thought in its conventional sense, miss the means by which the word *perfects* thought. However, the word itself is not a post-knowledge product but rather the performative execution of knowledge itself. This is an expansion and clarification of Heidegger's insight that it is language itself that speaks, for the questioner is bound to it in such a way that that the dialogue itself is spoken through it by those who are themselves engaged thereof. This does not, however, mean that language is merely a tool either, but is rather the universal horizon against which hermeneutic experience is possible. It is opinion that disrupts the self-correcting process of questioning by which criticism and refinement are ever working within the relation to their own light: as such it is unable to become schematized as a domesticated technique against the eternal and unchanging world around it. For "it is the power of opinion against which it is so hard to obtain an admission of ignorance. It is opinion that suppresses questions. Opinion has a curious tendency to propagate itself. It would always like to be the general opinion just as the word that the Greeks have for opinion, doxa, also means the decision made by the majority in the council assembly."[492]

---

491 Ibid., 359.
492 Ibid.

The realization of one's own ignorance and the questioning which flows in like a gust of wind following a door's opening comprise a sudden realization, like an idea striking us: "the real nature of the sudden idea is perhaps less that a solution occurs to us like an answer to a riddle than that a question occurs to us that breaks through into the open and thereby makes an answer possible. Every sudden idea has the structure of a question. But the sudden occurrence of the question is already a breach in the smooth front of popular opinion."[493] The question is like the negative dialectical nature of experience, which itself implies a question: unless a question arises, it does not seem as though there can be an experience, for it always already opens up the possibilities, where the experience as such is the determinate relation. This is because the experience expresses against the other possibilities which are negated. The conscious art of questioning is "reserved to the person who wants to know, i.e., who already has questions. The art of questioning is not the art of resisting the pressure of opinion; it already presupposes this freedom. It is not an art in the sense that the Greeks speak of techne, nor a craft that can be taught or by means of which we could master the discovery of truth."[494] It is rather an art of considering possibilities for those who already maintain the potential questionability of their own opinions. As such, since the art of questioning is always-already contained within the act of dialogue itself, it is constitutive of the relation such that the openness to truth is itself an openness to the Other. Thus

> the art of dialectic is not the art of being able to win every argument. On the contrary, it is possible that someone practicing the art of dialectic—i.e., the art of questioning and of seeking truth—comes off worse in the argument in the eyes of those listening to it. As the art of asking questions, dialectic

---

493 Ibid., 360.
494 Ibid.

> proves its value because only the person who knows how to ask
> questions is able to persist in his questioning, which involves
> being able to preserve his orientation towards openness. The
> art of questioning is the art of questioning even further—i.e.,
> the art of thinking. It is called dialectic because it is the art of
> conducting a real dialogue.[495]

This means that questioning is kept open by account of its resistance to domestication. Questioning can never become schematized by way of an orientation of the particular to the universal: it may never reveal an eternal technique that relates the individual to whatever sequence of norms that may lay in front of him.

It would be more proper to say that the actions of refinement, critique, formulation, deconstruction, and the like are all made possible in relation to questioning, for the process by which they are all made possible is illuminated *by the very light of questioning itself.* In authentic dialogue there is no attempt to outdo or one-up each other, there is no listening for the sake of seeking out vulnerabilities for manipulative personal gain, but rather a cooperative endeavor by which agreement is sought out at every level of the dialogue so that the unfolding truth of the conversation might be sustained. For "dialectic consists not in trying to discover the weakness of what is said, but in bringing out its real strength. It is not the art of arguing (which can make a strong case out of a weak one) but the art of thinking (which can strengthen objections by referring to the subject matter)."[496] The emergence of meaning as understanding relays the substantive position as that which is right, and as such is constitutive of the verbal process itself. It is through the interpretive act as a conceptual intrasubjective relation that one habitually reawakens the meaning of a text through

---

495 Ibid.
496 Ibid., 361.

understanding. This understanding is of course related to tradition as that which is historically given through our finite situation of being always-already in the world. This is because, within the process of the Platonic dialectic, "what is said is continually transformed into the uttermost possibilities of its rightness and truth, and overcomes all opposition that tries to limit its validity. Here again it is not simply a matter of leaving the subject undecided."[497] This is why the position of the interlocutors, and perhaps more pointedly of the questioner himself, is that of non-neutral openness: for the dialectical structure of question-and-answer is such that the horizons of each are habitually fused. This is so that within the finite present, in tandem with the tradition in which the questioning is taking place, the matter at hand is brought to its proper presence wherefrom understanding takes place within this very fusion of horizons. We find that

> the maieutic productivity of the Socratic dialogue, the art of using words as a midwife, is certainly directed toward the people who are the partners in the dialogue, but it is concerned merely with the opinions they express, the immanent logic of the subject matter that is unfolded in the dialogue. What emerges in its truth is the logos, which is neither mine nor yours and hence so far transcends the interlocutors' subjective opinions that even the person leading the conversation knows that he does not know.[498]

The very nature of dialogue reveals the teleology (if it can be called that) of the dialectic in general: for it was the aim of Hegel to produce the content of this transhistorical process by way of the sheer determination of the logic of self-consciousness.

---

497 Ibid.
498 Ibid.

The aim of Hegel's logic . . . [was] the attempt to comprehend within the great monologue of modern "method" the continuum of meaning that is realized in every particular instance of dialogue. When Hegel sets himself the task of making the abstract determinations of thought fluid and subtle, this means dissolving and remolding logic into concrete language, and transforming the concept into the meaningful power of the word that questions and answers—a magnificent reminder, even if unsuccessful, or what dialectic really was and is. Hegel's dialectic is a monologue of thinking that tries to carry out in advance what matters little by little in every genuine dialogue.[499]

It is from interpretation which occurs in genuine dialogue that meaning addresses our fundamental prejudices and insights, such that experience itself may authentically be other than that which our view (or thought) constructs it to be. It is the very possibility that our understanding may be fitted to that which we are seeking to understand *by the matter at hand.* "Thus, interpretation always involves a relation to a question that is asked of the interpreter,"[500] meaning that understanding another is to understand this 'the matter-at-hand' as an answer to this question, the contours of which, the "horizon of the question," is that transcendent feature which determines the sense of the matter-at-hand. This horizon is that which "as such, necessarily includes other possible answers. Thus the meaning of a sentence is relative to the question to which it is a reply, but that implies that its meaning necessarily exceeds what is said in it."[501] To understand the question behind what is said is to transcend what is

---

499 Ibid., 363.
500 Ibid.
501 Ibid.

said, so that we might come to see meaning as that which exceeds it. Thus, understanding can only be retroactively constituted by not simply understanding what is said, but what that which is said is in answer to, namely, a question. Once again, this phenomenological relation is that by which all understanding comes about, one which situates understanding within the relation to a question that proceeds it, as in the case of its fore-conception of completeness. And "yet one cannot conceal the fact that the logic of question and answer has to reconstruct two different questions that have two different answers."[502] There is a double move involved in the question which has been ignored by both deconstructionists and structuralists in their attempt to displace the privilege of the search wholly onto either the author or the work, and in that sense cripple their understanding. It is true that "our understanding of written tradition per se is not such that we can simply presuppose that the meaning we discover in it agrees with what the author intended . . . [for] the sense of a text in general reaches far beyond what the author originally intended."[503] In order to achieve understanding of "the meaning of a sentence – i.e., have reconstructed the question to which it really is the answer—it must be possible to inquire also about the questioner and his intended question, to which the text is perhaps only an imagined answer."[504] However, the question in relation to history is differentiated in character by its web through which the variety of motives seldom seem to conform to the unilateral clarity that one would expect from a rather uncomplicated individual.

Due to the intentionality and execution of motives, we come to find that experience tends to changes our plans, for the events therein are necessarily intrasubjective. Understanding a text does not explicitly involve the real distinction between the question that the text intended

502 Ibid., 364.
503 Ibid.
504 Ibid. 365

to answer and the question that the text winds up answering. What is perhaps a larger mistake to make is the one made by historicism, where it mistakenly follows the methodology of science in attempting to artificially reproduce the process that it studies. However, by now it should be clear to us that

> every historian and philologist must reckon with the fundamental non-distinctiveness of the horizon in which his understanding moves. Historical tradition can be understood only as something always in the process of being defined by the course of events. Similarly, the philologist dealing with poetic or philosophical texts knows that they are inexhaustible. In both cases it is the course of events that brings out new aspects of meaning in historical material. By being re-actualized in understanding, texts are drawn into a genuine course of events in exactly the same way as are events themselves . . . Every actualization in understanding can be regarded as a historical potential of what is understood. It is part of the historical finitude of our being that we are aware that others after us will understand in a different way. And yet it is equally indubitable that it remains the same work whose fullness of meaning is realized in the changing process of understanding, just as it is the same history whose meaning is constantly in the process of being defined.[505]

This is because, again, every encounter with a question is essentially a new experience with the property of negativity, such that the individual who encounters it does so as if the question is *his own*. And yet again it must be stressed here that the task of interpretation (from which all understanding unfolds) should not be read as a radical subjectivity

---

505 Ibid., 366.

or relativism. It is a middle ground which is neither reproductive or productive as it seeks to ask not only what the text says presently, but also what it mean at its genesis. This is because there is somehow still a belief in the totality of understanding being explicitly represented by the false dichotomy of either unilateral determination of meaning by a specific author or world-historical individual, or else there is a collapse of meaning where any reading is legitimate. However, given the radical multiplicity of situations that are temporally related to the work, there will be both/neither an infinite sequence of meanings which are still within the purview of the horizon determined by the question-and-answer of the text itself. This is what it means to say that meaning is unfolded across the plane of history, which is itself forever unfolding. Understanding necessarily relates the intrinsic self-mediation of the facticity of the individual in the present and the traditionary such that "the voice that speaks to us from the past—whether text, work, trace—itself poses a question and places our meaning in openness. In order to answer the question put to us, we the interrogated must ourselves begin to ask questions."[506]

The ever new signification of the present coincides with the actualization of the history of the effects of tradition, where meaning and definitions are always-already related from within the process of the event of understanding. To understand something as questionable is already itself engaged in the process of questioning. When answering the question put to us, we find that it is the very act of questioning which always brings about the possibilities of the matter-at-hand—it is the horizon that always-already includes us as questioners such that the unquestioned assumptions of the author of the answer, as well as the reconstruction of his question, are extraneous to the original horizon. "To understand a question means to ask it. To understand meaning is to understand it as the answer to a question. The logic of question and answer . . .

---

506 Ibid., 366-67.

puts an end to talk about permanent *problems,* as in the way the 'Oxford realists' approach to the classics of philosophy, and hence also an end to the concept of *history of problems* developed by neo-Kantianism."[507] In other words, there is no ahistorical position from which these problems, as mere abstractions of the context of the original question, can be resolved. Their decontextualized and unmotivated relation as such suppresses any potential sense they may otherwise contain. This is because "the problem that we re-cognize is not in fact simply the same if it is to be understood in a genuine act of questioning."[508] In other words, these long standing 'problems' are "insoluble, like every question that has no clear, unambiguous sense, because it is not really motivated and asked."[509]

The problems that persist do so *at the expense of being treated dialogically.* These problems do not arise by themselves, and are not real questions, as they retroactively seek to cover up these questions which brought about their status as a problem, and as such resist transformation into contextual questions which in-and-of-themselves actually contain a relation to the world such that an individual may actually be addressed by them. "This also confirms the origin of the concept of the problem. It does not belong in the sphere of those 'honestly motivated refutations' in which the truth of the subject matter is advanced, but in the sphere of dialectic as a weapon to amaze or make a fool of one's opponent."[510] Thus understanding, as the fusion of horizons, responds to historical tradition by making it speak and address us as with an authentic question belonging to the tradition itself, which is presupposed by our anticipation of an answer. As Gadamer tells us,

> The guiding idea of the following discussion is that the fusion
> of horizons that takes place in understanding is actually the

507 Ibid., 368.
508 Ibid., 369.
509 Ibid.
510 Ibid.

achievement of language. Admittedly, what language is belongs among the most mysterious questions that man ponders. Language is so uncannily near our thinking, and when it functions it is so little an object, that it seems to conceal its own being from us. In our analysis of the thinking of the human sciences, however, we came so close to this universal mystery of language that is prior to everything else, that we can entrust ourselves to what we are investigating to guide us safely in the quest. In other words we are endeavoring to approach the mystery of language from the conversation that we ourselves are.[511]

It is the entirety of the hermeneutic approach to understanding which is authentically after the truth of the matter-at-hand. Understanding, as we have said before, must take the form of language—for it is not a repackaging of our understanding that we get through language, but is the very coming-into-language of the truth of the thing itself. It is vital if we are to understand the constitutive import of the question as it stands for dialogue (and therein for understanding itself) that we demonstrate the linguistic nature of dialogue. We must understand

that the language in which something comes to speak is not a possession at the disposal of one or the other of the interlocutors. Every conversation presupposes a common language, or better, creates a common language. Something is placed in the center, as the Greeks say, which the partners in dialogue both share, and concerning which they can exchange ideas with one another. Hence reaching an understanding on the subject matter of a conversation necessarily means that a common language must first be worked out in the conversation.

511 Ibid., 370.

This is not an external matter of simply adjusting our tools; nor is it even right to say that the partners adapt themselves to one another but, rather, in a successful conversation they both come under the influence of the truth of the object and are thus bound to one another in a new community. To reach an understanding in a dialogue is not merely a matter of putting oneself forward and successfully asserting one's own point of view, but being transformed into a communion in which we do not remain what we were.[512]

Against Habermas, then, language cannot be restricted to a procedural telos—it is rather by way of the understanding which unfolds from the truth of the subject matter at hand that a presupposition as to the hybridity of both stability and change can be found in a single moment. Understanding proper belongs to the intellectually humble, who lose themselves in the ethical solidarity surrounding the dialectical/dialogical relation to the matter-at-hand. This, then, is itself *the* event which Gadamer calls the achievement of language.

512 Ibid., 371.

Psychoanalysis and the Theory of Beliefs

A one-to-one correlative theory of consciousness is undermined by the concepts of belief and desire, which the theory seems to require as simple and accessible to the individual. Upon examination, belief and desire seem, however, to present complexities which suggest a conceptual rather than noumenal status readily available to the individual. In fact, it seems as though the entire theoretical system generated by the encounter of the same with the other gives not only shape to these notions but fills out their meaning in relation to the whole of the system. It is through this recognition of the foundational theory of consciousness that we can make sense out of the fact that we can be wrong about our own beliefs and desires. This social network of coherence spies the relationality of internal systems utilizing both desire and belief in order to navigate the consistencies that inhere in neurological responses to our environment. This is perhaps first found in the Hegelian mythic encounter and struggle with the Other: the story in Hegel provides us with the possibility of describing this reflection of neurological trends in a way that mirrors our narrative about our own internality, neither image of which provides any particularly privileged access on our behalf.

Belief and desire are thus theoretical terms within the symbolic order that make it so that social relationships might be navigated at all by way of the fundamental theoretical predictability of both ourselves and the Other. In fact, desire and belief themselves are generated and conditioned by the very social relations that they, as theoretical tools, attempt to make sense of. This is where the analytic situation finds itself: isolating phenomena through a structure separate and distinct from subjectivity so that through dialogue, the ruptures and inconsistencies which unground meaning from the human subject might be mended. These ruptures and inconsistencies are fundamentally given the placeholder of the unanalyzable kernel of the symptom. As far back as Freud we read that the symptom is "a sign of, and a substitute for, an instinctual satisfaction which has remained in abeyance; it is a consequence of the process of repression."[513] However Lacan's progression from Freud is to see that primary repression is itself a structural feature of language which, by way of its incompleteness, disallows the very possibility of saying the truth about the truth. For Lacan, discourse is itself always-already marked as the site whereby we encounter resistance. However, Lacan also tells us, "to know what resistance is, one must know what blocks the advent of speech, and it is not some individual disposition, but rather an imaginary interposition which goes beyond the subject's individuality in that it structures his individualization as specified in the dyadic relation."[514] Another way of showing what's at issue here is by understanding that the interposition discussed above is that of the ego, which is the subject objectified within the imaginary order.

By necessity the ego manifests a narrative defense that disavows the notion of its own construction as a restrictive viewpoint on the subject. Thus, "the resistance in question projects its effects on to the system of the ego . . . The ego has a reference to the other. The ego is constituted in relation to the other. It is its correlative. The level on which the other is experienced locates exactly the level on which, quite literally, the ego exists for the subject."[515] In order, then, for analysis to be effective, we

---

513 Freud, *Complete Psychological Works*. 1926A, 91

514 Lacan, Jacques, "The Situation of Psychoanalysis and the Training of Psychoanalysts in 1956," in *Ecrits: The First Complete Edition in English* (New York: W. W. Norton, 2007), 386.

515 Lacan, *Freud's Papers on Technique*, 50.

understand that it must be operative on discourse itself, for recognition of resistance is found through "its effect in the verbalisation of chains of speech in which the subject constitutes his history."[516] Thus, just as we found Gadamer's focus on the dialogical Socratic relation, so too do we hear the echoes of Socrates from the *Gorgias* where he states: "I know how to provide one witness for what I say: the man himself to whom my speech [*logos*] is directed, while I bid the many farewell; and I know how to put the vote to one man, while I don't converse with the many either."[517]

It is the very particularity of the individual case by which understanding may be achieved, the dialogical relation which constitutes

> the reintegration by the subject of his history right up to the furthermost perceptible limits, that is to say into a dimension that goes well beyond the limits of the individual . . . History is not the past . . . The path of restitution of the subject's history takes the form of a quest for the restitution of the past. We should consider this restitution as the butt to be aimed at by the recourses of technique.[518]

This restitution is the process by which the repressed signifier is given a new translation such that it may link up with the chain of signifiers of the individual. Analysis then is a domain over which a discourse, in unification through *phronesis*, is given primacy, and it is from this status that discourse may produce understanding. With this in mind we come to see that "the analyst, because he cannot detach the experience of language from the situation which it implies (the situation of the interlocutor), touches on the simple fact that language, before signifying something,

---

516 Ibid., 277.
517 Nichols, James H., Jr., *Plato: Gorgias* (Ithaca, N.Y.: Cornell University Press, 1998), 474ab.
518 Lacan, *Freud's Papers on Technique*, 14.

signifies for someone."[519] A core insight, then, of Lacanian analysis is that a signifier of this representation represents the subject for another signifier, and that to speak is marked by the intention. We can imagine that it is through a 'restoration' of the past that an individual assumes the meaning of the symptoms which plague them personally. And it is from authentic dialogue that this restoration is at all possible—language is not (as many psychologizing reports would like us to imagine) primarily a mental phenomenon—it is itself relational in that it belongs to a community irreducible to particulars. This means that there intrinsically must be a community that habitually verifies the use of language such that its investigation occurs only when it breaks apart. It is *only* when there is an external reference of a community of language users that there can be fault, and that it may be found. Thus, the structure of a given community's customs with their language is given to individuals as knowhow, neither explicit nor articulated as such: not mechanistic, but living, and as such it is given to the individual through cues that are softly held within the community.

The pattern recognition that is found therein is not explicitly given within consciousness - there is no cognition of the relation of the communal network. It is when the customs are broken that the network of coherence is found: the limits of the communal relation are understood where they break apart. Philosophy as such is an emergent property and an offspring of dialogue whence questions arise. From this perspective, it is out of respect for the Other that discourse itself is allowed to proceed *as if it will* be without manipulation, and thus disclosure of the inter-subjective truth is possible. Anticipation and feigning ignorance based off of prior interactions are not tools that are available for the dialogical relation, for it is necessary to recreate the question that prompts dialogue with fresh perspectives upon each new interaction so as to produce true

---

519 Lacan, *The Language of the Self: The Function of Language in Psychoanalysis*, trans. Anthony Wilden (Baltimore: Johns Hopkins University Press, 1968), 76-77.

understanding. This is also, in part, because the analytic interposition is one that disregards questions of accuracy in reconstitution or the guarantee of consistency, for both Freud and Lacan showcase the relation of uncertainty to the greater potentiality of meaningfulness. This is because the incompleteness of language retroactively seeks to provide the appearance of coherence and completeness such that the ego, as captured by its environment, might meld into the world of meaning that surrounds it, however broken and dysfunctional it may be. We find, then, through the performative action of full dialogical speech that "an essential element of coming into being of the other is the capacity of speech to unite us to him,"[520] while the other half of this speech is named 'revelation,' which is a way of describing the truth-relation in psychoanalysis such that it may mean something akin to insight.

Another way of understanding this experiential relation of truth is through the concept of disclosure, discussed in earlier chapters. It is revelation or insight into this disclosure of truth which is ultimately sought after in the analytic experience. Lacan tells us to look out for speech which merely mediates, for "if speech then functions as mediation, it is on account of its revelation not having been accomplished. The question is always one of knowing at which level hooking on to the other occurs."[521] We should not confuse the speech act with the structure that is language itself (which exists prior to each individual's entry to it), but should recognize that there is already a split in the level of speech itself playing out here. It is at this level of the split, then, that we find the differentiation of something like the knowledge and understanding bifurcated within Lacan's teachings where he states:

> Two planes have always been distinguished within which the exchange of human speech is played out—the plane of

520 Lacan, *Freud's Papers on Technique*, 48.
521 Ibid., 49.

recognition in so far as speech links the subjects together into this pact which transforms them, and sets them up as human subjects communicating—the plane of communique, in which one can distinguish all sorts of levels, the call, discussion, knowledge, information, but which, in the final analysis, involves a tendency to reach an agreement on the object. The term 'agreement' is still there, but here the emphasis is placed on the object considered as external to the action of speech, it is already partially given in the system of objects, or objective system, in which one should include the accumulated prejudices which make up a cultural community, up to and including the hypotheses, the psychological prejudices even, from the most sophisticated generated by scientific work to the most naive and spontaneous, which most certainly do not fail considerably to influence scientific references, to the point of impregnating them.[522]

It is then through the plane of recognition that there is a true honoring of the Other as the site of external language whereby the individual may be recognized and heard.

Yet in order to arrive therein, the dialogical relation, in its initial step of analysis, works on the situatedness of the individual's alienation within the imaginary order, and by dissolving the structure of the ego it reintegrates the privileged images that constitute it back into the symbolic network. To skip this moment and leave them inert and stagnant as they are is to allow for the death of the dialogue itself. We can understand from the clinical perspective the same understanding when we read that

What merits the name resistance is the fact that the ego isn't identical to the subject, and it is in the nature of the ego to

---

522 Ibid., 108.

integrate itself into the imaginary circuit which determines the interruptions of the fundamental discourse. It is this resistance that Freud emphasises when he says that every resistance stems from the organisation of the ego. For it is in so far as it is imaginary, and not simply in so far as it is carnal existence, that the ego is, in analysis, the mainspring of the interruptions of this discourse, which simply asks to be put into action, into speech . . . The analyst partakes of the radical nature of the Other, in so far as he is what is most inaccessible. From then on, and beginning at this point in time, what leaves the imaginary of the ego of the subject is in accordance not with this other to which he is accustomed, and who is just his partner, the person who is made so as to enter into his game, but precisely with this radical Other which is hidden from him.[523]

It is through the intimate nature of the ego that self-reflection possesses such a major blind spot. There is a sense of alienation that occurs within the symbolic register of language whereby we are represented but not retroactively related. What's more is that man's birth through language necessarily finds holes in the discourse that he himself takes as his own. The synthetic wholeness of self-understanding then is feigned by way of the dialogical relationship which presses forth an insistent drive towards expression. Despite the fact that speech and behavior signify, they are never wholly subsumed by this signification which does not even grant us a proper identity; in every signification utilized there is always a margin of desire that escapes the meaning ascribed to it, thus maintaining some mysterious otherness. It is the operative character of desire that propels the dialogical relationship, which is extinguished through hasty conclusions and fudging the answers to its questions.

523 Ibid., 324.

While the dialogical relation aims at the good and the true, it does so while maintaining fidelity to the complex nature of desire that extends over-and-beyond it. Belief and desire fit into the transcendent character of our being bearers of knowledge that is separated from us and about which we are unconscious. This is in part why Lacan denotes the subject as a crossed-out or barred 'S,' because the positive identity lacks a substantial support, and as such the "concept of identification plays . . . a crucial role in psychoanalytic theory: the subject attempts to fill out its constitutive lack by means of identification, by identifying itself with some master signifier [that guarantees] its place in the symbolic network."[524] This is Derrida's famous center that is not the center, functioning both inside and outside of the system so as to found the system while controlling it. The supposed universal function which the master signifier gives 'meaning' to must *ipso facto* operate by way of its foundation, which is itself its own exception. This is the desire to have definite knowledge over the symbolic network: the illusion of a guarantee of certainty that knowledge (which is related to stale and dead objects) grants the individual when they apply it to whatever terrorizes them in its phantasmatic dimension. "And yet," Lacan tells us,

> if the subject commits himself to searching after truth as such, it is because he places himself in the dimension of ignorance— it doesn't matter whether he knows it or not. That is one of the elements making up what analysts call 'readiness to the transference.' There is a readiness to the transference in the patient solely by virtue of his placing himself in the position of acknowledging himself in speech, and searching out his truth to the end . . . The analyst's ignorance is also worthy of consideration. The analyst must not fail to recognise what I

---

524 Žižek, Slavoj, *Looking Awry: An Introduction to Jacques Lacan through Popular Culture* (Cambridge, Mass.: MIT Press, 2006), 100.

will call the dimension of ignorance's power of accession to being, since he has to reply to the person who, throughout his discourse, questions him in this dimension. He doesn't have to guide the subject to a Wissen, to knowledge, but on to the paths by which access to this knowledge is gained. He must engage him in a dialectical operation, not say to him that he is wrong since he necessarily is in error, but show him that he speaks poorly, That is to say that he speaks without knowing, as one who is ignorant, because what counts are the paths of his error. Psychoanalysis is a dialectic, what Montaigne, in book III, chapter VIII, calls an art of conversation. The art of conversation of Socrates in the Meno is to teach the slave to give his own speech its true meaning. And it is the same in Hegel. In other words, the position of the analyst must be that of an ignorantia docta . . . If the psychoanalyst thinks he knows something, in psychology for example, then that is already the beginning of his loss, for the simple reason that in psychology nobody knows much, except that psychology is itself an error of perspective on the human being.[525]

First and foremost, this showcases the dysfunction of 'systematic knowledge,' which is always deferred to the authority of the other. But beyond that is the way in which specificity of affect fails to be interpreted within the system of the particular individual being addressed. This is summed up by Lacan in reference to the *Meno* when he states:

What is highlighted in this dialogue is not simply that Meno doesn't know what he is saying, it is rather that he doesn't know what he is saying regarding virtue. Why?—because he was a bad pupil of the Sophists—he doesn't understand what

---

525 Lacan, *Freud's Papers on Technique*, 263-64.

the Sophists have to teach him, which isn't a doctrine which explains everything, but the use of discourse, which is really quite different. You can see how bad a pupil he is when he says—If Gorgias were here, he would explain all this to us. You would be knocked over by what Gorgias said. The system is always in the other.[526]

Just as significant is the way this highlights the divisive split of psychoanalysis from general psychology in that it refuses the systematization of knowledge which applies not only to the patient undergoing psychological treatment, but also the sustained relationship and the language used therein. It is radical for psychoanalysis to accept this position of the *ignorantia docta* as that which leaves open the dialogical relation to take its 'theoretical' cue from what the signifiers within the relation itself reveal. It leaves open the potentiality from revelation of the inconsistencies in the self-narrative rather than the overlapping moments of their rehearsal. It is only in this way that the discourse of the individual and the other can be truly respected. In fact, Lacan takes this critique much further in ascribing the role of ideological manipulation to psychology at large, stating for example that "psychologists. . . as a group and *per se* are in the service of technocratic exploitation,"[527] stating even further that "as for psychology, it is striking that there is no shadow of it in things that are enlightening . . . It is a little montage that gets its value from its master signifiers, which is worthwhile because it is readable. No need in the least for psychology."[528]

This is because, in large part, psychology is that structure which observes and 'treats' the individual subject as a completely knowable

526 Lacan, *Ego in Freud's Theory,* 16.

527 Lacan, *Ecrits: The First Complete Edition,* 722.

528 Lacan, Jacques, *The Seminar of Jacques Lacan: The Other Side of Psychoanalysis,* trans. Russell Grigg (New York: W. W. Norton, 2007), 192.

object. This is why Lacan defines psychology proper as that which is "effectively a science of perfectly well-defined objects."[529] This science, however, understands neither that "the core of our being does not coincide with the ego," nor that the ego is "a particular object within the experience of the subject. Literally, the ego is an object —an object which fills a certain function which we here call the imaginary function."[530] This form of psychology prioritizes the ego in its equation with the self. It believes the illusion of wholeness and ascendance that the ego asserts, yet which psychoanalysis has found as misrecognition of the ego which in turn refuses the truth of its own fragmentation and alienation. In other words, psychology, like academic philosophy and popular culture, structures a system of 'scientific' knowledge such that it is properly diffused, reproduced, and conserved by the masses. What psychology is missing, then, is the fundamental notion of psychoanalysis, which sees man as overidentificatory and from which we find the dialectical relation of the ego to knotty social conditions. It is in this way (among others) that psychoanalysis resists becoming a discipline proper with systematic knowledge and tools, and rather maintains its status as a relational-ethical practice.

This is why, when Lacan compares himself to Aristotle (in his lecture "My Teaching, Its Nature and Its Ends") by distinguishing himself as Aristotle was distinguished, he is indicating their shared separation from the discipline that surrounded them. Both Lacan and Aristotle keep their eyes on the life of the logic before them—forming not so much a theory of the world, but of how in our daily lives we experience this life that surrounds us. They both maintain a hermeneutic approach that allows for authentic analysis, which Lacan calls "psychoanalysis giv[ing] us a

---

529 Lacan, Jacques, and Jacques-Alain Miller, *The Seminar of Jacques Lacan: The Psychoses* (New York: Norton, 1988), 243.
530 Lacan, *Ego in Freud's Theory*, 44.

chance, a chance to start again,[531] in the place in which philosophy had dried up and died in Aristotle's attempt. It is from here that we find the ethical position as Lacan's starting point when he states, "Confusing the subject with the message is one of the great characteristics of all the stupid things that are said about the so-called reduction of language to communication. The communication function has never been the most important aspect of language."[532] Thus, the ethical relation of psychoanalysis requires a hermeneutic approach to moral phenomena due to their nature as overdetermined: because of this, we find the stress on attention to language, for the "technique [of the psychoanalyst] cannot be understood, nor therefore correctly applied, if one misunderstands the concepts on which it is based . . . these concepts take on their full meaning only when oriented in a field of language and ordered in relation to the function of speech."[533] Thus there is a sensitivity that resists the corruption of thought found in knowledge-oriented dogmatism, which is imposed by the methodology of a discipline. Interestingly, in Aristotle's theory of the ethical, which Lacan clearly held in high regard (calling it "one of the most eminent forms of ethical thought"[534]) we find the failure to fully consider the overdetermined nature of the moral situation whereby Aristotle's ethics are revealed to be overly severe. It showcases this failure of thought explicating the master's discourse and ignoring the openness of ethics as they are habitually reintegrated in ever-new situations within human life. Thus, despite the usefulness of Aristotle's ethics, Lacan turns his work toward a notion of ethics that is forever open: impossible to complete as it is in the lives of human

---

531 Lacan, Jacques, "My Teaching, Its Nature and Its Ends" (London: Verso, 2009), 76.

532 Ibid., 84.

533 Lacan, *Ecrits: The First Complete Edition*, 205.

534 Lacan, Jacques, *The Seminar of Jacques Lacan: The Ethics of Psychoanalysis* (New York: Norton, 1992), 43.

beings, yet forever demanding the individual comport himself toward its completion.

In addition to respect for the other, we find here a profound respect toward language such that the variety of life, just as the variety of ethical situations, may be approached without reductive rigid categories over-determining the individual and the situation. The central idea at the heart of this dialogical analysis is that the symptom, found at the start of analysis, is there again at its very end revolutionized by the process. The beginning of analysis is the individual's belief in his symptom, and the issues caused by his inability to integrate this symptom within his broader symbolic chain of meaning. Thus "if anything constitutes the originality of the analytic treatment, it is rather to have perceived at the beginning, right from the start, *the problematical relation of the subject to himself.* The real find, the discovery . . . is *to have conjoined this relation with the meaning of the symptoms.*"[535] *It* is the cause and knowledge behind the symptom that plagues the individual, who assumes that its justification is secured in an authority on the matter, and that he may restore meaning by having the knowledge or understanding thereof revealed to him. This is why speech can nearly be thought of as the tool by which a symptom seeks out its meaning. Analysis, as a project that involves seeking out the truth (which is not necessarily always beneficial) finds "the true termination of an analysis is that which prepares you to become an analyst."[536] This is the closed loop of analysis which procures the situatedness of the individual from analysand to analyst by traversing his fantasy. At its 'end' we once again see the Socratic parallel where we have already seen Lacan invoke the *docta ignorantia*, and here through the analytic process the individual has found a position from which to embark upon his life of a beginner.

---

535 Lacan, *Freud's Papers on Technique*, 29.
536 Lacan, *The Ethics of Psychoanalysis*, 303.

ONE FINAL ACT OF WILLING

I t is a sorrowful and triumphant picture that Sartre paints of the individual before the fabric of his Being with dizzying freedom. This portrait is founded through Heidegger's notion of anxiety resulting from our position of care toward ourselves. Disclosure in this sense is determined in part by our choices from this wellspring of freedom. In this way the fundamental nature of the very world is determined before us. It is, as Levinas tells us, a position where "the founding of truth on freedom . . . [implies] a freedom justified by itself."[537] It is thus a spell which redirects the gaze placed on the glaring hole of its irrational founding. To observe its fantastical construction is to recognize the necessity, as Levinas spent his career trying to show us, in the approach toward the Other which calls our Being—be that our freedom, or the meaning of action derived therefrom in the previous picture—into question. It is *the* call for justification which cannot be derived from itself as unending freedom. It is through the social relation that this call is given to man: meaning, being-towards-death, self-consciousness, and understanding spring forth. It is the very means by which the difference between beings brings about the difference of their Being: for the presence of the other is by way of his difference *as such*, what keeps the individual from achieving 'full self-identity,' and yet it is by way of the social relation as *intersubjective* that subjectivity, which is consciousness, is brought about. It is by way of the intersubjective relation that the psychic economy of knowledge (which mirrors the Hegelian concept of desire *of* the other's desire) finds the production of understanding to

---

537 Levinas, *Totality and Infinity*, 34.

392 IDEOLOGY AND UNDERSTANDING

be contingent upon the knowledge of the other's knowledge as it exists purely in their own subjectivity.

The story of the twentieth century that found ideologies competing for control of hegemony in the wake of the theoretical 'death of God' had become addressed by the obverse issue recalled in the fight against ideology. The start of the twenty-first century finds this problem exacerbated by the existentialist problem of individuality, or particularity in the face of such totalizing, absolute normative claims of ideology. The shift from the problems of the twentieth century to the twenty-first century are then simply a shift in privileging the universal over the particular. And yet, as the twenty-first century enters its early adulthood it becomes all too clear that this shift in privilege maintains the feedback loop of the universal and particular such that focus on the one shifts into a demand of the other. The worry, then, is not one of reconciling the absolute and the particular as such, for as Žižek shows us,

> The difference is not on the side of particular content (as the traditional *differentia specifica*), but on the side of the Universal. The Universal is not the encompassing container of the particular content, the peaceful medium-background of the conflict of particularities; the Universal "as such" is the site of an unbearable antagonism, self-contradiction, and (the multitude of) its particular species are ultimately nothing but so many attempts to obfuscate/reconcile/master this antagonism. In other words, the Universal names the site of a Problem-Deadlock, of a burning Question, and the Particulars are the attempted but failed Answers to this Problem. The concept of State, for instance, names a certain problem: how to contain the class antagonism of a society? All particular forms of State are so many (failed) attempts to propose a solution to this problem.[538]

---

538 Žižek, *The Parallax View*, 35.

This brutal tension is what Gadamer's non-neutral stance of openness refuses to participate in. It is the recognition that it is not through a more universal particularity that truth is accessed, but rather it is by way of the site of what Žižek calls an "antagonism that cuts diagonally across all particular groups."[539] He states that "true universality and partiality do not exclude each other, but *universal Truth is accessible only from a partial engaged subjective position.*"[540] The call to action from the Other is the ethical relation as it is sustained by the very relation in its moment of Being. This is the very image of the ethical we have painted throughout this text: both the ethical relation to the Other and to the self. The intersubjective relation is that by which the ethical is founded by the bisection of the universal and the particular: it is the fusion of horizons whereby the particularities are enjoined in such a way that seem paradoxical from the subjectivist or objectivist viewpoints: the tension of this perspectival difference is maintained through the fusion as such. Where there is, at the core of the Other, forever the distance that separates their being from yours (this can be seen in the popular quotation of Miles Davis, "If you understood everything I said you'd be me,") understanding reveals to each a shared relation towards the truth of the matter-at-hand: it is an enframing that makes communication possible.

Despite this, the risk of venturing forward into this relation is done with full knowledge of the incommensurability of the Other with the self, and that despite shared understandings, there is forever at the core of the individual's Being a potentiality such that the agreement thereof is barred. The process of realization, whereby appropriation of the truth of the relation is made by the individual, is not something founded by either the subjectivity of the individual alone, nor a leap of faith into the absolute, but through a sharing of the relation itself. It is an alignment of the individual as messenger and as translator that finds the relation

539 Ibid., 9.
540 Ibid., 35.

of his statements true: understanding is generated from dialogue rather than from facts. It is the intersubjective relation —which is itself a site of truth—whereby understanding bears the truth rather than facts as they are in-and-for-themselves. We may even say that it is by this very shift that ideology becomes so powerful: ideology is not the temptation to do evil for its own sake, but it is rather the fidelity of the individual to a wrongful perspective of the right. It is the formal structure, which parallels the good and the true, whereby the wrong and the false are given their persuasive power. However, the risk of the relation extends even beyond this, for there is the possibility that the individual might find himself placed within the position of truth, and yet remaining fundamentally barred from assenting thereto.

Regardless, this does not reduce the event-site of truth to that of objectivity, for it is fundamentally relational and as such is caught up in the network of a community *as such*. Thus, when one gets down to the bare-bone difference between fundamental beliefs, it is *the* quintessential challenge is what comprises the conditions of assent. As seen in many of the greatest debates between public thinkers, the expression of difference is enumerated all throughout the expressions of belief: and yet, at the core of their true fundamental positions is something radically incommensurate and irreconcilable in relation to the position of each other. It seems, then, that once we have seen how understanding is a relational production, and once we have seen the way that openness, humility and the priority of the question lead the individual toward the widest horizon of the true, we must interrogate the nature of ascent to belief and if persuasion therein is itself possible. It's obvious that ascension to belief must be distinct from belief itself, which seems related to the experience of habitual causal or consonant conjunctions repeatedly contained in the present impressions of an individual. Belief can also be stretched to encompass immediate sense-impressions which demand attention, like that of an object seemingly flying towards an individual. It can also be found in induction and other synthetic relations of probability which condition a great deal of human life. The question exceeds the notions inhering in our common conception of belief as practically embodied justification, for not only does belief often seem to fly in the face of facts, but it is also conditioned through the relation of domination by ideology.

When speaking about fundamentally held beliefs we look to the propulsive condition whereby one is motivated into or kept from ascension. It is self-evident that the relation of man toward belief is complicated beyond all current conceptions: through his past, his family, friends, ideology, neurological and biological conditions, etc. Many would like to draw a distinction here between the holding of a belief and its acceptance, and, through the language of ascendance to a belief, many might imagine that what is being asked here is of a similar order of interrogation. However, such a distinction seems ultimately to falsely bifurcate a justification founded by its acceptance and the holding of a belief (which may happen before the individual actually manages to accept the belief by introducing its justification). This notion of belief involves approximating an adequation of the true such that inquiry can be halted and the individual may act as though the matter is in fact settled without ever actually 'believing' it to be so. Ultimately, if this is the way one approaches belief, one may find oneself unwittingly falling into belief (as we have already found in the formula of Blaise Pascal). To hold this view forces us to admit that the individual who sees the results of understanding in its production of a convincing account of the matter of hand would be free in some arbitrary regard to reject the results. However, it ultimately follows in application that ascent thereto would be produced almost regardless. This is because, as Bernard Berofsky tells us,

> Autonomy is essentially constituted by the manner in which an agent is engaged in her world rather than the metaphysical origin of her motivations. If we say of a person who finds meaning in an activity he has hitherto been unable to

appreciate that he is now really expressing his true nature, we are just redescribing this open relation to the world in a misleading metaphysical way. When the self is absorbed in the other, there is potentiality for a form of delight unfettered by a fear of inauthenticity and enriched by a flow of activity that is both spontaneous, yet governed by its own internal logic. When this potentiality is realized, we tend to speak of self-realization as if we are offering an explanation when in truth we are producing a metaphor.[541]

This is an applied notion of what autonomy looks like in the engaged practical wisdom we have been exploring as the backdrop against which relationality produces understanding. It is self-evident that this notion of autonomy includes already within it the demand of a sort of independence from another individual person: but yet so too does the conditionality of the community, the tribe, family, and the like always-already determine the individual in respect to tradition and authority. Included within the most fully autonomous individual must be the notion of habitual examination of these values and beliefs given to him from the communities which condition his maturation. This is not to say that this is a possibility in every situation, but rather that self-reflection and openness toward relating the self to ever-new experiences and relations are seemingly necessary conditions of autonomy in a conception that most seriously honors the character inhering therein.

In addition we have noted that to confuse the ego with the individual for whom it exists is a grave mistake, and thus we must assert that to imagine that the autonomy of which we speak belongs to the relation of the ego's independence from the *id* or even the superego is to commit the same error. In seeking the potentiality of man to choose or alter assent to the beliefs which are in some sense more fundamental, we

---

541 Berofsky, *Liberation from Self*, 1–2.

are asking to delineate that which is not separate or distinct from the overall ongoing process of understanding which always-already contains within itself application and concept formation. As Gadamer tells us, "The interpreter does not use words and concepts like a craftsman who picks up his tools and then puts them away. Rather, we must recognize that all understanding is interwoven with concepts."[542] In some greater sense, then, understanding itself must actually be free from containing absolute purposefulness on the behalf of the individuals who are engaged in its production.

This is what is at stake when there is an attempt to draw a semblance of the relations between the cultural and the personal histories involved therein, such that language becomes the emotion of an animalistic relation of wills. It is clear, however, that to do so is to introduce innumerable ruptures into what a coherent notion of understanding looks like. This is because

> coming to an understanding as such, rather, does not need any tools, in the proper sense of the word. It is a life process in which a community of life is lived out. To that extent, coming to an understanding through human conversation is no different from the understanding that occurs between animals. But human language must be thought of as a special and unique life process since, in linguistic communication, "world" is disclosed. Reaching an understanding in language places a subject matter before those communicating like a disputed object set between them. Thus the world is the common ground, trodden by none and recognized by all, uniting all who talk to one another. All kinds of human community are kinds of linguistic community: even more, they form language. For language is by nature the language

---

542 Gadamer, *Truth and Method*, 404.

of conversation; it fully realizes itself only in the process of coming to an understanding. That is why it is not a mere means in that process.[543]

What many would deem the core beliefs of an individual seem to be rather the accretion of a high volume of concurrent and parallel conversations held with a wide variety of sources. It is through the commitment (perhaps to the understanding produced by these relations) that the language which constitutes an incommensurable dialectic is rather itself from the start foreign.

While the Real might be 'without fissure' and thus may be considered without category, it is the differential function of the symbolic to which the Real as impossible to integrate therein persists as traumatic in that it absolutely resists symbolization in any form. In Lacanian psychoanalytic terms, the subject split by both his conscious imaginary and subconscious symbolic relations finds traces that recall the Real as beyond the traumatic gaps of each order as such. We can see, then, that through the absolutizing of the relation of the *objet petit a* to its master-signifier, or in the absolutizing of the particularity thereof in an aversion to the big Other. We find one instance imaging the master-signifier to be perfect and without rupture, and in the other the individual is given as wholly autonomous, and we find that their autonomy is granted a universality to the particularity *as particular* such that it mirrors the Enlightenment's fetishization of reason only now with individuality via autonomy.

In relating the ego to the world, the individual constructs fantasies which cohere with a particular narrative that functions through denying the failure of the master-signifier to cover the whole of the real, the authority of the symbolic order or the big Other in its entirety. Through these narratives we see the pathological loss of the individual to his

---

543 Ibid., 443.

fantasy such that, in its construction, the individual either loses the ability to cope with otherness and the world or their identity as such. Here Gadamer's notion of the potentiality of understanding provides the non-neutral openness necessary to give understanding as a relational production the basis for practically engaged wisdom which is involved in our actual day-to-day relationships. He tells us:

> In every worldview the existence of the world-in-itself is intended. It is the whole to which linguistically schematized experience refers. The multiplicity of these worldviews does not involve any relativization of the "world." Rather, the world is not different from the views in which it presents itself. The relationship is the same in the perception of things. Seen phenomenologically, the "thing-in-itself" is, as Husserl has shown, nothing but the continuity with which the various perceptual perspectives on objects shade into one another. A person who opposes "being-in-itself" to these "aspects" must think either theologically—in which case the "being-in-itself" is not for him but only for God—or he will think like Lucifer, like one who wants to prove his own divinity by the fact that the whole world has to obey him. In this case the world's being-in-itself is a limitation of the omnipotence of his imagination. In the same way as with perception we can speak of the "linguistic shadings" that the world undergoes in different language-worlds. But there remains a characteristic difference: every "shading" of the object of perception is exclusively distinct from every other, and each helps co-constitute the "thing-in-itself" as the continuum of these nuances—whereas, in the case of the shadings of verbal worldviews, each one potentially contains every other one within it—i.e., each worldview can be extended into every

other. It can understand and comprehend, from within itself,
the "view" of the world presented in another language.[544]

While it may be true that the fundamental character of Being against
the backdrop of the real is that of pure difference as such, so too do we
understand that exclusivity is not the hard limit of perspectives. For it
is due to our finitude and historicity that we always-already think from
within the domain given to us, and yet we are ever propelled forward
such that by way of our being-with-others, we are given as attentive to
these prejudices and traditions.

In this way, due to the contemplative reflection and necessity of action
drawn in by the presence of the Other, examination is also always a part
of the will which extends over and beyond its initial given moment such
that it reaches toward the worldview of the Other. It is through understanding that coming to an agreement is formed through an enjoined
common language; it is through the conversation that the process of
understanding finds its interlocutors already caught up in the attentiveness toward both the self and the Other. It is through the event-site of
understanding that both what persists and what changes are reflected.
This is because not only does that which persists maintain its nature as
a live option by persisting *as such*, but so too is it always-already caught
up with the relation to the world and the other, such that change is itself
ever present. In many ways this notion of the fusion of horizons reveals
the idealism which informs many of the lifelong categorical struggles of
the discipline of philosophy (as opposed to philosophy proper).

The linguisticality of understanding can be understood as always-
already containing within it its own application, for it also is caught up
with shaping the world as much as the world shapes it: application then
is co-determinate in the relation of understanding itself. Intersubjective
relationality is the means by which understanding gives our finite limita-

---

544 Ibid., 444-45.

tions over to the potentiality whereby they can be habitually traversed through continual reexamination and non-neutral openness, for

> By entering foreign language-worlds, we overcome the prejudices and limitations of our previous experience of the world, [however] this does not mean that we leave and negate our own world. Like travelers we return home with new experiences. Even if we emigrate and never return, we still can never wholly forget. Even if, as people who know about history, we are fundamentally aware that all human thought about the world is historically conditioned, and thus are aware that our own thought is conditioned too, we still have not assumed an unconditional standpoint. In particular it is no objection to affirming that we are thus fundamentally conditioned to say that this affirmation is intended to be absolutely and unconditionally true, and therefore cannot be applied to itself without contradiction. The consciousness of being conditioned does not supersede our conditioned-ness. It is one of the prejudices of reflective philosophy that it understands matters that are not at all on the same logical level as standing in propositional relationships. Thus the reflective argument is out of place here. For we are not dealing with relationships between judgments which have to be kept free from contradictions but with life relationships. Our verbal experience of the world has the capacity to embrace the most varied relationships of life.[545]

Our fundamental orientation is a givenness which is supremely intimate and which always-already by nature of its dialogical relation possesses this capacity to embrace. Verbal experience of the world is such that it

---

545 Ibid., 445.

embraces all Being in every subjectivity that it manifests. This means that in addition to both truth and meaning, so too does the thing itself come into being through language. The world is thus related to language, for man is not the master of primordial language, but rather is given to it; and as such it is prior to man in a significant way that finds incoherent the notion that the world is the object of language of which we can speak but are forever kept from.

Instead, the world horizon of language is such that disclosure is itself inherent to the concrete world-language which we are caught up in. It is through understanding itself that analytic experience is located. It is the 'transcendental conditions' that primordially give over to us our language which is the means by which understanding is able to 'reach across the aisle.' In this way, language prefigures human experience such that it remains intact after our game-like participation therein. It might be said that experience is predicated on language, through which understanding is made possible. This is why trauma insists and repeats itself until it is made a part of the verbal understanding of man. Bracketing our own language, were it not an impossibility, would actually hamper understanding itself. It is this very same principle which allows understanding to reach out into the past which continues to engage dialogically in determining and framing contemporary experience. This is why Gadamer says that

> The sun has not ceased to set for us, even though the Copernican explanation of the universe has become part of our knowledge. Obviously we can keep seeing things in a certain way while at the same time knowing that doing so is absurd in the world of understanding. And is it not language that operates in a creative way, reconciling these stratified living relationships? When we speak of the sun setting, this is not an arbitrary phrase; it expresses what really appears to be the case. It is the appearance presented to a man who is not himself in motion. It is the sun that comes and goes as its rays reach or leave us. Thus, to

our vision, the setting of the sun is a reality (it is "relative to Dasein"). Now, by constructing another model, we can mentally liberate ourselves from the evidence of our senses, and because we can do this we can see things from the rational viewpoint of the Copernican theory. But we cannot try to supersede or refute natural appearances by viewing things through the "eyes" of scientific understanding. This is pointless not only because what we see with our eyes has genuine reality for us, but also because the truth that science states is itself relative to a particular world orientation and cannot at all claim to be the whole. But what really opens up the whole of our world orientation is language, and in this whole of language, appearances retain their legitimacy just as much as does science.[546]

For science, the object of the world is objectified, and as such can never really be comprehensively given through experience. In this way, science set itself up in opposition to the position it had previously occupied as a 'natural' expansion of man's experience of the world, and instead founded a scientific cognition which was justified by a type of radical scientific-realism.

The scope of the study of science, as with any other specialized field, cannot by itself be extracted to encompass the whole which surrounds it, and of which it is a mere part. Biology can never get beyond the analytic condition which forms it: it cannot, for example, make psychological inferences, nor can it tell us about the sonic history of the counterpoint. The diachronic dimension of conceptuality finds concept formation and adjustment a natural process, for it is within the language itself that we understand the previous achievements of thought, which retain negated material *as* negated, which is itself represented by the very nature of sublation as such. Each of these linguistic communities construct a relationship to the object of their study such that it contains

---

546 Ibid., 445-46.

already within its point of view the inability to take account of itself from the outside. To allow the scope of study to be radically expanded in privileging any particular specialization is to restrict language to an arbitrary system of signs, from which a new epistemological theory must be founded to account for its prior loss. Rather,

> Every language has a direct relationship to the infinity of beings. To have language involves a mode of being that is quite different from the way animals are confined to their habitat. By learning foreign languages men do not alter their relationship to the world, like an aquatic animal that becomes a land animal; rather, while preserving their own relationship to the world, they extend and enrich it by the world of the foreign language. Whoever has language "has" the world.[547]

The factuality which belongs to language is distinct from the creation of an objectified internal universe of beings that belongs to both mathematics and science. This can be seen in the fact that Gadamer does not merely transpose language into the position of the absolute, but rather recognizes it as the medium which holds the totality of beings as well as their infinity. This is because the world is not a concrete totality as such, but rather that is what 'my' world is, which is habitually enlarged as it both preserves what is true within what has already been encountered, but so too does it make room for what is, by nature of life itself, ever new. Preservation and revolution are caught up in the interpretative process which is common to all understanding: this is understanding's speculative dialectic which finds the familiar and the foreign in conversation and translation with one another.

It is through sublation, which again maintains the sublated material as negated, such that we are not found to be inescapably captive

---

547 Ibid., 449.

by our history, prejudices, or language. This is what the fusion of horizons can achieve by uniting the familiar and the foreign through understanding, for language always involves the world and the Otherness of others such that it can in fact be understood as the universal horizon of hermeneutic experience (which, is itself universal: the *logos* is common to all). This is again the moment of delineation from the objectivity found in mathematics and science, for this universality is not the concrete totality belonging to the knowledge that is itself the achievement of objectivity. The universal horizon of the hermeneutic experience is such that expanding a worldview is the principal move of understanding, rather than abandonment of an old view and adoption of a new view, which is in effect strictly an impossibility. Contained then within the notion of the horizon of a worldview is both the relativity of the position, but the capturing of the object, albeit not exhaustively or completely. To imagine that we can understand a whole exhaustively and universally would be to imagine that we can achieve an understanding *beyond understanding*.

However, considering that understanding is the site of intelligibility, such a notion is itself simply incoherent outside of the echoes and reverberations which words carry from their finitude as an event, and yet in its relation to Being it is a moment with speculative reflection into the infinity thereof. The hermeneutical event, then, is the coming-into-language of what has been said within tradition from which it speaks: it is the way that "language speaks us" and the way in which the event is the true act of the thing itself. It is the fact that "the dialectic of question and answer always precedes the dialectic of interpretation," which "determines understanding as an event."[548] We are captivated by the relation of what we encounter paralleled by understanding in that of the beautiful. "In understanding we are drawn into an event of truth and arrive, as it were, too late, if we want to know what we are supposed to

---

548 Ibid., 467.

believe."[549] This is because, like speech, understanding guides us beyond where we know for certain what will follow. This means that in some sense, for speech, risk is involved in that conclusions follow beyond the necessary intention of the individual, which is given more obviously in understanding. This is because

> language is the single word, whose virtuality opens for us the infinity of discourse, of speaking with one another, of the freedom of "expressing oneself" and "letting oneself be expressed." Language is not its elaborated conventionalism, nor the burden of pre-schematization with which it loads us, but the generative and creative power to unceasingly make this whole once again fluent.[550]

We find again in language the creative power of free association of dialogue through which interlocutors are guided should they submit to the process rather than attempting to wrest control of it. This element of the hermeneutic experience reflects the achievements of psychoanalysis such that one finds within the dialogical relation ready-to-hand not only self-reflection but transference, not only countertransference but the impetus to traverse fantasy. While psychoanalysis might be differentiated from hermeneutic practices due to the clinical setting, and the relation of the truth and subject among other things, it does find harmony in another regard. It is the notion of interpretation which ventures forth from an original agreement, only in the hermeneutic position is this done by both parties, and as such understanding is achieved. This is done in both situations by not only the agreements of the meanings of words, but so too are the rules of the spoken language generally agreed upon as well as the matter-at-hand that is under interpretation.

---

549 Ibid., 484.
550 Ibid., 553.

In fact, there is further agreement as to the hidden texture of presuppositions which condition the interpretation taking place: furthermore, Gadamer and Lacan seem radically skeptical about the Enlightenment's championing of reason in order to do away with these presuppositions and prejudices. There is even agreement, although from differing directions, about understanding being unified with one's opinions on the matter. Through Gadamer's words on his distinction from critical theory, however, we can begin to see the ontological primordiality of the hermeneutic position when he states that

> what one understands always speaks for itself as well. On this depends the whole richness of the hermeneutic universe, which includes everything intelligible. Since it brings this whole breadth into play, it forces the interpreter to play with his own prejudices at stake. These are the winnings of reflection that accrue from practice, and practice alone . . . In truth hermeneutic experience extends as far as does reasonable beings' openness to dialogue.[551]

Here, in contrast to ideological monologues, authentic dialogue generates maximal stakes in understanding, which is not only in keeping with its pursuit of the good and the true instead of mere dumb and deaf repetition of drives, but in keeping with the broadest possible application of practical individual autonomy. Authentic dialogue asks us to engage in diachronic engagement with our traditions and synchronic engagement with others in order that we may be addressed in our historical situation with a continuity that allows practical co-creation of the events of understanding. This practice of understanding is dependent on what has come down to us from the past being made conscious and freely adopted in coordination with both the contemporary influence of the social order

---

551 Ibid., 570.

on the right, and Otherness as such. The event of understanding is then the achievement of the participation in one's life—the dialogue that gives birth to it is, in some sense, the rapturous playing of a game—the results are a true affirmation of life which blooms through and around oneself.

The philosopher is one who, having undertaken this journey, has emerged a joyful radical: one whose extremism appears betrayed by the delight with which conversation is engaged. Cast as he may be by those around him in various shades which attempt to justify their position within an ideological struggle, and called as he is to engorge himself on the productions therefrom, he stands resolute in his inquiry and creation of this a new life as the achievement of his Herculean occupation and inventive play. The philosopher's life is both an artistic life of discipline and training which is aimed at seeking the good and the true, but so too it is the humble and careful life of resolve in the face of the momentous task of interrogating the productions of their tradition to keep them from calcifying into mere ideology. Thus, through the quiet and resolute life of the philosopher, new life is supplied to those prejudices that remain a live option due to their inability as such to be resolved into higher unities or simpler parts. This establishes the radical nature of this life as one whose words simultaneously cleave creation and destruction by authentic engagement in dialogue. It is in this way that the true and the good may be secured to the throne of any particular community, rather than hitching it on the heels of a group who strive for either pure victory or mere sensuous pleasure. To join ourselves to this pursuit is to venture forth into the immense open space of being, whose co-construction is the work of our very lives.

BIBLIOGRAPHY

Abramson, Seth. "Metamodernism: The Basics." *The Huffington Post.* October 12, 2014. Adorno, Theodor. *Negative Dialectics.* Translated by E. B. Ashton. London: Routledge & Kegan Paul, 1973.

------. *Prisms.* Translated by Samuel and Shierry Weber. London: N. Spearman, 1967.

Adorno, Theodor W., and J. Bernstein. "Culture Industry Reconsidered." In *The Culture Industry: Selected Essays on Mass Culture.* Translated by Anson Rabniach. London: Routledge, 2001.

Adorno, Theodor, W., and Max Horkheimer. "Culture Industry: Enlightenment as Mass Deception." In their *Dialectic of Enlightenment.* Translated by Edmund Jephcott. Frankfurt Am Main: Fischer Verlag, 2006.

Agnew, C. R., et al. "Cognitive Interdependence: Commitment and the Mental Representation of Close Relationships." *Journal of Personality and Social Psychology* 74 (1998).

Althusser, Louis. *Essays in Self-Criticism.* Translated by Grahame Lock. London: New Left, 1976.

------. *Lenin and Philosophy and Other Essays.* Translated by Ben Brewster. New York: Monthly Review, 2001.

------. "The States." *On the Reproduction of Capitalism: Ideology and Ideological State Apparatuses.* Translated by G. M. Goshgarian. London: Verso, 2014.

Appel, Markus, and Tobias Richter. "Persuasive Effects of Fictional Narratives Increase Over Time." *Media Psychology* 10, no. 1 (2007).

Aronowitz, Stanley. *False Promises; the Shaping of American Working Class Consciousness*. New York: McGraw-Hill, 1973.

Arthos, John. "Introduction." *The Inner Word in Gadamer's Hermeneutics*. Notre Dame, Ind.: University of Notre Dame Press, 2009.

Aslan, Reza. "Why Richard Dawkins, Sam Harris and the 'New Atheists' Aren't Really Atheists." *Alternet*. November 21, 2014.

Badiou, Alain. "Paul: Our Contemporary." *Saint Paul: The Foundation of Universalism*.

Translated by Ray Brassier. Stanford, Calif.: Stanford University Press, 2003.

Barth, Hans. "The Ideology of Destutt De Tracy and Its Conflict with Napoleon Bonaparte." *Truth and Ideology*. Berkeley: University of California Press, 1977.

Barthes, Roland. "The Rhetoric of the Image." In *Image-Music-Text*, translated by S. Heath. London: Wm. Collins Sons and Co., 1964.

Berofsky, Bernard. "Values and the Self." In *Liberation from Self: A Theory of Personal Autonomy*. Cambridge: Cambridge University Press, 1995.

Blackmore, Susan J. "Strange Creatures." In *The Meme Machine*. Oxford: Oxford University Press, 1999.

Braverman, Harry. *Labor and Monopoly Capital*. New York: Monthly Review Press, 1974.

Brenner, Charles. *An Elementary Textbook of Psychoanalysis*. New York: International Universities, 1973.

Brown, Jane D. "Mass Media Influences on Sexuality." *The Journal of Sex Research* 39, no. 1 (2002).

Brown, Wendy. "Wounded Attachments." In *States of Injury: Power and Freedom in Late Modernity*. Princeton, N.J.: Princeton University Press, 1995.

Bunnell, Noah. "Oscillating from a Distance: A Study of Metamodernism In Theory and Practice." *Undergraduate Journal of Humanistic Studies* 1 (2015).

Butler, Judith. *Gender Trouble: Feminism and the Subversion of Identity*. New York: Routledge, 1990.

Carol, Hanisch. "The Personal Is Political: The Original Feminist Theory Paper at the Author's Web Site." *Carol Hanisch of the Women's Liberation Movement*. 2016.

Chiesa, Lorenzo. "The Subject of the Imaginary (Other)." In *Subjectivity and Otherness*. Cambridge, Mass.: MIT Press, 2007.

Chilton, David. "God's Law and the State." *Productive Christians in an Age of Guilt-manipulators: A Biblical Response to Ronald J. Sider*. Tyler, Tex.: Institute for Christian Economics, 1985.

Chomsky, Noam, and Michel Foucault. *Chomsky-Foucault Debate: On Human Nature*. New York: New Press, 2006.

Davis, Lennard J. "Resisting the Novel." In his *Resisting Novels: Ideology and Fiction*. New York: Methuen, 1987.

Dawkins, Richard. *The Selfish Gene*. Oxford: Oxford University Press, 1989. de Beauvoir, Simone. "II Personal Freedom and Others." In *The Ethics of Ambiguity*. Translated by Bernard Frechtman. Citadel Press, 1975.

Debord, Guy. *The Society of the Spectacle*. Translated by Donald Nicholson-Smith. New York: Zone Books, 1995.

D'Emilio, John, and Estelle B. Freedman. "The Rise and Fall of Sexual Liberalism: 1920 to the Present." In *Intimate Matters: A History of Sexuality in America*. Chicago: University of Chicago Press, 2012.

Dennett, D. C. "Multiple Drafts Versus the Cartesian Theater." In *Consciousness Explained*. Boston: Little, Brown, 1991.

Derrida, Jacques. "Linguistics and Grammatology." In *Of Grammatology*. Translated by Gayatri Chakravorty Spivak. Baltimore: Johns Hopkins University Press, 1976.

------. "Meaning and Representation." In *Speech and Phenomena: And Other Essays on Husserl's Theory of Signs*. Translated by David B. Allison. Evanston, Ill.: Northwestern University Press, 1973.

Diels, Hermann, and Walther Kranz. *Die Fragmente der Vorsokratiker*. Available at https://www.wilbourhall.org/pdfs/die_fragmente_der_vorsokratiker.pdf.

Dillon, M. C. *Merleau-Ponty's Ontology*. Evanston, Ill.: Northwestern University Press, 1988.

Dilworth, Dianna. "Interview with Slavoj Žižek." *The Believer* (July 2004).

Drexler, Peggy. "The New Face of Infidelity." *The Wall Street Journal*. October 19, 2012. Dreyfus, Hubert. *Kierkegaard & the Information Highway*. Berkeley: University of California Press, 1997.

Dreyfus, Hubert, and Mark A. Wrathall. "Nihilism on the Information Highway." In *Background Practices: Essays on the Understanding of Being*. Oxford: Oxford University Press, 2017. Eagleton, Terry. "Ideological Strategies." In *Ideology: An Introduction*. London: Verso, 1991. Eckhart, Meister, and Matthew Fox. *Meditations with Meister Eckhart*. Santa Fe, N.M.: Bear, 1983.

Escudero, Jesús Adrián. "Heidegger on Selfhood." *American International Journal of Contemporary Research* 4, no. 2 (2014).

Farber, Daniel A., and Suzanna Sherry. *Beyond All Reason: The Radical Assault on Truth in American Law*. Oxford: Oxford University Press, 1998.

Felluga, Dino. "Terms Used by Psychoanalysis." In "Introductory Guide to Critical Theory." Purdue University lecture, January 31, 2011.

Foucault, Michel. "The Subject and Power." In *Art after Modernism: Rethinking Representation*. New York: New Museum of Contemporary Art, 1984.

Freud, Sigmund. *The Standard Edition of the Complete Psychological Works of Sigmund Freud*. Translated by James Strachey. 24 vols. London: Hogarth, 1953-74.

Gadamer, Hans-Georg. *Hermeneutics, Religion, and Ethics*. Translated by Joel Weinsheimer. New Haven, Conn.: Yale University Press, 2012.

------. Language and Understanding. In *Theory, Culture & Society*.

------. *Truth and Method*. Translated by John Cumming. 2nd ed. New York: Seabury Press, 1975.

Gadamer, Hans-Georg, and David Linge. "Semantics and Hermeneutics." In *Philosophical Hermeneutics*. Berkeley: University of California Press, 2008.

Gadamer, Hans-Georg, and Joel Weinsheimer. *Language as the Medium of Hermeneutic Experience*. London: Continuum, 2011.

Gadamer, Hans-Georg, and Robert Bernasconi. "The Relevance of the Beautiful." In *The Relevance of the Beautiful and Other Essays*. Cambridge: Cambridge University Press, 2002. Gadamer, Hans-Georg, and Richard E. Palmer. "The Universality of the Hermeneutical Problem." In *The Gadamer Reader: A Bouquet of the Later Writings*. Evanston, Ill.: Northwestern University Press, 2007.

Macey, Marie, and Eileen Moxon. "An Examination of Anti-Racist and Anti-Oppressive Theory and Practice in Social Work Education." *The British Journal of Social Work* 26, no. 3 (June 1996).

Grimes, Robert G. "GENERAL SEMANTICS AND MEMETICS: A Tentative Relationship?" *ETC: A Review of General Semantics* 55, no. 1 (1998).

Hahn, Songsuk Susan. "Hegel's Final Synthesis." *Contradiction in Motion: Hegel's Organic Concept of Life and Value*. Ithaca, N.Y.: Cornell University Press, 2007.

Hawkes, Terence. "Introduction." In *Structuralism and Semiotics*. London: Routledge, 2005.

Hegel, G. W. F. "Dogmatic and Skeptical Philosophy." In *Lectures on the History of Philosophy 1825-26*. Translated by Robert Brown. Oxford: Clarendon Press, 2006.

------. *The Phenomenology of Mind*. Translated by J. B. Bailleie. 2nd ed. New York: Humanities Press, 1964.

------. *Phenomenology of Spirit*. Translated by A. V. Miller. Oxford: Clarendon Press, 1979.

------. *Phenomenology of Spirit*. Translated by A. V. Miller. New Delhi: Shri Jainendra, 1998.

------. *The Philosophy of History*. Translated by J. Sibree. New York: Dover, 1956.

------. *The Science of Logic*. Translated by A. V. Miller. Cambridge: Cambridge University Press, 2015.

Heidegger, Martin. *Basic Writings*. Translated and edited by David Krell. New York: Harper and Row, 1977.

------. *Being and Time*. Translated by John Macquarrie and Edward Robinson. New York: Harper Collins, 1962.

------. *On the Way to Language*. Translated by Peter D. Hertz. New York: Harper and Row, 1982.

------. *The Origin of the Work of Art.* Translated by David Farrell Krell. Waterloo: University of Waterloo Press, 1977.

Hucheon, L. *The Politics of Postmodernism.* New York: Routledge, 2002.

Huntington, Samuel P. "The Clash of Civilizations?" *The Clash of Civilizations and the Remaking of World Order.* New York: Simon & Schuster, 1996.

Ioana, Cristea. "Antonio Gramsci's Concept of Ideology." *South-East European Journal of Political Science* 1, no. 3 (2013).

Jappe, Anselm. *Guy Debord.* Berkeley: University of California Press, 1999.

Johns, Lindsay. "Why Lee Jasper Is Wrong: White People Don't Have a Monopoly on Racism." *Daily Mail Online*, May 1, 2012.

Kant, Immanuel. "Of Duties to the Body in Regard to the Sexual Impulse." Translated by Peter Heath. In *Lectures on Ethics.* Cambridge: Cambridge University Press, 2008.

------. "On the Right of Domestic Society Title I: Marriage Right." In *The Metaphysics of Morals.* Translated by Mary Gregor. Cambridge: Cambridge University Press, 1991.

------. "What Is Enlightenment?" Translated by Mary C. Smith. Available at www.columbia.edu/acis/ets/CCREAD/etscc/kant.html.

Kierkegaard, Søren. *The Concept of Anxiety: A Simple Psychologically Orienting Deliberation on the Dogmatic Issue of Hereditary Sin.* Translated by Reidar Thomte and Albert Anderson. Princeton, N.J.: Princeton University Press, 1980.

------. *The Present Age.* New York: Harper Perennial, 1962.

Kimball, A. Samuel. *The Infanticidal Logic of Evolution and Culture.* Newark: University of Delaware, 2007.

Kögler, Hans-Herbert. "The Crisis of a Hermeneutic Ethic." *Philosophy Today* 58, no. 1 (2014). Kojeve, Alexandre, and Raymond Queneau. "In Place of an Introduction." *Introduction to the Reading of Hegel: Lectures on the Phenomenology of Spirit.* Translated by James H. Nichols, Jr. New York: Basic, 1969.

Kolakowski, Leszek. "Althusser's Marx." *Socialist Register* (1971).

Kruks, Sonia. "The Politics of Recognition." In *Retrieving Experience: Subjectivity and*

Recognition in Feminist Politics. New York: Cornell University Press, 2001.

Lacan, Jacques. *Ecrits: A Selection.* New York: W. W. Norton, 1977.

------. *The Ego in Freud's Theory and in the Technique of Psychoanalysis: 1954-1955.* Translated by Jacques-Alain Miller. New York: Norton, 1991.

------. *Freud's Papers on Technique 1953-1954.* In *The Seminar of Jacques Lacan, Book 1.*

Translated by John Forrester, edited by Jacques-Alain Miller. New York: Norton, 1991.

------. *The Language of the Self: The Function of Language in Psychoanalysis.* Translated by Anthony Wilden. Baltimore: Johns Hopkins University Press, 1968.

------. *My Teaching.* Trans. David Macey. London: Verso, 2009.

------. *The Seminar of Jacques Lacan: The Ethics of Psychoanalysis.* Translated by Dennis Potter.

New York: W. W. Norton, 1992.

------. *Seminar XI: The Four Fundamental Concepts of Psycho-Analysis.* Edited by Jacques-

Alain Miller. Translated by Alan Sheridan. New York: W. W. Norton, 1981.

------. *The Seminar of Jacques Lacan: The Other Side of Psychoanalysis.* Translated by Russell Grigg. New York: W. W. Norton, 2007.

Lacan, Jacques, and Jacques-Alain Miller. *The Seminar of Jacques Lacan: The Psychoses.* Translated by Russell Grigg. New York: Norton, 1988.

Laclau, Ernesto, and Chantal Mouffe. *Hegemony and Socialist Strategy: Towards a Radical Democratic Politics.* London: Verso, 2014.

Lantz, Herman R., et al. "The American Family in the Preindustrial Period: From Base Lines in History to Change." *American Sociological Review* 40, no. 1 (1975).

Levinas, Emmanuel. "Ethics as First Philosophy." In *The Continental Philosophy Reader*, edited by Richard Kearney and Mara Rainwater. London: Routledge, 1996.

------. *Totality and Infinity: An Essay on Exteriority.* Translated by Alphonso Lingis. Pittsburgh, Pa.: Duquesne University Press, 1969.

Lukács, György. *History and Class Consciousness Studies in Marxist Dialectics.* Translated by Rodney Livingstone. London: Merlin, 1971.

MacIntyre, Alasdair. *After Virtue.* Notre Dame, Ind.: University of Notre Dame Press, 1984.

Mannheim, Karl. *Ideology and Utopia.* London: Routledge & Kegan Paul, 1966.

Marcuse, Herbert. *One-Dimensional Man: Studies in the Ideology of Advanced Industrial Society.* Boston: Beacon, 1964.

Marx, Karl. *Capital: A Critique of Political Economy*, vol. 1. Translated by Ben Fowkes. New York: Vintage, 1976.

------. *Introduction to "A Contribution to the Critique of Hegel's Philosophy of Right."* In *Collected Works*, vol. 3. Translated by Jack Cohen. New York: Oxford University Press, 1976.

------. *Selected Writings.* New York: Oxford University Press, 2000.

Marx, Karl, and Friedrich Engels. *The Collected Works of Karl Marx and Frederick Engels: Early Works, 1835-1844: vol. 3.* Charlottesville, Va.: InteLex Corporation, 2001.

------. *The German Ideology.* Moscow: Progress, 1976.

Merleau-Ponty, Maurice. *Phenomenology of Perception.* New York: Routledge, 2014.

Merricks, Trenton. *Objects and Persons.* Oxford: Clarendon, 2001.

National Education Association. "Education and Racism." Washington, D.C., 1973.

Nietzsche, Friedrich. *The Gay Science with a Prelude in Rhyme and an Appendix of Songs.* Translated by Walter Kaufmann. New York: Vintage, 1974.

------. *On the Genealogy of Morals / Ecce Homo.* Translated by Walter Kaufmann and R. J. Hollingdale. New York: Vintage, 1989.

------. *The Will to Power.* Translated by Walter Kaufmann and R. J. Hollingdale. New York: Vintage Books, 1967.

Origen. *Commentary on John.* Cited in Papanikolaou, Athanasios, *Theology: Quarterly Edition of the Holy Synod of the Church of Greece* 45, no. 2 (1974).

Pilgrim, David. *Question of the Month.* Jim Crow Museum (March 2009).

Plato. *Gorgias.* Translated by James H. Nichols, Jr. Ithaca, N.Y.: Cornell University Press, 1998.

------. *Plato in Twelve Volumes.* Vol. 1, translated by Harold North Fowler. Cambridge, Mass.: Harvard University Press, 1966.

Poulard, Étienne. "Shakespeare's Politics of Invisibility: Power and Ideology in The Tempest." *International Journal of Žižek Studies* 4, no. 1 (2010). Ragland-Sullivan, Ellie. *Jacques Lacan and the Logic of Structure: Topology and Language in Psychoanalysis*. London: Routledge, 2015.

Ricoeur, Paul, and George Taylor. *Lectures on Ideology and Utopia*. New York: Columbia University Press, 1986.

Roderick, Rick. "Philosophy and Post-Modern Culture." *Philosophy and Human Values* (1990). "Romans." *The Holy Bible: New International Version*. London: Hodder & Stoughton, 1979. Rothenberg, Molly Anne. *The Excessive Subject: A New Theory of Social Change*. Polity, 2013. Sartre, Jean-Paul. *Being and Nothingness: An Essay on Phenomenological Ontology*. Translated by Hazel E. Barnes. New York: Philosophical Library, 1956.

Scheler, Max, and Hans Meyerhoff. *Man's Place in Nature*. New York: Farrar, Straus and Cudahy, 1961.

Schrag, Calvin O. *Philosophical Papers: Betwixt and Between*. Albany: State University of New York Press, 1994.

Sedikides, Constantine, and Marilynn B. Brewer. *Individual Self, Relational Self, Collective Self*. Philadelphia: Psychology, 2001.

Sextus Empiricus. *Against the Professors*. Translated by Robert Gregg Bury. Cambridge, Mass.: Harvard University Press, 1961.

------. *Outlines of Scepticism*. Translated by Julia Annas and Jonathan Barnes. Cambridge: Cambridge University Press, 1994.

Steinkraus, Warren E. "Hegel's Ideas about Tragedy." In *New Studies in Hegel's Philosophy*. New York: Holt, Rinehart and Winston, 1971.

Stevenson, Nick. *Understanding Media Cultures: Social Theory and Mass Communication*. 2nd ed. London: Sage, 2006.

Stiegler, Bernard, et al. *Technics and Time*. Translated by Richard Beardsworth and George Collins. Stanford, Calif.: Stanford University Press, 1998.

Taylor, Mark C. *Erring: A Postmodern A/theology*. Chicago: University of Chicago Press, 1984. Turner, Luke. *The Metamodernist Manifesto*.

Available at www.metamodernism.org. Vermeulen, Timotheus, and Robin Van Den Akker. "Notes on Metamodernism." *Journal of Aesthetics & Culture* 2, no. 1 (2010).

Voegelin, Eric. *The Collected Works of Eric Voegelin*. Edited by E. Sandoz. Baton Rouge: Louisiana State University Press, 1989.

Wachterhauser, Brice. "Getting It Right: Relativism, Realism, and Truth." In *The Cambridge Companion to Gadamer*, edited by Robert J. Dostal. Cambridge: Cambridge University Press, 2010.

Wallace, David Foster. "E Unibus Pluram: Television and U.S. Fiction." *Review of Contemporary Fiction* 13, no. 2 (Summer 1993).

White, Hayden. *The Historical Imagination in Nineteenth-Century Europe*. Baltimore: Johns Hopkins University Press, 1975.

Wittgenstein, Ludwig, and Cyril Barrett. *Lectures & Conversations on Aesthetics, Psychology, and Religious Belief*. Berkeley: University of California Press, 1966.

Wright, Erik Olin, and Joel Rogers. *American Society: How It Really Works*. New York: W. W. Norton, 2011.

Wright, N. T. "The New Testament and the 'State.'" *Theological Studies* (1990).

------. "What Do You Mean by Literal?" BioLogos, September 8, 2010; available at www.youtube.com/watch?v=fxQpFosrTUk.

Yoder, John Howard. "Let Every Soul Be Subject." In *The Politics of Jesus: Vicit Agnus Noster*. Grand Rapids, Mich.: Eerdmans, 2008.

Young, Cathy. "You Can't Whitewash The Alt-Right's Bigotry." *The Federalist*, April 20, 2016. Žižek, Slavoj. "Disorder Under Heaven." European Graduate School Video Lectures, Evening Lecture, June 13, 2019.

------. *The Fragile Absolute, Or, Why Is the Christian Legacy Worth Fighting For?* London: Verso, 2000.

------. *Living in the End Times*. London: Verso, 2010.

------. *Looking Awry: An Introduction to Jacques Lacan through Popular Culture*. Cambridge, Mass.: MIT Press, 1991.

------. *Mapping Ideology*. London: Verso, 2012.

------. *The Parallax View*. Cambridge, Mass.: MIT Press, 2009.

------. *RETHINKING REVOLUTION: Socialist Register 2017*. Halifax: Fernwood, 2016.

------. *The Sublime Object of Ideology*. London: Verso, 1989.

------. *Tarrying with the Negative: Kant, Hegel, and the Critique of Ideology*. Durham, N.C.: Duke University Press, 1993.

------. *Violence: Six Sideways Reflections*. New York: Picador, 2008.

------. *Welcome to the Desert of the Real*. London: Verso, 2013.

Žižek, Slavoj, Rex Butler, and Scott Stephens. *Interrogating the Real*. London: Bloomsbury Academic, 2013.

INDEX

D

grammar (*grammatical,
grammatistic*) 110, 156-9
Gramsci 200, 206, 210-1
guilt 62, 93, 97, 202, 253

H

Habermas 14-5, 215-7, 258, 377
habits (*habitual, habituate*) 34-5,
39, 55, 69, 82, 98-9, 105, 108-9,
117, 134, 139-40, 168, 173, 189,
197, 213, 229, 231, 238-9, 252,
271, 327, 331, 335, 369, 370,
381, 389, 394, 396, 401, 404
hate (*hateful, hatred*) 78, 92, 156,
255, 284
Hegel (*Hegelian*) 16-7, 27, 32, 42,
45-7, 55-7, 66, 74, 81, 83, 94,
108, 113-4, 131, 150, 199, 207,
220-1, 242, 246, 248, 252, 265-7,
269, 271, 274, 290, 292-3, 299,
301-3, 311, 315, 351-4, 359,
370-1, 378, 386, 391
hegemony (*hegemonic*) 27, 43, 54,
61, 63, 65, 76, 81, 86-9, 91, 93-4,
96, 101-2, 106, 112, 127, 133,
134, 136-9, 142-6, 172, 174, 176,
181, 183-6, 190, 192-3, 197-8,
202, 204, 210-5, 219, 221, 224,
231-2, 234-6, 238-9, 294, 346-7,
350, 392
Heidegger (*Heideggerian*) 33-4, 44,
113, 250, 253, 256-7, 270, 274-5,
299, 307, 310-1, 313, 316, 321,
329-30, 337, 339, 340-1, 367,
391

Heraclitus 229, 295-6, 352
hermeneutic 12, 14-5, 81, 270,
273, 287, 290, 295, 309, 316-7,
322, 326-9, 338, 343, 345, 353,
355-8, 362, 367, 376,
388-9, 405-7
historicism (*historicity*) 18, 134,
185, 305, 308, 313, 317, 320,
350, 352, 354, 356, 373, 400
Horkheimer 212-3
humanism 62, 78, 217, 219, 274
Husserl 173, 350, 358, 399

I

icon (*iconography*) 58, 84, 103,
124, 144, 146-7, 197-8, 231,
235-8, 246, 263, 347
ideal (*idealism, idealistic*) 12, 14,
17, 21-2, 30, 31, 48, 54, 57, 65,
67, 103, 112, 140, 142-3, 147-8,
166-7, 169, 171, 222, 232, 249,
276, 298-9, 301, 315, 319, 350,
360, 400
identification 31, 36, 41, 64, 104,
108, 113, 119-22, 125, 131, 142,
144, 185-6, 190, 231, 267,
299, 385
identifiers (*identify*) 103, 120-2,
142, 148, 187, 224, 236, 295,
360, 385
identitarian 50-2, 236, 240,
242, 290-1
identity 16, 18, 20, 41, 48, 50-3,
59, 60, 65, 86, 90, 102-5, 109,
112-3, 136, 141, 143-6, 148-9,

N

O

P

169, 188-90, 193, 214, 220, 234,
325, 381, 383, 386-8, 403
Pyrrhonian 150-60, 162
Pythagorean 154-5

R

race (*racial*) 64, 67, 92-3,
123, 282-4
racism (*racist*) 78, 84, 91-2, 281-5
radicalization 81, 279, 320
reactionary 49, 50, 69, 77, 86-8,
94, 99, 100, 102-3, 112, 133,
138, 174, 179, 213, 223, 278,
319, 322
reformation 89, 126, 179-80,
210, 212
reification 62, 71, 81, 124, 127,
132, 139, 166, 176, 207-9, 285
relation (*relationality*) 11, 15,
18,-20, 22, 30-3, 36-7, 39,
41, 45, 47, 50, 52-3, 59, 65-7,
69-72, 74, 77-80, 82-5, 87-8, 93,
96-102, 106, 108, 110-11, 113,
117, 120-2, 126, 127, 131-3,
135-7, 140-1, 144-5, 153-4, 160,
162-7, 170,-5, 178, 182, 184,
188, 191-4, 197, 203, 208, 211,
224, 230-1, 233-5, 237, 239-43,
249-52, 259, 267, 270, 272,
275-6, 281-2, 285-6, 289-90,
292-3, 295, 298-301, 309-11,
313-4, 316, 321, 327-9, 332,
334-46, 348-50, 353-63, 365,
367-9, 371-2, 375, 377-83, 385,
387-91, 393-401, 405-6

religion (*religious*) 11, 22, 35, 51-2,
58, 60, 63, 64, 67-70, 73, 77, 85,
130, 131, 176, 189, 202, 222,
254, 260, 292, 309, 318
repression 85, 178, 213, 219,
276, 379-80
revolution (*revolutionize,
revolutionary*) 43, 49-50, 59, 63,
86, 88, 96, 101-3, 112-3, 115-6,
135, 198, 204, 206, 209-12, 215,
223-4, 237-8, 244, 264, 278,
286, 288, 321-2, 404
rhetoric 75, 102-4, 178, 180,
269-70, 340
Ricoeur 291
romanticism 317-320, 84
Russell 387

S

Sartre 29, 54, 83, 358, 391
Scepticism
schematized 13, 186, 212, 333,
365, 367, 369, 399, 406
science (*scientific*) 12, 21, 27-8,
51, 81, 92, 135, 160, 200-2, 208,
215, 217-9, 283, 286, 292, 297-8,
301, 306-8, 318, 320, 326, 350,
352, 373, 376, 383, 388, 403-5
scientism 15, 68
secular 11, 77, 87, 183, 346
self-consciousness 33, 36, 46, 47,
48, 56, 109, 130, 143, 146, 239,
251, 302, 303, 353, 370, 391
self-narrative 40, 71, 82, 143,
145-7, 197, 387

totality (*totalization*) 12, 14, 16-7,
  21-2, 27, 36-7, 46-7, 49, 53,
  60-1, 72, 74-5, 79, 82, 86, 96,
  102, 106-7, 109, 120, 122, 133,
  135-6, 141, 165-7, 170, 196,
  199, 205, 209, 215, 229, 232,
  238-42, 246-8, 256, 260, 264-5,
  268, 274, 279, 281, 283, 286-7,
  288-9, 297-301, 304, 306, 308,
  325-6, 331, 336, 338, 346-7,
  362, 365, 374, 392, 404-5
tradition 13-5, 59-61, 64, 67,
  115, 202, 206, 211-2, 214, 220,
  270, 276-9, 282, 286-7, 291,
  294, 313, 317, 319, 320-2, 326,
  328-30, 334, 348-50, 354-7, 360,
  362, 370, 372-5, 396, 405, 408
transcendence (*transcendental*) 65,
  103, 108, 167, 237, 240-1, 252,
  263, 274, 276, 300, 305, 316,
  318, 331, 335-9, 345, 350, 359,
  361, 370-1, 385, 402
transference 125, 127, 151, 178,
  185, 292, 337, 385, 406
truth 8, 11, 14-20, 22, 27-8, 34,
  38, 40, 43-4, 46-8, 50-1, 54-5,
  57, 64-5, 67, 69, 72-5, 79-82,
  84, 88-9, 94, 96, 98-9, 103,
  105, 107, 115, 117, 120, 126,
  130-1, 136-8, 140, 142, 149,
  151-6, 159-61, 164, 166-8, 171,
  175, 180, 182, 184, 187, 194-6,
  198-9, 204-6, 211, 218, 222-4,
  236-7, 262, 273, 279, 281, 283,
  287, 291-2, 294-5, 299-301,
  303, 305, 307-14, 316, 318-9,
321-2, 332-3, 335-9, 341, 345-6,
  348, 351, 353-7, 362, 364, 366,
  368-70, 372, 375-7, 379, 381-3,
  385-6, 388, 390-1, 393-6, 400-8
tyranny 59, 63, 160, 253

U

unconscious 56, 71, 78, 103, 106,
  119, 176, 186, 213, 221, 229,
  245, 283, 286, 317, 319,
  367, 385
universalism 186, 263, 349
universalizing 21, 204, 235-6, 238,
  262, 320, 332, 343
utilitarian 304
utility 84, 154, 213, 224, 238,
  243, 251-2, 307-8
utopian 187, 359

V

value 28-9, 43, 47, 65, 84, 98, 99,
  104-6, 109, 111, 114, 124, 132,
  139, 154, 160, 161, 182, 183,
  189, 197-8, 208, 211, 221, 249,
  250, 255, 261, 269, 278, 291,
  301, 318, 319, 321, 329, 354,
  359, 361, 369, 387 396,
virtue 18, 20, 28, 76-7, 81, 103,
  116, 143, 155, 191, 232, 237,
  243, 246, 254, 266, 299, 334-5,
  338, 342-3, 385, 386

W

war 13, 89, 101, 106-7, 112-3,
140, 143-4, 206, 246, 269
will (*willing*) 13, 22-3, 47, 63, 81,
98, 211, 241, 251, 254, 260, 304,
350, 360, 362-4, 397, 400,
Wittgenstein 27, 73-4
worldview 13, 15-6, 87, 140, 399-
400, 405
Wright 60, 144, 296

Z

Žižek 22, 63, 64, 105, 115-7, 148,
181, 184, 206, 222-4, 346, 348,
385, 392-3

www.ingramcontent.com/pod-product-compliance
Lightning Source LLC
Chambersburg PA
CBHW022042020426
42335CB00012B/503